2018 SAT® READING: WORLD LITERATURE

ies TEST PREP

ADVANCED PRACTICE SERIES

50 PASSAGES

500 QUESTIONS

2000 DETAILED ANSWER EXPLANATIONS

A CURATED COLLECTION OF WORKS BY INTERNATIONAL AUTHORS

- ◆ FEATURING BOTH CLASSIC AND MODERN LITERATURE
- ◆ REFLECTING A DIVERSITY OF CULTURES AND SOCIETIES
- ◆ DISPLAYING A VARIETY OF WRITING STYLES AND GENRES

PROVIDES RIGOROUS PREPARATION FOR THE WORLD LITERATURE COMPONENT OF THE SAT READING SECTION

Authors
Khalid Khashoggi, CEO IES
Arianna Astuni, President IES

Editorial
Patrick Kennedy, Executive Editor
Christopher Carbonell, Editorial Director
Rajvi Patel, Senior Editor
Cassidy Yong, Assistant Editor

Design
Christopher Carbonell

Contributors
Margaret Cheng
Audrey Dunn
Chris Holliday
Sophie Osorio
Dina Peone

Published by IES Publications
www.IESpublications.com
© IES Publications, 2017

ON BEHALF OF

Integrated Educational Services, Inc.
355 Main Street
Metuchen, NJ 08840
www.iestestprep.com

We would like to thank the IES Publications team as well as the teachers and students at IES Test Prep who have contributed to the creation of this book.

The SAT® is a registered trademark of the College Board, which was not involved in the production of, and does not endorse, this product.

ISBN-10: 1548225010

ISBN-13: 978-1548225018

QUESTIONS OR COMMENTS? Visit us at iestestprep.com

TABLE OF CONTENTS

Dear student,

When we at Integrated Educational Services set out to
create this book, we did so with two purposes in mind.
The first is fairly straightforward, and is constant across
all of the books in the SAT Advanced Practice Series: to
target an element of the test that has proven especially
challenging to the students we instruct, and to all students
who take the test. Indeed, one of the most subtle and
unpredictable element of recent tests has been the World
Literature content, which is normally the first SAT
Reading passage that a student will see. This passage can
set the tone for the test-taking experience as a whole; it
also involves an array of questions—from remarkably nuanced word-in-context items
to broader considerations of theme and structure—that can be unparalleled in difficulty.
With the demands it makes in student attention and discipline, it was a section that
demanded its own book.

The second purpose of this book, however, is somewhat different. In college, you
will have the opportunity to take literature courses that will revolutionize the way
you think—that open your mind to new branches of world culture, and radically new
perspectives on human nature. Why not begin that revolution here. The 50 passages in
this book were chosen not simply because they fit the demands of the most recent tests,
but because they capture the essence of authors from all eras, from all over the globe.
Perspectives on society, memory, greed, power, and love—the entire human condition—
are at your fingertips, delivered by the men and women who have defined the literature
of the United States, Russia, China, and many more.

As you work your way through this book, you will come across gripping storylines
and unforgettable characters. Sometimes you will yearn to read more, to figure out
how the entire plot behind an excerpt unfolds: that, after all, is what defines captivating
literature. Yet no matter where this survey of world literature takes you as a reader, it
will take you—as a student preparing for the SAT—that much closer to your ideal score.
Read, enjoy, and control the test!

Wishing you all the best in your test-taking endeavors.

-Khalid Khashoggi

INTRODUCTION

The World Literature passage is the first passage on the SAT. The passage is an excerpt from either a work of fiction or a memoir. Usually, there is a central character with whom one or two other characters might interact.

Upon closer examination, we noticed that the College Board tends to ask certain questions focusing on different aspects of the passage (characterization, theme, plot, main idea, etc.). These questions test the reader's understanding of how such aspects relate to the overall idea of the passage.

After looking at the mix of questions that accompany the various types of literature passages, we've determined that they can be broken down into four groups, each prompting a different set of questions: Personal Narrative, Character Portrait, Story Based, and Relationship Dynamics.

PERSONAL NARRATIVE

In this category, the events of the passage prompt the narrator to reflect within himself or herself. While there might be other characters, they are presented in relation to how they affect the narrator, and the narrator's commentary on them will often reveal something about his or her perspective on life, resulting in an indirect characterization of the narrator.

Examples of passages in the Personal Narrative category include:
- *Don't Ask Me Where I'm From* by Sophie Osorio
- *Indian Boyhood* by Ohiyesa
- *The Bald Truth* by Chris Holliday
- *The Angel's Game* by Carlos Ruiz Zafón (College Board Test 8)

CHARACTER PORTRAIT

In this category, the events and setting of the passage serve to highlight the motives and perspectives of a central character. The main role of the narrator in a Character Portrait passage is to characterize the central character through description or interaction. Because of this, the Character Portrait is the direct opposite of the Personal Narrative, in which the other characters of the passage are used to characterize the narrator.

Examples of passages in the Character Portrait category include:
- *Kung I-Chi* by Lu Hsun
- *Mother* by Maxim Gorky
- *Paul's Case* by Willa Cather
- *The Schartz-Metterklume Method* by Saki (College Board Test 3)

STORY BASED

In this category, the passage revolves around a series of events that affects a character or group of characters. Their actions as a result of these events are the main focus of the story. While there may be characters in a Story Based passage, they are primarily plot devices, and any characterization only serves to advance the story.

Examples of passages in the Story Based category include:
- *The Extraordinary Adventures of Arsène Lupin, Gentleman-Burglar* by Maurice Leblanc
- *The Vengeance of Felix* by José Medeiros E Albuquerque
- *The Canterville Ghost* by Oscar Wilde
- *The Strangeness of Beauty* by Lydia Minatoya (College Board Test 1)

RELATIONSHIP DYNAMICS

In this category, the passage explores the connection between two or more characters and the influence they may have on each other. In the Relationship Dynamics passage, characterization provides context for the interactions that occur between the characters, thereby revealing the nature of their relationship.

Examples of passages in the Relationship Dynamics category include:
- *The Fortune Teller* by Joaquim Maria Machado de Assis
- *The Castaway* by Rabindranath Tagore
- *A Service of Love* by O. Henry
- *Silas Marner* by George Eliot (College Board Test 7)

CHAPTER ONE

Questions 1-10 are based on the following passage.
Chapter 1.1
Adapted Rabindranath Tagore, "The Postmaster."
Printed in *Stories from Tagore* (1918).

The postmaster first took up his duties in the
village of Ulapur. Though the village was a small one,
there was an indigo factory near by, and the proprietor,
Line an Englishman, had managed to get a post office
5 established.

Our postmaster belonged to Calcutta. He felt like
a fish out of water in this remote village. His office and
living-room were in a dark thatched shed, not far from
a green, slimy pond, surrounded on all sides by a dense
10 growth.

The men employed in the indigo factory had
no leisure; moreover, they were hardly desirable
companions for decent folk. Nor is a Calcutta boy
an adept in the art of associating with others. Among
15 strangers he appears either proud or ill at ease. At any
rate, the postmaster had but little company; nor had he
much to do.

At times he tried his hand at writing a verse or
two. That the movement of the leaves and the clouds
20 of the sky were enough to fill life with joy—such were
the sentiments to which he sought to give expression.
But God knows that the poor fellow would have felt it
as the gift of a new life, if some genie of the Arabian
Nights had in one night swept away the trees, leaves
25 and all, and replaced them with a macadamized road,
hiding the clouds from view with rows of tall houses.

The postmaster's salary was small. He had to cook
his own meals, which he used to share with Ratan, an
orphan girl of the village, who did odd jobs for him.
30 When in the evening the smoke began to curl up
from the village cowsheds, and the cicadas chirped in
every bush; when the mendicants of the Baül sect sang
their shrill songs in their daily meeting-place, when
any poet, who had attempted to watch the movement
35 of the leaves in the dense bamboo thickets, would have
felt a ghostly shiver run down his back, the postmaster
would light his little lamp, and call out "Ratan."

Ratan would sit outside waiting for this call, and,
instead of coming in at once, would reply, "Did you
40 call me, sir?"

"What are you doing?" the postmaster would ask.
"I must be going to light the kitchen fire," would
be the answer.

And the postmaster would say: "Oh, let the
45 kitchen fire be for awhile; light me my pipe first."

At last Ratan would enter, with puffed-out
cheeks, vigorously blowing into a flame a live coal
to light the tobacco. This would give the postmaster
an opportunity of conversing. "Well, Ratan," perhaps
50 he would begin, "do you remember anything of your
mother?" That was a fertile subject. Ratan partly
remembered, and partly didn't. Her father had been
fonder of her than her mother; him she recollected
more vividly. He used to come home in the evening
55 after his work, and one or two evenings stood out
more clearly than others, like pictures in her memory.
Ratan would sit on the floor near the postmaster's
feet, as memories crowded in upon her. She called to
mind a little brother that she had—and how on some
60 bygone cloudy day she had played at fishing with
him on the edge of the pond, with a twig for a make-
believe fishing-rod. Such little incidents would drive
out greater events from her mind. Thus, as they talked,
it would often get very late, and the postmaster would
65 feel too lazy to do any cooking at all. Ratan would then
hastily light the fire, and toast some unleavened bread,
which, with the cold remnants of the morning meal,
was enough for their supper.

On some evenings, seated at his desk in the corner
70 of the big empty shed, the postmaster too would call
up memories of his own home, of his mother and his
sister, of those for whom in his exile his heart was
sad—memories which were always haunting him,
but which he could not talk about with the men of the
75 factory, though he found himself naturally recalling
them aloud in the presence of the simple little girl. And
so it came about that the girl would allude to his people
as mother, brother, and sister, as if she had known them
all her life. In fact, she had a complete picture of each
80 one of them painted in her little heart.

One noon, during a break in the rains, there was a
cool soft breeze blowing; the smell of the damp grass
and leaves in the hot sun felt like the warm breathing
of the tired earth on one's body. A persistent bird went
85 on all the afternoon repeating the burden of its one
complaint in Nature's audience chamber.

The postmaster had nothing to do. The shimmer of
the freshly washed leaves, and the banked-up remnants
of the retreating rain-clouds were sights to see, and
90 the postmaster was watching them and thinking to
himself: "Oh, if only some kindred soul were near—
just one loving human being whom I could hold near
my heart!" This was exactly, he went on to think, what
that bird was trying to say, and it was the same feeling
95 which the murmuring leaves were striving to express.

CONTINUE

1

Which of the following best describes a major theme of the passage?

A) The yearning for companionship from a life of isolation

B) The slow passage of time in a life devoid of activity

C) The strength of a connection forged through crisis

D) The restorative power of sharing childhood memories

2

Over the course of the passage, there is a significant shift from

A) the postmaster's reliance on poetry for enlightenment to his discovery of it through memories alone.

B) the postmaster's inability to write poetry to a sudden discovery of this aptitude.

C) the postmaster's feeling of disconnection from society to a recognition of his predicament reflected in the nature that surrounds him.

D) the postmaster's independence from others to his desperate attachment to a companion.

3

The role of Ratan in the postmaster's life can best be described as

A) a figment of his imagination.

B) a former companion.

C) a current employee.

D) an adopted daughter.

4

Which choice provides the best evidence for the claim that the postmaster wished to return to a life in the city?

A) Lines 6-10 ("He felt...growth")

B) Lines 13-17 ("Nor is...do")

C) Lines 22-26 ("But God...houses")

D) Lines 69-73 ("On some...sad")

5

The main function of the third paragraph is to

A) defend the postmaster's aloofness towards the villagers.

B) juxtapose the qualities of two socio-economic classes.

C) provide context for the postmaster's loneliness.

D) describe the inhabitants of the postmaster's village.

6

The repetition of the word "would" in lines 38-49 primarily has the effect of

A) portraying the hypothetical nature of a relationship.

B) stressing the drudgery of a life in the village.

C) highlighting the permanence of a relationship.

D) depicting a former series of events as routine.

7

Which choice best characterizes Ratan's memories?

A) She recalled trivial details while significant occurrences eluded her.

B) Her bias towards certain family members affected her memories of them.

C) She tended to recall only happy memories while suppressing traumatic ones.

D) Her memories were gradually supplanted by those of the postmaster.

8

Which choice provides the best evidence for the answer to the previous question?

A) Lines 54-56 ("He used...memory")

B) Lines 57-58 ("Ratan would...her")

C) Lines 62-63 ("Such little...mind")

D) Lines 77-79 ("so it...life")

CONTINUE

9

As used in line 75, "naturally" most nearly means

A) unconsciously.

B) logically.

C) habitually.

D) easily.

10

The narrator uses the phrase "she had a complete picture of each one of them" (lines 79-80) to depict Ratan as

A) having been adopted as the postmaster's own daughter.

B) yearning for a sense of belonging in a family.

C) having an extraordinarily vivid imagination.

D) feeling a sense of kinship with the postmaster.

CONTINUE

Questions 1-10 are based on the following passage.
Chapter 1.2
The following is an excerpt from *The Fortune Teller* (1880) by Joaquim Maria Machado de Assis.

Villela, Camillo and Rita: three names, <u>one</u> <u>adventure and no explanation of how it all began</u>. Let us proceed to explain. The first two were friends since
Line earliest childhood. Villela had entered the magistracy.
5 Camillo found employment with the government, against the will of his father, who desired him to embrace the medical profession. But his father had died, and Camillo preferred to be nothing at all, until his mother had procured him a departmental position.
10 At the beginning of the year 1869 Villela returned from the interior, where he had married a silly beauty; he abandoned the magistracy and came hither to open a lawyer's office. Camillo had secured a house for him near Botafogo and had welcomed him home.
15 "Is this the gentleman?" exclaimed Rita, offering Camillo her hand. "You can't imagine how highly my husband thinks of you. He was always talking about you."
Camillo and Villela looked at each other tenderly.
20 They were true friends. Afterwards, Camillo confessed to himself that Villela's wife did not at all belie the enthusiastic letters her husband had written to him. Really, she was most prepossessing, lively in her movements, her eyes burning, her mouth plastic
25 and piquantly inquiring. Rita was a trifle older than both the men: she was thirty, Villela twenty-nine and Camillo twenty-six. The grave bearing of Villela gave him the appearance of being much older than his wife, while Camillo was but a child in moral and practical
30 life. He possessed neither experience nor intuition.
The three became closely bound. Propinquity bred intimacy. Shortly afterwards Camillo's mother died, and in this catastrophe, for such it was, the other two showed themselves to be genuine friends of his. Villela
35 took charge of the interment, of the church services and the settlement of the affairs of the deceased; Rita dispensed consolation, and none could do it better.
Just how this intimacy between Camillo and Rita grew to love he never knew. The truth is that
40 he enjoyed passing the hours at her side; she was his spiritual nurse, almost a sister,—but most of all she was a woman, and beautiful. The aroma of femininity: this is what he yearned for in her, and about her, seeking to incorporate it into himself.
45 They read the same books, they went together to the

theatre or for walks. He taught her cards and chess, and they played of nights;—she badly,—he, to make himself agreeable, but little less badly. Thus much, as far as external things are concerned. And now came
50 personal intimacies, the timorous eyes of Rita, that so often sought his own, consulting them before they questioned those of her own husband,—the touches of cold hands, and unwonted communion. On one of his birthdays he received from Villela a costly cane, and
55 from Rita, a hastily pencilled, ordinary note expressing good wishes. It was then that he learned to read within his own heart; he could not tear his eyes away from the missive. Commonplace words, it is true; but there are sublime commonplaces,—or at least, delightful
60 ones. The old chaise in which for the first time you rode with your beloved, snuggled together, is as good as the chariot of Apollo. Such is man, and such are the circumstances that surround him.
Camillo sincerely wished to flee the situation, but
65 it was already beyond his power. Rita, like a serpent, was charming him, winding her coils about him; she was crushing his bones, darting her venomous fangs into his lips. He was helpless, overcome. Vexation, fear, remorse, desire,—all this he felt, in a strange
70 confusion. But the battle was short and the victory deliriously intoxicating. Farewell, all scruple! The shoe now fitted snugly enough upon the foot, and there they were both, launched upon the high road, arm in arm, joyfully treading the grass and the gravel,
75 without suffering anything more than lonesomeness when they were away from each other. As to Villela, his confidence in his wife and his esteem for his friend continued the same as before.

CONTINUE

1

Which choice best describes what happens in the passage?

A) An old friendship between two characters becomes strained as one of them begins an affair with the other's wife.

B) One character unwittingly ignites a romance between himself and his best friend's wife by showing her common courtesy.

C) One character is tormented by feelings he develops for his best friend's wife who is at once attractive and flirtatious.

D) A change of circumstances in the lives of three characters leads to a secret romance between two of them.

2

Which statement best describes a technique the narrator uses to represent the relationship between Rita and Camillo?

A) The narrator illustrates the compatibility between Rita and Camillo by comparing their relationship to a perfectly fitted shoe.

B) The narrator hints at the codependence between Rita and Camillo by describing them as overwhelmingly lonely when separated.

C) The narrator emphasizes the intoxicating power Rita has over Camillo by depicting her as an alluring yet deadly snake.

D) The narrator demonstrates the positive influence Rita has on Camillo by portraying him as immature and naive before meeting her.

3

Which choice provides the best evidence for the conclusion that Camillo had been informed of Rita's qualities prior to meeting her?

A) Lines 10-11 ("At the...beauty")

B) Lines 13-14 ("Camillo had...home")

C) Lines 16-18 ("You can't...you")

D) Lines 20-22 ("Afterwards, Camillo...him")

4

The narrator indicates that the primary quality of Rita which caused Camillo to fall in love with her was

A) the attention she gave him.

B) the compassion she showed Villela.

C) the sensual aura she evoked.

D) the mental stimulation she provided.

5

Which choice provides the best evidence for the answer to the previous question?

A) Lines 23-25 ("Really, she...inquiring")

B) Lines 39-41 ("The truth...sister")

C) Lines 42-44 ("The aroma...himself")

D) Lines 56-58 ("It was...missive")

6

The main purpose of lines 31-37 ("The three...better") is to

A) describe an event that would place Camillo in a vulnerable position.

B) illustrate the strength of the bond that ties Camillo to his friends.

C) indicate when the friendship between Camillo and Rita turns to love.

D) depict a turning point in the dynamic between Rita and Camillo.

7

In describing the development of the relationship between Camillo and Rita, the narrator primarily presents a shift from

A) the activities Rita and Camillo participate in as friends to the gestures that betray their deeper romantic feelings.

B) the timidity of Camillo before his relationship with Rita to his newfound confidence when he discovers her love for him.

C) the security Camillo feels about his friendship with Villela to the conflict he undergoes when he develops feelings for Rita.

D) the extended and slow nature of the courtship between Rita and Camillo to the intense and fleeting quality of their affair.

CONTINUE

8

As used in line 55, "ordinary" most nearly means

A) familiar.

B) generic.

C) offhand.

D) unoriginal.

9

In describing Camillo's reaction to Rita's birthday note, the narrator draws a comparison between the "old chaise" and the "chariot of Apollo" in lines 60-63 most likely to

A) emphasize the extent to which Camillo ascribed meaning to the note.

B) suggest that Camillo had reacted in a way typical of a man in love.

C) hint that Camillo was misinterpreting the significance of Rita's letter.

D) underscore the effectiveness of Rita's succinct and elegant writing style.

10

The narrator uses the interjection "Farewell, all scruple!" (line 71) to imply that

A) Camillo finally succumbs to Rita's charms after a period of conflicting emotions.

B) Camillo has chosen his love for Rita over his longstanding friendship with Villela.

C) Camillo undergoes a transformation by which he is liberated from moral constraint.

D) Camillo is entering an affair with Rita unaware of the potential consequences.

CONTINUE

Questions 1-10 are based on the following passage.
Chapter 1.3
Adapted from Sophie Osorio *Don't Ask Me Where I'm From* (2016).

"If I don't get into Cornell, my parents might actually disown me," one said. "My aunt got her law degree at Duke, so it's always been my dream to follow
Line in her footsteps," another added. "Literally, all I wear
5 is Harvard apparel because of my siblings," the third responded. I slid deeper and deeper into my seat at the lunch table that day, hoping that my friends wouldn't try to include me in their oh-so-fascinating college conversation.
10   "What about you? Where did your family members go?"
    Oh, great, I thought to myself. Not this again. Don't they know better than to assume that every girl's parents went to some Ivy? My friends, noticing my quivering
15 fingers, exchanged those "uh oh" glances that we all know too well. I took a shaky breath and said, "Neither one of my parents went to college. They both went straight from high school to medical school in Serbia." I expected them to put on those fake, sympathetic smiles,
20 and to lightly touch my arm as a way of saying, "We're sorry that you're different." For some reason, I didn't get that response. Instead, they tossed a "How cool!" and a "Wow, my family is so boring in comparison!"
    What was I so afraid of? What was so wrong with
25 being Serbian?
    If someone asked me that ten years ago, the answer would've been "everything." I was the foreign kid in the sea of bubbly classmates dancing around with their golden curls. Like every lower school girl, all I wanted
30 was to be "in with the crowd." I would get the same backpack, wear the same hairstyles, and use the same school supplies as all the other cool girls in my class. Since we all became replicas of each other, I never felt separated. Well, that was short lived.
35   "Why does your mom have an accent?"
    Those seven words were enough to blow my self-confidence to pieces. Did my friends really mean to hit that nerve? Probably not. It didn't matter how they meant it because, to me, it was no different than
40 plastering the words "I'M AN ALIEN!" across my forehead.
    Why couldn't I be French, German, or even Swedish? I would ask myself. My life would be so much easier if that were the case. People actually know where
45 those countries are. All I have as reference is the tennis player, Novak Djokovic, but he's just known as that

annoying guy who defeated America's favorite, Rafael Nadal. To prove how American I was, I pretended that the Super Bowl was the best sporting event of the
50 year, just because I knew that my best friends would be watching. In French class, I kept my English accent while pronouncing the French words because that's what the Americans do.
    Then there was that time when we stood in our
55 pews at our winter music concert and my second-grade best friend said, "Look, some old lady is waving to us over there. I can't understand what she's saying. Is that your grandma?" Drenched in sweat from embarrassment, I said a quick "zdravo" (hello) to my
60 grandma and then slipped under a crowd of people to reunite with my classmates—just because I was scared that they'd make fun of me for speaking in what seemed like gibberish to them.
    When friends came over after school, my grandma
65 would prepare traditional dishes such as Moussaka (potato dish) and Gibanica (cheese pie), but after a telling crinkling of their noses, I knew I had to ask for hot dogs instead. "Ew, what's that? Can you tell your grandma that I just want something normal and simple?"
70 they would occasionally add. I began to ask myself what "normal" really meant. If our dishes were weird, the language didn't sound real, and my mother's American dialect was sometimes unrecognizable, did that mean that I wasn't normal?
75   My initial reaction to moments where I'm the odd one out—putting up defensive walls—hasn't changed, and most likely won't. I've learned, though, to take them down when I remember that the people trying to open the locked-up Serbian identity box aren't trying to make
80 me feel bad for being different. This part of my identity will always be sore, but with maturity and time, I can at least now accept it as part of who I am. Being the odd one out makes a person more interesting; the only one criticizing me for my culture is myself.

CONTINUE

1

Which of the following best describes the passage?

A) A character details her friends' discrimination of her culture

B) A character comes to a conclusion about herself

C) A character reminisces embarrassing moments in her childhood

D) A character shows her annoyance with her family

2

With respect to her Serbian ethnicity, the narrator experiences a shift in perspective from feeling

A) insecurity to open pride.

B) embarrassment to qualified acceptance.

C) alienation to solidarity with her peers.

D) denial to reluctant resignation.

3

Which of the following provides the best evidence for the answer to the previous question?

A) Lines 6-9 ("I slid...conversation")

B) Lines 36-38 ("Those seven...nerve")

C) Lines 71-74 ("If our...normal")

D) Lines 80-83 ("This part...am")

4

The first paragraph (lines 1-9) serves mainly to

A) characterize the narrator as self-conscious.

B) introduce the narrator's friends as new characters.

C) list examples of schools the narrator wishes her parents had attended.

D) display the narrator's fear of going to college.

5

In the third paragraph (lines 12-23), Osorio creates a contrast between

A) the Ivy League education of her friends' parents and the lesser known schools Osorio's parents attended.

B) her friends' exasperation with attending college in America and their fascination with universities in Serbia.

C) her friends' nonchalant attitudes towards college and the pressure faced by Osorio to attend a prestigious university.

D) Osorio's prediction of a condescending reaction from her friends and the response that occurred in reality.

6

According to the passage, the narrator's insecurity with her culture affected her in what way?

A) She felt obliged to tell her friends that her parents attended Ivy schools.

B) She felt compelled to act a certain way so that she could be included.

C) She was criticized and excluded by her classmates when she was young.

D) She felt ashamed of her family members and sought to avoid them.

7

Which of the following provides the best evidence for the answer to the previous question?

A) Lines 12-14 ("Don't they...Ivy")

B) Lines 35-37 ("Why does...pieces")

C) Lines 51-53 ("In French...do")

D) Lines 66-68 ("after a...instead")

19

CONTINUE

8

The narrator's greeting to her grandmother in line 59 serves to

A) provide the English translation for a Serbian civility.

B) sarcastically comment on the intolerance of Osorio's peers.

C) underscore Osorio's feeling of shame and alienation.

D) highlight the cultural discrepancy between the generations.

9

The author's use of which of the following techniques conveys her character as analytical?

A) rhetorical questions.

B) extended analogies.

C) conversational tone.

D) personal anecdotes.

10

In line 81, "sore" most nearly means

A) aching.

B) damaged.

C) sensitive.

D) traumatic.

CONTINUE

Questions 1-10 are based on the following passage.
Chapter 1.4
Adapted from W.M. Thackeray, *Vanity Fair* (1848).

By the side of many tall and bouncing young ladies in Miss Pinkerton's school, Rebecca Sharp looked like a child. But she had the dismal precocity of
Line poverty. Many a debt collector had she talked to, and
5 turned away from her father's door; many a tradesman had she coaxed and wheedled into good-humour, and into the granting of one meal more. She sate commonly with her father, who was very proud of her wit, and heard the talk of many of his wild companions—often
10 but ill-suited for a girl to hear. But she never had been a girl, she said; she had been a woman since she was eight years old. Oh, why did Miss Pinkerton let such a dangerous bird into her cage?

The fact is, the old lady believed Rebecca to be
15 the meekest creature in the world, so admirably, on the occasions when her father brought her to Chiswick, used Rebecca to perform the part of the ingenue; and only a year before the arrangement by which Rebecca had been admitted into her house, and when Rebecca
20 was sixteen years old, Miss Pinkerton majestically, and with a little speech, made her a present of a doll . . . How the father and daughter laughed as they trudged home together after the evening party (it was on the occasion of the speeches, when all the
25 professors were invited) and how Miss Pinkerton would have raged had she seen the caricature of herself which the little mimic, Rebecca, managed to make out of her doll. Becky used to go through dialogues with it; it formed the delight of Newman Street, Gerrard
30 Street, and the Artists' quarter: and the young painters, when they came to take their gin-and-water with their lazy, dissolute, clever, jovial senior Mr. Sharp, used regularly to ask Rebecca if Miss Pinkerton was at home: she was as well known to them, poor soul! as
35 Mr. Lawrence or President West. . .

Catastrophe came, and she was brought to Miss Pinkerton's school as to her home. The rigid formality of the place suffocated her: the prayers and the meals, the lessons and the walks, which were arranged with
40 a conventual regularity, oppressed her almost beyond endurance; and she looked back to the freedom and the beggary of the old studio in Soho with so much regret, that everybody, herself included, fancied she was consumed with grief for her deceased father.
45 She had a little room in the garret, where the maids heard her walking and sobbing at night; but it was

with rage, and not with grief. She had not been much of a dissembler, until now her loneliness taught her to feign. She had never mingled in the society of
50 women: her father, reprobate as he was, was a man of talent; his conversation was a thousand times more agreeable to her than the talk of such of her own sex as she now encountered. The pompous vanity of the old schoolmistress, the foolish good-humour of her sister,
55 the silly chat and scandal of the elder girls, and the frigid correctness of the governesses equally annoyed her; and she had no soft maternal heart, this unlucky girl . . . She determined at any rate to get free from the prison in which she found herself, and now began to
60 act for herself, and for the first time to make connected plans for the future.

She took advantage, therefore, of the means of study the place offered her; and as she was already a musician and a good linguist, she speedily went
65 through the little course of study which was considered necessary for ladies in those days. Her music she practised incessantly, and one day, when the girls were out, and she had remained at home, she was overheard to play a piece so well that Miss Pinkerton thought,
70 wisely, she could spare herself the expense of a master for the juniors, and intimated to Miss Sharp that she was to instruct them in music for the future.

The girl refused; and for the first time, and to the astonishment of the majestic mistress of the school. "I
75 am here to speak French with the children," Rebecca said abruptly, "not to teach them music, and save money for you. Give me money, and I will teach them."

Miss Pinkerton was obliged to yield, and, of
80 course, disliked her from that day. "For five-and-thirty years," she said, and with great justice, "I never have seen the individual who has dared in my own house to question my authority. I have nourished a viper in my bosom."
85 "A viper—a fiddlestick," said Miss Sharp to the old lady, almost fainting with astonishment. "You took me because I was useful. There is no question of gratitude between us. I hate this place, and want to leave it. I will do nothing here but what I am obliged
90 to do."

It was in vain that the old lady asked her if she was aware she was speaking to Miss Pinkerton? Rebecca laughed in her face, with a horrid sarcastic demoniacal laughter, that almost sent the
95 schoolmistress into fits. "Give me a sum of money," said the girl, "and get rid of me."

CONTINUE

1

Which choice best summarizes the passage?

A) One character facing adversity is placed in an institution where she eventually thrives.

B) One character attempts to escape a situation forced upon her by an unfortunate circumstance.

C) One character who has lost her father seeks purpose and refuge in spirituality and education.

D) One character reunites with and is oppressed by a recurring figure from her childhood.

2

Over the course of the passage, the main focus shifts from a

A) depiction of Rebecca as a child to an analysis of her as a young woman.

B) description of the hardships faced by Rebecca to their effects on her character.

C) series of scenes from Rebecca's life with her father to her experiences after his death.

D) recounting of loosely related anecdotes to a reflection on an influential event.

3

The primary impression created by the narrator's description of Rebecca's father is that he is

A) infamous.

B) corrupt.

C) mischievous.

D) respectable.

4

Which choice best supports the conclusion that Rebecca is manipulative?

A) Lines 5-7 ("many a...more")

B) Lines 12-15 ("Oh, why...world")

C) Lines 47-49 ("She had...feign")

D) Lines 58-61 ("She determined...future")

5

The narrator uses the phrase "How the father and daughter laughed as they trudged home together after the evening party" (lines 22-23) mostly to

A) comment on the poor parenting and negative influence of Rebecca's father.

B) demonstrate Rebecca and her father's enthusiasm about leaving the party.

C) display the irony of Rebecca and her father's enjoyment of an immoral ruse.

D) characterize Rebecca and her father as accomplices in a deceptive performance.

6

It can reasonably be inferred from the passage that the main reason Rebecca considered Miss Pinkerton's school to be a "prison" (line 59) was because

A) she fought with the other girls at the school.

B) she was prevented from seeing her father.

C) she felt stifled by its strict conventions.

D) she felt that she was being exploited.

7

Which choice provides the best evidence for the answer to the previous question?

A) Lines 37-41 ("The rigid...endurance")

B) Lines 49-53 ("She had...encountered")

C) Lines 53-57 ("The pompous...her")

D) Lines 74-78 ("I am...them")

CONTINUE

8

The passage implies that Rebecca practiced the piano "incessantly" (line 67) in order to

A) acquire skills useful to her eventual independence from the school.

B) secure a position within the school as a music teacher.

C) justify her avoidance of the other girls by staying at the school.

D) make her life bearable by passing the time in an enjoyable pursuit.

9

As used in line 81, "justice" most nearly means

A) vengeance.

B) humiliation.

C) righteousness.

D) offense.

10

In the context of the exchange between Rebecca and Miss Pinkerton, Rebecca's remarks in lines 85-96 ("A viper...me") serve to

A) present the particular moment Rebecca leaves the school.

B) account for the hostility between Rebecca and Miss Pinkerton.

C) underscore the nature of Rebecca's relationship with Miss Pinkerton.

D) signify a turning point in Rebecca's stance about the school.

CONTINUE

Questions 1-10 are based on the following passage.
Chapter 1.5
Adapted from Maurice Leblanc, *The Extraordinary Adventures of Arsène Lupin, Gentleman-Burglar* (1907).

On the second day, at a distance of five hundred miles from the French coast, in the midst of a violent storm, we received the following message by means of
Line the wireless telegraph:
5   "Arsène Lupin is on your vessel, first cabin, blonde hair, wound right fore-arm, traveling alone under name of R........"
At that moment, a terrible flash of lightning rent the stormy skies. The electric waves were interrupted.
10 The remainder of the dispatch never reached us. Of the name under which Arsène Lupin was concealing himself, we knew only the initial. . .
Arsène Lupin in our midst! the irresponsible burglar whose exploits had been narrated in all the
15 newspapers during the past few months! the mysterious individual with whom Ganimard, our shrewdest detective, had been engaged in an implacable conflict amidst interesting and picturesque surroundings. Arsène Lupin, the eccentric gentleman who operates
20 only in the chateaux and salons, and who, one night, entered the residence of Baron Schormann, but emerged empty-handed, leaving, however, his card on which he had scribbled these words: "Arsène Lupin, gentleman-burglar, will return when the furniture
25 is genuine." Arsène Lupin, the man of a thousand disguises: in turn a chauffer, detective, bookmaker, Russian physician, Spanish bull-fighter, commercial traveler, robust youth, or decrepit old man.
Then consider this startling situation: Arsène
30 Lupin was wandering about within the limited bounds of a transatlantic steamer; in that very small corner of the world, in that dining saloon, in that smoking room, in that music room! Arsène Lupin was, perhaps, this gentleman.... or that one.... my neighbor at the table....
35 the sharer of my stateroom....
"And this condition of affairs will last for five days!" exclaimed Miss Nelly Underdown, next morning. "It is unbearable! I hope he will be arrested."
Then, addressing me, she added:
40   "And you, Monsieur d'Andrézy, you are on intimate terms with the captain; surely you know something?"
I should have been delighted had I possessed any information that would interest Miss Nelly. She was
45 one of those magnificent creatures who inevitably attract attention in every assembly. Wealth and beauty form an irresistible combination, and Nelly possessed both. . .
"I have no definite knowledge, mademoiselle,"
50 I replied, "but can not we, ourselves, investigate the mystery quite as well as the detective Ganimard, the personal enemy of Arsène Lupin?"
"Oh! oh! you are progressing very fast, monsieur."
"Not at all, mademoiselle. In the first place, let me
55 ask, do you find the problem a complicated one?"
"Very complicated."
"Have you forgotten the key we hold for the solution to the problem?"
"What key?"
60   "In the first place, Lupin calls himself Monsieur R———."
"Rather vague information," she replied.
"Secondly, he is traveling alone."
"Does that help you?" she asked.
65   "Thirdly, he is blonde."
"Well?"
"Then we have only to peruse the passenger-list, and proceed by process of elimination."
I had that list in my pocket. I took it out and
70 glanced through it. Then I remarked:
"I find that there are only thirteen men on the passenger-list whose names begin with the letter R."
"Only thirteen?"
"Yes, in the first cabin. And of those thirteen, I
75 find that nine of them are accompanied by women, children or servants. That leaves only four who are traveling alone. First, the Marquis de Raverdan———"
"Secretary to the American Ambassador," interrupted Miss Nelly. "I know him."
80   "Major Rawson," I continued.
"He is my uncle," some one said.
"Mon. Rivolta."
"Here!" exclaimed an Italian, whose face was concealed beneath a heavy black beard.
85   Miss Nelly burst into laughter, and exclaimed: "That gentleman can scarcely be called a blonde."
"Very well, then," I said, "we are forced to the conclusion that the guilty party is the last one on the list."
90   "What is his name?"
"Mon. Rozaine. Does anyone know him?"
No one answered. But Miss Nelly turned to the taciturn young man, whose attentions to her had annoyed me, and said:
95   "Well, Monsieur Rozaine, why do you not answer?"
All eyes were now turned upon him. He was a

CONTINUE

blonde. I must confess that I myself felt a shock of
surprise, and the profound silence that followed her
100 question indicated that the others present also viewed
the situation with a feeling of sudden alarm. However,
the idea was an absurd one, because the gentleman
in question presented an air of the most perfect
innocence.

105   "Why do I not answer?" he said. "Because,
considering my name, my position as a solitary traveler
and the color of my hair, I have already reached the
same conclusion, and now think that I should be
arrested."

110   He presented a strange appearance as he uttered
these words. His thin lips were drawn closer than usual
and his face was ghastly pale, whilst his eyes were
streaked with blood. Of course, he was joking, yet his
appearance and attitude impressed us strangely.

1

Which choice best describes what happens in the passage?

A) A group of characters falls under suspicion when it is
revealed a fugitive is among them.

B) Characters traveling on a ship amuse themselves at
playing detective.

C) One character successfully identifies another character
as a wanted criminal.

D) One character's arrival on a ship sends the other
passengers into a frenzy.

2

It can be inferred from the passage that Arsène Lupin
has successfully avoided capture throughout his criminal
career mostly because

A) He is adept at changing his appearance.

B) He blends in with any surrounding.

C) He never stays in one place for long.

D) He never reveals his true identity.

3

Which choice provides the best evidence for the answer to
the previous question?

A) Lines 10-12 ("Of the...initial")

B) Lines 15-18 ("The mysterious...surroundings")

C) Lines 25-28 ("Arsène Lupin...man")

D) Lines 33-35 ("Arsène Lupin...stateroom")

4

The main purpose of the fourth paragraph (lines 13-28)
is to

A) illustrate the mystique that surrounds a character.

B) introduce a character who is essential to the narrative.

C) express the narrator's judgments on a character.

D) outline all the crimes committed by a character.

5

The narrator describes the "startling situation" in lines
29-35 ("Then consider...stateroom") most likely to
convey his

A) confusion about Lupin's whereabouts.

B) astonishment at Lupin's proximity.

C) panic shared with the other passengers.

D) suspicions about certain passengers.

6

Which choice provides the best evidence for the claim
that the narrator is confident in his ability to ferret out
Arsène Lupin from among the passengers?

A) Lines 40-42 ("And you...something")

B) Lines 50-52 ("but can...Lupin")

C) Lines 57-58 ("Have you...problem")

D) Lines 87-89 ("Very well...list")

7

In their attempts to discover the identity of Arsène
Lupin, the characters rely mostly on

A) intuition.

B) rumor.

C) interrogation.

D) deduction.

CONTINUE

8

The exchanges in lines 78-84 ("Secretary to...beard") primarily serve to

A) place the suspect outside everyone's social circle.

B) underscore the absurdity of the search.

C) identify the potential suspects by name.

(D) eliminate certain personalities as suspects.

9

When the process of elimination reveals the suspect as one of the group members, the narrator reacts with

A) dread, then amusement.

B) excitement, then fear.

(C) astonishment, then denial.

D) outrage, then bewilderment.

10

As used in line 93, "attentions to" most nearly means

A) affinity for.

(B) preoccupation with.

C) perception of.

D) closeness with.

Answer Key: CHAPTER ONE

Chapter 1.1
1. A
2. C
3. B
4. C
5. C
6. D
7. A
8. C
9. D
10. D

Chapter 1.2
1. D
2. C
3. D
4. C
5. C
6. D
7. A
8. B
9. A
10. A

Chapter 1.3
1. B
2. B
3. D
4. A
5. D
6. B
7. C
8. C
9. A
10. C

Chapter 1.4
1. B
2. C
3. C
4. A
5. D
6. C
7. A
8. A
9. D
10. C

Chapter 1.5
1. B
2. A
3. C
4. A
5. B
6. C
7. D
8. D
9. C
10. B

Answer Explanations

Chapter 1

Chapter 1.1 | *The Postmaster*

1) CORRECT ANSWER: A
The passage as a whole describes the postmaster, a man who "felt like a fish out of water" (lines 6-7) and "had nothing to do" (line 87); his only apparent companion, an orphan girl named Ratan, is no longer available. This information supports A as a major theme of the passage, while the postmaster does in fact have professional duties or activities (eliminating B) and is no longer in contact with Ratan (eliminating C and D, which both indicate that their contact had a more enduring or therapeutic effect).

2) CORRECT ANSWER: C
Early on, the passage focuses on the fact that "the postmaster had but little company" (line 16); while Ratan temporarily gives him some human contact, he loses even her company and finds himself "watching" nature (line 90) and reflecting on his loneliness. This information supports C. As described early in the passage, the postmaster's "verse" (line 18) is a diversion from his loneliness, not a positive source of enlightenment (eliminating A) or a negative source of a sense of failure or inability (eliminating B). D is inaccurate because the postmaster has learned to live without Ratan (rather than feeling desperate attachment) even if he would still like a companion.

3) CORRECT ANSWER: B
Ratan is "an orphan girl of the village, who did odd jobs" (lines 28-29) for the postmaster and shared recollections with him, but is no longer available to keep him company. This information supports B and eliminates A (since Ratan is real) and C (since Ratan has left). D relies on a misreading of the passage; the postmaster may seem like a father figure to Ratan, but he is not her ACTUAL father.

4) CORRECT ANSWER: C
In lines 22-26, the narrator explains that the postmaster would have felt a sense of "new life" if his rural surroundings could be replaced with the features of a city, particularly macadamized roads and tall buildings. This information supports C. A indicates that the postmaster is uncomfortable in his new surroundings, B only indicates that the postmaster is lonely and does not fit in, and D indicates that the postmaster is preoccupied with memories of home. Although these answers apply appropriate negative tones to the postmaster's current circumstances, they do NOT explicitly indicate that he wants to return to the city as a remedy, and should thus be eliminated.

5) CORRECT ANSWER: C

The relevant paragraph indicates that the postmaster's only options for companionship are the undesirable "men employed in the indigo factory" and that the postmaster is not "adept in the art of associating with others". Such factors explain why the postmaster has no companions, so that C is an effective answer. The paragraph indicates that the postmaster is indeed aloof (but does not praise or defend this quality, eliminating A) and is MAINLY concerned with the postmaster's unique situation. The narrator only briefly references the social class of the factory workers and the inhabitants of the village to explain that situation, so that B and D should be eliminated as answers that do not capture the paragraph's main function.

6) CORRECT ANSWER: D

The word "would" is repeated as the author describes how the postmaster and Ratan habitually interacted "in the evening" (line 30); Ratan has a set of duties that includes "going to light the kitchen fire" (line 42) but also keeps the postmaster company on a regular basis. The word "would" thus construes certain actions as repeated or routine: thus, choose D and eliminate A, since the narrator is describing the ACTUAL relationship that once existed between the postmaster and Ratan. The postmaster appreciates the evening routine (eliminating the negative B, which also wrongly focuses on the village at large) while Ratan is no longer a part of the postmaster's day-to-day life (eliminating C, which wrongly introduces the idea of permanence).

7) CORRECT ANSWER: A

In lines 62-63, the narrator indicates that when Ratan is thinking, "little incidents" take priority over "greater events". This information supports A. B distorts the idea that Ratan's father was biased towards her (as the passage does indicate) into the idea that she was biased towards HIM, C misrepresents the kinds of memories that Ratan prioritizes (small, but not necessarily happy, memories), and D misrepresents the idea that Ratan felt an emotional connection to the postmaster's memories as the idea that Ratan ELIMINATED her own memories in favor of the postmaster's.

8) CORRECT ANSWER: C

See above for the explanation of the correct answer. A indicates that Ratan had a few especially vivid memories of her father, B indicates that Ratan's memories were vivid and perhaps overwhelming, and D indicates that Ratan felt an emotional connection to figures from the postmaster's life. Make sure not to wrongly take D as evidence for Question 7 D, which indicates that Ratan connected to the postmaster's memories but wrongly states that she did so by "supplanting" or removing her own.

9) CORRECT ANSWER: D

The word "naturally" refers to how the postmaster would "recall" memories of his past in Ratan's presence; he has no trouble talking to her (while he is more reserved among the factory men) and thus speaks to her easily. D is the best answer, while A wrongly indicates that he is unaware of what he is doing or saying and B wrongly indicates that the memories follow a specific system or logic (when in fact they arise spontaneously). C is a trap answer; recalling the memories is indeed one of the postmaster's "habits", but the SPECIFIC line reference is meant to call attention to a different theme: the "ease" of his conversations with Ratan.

10) CORRECT ANSWER: D

Ratan is able to form complete pictures of the postmaster's relatives because he talks openly to her about them and makes her feel "as if she had known them all her life" (lines 78-79). D is thus an effective answer, while A wrongly indicates that the postmaster has an ACTUAL familial relationship with the absent Ratan. B is inaccurate because Ratan does have a family and some vivid memories of her own, while C is inaccurate because Ratan's imagination is not compared to that of any other child (making any evaluative judgment of it as "extraordinary" automatically out of scope).

Chapter 1.2 | *The Fortune Teller*

1) CORRECT ANSWER: D

The passage describes the shared lives of three characters and the events that occurred after "Camillo's mother died" (line 32); the central one of these events is the "intimacy between Camillo and Rita" (line 38-39). D is thus the best answer, while A wrongly indicates that Villela (who is oblivious to the romance) is troubled by his wife's intimacy with Camillo. B is contradicted by the fact that Camillo "never knew" (line 39) how the intimacy developed, while C only would only refer to Camillo's feelings in the final paragraph, NOT to the nature of the entire passage.

2) CORRECT ANSWER: C

The narrator explains, regarding Camillo, that "Rita, like a serpent, was charming him" (lines 65-66) and destroying him even as he found her alluring. This evidence supports C, while Camillo's continued helplessness and impulsiveness can be used to eliminate an overly positive answer such as D. A refers to an image from the final paragraph that indicates the finality and fatefulness of the relationship between Camillo and Rita (not their "compatibility"), while B overstates the extent to which separation negatively affects these two characters (lines 75-76, which do not identify separation as a crippling or "overwhelming" problem).

3) CORRECT ANSWER: D

In lines 20-22, the narrator explains that Rita lives up to the depiction of her in Villela's "enthusiastic letters", as Camillo finds upon first meeting her. The letters thus gave him news of her qualities in advance, so that D is the best answer. A describes Rita as silly (and is too negative to fit the question), B indicates that Camillo welcomes Villela (NOT necessarily Rita), and C indicates Villela's high regard for Camillo (NOT Camillo's regard for Rita's qualities).

4) CORRECT ANSWER: C

In lines 42-44, the narrator explains that Camillo "yearned" for the "aroma of femininity" that made Rita so sensual or intriguing, so that C is the answer that best explains how the contact between Rita and Camillo "grew to love" (line 39). A, B, and D all describe qualities that Camillo enjoyed or would admire, but that are not directly cited by the narrator as the sources of his "love" for Rita.

5) CORRECT ANSWER: C

See above for the explanation of the correct answer. A indicates that Rita is attractive and lively in appearance, B indicates that Camillo bonded with Rita (but not WHY he loved her), and D indicates that Camillo reacts strongly to Rita's missive. Because these answers do not directly mention Camillo's love or yearning in the manner of C, they should be eliminated as poorly aligned to the demands of the previous question.

6) CORRECT ANSWER: D

While the paragraph begins with a discussion of "The three" (line 31) closely-bound characters, it ends with an explanation of how Rita and Camillo began (as a result of the death of Camillo's mother) to form an exclusive relationship that led to romance. The paragraph thus describes a turning point, so that D is the best answer. A is problematic because the death of Camillo's mother is only briefly mentioned (not described in the paragraph as a whole). B refers to a subject that is mostly addressed BEFORE the relevant paragraph, while C refers to a subject that is mainly analyzed AFTER, since the love between Camillo and Rita has not yet been directly discussed.

7) CORRECT ANSWER: A

While the narrator begins to explain the relationship between Camillo and Rita by describing shared activities (reading and recreation in lines 45-48), the narrator later shifts to gestures such as looks and touches (lines 49-53) that communicate the characters' closeness. This information supports A, while B wrongly criticizes Camillo (who is at most saddened by his mother's death) as timid. C wrongly attributes Villela's security about his friendship (line 77) to Camillo, who is not analyzed where this topic is concerned; D wrongly indicates that the affair has ended (is "fleeting" or short-lived), when in fact the affair is still in progress at the end of the passage.

8) CORRECT ANSWER: B

The word "ordinary" refers to the note expressing "good wishes" (line 56) that Rita sends to Camillo; the "hastily pencilled" (line 55) note is standard and unremarkable or "generic" in its contents. Choose B and eliminate A, since Camillo is just receiving the note and thus cannot be familiar with it. C (meaning careless) and D (a strong negative) would harshly and incorrectly criticize Rita and her attempt to reach out to Camillo.

9) CORRECT ANSWER: A

The narrator notes that the old chaise "is as good" (line 61) as the loftier chariot of Apollo: this attribution of grand qualities to something lowly or unremarkable is used to explain why Camillo holds Rita's ordinary note in such high regard. Choose A and eliminate D, since the comparison mostly involves interpretation (NOT the nature of the writing itself). B refers to a theme that is addressed only in the FOLLOWING portions of the passage (the typicality of Camillo's reaction, lines 62-63), while C criticizes Camillo (rather than explaining or analyzing his reaction).

10) CORRECT ANSWER: A

The relevant line reference occurs immediately after Camillo's struggle with "Vexation, fear, remorse, desire" (lines 68-69), and leads into the discussion of Camillo's accepted relationship with Rita. A is the best answer, while the relationship between Camillo and Villela DOES in fact continue (lines 76-78, eliminating B). C wrongly indicates that Camillo has become entirely immoral (not that he has committed a single transgression in forming a relationship), while D wrongly indicates that Camillo is not aware of the consequences (which he has, in fact, most likely considered in his state of "Vexation" but decided to disregard).

Chapter 1.3 | *Don't Ask Me Where I'm From*

1) CORRECT ANSWER: B
After considering her family's Serbian roots at length, the narrator determines that "This part of my identity will always be sore" (lines 81-82) but is something that she can "at least now accept" (lines 81-82). This sense that the narrator has arrived at a conclusion supports B, while the friends' acceptance of the narrator's background (lines 22-25) can be used to eliminate A. Although childhood moments and moments of annoyance are PARTS of the narrator's discussion, they do not make up the passage as a whole: eliminate C and D as inaccurate descriptions of the entire passage.

2) CORRECT ANSWER: B
In lines 80-83, the narrator notes that her Serbian identity makes her "sore" but that she can accept it "as part of who I am", a shift that is reflected in the passage as a whole. This evidence supports B. A overstates the narrator's shift towards a more positive emotion, C wrongly indicates that the narrator feels the SAME ("solidarity") as her peers when she in fact realizes that her identity sets her apart, and D wrongly states that the narrator "denied" being Serbian, rather than being uncomfortable with an identity that she was compelled to acknowledge.

3) CORRECT ANSWER: D
See above for the explanation of the correct answer. A indicates the narrator's hope that she will not be brought into a conversation, B indicates the narrator's sensitivity about her family background, and C records the narrator's doubts that she is "normal" on account of her background. While these line references involve strong emotions, they do not describe clear SHIFTS in emotion and thus do not fit the previous question.

4) CORRECT ANSWER: A
In the first paragraph, the narrator listens to a conversation about colleges and hopes that her friends "wouldn't try to include" (lines 7-8) her; she is conscious that she is different from them in an uncomfortable way, so that A is the best answer. The narrator's friends are not given specific names or well-developed identities (and are thus not being introduced here as important characters, eliminating B). C focuses too much attention on the narrator's parents (who have not been mentioned yet), while D attributes the wrong fear to the narrator (who doesn't want to TALK about colleges, but is not clearly afraid of attending college herself).

5) CORRECT ANSWER: D
While the narrator expects the friends to put on "fake, sympathetic smiles" and to condescend to her in other ways, they in fact are interested in and impressed by her background, so that D is the best answer. A wrongly assumes that the schools attended by the narrator's parents are not well known (an issue that is not addressed and that is LESS important than the fact that the schools are not American). B wrongly attributes a negative tone to the friends' ideas about college, while C wrongly indicates that the narrator feels anxiety about attending college herself, when in fact she feels anxiety about discussing her family.

6) CORRECT ANSWER: B
In lines 51-53, the narrator explains that she kept her "English accent while pronouncing the French words"; this is one example of a way in which she modified her behavior to

indicate that she was American, so that B is the best answer. A is contradicted by the narrator's admission that her parents did NOT go to Ivy League schools, while C is contradicted by the fact that the narrator felt different but was not socially ostracized in any cruel or systematic way. D involves a misreading of the narrator's account with her grandmother: the narrator does not avoid the grandmother completely, and is embarrassed MAINLY by the prospect of seeming unusual herself. Keep in mind, also, that the scene in which the narrator dodges the grandmother does not get a line reference in the question that follows.

7) CORRECT ANSWER: C

See above for the explanation of the correct answer. A indicates that the narrator's parents did not attend Ivy League schools, B indicates that the narrator is sensitive to her mother's accent and her peers' opinions, and D indicates that the narrator and her friends reacted poorly to the grandmother's cooking. Make sure not to take A as evidence for Question 6 A, B as evidence for Question 6 C or Question 6 D, or D as evidence for Question 6 D.

8) CORRECT ANSWER: C

The narrator's greeting is accompanied by "embarrassment" (line 59) and is quick because the narrator fears that her friends will make fun of her for speaking a foreign language. C thus appropriately captures the narrator's negative sentiments; A is wrongly neutral in tone. It is not clear from the greeting that the peers are intolerant (only that the narrator expects them to be, eliminating B), while the real discrepancy involves the narrator's background and the background of her classmates (not "generations", eliminating D).

9) CORRECT ANSWER: A

In lines 12-14, the narrator asks whether her friends knew better than to "assume that every's girl's parents went to some Ivy": the friends in fact do know better. Later, the narrator asks what was wrong with being Serbian (lines 24-25) and whether her friends meant to raise a specific sore point (lines 37-38), then promptly answers her own question in each case. Questions with such evident answers are known as rhetorical questions, and are used by the narrator to analyze her cultural situation: A is the best answer. B is problematic because the narrator relies on DIFFERENT scenarios and modes of comparison (not on a single EXTENDED analogy) to make her points. C and D describe actual features of the passage, but NOT features that clearly indicate that the narrator is analytical: in fact, conversational tones and anecdotes can indicate that a narrator is easygoing, informal, and NOT analytical.

10) CORRECT ANSWER: C

The word "sore" refers to a part of the narrator's identity, her Serbian heritage, which has proven to be a source of anxiety or a "sensitive" topic. C is the best answer. A and B both describe physical objects or conditions of weakness, while D ("traumatic") refers to a shocking and psychologically scarring occurrence, not to an issue that simply causes embarrassment over time.

Chapter 1.4 | *Vanity Fair*

1) CORRECT ANSWER: B

According to the passage, Rebecca was brought to Miss Pinkerton's school as a result of the "Catastrophe" (line 36) of her father's death; she dislikes her new surroundings and, after some time, desires for Miss Pinkerton to give her "a sum of money" and "get rid" of her (lines 95-96). This evidence supports B, while A and C both apply inappropriate positive tones to Miss Pinkerton's school (where Rebecca feels imprisoned and alienated). D wrongly identifies Miss Pinkerton as "oppressive": her SCHOOL is oppressive to Rebecca, while Miss Pinkerton herself does nothing to consciously harm her.

2) CORRECT ANSWER: C

The early stages of the passage describe how Rebecca interacted "with her father" (line 8) and mocked Miss Pinkerton with him, while the later segments explain how Rebecca fared at Miss Pinkerton's school after her father was "deceased" (line 44). This information supports C. A is inaccurate because Rebecca is depicted as a teenager throughout (so that there is not a pronounced shift in age), while B is problematic because Rebecca did not face "hardships" with her father and instead enjoyed his company. D is inaccurate because the early anecdotes are all "related" to the theme of Rebecca's clever and cynical nature, while the ultimate influence of the later "event" (Miss Pinkerton's offer) is not clearly explained.

3) CORRECT ANSWER: C

Rebecca's father is described as "lazy, clever, dissolute, [and] jovial" (line 32). He is both resourceful (clever) and committed to negative ends (dissolute), so that "mischevious" would be an appropriate description. Choose C and eliminate the positive D. A indicates that Mr. Sharp is extremely well known for evil deeds (not simply known and liked among somewhat shady acquaintances), while B is a harsh criticism that implies strong moral degeneracy (when in fact he is a lively or "jovial" man and has raised a daughter without horrific results).

4) CORRECT ANSWER: A

In lines 5-7, the narrator indicates that the juvenile Rebecca was able to manipulate ("coaxed and wheedled") adults into giving her the results she desired, such as meals. This information makes A the best answer. B indicates that Miss Pinkerton deluded herself into believing that Rebecca was innocent (not that Rebecca MANIPULATED her into having this false impression), C indicates that Rebecca learned put up false appearances (not that these false appearances were SUCCESSFUL as manipulation), and D indicates that Rebecca is forming a plan, but not that manipulation is central to this new effort.

5) CORRECT ANSWER: D

Rebecca and her father laugh after Miss Pinkerton makes Rebecca "a present of a doll" (line 21) and Rebecca eventually uses the doll itself to make a mockery of Miss Pinkerton in a routine that her father enjoys. D is the best answer. The narrator does not explicitly condemn the morals of either Rebecca or her father in the mostly descriptive line reference of them leaving and laughing (eliminating both A and D), while Rebecca and her father are enthusiastic about making a mockery of Miss Pinkerton, not about the act of leaving the party itself (eliminating B).

6) CORRECT ANSWER: C

In lines 37-41, Rebecca is described as reacting negatively to the "rigid formality" and "conventional regularity" of Miss Pinkerton's school, so that C effectively explains why Rebecca felt oppressed or saw the school as a "prison." A incorrectly identifies Rebecca's dislike of her companions as actual, physical aggression towards them, B is illogical because her father dies before she enters the school, and D misstates her actual complaints: she raises the POSSIBILITY of exploitation in lines 74-78, but does not claim that Miss Pinkerton IS exploiting her.

7) CORRECT ANSWER: A

See above for the explanation of the correct answer. B indicates Rebecca's preference for her father and aversion to her female companions, C lists specific women in the school whom Rebecca dislikes, and D indicates that Rebecca dislikes Miss Pinkerton's proposal. Make sure not to take B as evidence for Question 6 B, C as evidence for Question 6 A, or D as evidence for Question 6 D.

8) CORRECT ANSWER: A

The narrator establishes that Rebecca, regarding Miss Pinkerton's school, "determined at any rate to get free from the prison in which she found herself" (lines 58-59) and thus took advantage of the music curriculum to refine her skills and ensure later independence in life. Her "incessant practice" of music would thus lead to freedom from the school; choose A and eliminate B and C, which both wrongly assume that Rebecca wants to stay at Miss Pinkerton's school. D wrongly indicates that Rebecca finds the music enjoyable on its own, when in fact it is positive to her primarily because it is USEFUL as a means to an end.

9) CORRECT ANSWER: D

The word "justice" refers to Miss Pinkerton's sentiments towards Rebecca; she "disliked" (line 80) Rebecca and compared her to a "viper" (line 83) on account of Rebecca's bold and insulting manner. Miss Pinkerton is thus offended by Rebecca's conduct: D is the best answer, while A wrongly assumes that she will take action to harm Rebecca in response. B wrongly indicates that Miss Pinkerton sees herself as being in the wrong and is humbled, while C does not fit the exact context: a reader may believe that Miss Pinkerton is right, but Miss Pinkerton's primary sentiment is distaste for Rebecca (not righteous self-defense).

10) CORRECT ANSWER: C

The relevant line reference indicates that Miss Pinkerton found Rebecca "useful" (line 87), and that Rebecca herself has no respect for Miss Pinkerton and deeply dislikes life at the school. These lines thus encapsulate the terms of the relationship between these two characters: C is the best answer. A is inaccurate because it is only indicated that Rebecca WANTS to leave the school (not that she in fact does), B neglects the fact that Rebecca's hostility towards Miss Pinkerton emerged earlier (when she was living with her father), and D wrongly indicates that Rebecca's attitude toward the school has changed (when in fact she is simply voicing negative feelings that she has harbored for a considerable time).

Chapter 1.5 | *The Extraordinary Adventures of Arsène Lupin, Gentleman-Burglar*

1) CORRECT ANSWER: B

The passage describes the apparent presence of a whimsical burglar on a transatlantic steamer; a few characters who receive word of Lupin's presence decide to "investigate the mystery" (lines 50-51) themselves, and do so in an open and at times laughing manner. This information supports B. A is incorrect because Lupin is a burglar (not a fugitive) and because no group stays under suspicion for long, C is incorrect because the young man at the end (though he fits certain conditions) is not DEFINITIVELY identified as Lupin, and D is incorrect because the passengers at large remain calm, despite the narrator's initial, dramatic reaction to the news of Lupin's presence.

2) CORRECT ANSWER: A

In lines 25-28, the narrator claims that Lupin is "the man of a thousand disguises" and indicates that Lupin can successfully adapt to take on dramatically different appearances. This information supports A, while B employs faulty logic: Lupin may in fact "stand out" by taking on a strange disguise or a prominent identity, but will not be IDENTIFIED as Lupin. C is out of scope: the narrator never indicates that Lupin is ALWAYS moving. After all, Lupin may in fact stay in one place if he no longer feels threatened. D neglects the fact that the burglar's true identity (Arsène Lupin) is known by almost everyone in the passage, and can be eliminated for this reason.

3) CORRECT ANSWER: C

See above for the explanation of the correct answer. A indicates that Lupin is on the ship and that his assumed identity is not fully known, B indicates that an accomplished detective has been pursuing Lupin, and D indicates that Lupin could be any one of a few nearby passengers. Make sure not to take B as evidence for Question 2 C or D as question for Question 2 B.

4) CORRECT ANSWER: A

The relevant paragraph explains that Lupin is a "mysterious individual" (lines 15-16) and indicates why he is noteworthy, describing his secretive exploits and his aptitude in taking on different appearances. This information supports A, while B is inaccurate because Lupin was first mentioned or "introduced" in line 5. Keep in mind that the narrator, though fascinated by Lupin, does not offer a strong positive or negative judgment of him (eliminating C) and only provides a few highlights of his career (not a listing of ALL of Lupin's crimes, eliminating D).

5) CORRECT ANSWER: B

The narrator has already established (lines 13-28) that Lupin is an unusual and intriguing character; lines 29-35 indicate that Lupin could, to the surprise of the narrator, be disguised as one of the men nearby. B is thus the best answer, while A is problematic because Lupin is apparently on the steamer, so that his "whereabouts" are not entirely unknown. The narrator also moves on to calmly consider which passenger might be Lupin (instead of displaying "panic," eliminating C) and only names passengers who have SOME remote possibility of passing for Lupin in lines 29-35 (rather than indicating strong, negative "suspicions" about any of them, eliminating D).

6) CORRECT ANSWER: C

In lines 57-58, the narrator tells Miss Nelly that the two of them hold the key "for the solution to the problem". This statement indicates that the narrator has confidence in his abilities, so that C is the best answer. A records a question from Miss Nelly herself (not a statement regarding the narrator's talents), B mostly indicates that the narrator can investigate the case (and in fact compares him to a detective who has FAILED to catch Lupin), and D indicates that the narrator has narrowed down the possibilities for which passenger is really Lupin (not that the narrator has confidently or definitely CAUGHT Lupin).

7) CORRECT ANSWER: D

In their effort to discover Lupin, the narrator and Miss Nelly use a set of clues to "proceed by process of elimination" (line 68) and arrive at a logical conclusion. "Deduction" is a reasoning process that involves starting with broad premises or broad bodies of information in order to systematically reason towards a specific result; D is thus the best answer. The narrator and Miss Nelly in fact AVOID courses of action that are more approximate and emotional, such as "intuition" (A) and "rumor" (B). "Interrogation" (C) involves asking questions; however, the two characters MOSTLY consult a list and work through many possibilities without consulting the other passengers.

8) CORRECT ANSWER: D

The relevant lines describe how the narrator and Miss Nelly determine how other passengers (who are either traveling alone or are already known and trusted) are NOT Lupin. D is thus the best answer, while the single, final "suspect" is not definitively identified in this portion of the passage (eliminating A). B mistakes the sometimes lighthearted tone of the passage for "absurdity" (and neglects the fact that the search uses logical principles, eliminating B), while only a few of the people mentioned are identified by name (and are quickly removed from the list of "potential suspects" in any case, eliminating C).

9) CORRECT ANSWER: C

The first revelation of the suspect causes the narrator to feel a "shock of surprise" (lines 98-99); this initial reaction, however, is soon followed by the narrator's sense that it is "absurd" (line 102) to take the innocent-looking man for the disguised Lupin. This information supports C, while A and D both wrongly identify strongly negative initial reactions and B wrongly indicates that the narrator's final reaction (a positive denial of the man's seeming guilt) is negative.

10) CORRECT ANSWER: B

The phrase "attentions to" describes how the quiet young man has responded to Miss Nelly; these "attentions" annoy the narrator, who himself admires Miss Nelly (lines 46-48) and wants her company. It can be concluded that the young man is himself "preoccupied" with the woman whose company the narrator wants for himself. B is an effective answer, while A and D indicate that Miss Nelly (who in fact seems closer to the narrator) has become close to the young man. C refers to how the young man himself would see or regard Miss Nelly, not to a social action that might elicit the narrator's annoyance.

CHAPTER
TWO

Questions 1-10 are based on the following passage.
Chapter 2.1
The following excerpt is from *Kung I-Chi* (1919) by Lu Hsun.

At the age of twelve I started work as a waiter in Prosperity Tavern. The tavern keeper said I looked too foolish to serve the long-gowned customers, so
Line I was given work in the outer room. Although the
5 short-coated customers there were more easily pleased, they would insist on watching as the yellow wine was ladled from the keg, looking to see if there were any water at the bottom of the wine pot. Under such keen scrutiny, it was very difficult to dilute the wine. After a
10 few days my employer decided I was not suited for this work, and I was transferred to warming wine.

Thenceforward I stood all day behind the counter. Although I gave satisfaction at this work, I found it monotonous and futile. Our employer was a fierce-
15 looking individual, and the customers were a morose lot. Only when Kung I-Chi came to the tavern could I laugh a little. That is why I still remember him.

Kung was the only long-gowned customer to drink his wine standing. He was a big man, strangely
20 pallid, and scars often showed among the wrinkles of his face. Although he wore a long gown, it was dirty and tattered, and looked as if it had not been washed or mended for over ten years.

Kung would come to the counter to order two
25 bowls of heated wine and a dish of peas flavoured with aniseed. And he would produce nine coppers. Someone else would then call out, in deliberately loud tones,

"Kung I-Chi! There are some fresh scars on your face! You must have been stealing again!"

30 "Why spoil a man's good name groundlessly?" he would ask, opening his eyes wide.

"Good name indeed! Day before yesterday I saw you with my own eyes being beaten for stealing books from the Ho family!"

35 Kung would flush, the veins on his forehead standing out. Then followed quotations from the classics, like "A gentleman keeps his integrity even in poverty," and a jumble of archaic expressions till everybody was roaring with laughter.

40 From gossip I heard, Kung I-chi had studied the classics but had never passed the official examinations. With no way of making a living, he grew poorer and poorer, until he was practically reduced to beggary. He was a good calligrapher, and could get enough
45 copying work to support himself. Unfortunately he had failings: he liked drinking and was lazy. So after

a few days he would invariably disappear, taking books, paper, brushes and inkstand with him. And after this had happened several times, nobody wanted
50 to employ him as a copyist again. Then there was no help for him but to take to occasional pilfering. In our tavern his behaviour was exemplary. He never failed to pay up, although sometimes, when he had no ready money, his name would appear on the board where we
55 listed debtors. However, in less than a month he would always settle, and his name would be wiped off the board again.

After drinking half a bowl of wine, Kung would regain his composure. But then someone would ask:
60 "Kung I-chi, do you really know how to read?"

When Kung looked as if such a question were beneath contempt, they would continue: "How is it you never passed even the lowest official examination?"

At that Kung would look disconsolate and ill at
65 ease. His face would turn pale and his lips move, but only to utter those unintelligible classical expressions. Then everybody would laugh heartily again, and the whole tavern would be merry. At such times, I could join in the laughter without being scolded by my
70 master. In fact he often put such questions to Kung himself, to evoke laughter.

Knowing it was no use talking to them, Kung would chat to us children. Once he asked me: "Have you had any schooling?"

75 When I nodded, he said, "Well then, I'll test you. How do you write the character *hui* in *hui-hsiang peas?"

I thought, "I'm not going to be tested by a beggar!" So I turned away and ignored him. After
80 waiting for some time, he said very earnestly:

"I'll show you how. Mind you remember! When you have a shop of your own, you'll need to make up your accounts."

It seemed to me I was still very far from owning a
85 shop; besides, our employer never entered *hui-hsiang* peas in the account book. Amused yet exasperated, I answered listlessly: "Isn't it the character *hui* with the grass radical?"

Kung was delighted, and tapped two long
90 fingernails on the counter. "Right, right!" he said, nodding. "Only there are four different ways of writing *hui*. Do you know them?" My patience exhausted, I scowled and made off. Kung had dipped his finger in wine, in order to trace the characters on the counter;
95 but when he saw how indifferent I was, he sighed and looked most disappointed.

*hui-hsiang: Chinese word for aniseed.

CONTINUE

1

Which choice best describes the developmental pattern of the passage?

(A) A reflective depiction of a memorable character
B) A lighthearted description of a diverse clientele
C) A candid account of a meaningful encounter
D) A nostalgic narration of a heartfelt moment

2

Which of the following statements about Kung I-Chi is best supported by the passage?

(A) He harbors a true appreciation of knowledge.
B) He enjoys playing the role of the tavern fool.
C) He disapproves of the other tavern customers.
D) He has resigned himself to the life of a beggar.

3

The main purpose of lines 4-9 ("Although...wine") is to

A) portray the customers of the tavern as having refined tastes.
(B) suggest that the customers suspect the tavern of cheating them.
C) contrast the upper class and lower class customers of the tavern.
D) indicate that the customers of the tavern are easily entertained.

4

The narrator's attitude towards Kung I-Chi can best be described as

A) sympathetic.
B) intrigued.
C) indifferent.
(D) condescending.

5

Which choice provides the best evidence for the answer to the previous question?

A) Lines 16-17 ("Only when...him")
B) Lines 45-46 ("Unfortunately he...lazy")
(C) Lines 78-79 ("I thought...him")
D) Lines 95-96 ("when he...disappointed")

6

According to the passage, the other customers at Prosperity Tavern pose questions to Kung I-Chi most likely to

A) mock him for his failed education.
(B) provoke him for their own amusement.
C) expose him as a man without integrity.
D) include him as a member of the community.

7

Which choice provides the best evidence for the answer to the previous question?

A) Lines 32-34 ("Good name...family")
B) Lines 64-65 ("At that...ease")
(C) Lines 65-68 ("His face...merry")
D) Lines 70-71 ("In fact...laughter")

8

In lines 40-57 ("From gossip...again") the narrator presents a contrast primarily between Kung I-Chi's

(A) irresponsible conduct outside of the tavern and his concern for his credit in the tavern.
B) apparent skill as a calligrapher and his inability to secure work as a copier.
C) former life as a scholar and his current life as a beggar.
D) widespread reputation as a thief and his underlying integrity.

CONTINUE

9

The passage indicates that Kung I-Chi is no longer able to support himself through his copying work primarily because he has earned a reputation of one who is

A) indolent.

B) manipulative.

C) unskilled.

D) untrustworthy.

10

As used in line 56, "settle" most nearly means

A) find a way out.

B) negotiate a compromise.

C) submit to pressure.

D) pay his dues.

CONTINUE

Questions 1-10 are based on the following passage.
Chapter 2.2
Adapted from Willa Cather's *Paul's Case* (1905).

It was Paul's afternoon to appear before the faculty
of the Pittsburgh High School to account for his various
misdemeanors. He had been suspended a week ago,
Line and his father had called at the Principal's office and
5 confessed his perplexity about his son. Paul entered
the faculty room suave and smiling. His clothes were a
trifle outgrown, and the tan velvet on the collar of his
open overcoat was frayed and worn; but for all that there
was something of the dandy about him, and he wore an
10 opal pin in his neatly knotted black four-in-hand, and a
red carnation in his buttonhole. This latter adornment
the faculty somehow felt was not properly significant
of the contrite spirit befitting a boy under the ban of
suspension.
15 Paul was tall for his age and very thin, with high,
cramped shoulders and a narrow chest. His eyes were
remarkable for a certain hysterical brilliancy, and
he continually used them in a conscious, theatrical
sort of way, peculiarly offensive in a boy. The pupils
20 were abnormally large, as though he were addicted to
belladonna, but there was a glassy glitter about them
which that drug does not produce.
When questioned by the Principal as to why he
was there Paul stated, politely enough, that he wanted to
25 come back to school. This was a lie, but Paul was quite
accustomed to lying; found it, indeed, indispensable for
overcoming friction. His teachers were asked to state
their respective charges against him, which they did
with such a rancor and aggrievedness as evinced that
30 this was not a usual case, Disorder and impertinence
were among the offenses named, yet each of his
instructors felt that it was scarcely possible to put into
words the real cause of the trouble, which lay in a sort of
hysterically defiant manner of the boy's; in the contempt
35 which they all knew he felt for them, and which he
seemingly made not the least effort to conceal. Once,
when he had been making a synopsis of a paragraph at
the blackboard, his English teacher had stepped to his
side and attempted to guide his hand. Paul had started
40 back with a shudder and thrust his hands violently
behind him. The astonished woman could scarcely have
been more hurt and embarrassed had he struck at her.
The insult was so involuntary and definitely personal
as to be unforgettable. In one way and another he had
45 made all his teachers, men and women alike, conscious
of the same feeling of physical aversion. In one class
he habitually sat with his hand shading his eyes; in

another he always looked out of the window during the
recitation; in another he made a running commentary on
50 the lecture, with humorous intention.
His teachers felt this afternoon that his whole
attitude was symbolized by his shrug and his flippantly
red carnation flower, and they fell upon him without
mercy, his English teacher leading the pack. He stood
55 through it smiling, his pale lips parted over his white
teeth. (His lips were continually twitching, and he had
a habit of raising his eyebrows that was contemptuous
and irritating to the last degree.) Older boys than Paul
had broken down and shed tears under that baptism of
60 fire, but his set smile did not once desert him, and his
only sign of discomfort was the nervous trembling of the
fingers that toyed with the buttons of his overcoat, and
an occasional jerking of the other hand that held his hat.
Paul was always smiling, always glancing about him,
65 seeming to feel that people might be watching him and
trying to detect something. This conscious expression,
since it was as far as possible from boyish mirthfulness,
was usually attributed to insolence or "smartness."
As the inquisition proceeded one of his instructors
70 repeated an impertinent remark of the boy's, and the
Principal asked him whether he thought that a courteous
speech to have made a woman. Paul shrugged his
shoulders slightly and his eyebrows twitched.
"I don't know," he replied. "I didn't mean to be
75 polite or impolite, either. I guess it's a sort of way I have
of saying things regardless."
The Principal, who was a sympathetic man, asked
him whether he didn't think that a way it would be well
to get rid of. Paul grinned and said he guessed so. When
80 he was told that he could go he bowed gracefully and
went out. His bow was but a repetition of the scandalous
red carnation.

CONTINUE

1

Over the course of the first paragraph, the primary focus shifts from

A) an objective characterization of Paul to observations about him made by other characters.

B) the confusion of Paul's father about the situation to the thoughts of the faculty members.

C) the reasons Paul had been suspended from school to Paul's reaction following his suspension.

D) the cause behind Paul's appearance at the faculty room to a description of Paul's clothing.

2

As used in line 1, "appear before" most nearly means

A) face.

B) approach.

C) confront.

D) withstand.

3

The passage states that Paul's red carnation struck the faculty as

A) stylish.

B) untidy.

C) cheerful.

D) inappropriate.

4

Which choice provides the best evidence for the answer to the previous question?

A) Lines 5-6 ("Paul entered...smiling")

B) Lines 6-8 ("His clothes...worn")

C) Lines 8-11 ("but for...buttonhole")

D) Lines 11-14 ("This latter...suspension")

5

The narrator uses an image of Paul's eyes (lines 16-22) to present Paul as

A) intellectual.

B) playful.

C) impudent.

D) unstable.

6

In context of the passage as a whole, the third paragraph (lines 23-50) mainly serves to

A) indicate the various misdemeanors Paul has been held accountable for.

B) reveal Paul's true feelings towards his teachers as the cause of his behavior.

C) show that Paul lied often to authority figures as a means of evading suspicion.

D) indicate a significant alteration in the relationship between Paul and his teachers.

7

The narrator states that Paul's teachers shared which common sentiment about him?

A) Bitterness

B) Revulsion

C) Pity

D) Confusion

8

Which choice provides the best evidence for the answer to the previous question?

A) Lines 28-30 ("they did...case")

B) Lines 31-33 ("each of...trouble")

C) Lines 41-42 ("The astonished...her")

D) Lines 44-46 ("In one...aversion")

CONTINUE

9

In the fourth paragraph (lines 51-68) the narrator primarily creates a contrast between

A) The teachers' perception of Paul and Paul's perception of them.

B) Paul's cheerful and confident appearance and his inner discomfort about being criticized.

C) the faculty's vehement and disparaging remarks towards Paul and Paul's indifferent response.

D) Paul's intentional expressions and his involuntary movements.

10

According to the passage, the purpose of Paul's appearance before the faculty was to

A) determine whether Paul had caused enough disruption to warrant expulsion.

B) give Paul a chance to appeal his suspension by explaining his behavior.

C) pacify Paul's teachers by giving them an opportunity to vent their frustration.

D) lay the foundations for Paul's education in correct manners.

CONTINUE

Questions 1-10 are based on the following passage.
Chapter 2.3
The following is an excerpt from a memoir in progress (2017) by Dina Peone.

When I first spotted Serena, she was bent over in a hot pink tutu. I had heard her squeal from a joke told by one of the six or seven young men that surrounded
Line her. Her hourglass torso sprang upright, revealing a
5 dyed-pink and blonde 'scene kid' haircut. She seemed unreal, like a hologram of an anime character. She exuded joy with a boyish charm. I decided she was the girl of my dreams.

I slinked behind her in a semi-circle, hoping to
10 get a better view of her face without appearing too obvious. When Serena laughed, her dark eyes vanished behind a glare on her nerdy square-rimmed glasses. On either side of her full, ruby-painted lips: dimples! I sank into them. She was so petite that she seemed
15 easily broken. Her neck was slim under a well-defined jaw, which, in light of my turtle-like chin pulling in a straight line of scarring to my chest, I envied. Between two broad but dainty shoulders, her collarbones protruded. Long, slender arms revealed the perfect
20 fingers. I almost forgot my own body, amputations included, the attraction to hers was so strong.

I spent the rest of the evening following Serena from room to room. She did not seem to notice me. Eventually, I worked up the courage to join her
25 outside; I complimented her rainbow bracelet and she thanked me. When I caught her looking at my sling, I reflexively explained that I had just had surgery in Boston. Serena replied that she too lives in Boston. I don't know why, but she gave me her number. I could
30 hardly conceal my excitement.

I waited two weeks to call Serena. When the machine picked up, I hung up and practiced the message I would leave. In it, trying not to sound too hoarse, I suggested a meeting for coffee. Weeks went
35 by without my hearing back from her, so I called again and left another message. This one focused on how I was unsure if I'd had the right number but if I did then I would like to hang out sometime. I might have even called Serena a third time but she finally responded.
40 There was a note of despair (or was it reluctance?) in her voice. We made plans for her to visit my apartment in Charlestown during the coming weekend. For days, I fretted over what I could wear that would conceal the majority of my bandages while preserving some
45 measure of attractiveness.

That weekend, Serena got lost near my apartment

building. I went out and found her near the bus stop, looking tipsy (or was it nervous?) and painfully gorgeous. Her hair was a flawless mess, her makeup
50 seemed like it had been done professionally, and her bare legs practically stabbed my eyes. Once we settled inside my room, Serena offered me a sip from her flask and I declined. I felt relieved that she had at least one weakness. The moment of silence that followed would
55 prove to be longer and more uncomfortable than a technical error that occurred onstage while I was acting seven years later: the gun that was supposed to "kill" me halfway through my line failed to fire, which left me clinging mid-fall to the air, suspending my scream
60 for what seemed like several minutes.

At some point in our awkward getting-to-know-you conversation, she asked if the nearby keyboard was mine. When I said yes, she jumped up and sat next to me on my bed.
65 "Do you play?" she asked, the bed still bouncing. Her body odor was pungent and undisguised by artificial scents. I felt lightheaded with longing.

"Yes, sort of. I try... I used to be better before my burn injury."
70 "That's so cool that you still play. My boyfriend and I have a band. He plays drums and I sing and play keyboard. We have some recordings online if you're curious."

I was disappointed to hear the B word, but I
75 gave an enthusiastic yes. She smiled and leaned in to type the URL on my laptop. I inhaled slowly, deeply, and clicked on the first song: "Complications." The opening was simple enough, but by the second measure, a voice cracked open like hard candy and
80 oozed, uncontainable. A wave of girlish shrieks and deathbed moans underneath a frantic minor scale made me shudder. Serena sounded like Barbie if Barbie got into a rolling car crash. I was seriously impressed.

I complimented her thoroughly and then confessed
85 that I used to sing better before the smoke damage to my lungs. The more I talked about the fire, the more relaxed I felt and the more that Serena drank. At some point, she confessed that she had been ignoring my calls but she didn't say why. The more she drank, the
90 sadder she got. How someone could be so beautiful and so troubled seemed unfair to me. I wanted to slap her and tell her to appreciate her body. But, inside, I knew, she was also at war with herself.

CONTINUE ▶

1

Which choice best describes the developmental pattern of the passage?

A) A lighthearted anecdote about a new relationship

B) A careful analysis of a complex character

C) A heartfelt recounting of a personal tragedy

D) A detailed depiction of a meaningful encounter

2

According to the passage, the narrator initially observes Serena with

A) wariness.

B) detachment.

C) amusement.

D) keenness.

3

The passage suggests that one consequence of Serena's beauty is that

A) she is stifled by the excessive attention she draws.

B) she has not been able to experience true happiness.

C) the narrator is overwhelmed with feelings of resentfulness.

D) the narrator feels a momentary reprieve from her own condition.

4

Which choice provides the best evidence for the answer to the previous question?

A) Lines 15-17 ("Her neck...envied")

B) Lines 20-21 ("I almost...strong")

C) Lines 47-49 ("I went...gorgeous")

D) Lines 90-91 ("How someone...me")

5

The parenthetical statements in lines 40 and 48 primarily serve to convey the narrator's

A) doubt about her assessments of Serena.

B) concerns about Serena's motives.

C) tendency to overanalyze every situation.

D) observation of an unpredictable personality.

6

Which choice best supports the conclusion that Serena is mindful of her appearance?

A) Lines 1-2 ("When I...tutu")

B) Lines 5-6 ("She seemed...character")

C) Lines 25-26 ("I complimented...me")

D) Lines 49-50 ("Her hair...professionally")

7

As used in line 54, "weakness" most nearly means

A) fixation.

B) fondness.

C) vulnerability.

D) disadvantage.

8

Over the course of the Serena's visit, the narrator presents a contrast between

A) Serena's apparent commitment to her boyfriend and the narrator's unrequited feelings for her.

B) her increasing calmness when discussing her tragic past and Serena's growing unease.

C) Serena's outward confidence in her appearance and the inner shame she feels about her body.

D) Serena's enthusiasm about pursuing a career in music and the narrator's loss of interest in such a path.

CONTINUE

9

Which statement best describes a technique the narrator uses to represent the quality of Serena's music?

A) The narrator illustrates the uninhibited quality of Serena's music by depicting Serena's voice as oozing uncontainably.

B) The narrator emphasizes the upbeat quality of Serena's music by comparing Serena's voice to that of a Barbie doll.

C) The narrator highlights the melancholy quality of Serena's music by describing her sounds as reminiscent of deathbed moans.

D) The narrator underscores the immature quality of Serena's music by hinting that her sounds are nothing more than girlish shrieks.

10

In context of the passage as a whole, the last sentence of the passage reveals the narrator's

A) compassion towards Serena.

B) connection to Serena.

C) judgment of Serena.

D) anxiety about Serena.

CONTINUE

Questions 1-10 are based on the following passage.
Chapter 2.4
Adapted from Emile Zola, *Therese Raquin* (1867).

A week after the marriage, Camille distinctly told his mother that he intended quitting Vernon to reside in Paris. Madame Raquin protested: she had arranged

Line her mode of life, and would not modify it in any way.

5 Thereupon her son had a nervous attack, and threatened to fall ill, if she did not give way to his whim.

"Never have I opposed you in your plans," said he; "I married my cousin Therese, I took all the drugs you gave me when I was ill. It is only natural, now, when I

10 have a desire of my own, that you should be of the same mind. We will move at the end of the month."

Madame Raquin was unable to sleep all night. The decision Camille had come to, upset her way of living, and, in despair, she sought to arrange another existence

15 for herself and the married couple. Little by little, she recovered calm. She reflected that the young people might have children, and that her small fortune would not then suffice. It was necessary to earn money, to go into business again, to find lucrative occupation for

20 Therese. The next day she had become accustomed to the idea of moving, and had arranged a plan for a new life.

At luncheon she was quite gay.

"This is what we will do," said she to her children.

25 "I will go to Paris to-morrow. There I will look out for a small shopkeeping business for sale, and Therese and myself will resume selling needles and cotton, which will give us something to do. You, Camille, will act as you like. You can either stroll about in the sun, or you

30 can find some employment."

"I shall find employment," answered the young man.

The truth was that an idiotic ambition had alone impelled Camille to leave Vernon. He wished to find a

35 post in some important administration. He blushed with delight when he fancied he saw himself in the middle of a large office, with lustring elbow sleeves, and a pen behind his ear.

Therese was not consulted: she had always

40 displayed such passive obedience that her aunt and husband no longer took the trouble to ask her opinion. She went where they went, she did what they did, without a complaint, without a reproach, without appearing even to be aware that she changed her place

45 of residence.

Madame Raquin came to Paris, and went straight to the Arcade of the Pont Neuf. An old maid at Vernon had sent her to one of her relatives who in this arcade kept a mercery shop which she desired to get rid of. The

50 former mercer found the shop rather small, and rather dark; but, in passing through Paris, she had been taken aback by the noise in the streets, by the luxuriously dressed windows, and this narrow gallery, this modest shop front, recalled her former place of business which

55 was so peaceful. She could fancy herself again in the provinces, and she drew a long breath thinking that her dear children would be happy in this out-of-the-way corner. The low price asked for the business, caused her to make up her mind. The owner sold it her for 2,000

60 francs, and the rent of the shop and first floor was only 1,200 francs a year. Madame Raquin, who had close upon 4,000 francs saved up, calculated that she could pay for the business and settle the rent for the first year, without encroaching on her fortune. The salary Camille

65 would be receiving, and the profit on the mercery business would suffice, she thought, to meet the daily expenses; so that she need not touch the income of her funded money, which would capitalise, and go towards providing marriage portions for her grandchildren.

70 She returned to Vernon beaming with pleasure, relating that she had found a gem, a delightful little place right in the centre of Paris. Little by little, at the end of a few days, in her conversations of an evening, the damp, obscure shop in the arcade became a palace;

75 she pictured it to herself, so far as her memory served her, as convenient, spacious, tranquil, and replete with a thousand inestimable advantages.

"Ah! my dear Therese," said she, "you will see how happy we shall be in that nook! There are three beautiful

80 rooms upstairs. The arcade is full of people. We will make charming displays. There is no fear of our feeling dull."

CONTINUE

1

Which choice best describes what happens in the passage?

A) Prompted by a career change, one character moves to a big city, resulting in his family's need to adapt.

B) One character responds to a threat to her lifestyle by immersing herself in an alternate plan.

C) Unwilling to grant independence to her newlywed children, a character follows them to settle in a new city.

D) One character creates a new business in a new location in anticipation of her family's marital needs.

2

The passage as a whole characterizes Madame Raquin as

A) overachieving.

B) closed-minded.

C) entrepreneurial.

D) assertive.

3

The narrator indicates that Camille wishes to move to Paris primarily in order to

A) start a new life with his family.

B) escape his overbearing mother.

C) pursue a dignified career.

D) seek a high-paying job.

4

Which of the following best supports the conclusion that Madame Raquin views Camille as having no significant role in her plans?

A) Lines 1-3 ("Camille distinctively...Paris")

B) Lines 12-15 ("The decision...couple")

C) Lines 28-30 ("You, Camille...employment")

D) Lines 33-35 ("The truth...administration")

5

The third paragraph (lines 12-22) functions primarily to

A) establish a character's primary values.

B) provide an explanation behind the couple's feeling of anxiety.

C) outline a thought process that leads to a resolution.

D) present an argument for a course of action.

6

It can be inferred from the passage that Therese is perceived by her family members as

A) a docile member whose views are not solicited.

B) an indispensable benefactor of the family.

C) a reliable source of emotional stability.

D) a financial burden to the rest of the household.

7

Which choice provides the best evidence for the answer to the previous question?

A) Lines 18-20 ("It was...Therese")

B) Lines 26-28 ("Therese and...do")

C) Lines 39-41 ("Therese was...opinion")

D) Lines 78-80 ("Ah! my...upstairs")

52

CONTINUE

8

As used in line 33, "idiotic" most nearly means

A) absurd.

B) bizarre.

C) illogical.

D) whimsical.

9

The passage states that Madame Raquin ultimately chose to buy the mercery shop regardless of its small size because

A) it would provide sufficient financial stability for her newlywed children.

B) it evoked a rural atmosphere in stark contrast to the chaos of Paris.

C) it represented something other than the typically pretentious Parisian storefront.

D) it was potentially self-sustaining and would not be a significant financial burden.

10

The narrator uses the word "palace" (line 74) to indicate that Madame Raquin

A) romanticizes her and her family's new life in the mercery shop.

B) is trying to convince herself that she made the right decision.

C) believes the shop will provide her family with upward social mobility.

D) feels the need to sway a reluctant Therese to agree with her plans.

CONTINUE

Questions 1-10 are based on the following passage.
Chapter 2.5
Adapted from Oscar Wilde's *The Canterville Ghost* (1887).

When Mr. Hiram B. Otis, the American Minister, bought Canterville Chase, every one told him he was doing a very foolish thing, as there was no doubt at all that the place was haunted. Indeed, Lord Canterville
5 himself, who was a man of the most punctilious honour, had felt it his duty to mention the fact to Mr. Otis when they came to discuss terms.

'We have not cared to live in the place ourselves,' said Lord Canterville, 'since my grandaunt, the
10 Dowager Duchess of Bolton, was frightened into a fit, from which she never really recovered, by two skeleton hands being placed on her shoulders as she was dressing for dinner, and I feel bound to tell you, Mr. Otis, that the ghost has been seen by several
15 living members of my family . . . After the unfortunate accident to the Duchess, none of our younger servants would stay with us, and Lady Canterville often got very little sleep at night, in consequence of the mysterious noises that came from the corridor and the
20 library.'

'My Lord,' answered the Minister, 'I will take the furniture and the ghost at a valuation. I come from a modern country, where we have everything that money can buy; and with all our spry young fellows painting
25 the Old World red, and carrying off your best actresses and prima-donnas, I reckon that if there were such a thing as a ghost in Europe, we'd have it at home in a very short time in one of our public museums, or on the road as a show.'

30 'I fear that the ghost exists,' said Lord Canterville, smiling, 'though it may have resisted the overtures of your enterprising impresarios. It has been well known for three centuries, since 1584 in fact, and always makes its appearance before the death of any member
35 of our family.'

'Well, so does the family doctor for that matter, Lord Canterville. But there is no such thing, sir, as a ghost, and I guess the laws of Nature are not going to be suspended for the British aristocracy.'

40 'You are certainly very natural in America,' answered Lord Canterville, who did not quite understand Mr. Otis's last observation, 'and if you don't mind a ghost in the house, it is all right. Only you must remember I warned you.'

45 A few weeks after this, the purchase was completed, and at the close of the season the Minister and his family went down to Canterville Chase. . . It was a lovely July evening, and the air was delicate with the scent of the pine-woods. Now and then they
50 heard a wood pigeon brooding over its own sweet voice, or saw, deep in the rustling fern, the burnished breast of the pheasant. Little squirrels peered at them from the beech-trees as they went by, and the rabbits scudded away through the brushwood and over the
55 mossy knolls, with their white tails in the air. As they entered the avenue of Canterville Chase, however, the sky became suddenly overcast with clouds, a curious stillness seemed to hold the atmosphere, a great flight of rooks passed silently over their heads, and, before
60 they reached the house, some big drops of rain had fallen.

Standing on the steps to receive them was an old woman, neatly dressed in black silk, with a white cap and apron. This was Mrs. Umney, the housekeeper,
65 whom Mrs. Otis, at Lady Canterville's earnest request, had consented to keep on in her former position. She made them each a low curtsey as they alighted, and said in a quaint, old-fashioned manner, 'I bid you welcome to Canterville Chase.' Following her, they
70 passed through the fine Tudor hall into the library, a long, low room, panelled in black oak, at the end of which was a large stained-glass window. Here they found tea laid out for them, and, after taking off their wraps, they sat down and began to look round, while
75 Mrs. Umney waited on them.

Suddenly Mrs. Otis caught sight of a dull red stain on the floor just by the fireplace and, quite unconscious of what it really signified, said to Mrs. Umney, 'I am afraid something has been spilt there.'

80 'Yes, madam,' replied the old housekeeper in a low voice, 'blood has been spilt on that spot.'

'How horrid,' cried Mrs. Otis; 'I don't at all care for blood-stains in a sitting-room. It must be removed at once.'

85 The old woman smiled, and answered in the same low, mysterious voice, 'It is the blood of Lady Eleanore de Canterville, who was murdered on that very spot by her own husband, Sir Simon de Canterville, in 1575. Sir Simon survived her nine
90 years, and disappeared suddenly under very mysterious circumstances. His body has never been discovered, but his guilty spirit still haunts the Chase. The blood-stain has been much admired by tourists and others, and cannot be removed.'

95 'That is all nonsense,' cried Washington Otis, the Minister's strapping young son; 'Pinkerton's Champion Stain Remover and Paragon Detergent will clean it up in no time,' and before the terrified

CONTINUE

housekeeper could interfere he had fallen upon his
100   knees, and was rapidly scouring the floor with a small
stick of what looked like a black cosmetic. In a few
moments no trace of the blood-stain could be seen.

1

Which choice best describes what happens in the passage?

A) A family is surprised to discover that their new home is occupied by a ghost.

B) A family is put in danger after having ignored warnings about their new home.

C) A family remains unconvinced about a ghost's existence in their new home.

D) A family becomes uneasy in their new home despite being cynical of a ghost there.

2

The main purpose of the third paragraph is to

A) emphasize Otis's determination to see the ghost.

B) imply that Otis views the ghost as a lucrative business opportunity.

C) show Otis's skepticism about the ghost's existence.

D) characterize Otis as brave in the face of unknown danger.

3

It can be reasonably inferred that Lord Canterville warns Mr. Otis of a ghostly presence at Canterville Chase most likely to

A) dissuade Otis from buying the property.

B) perpetuate the notoriety of the ghost.

C) remain consistent with his principles.

D) avoid blame for putting Otis in danger.

4

Which choice provides the best evidence for the answer to the previous question?

A) Lines 2-4 ("every one...haunted")

B) Lines 4-7 ("Indeed, Lord...terms")

C) Lines 8-11 ("We have...recovered")

D) Lines 42-44 ("if you...you")

5

Which choice provides the best evidence for the claim that Otis's disbelief in ghosts is based in a scientific perspective of the world?

A) Lines 21-22 ("I will...valuation")

B) Lines 22-24 ("I come...buy")

C) Lines 26-29 ("I reckon...show")

D) Lines 37-39 ("But there...aristocracy")

6

In context of his conversation with Lord Canterville, Mr. Otis's mention of "the family doctor" (line 36) serves to

A) sardonically dismiss Lord Canterville's claim about the ghost.

B) provide respite from a serious exchange with a lighthearted remark.

C) underscore his credibility by providing a personal anecdote.

D) point out that visitations before family deaths are common.

7

In lines 45-62, the narrator presents a contrast primarily between the

A) peaceful atmosphere outside Canterville Chase and the ominous mood created near it.

B) vibrant nature surrounding Otis's former home and the bleak desolation of Canterville Chase.

C) family's excitement about moving to Canterville Chase and their later uncertainty upon seeing it.

D) fair climate of Canterville Chase during the daytime and its unpleasant weather at night.

55

CONTINUE

8

The narrator indicates that Mrs. Umney remained at Canterville Chase mainly because

A) Lady Canterville had insisted that she stay to serve the Otis family.

B) she was able to educate the Otis family about the ghost's behaviors.

C) Mrs. Otis requested that she serve as the Otis family's housekeeper.

D) she was able to protect the Otis family from the ghost's harmful presence.

9

As used in line 77, "unconscious of" most nearly means

A) unsure of.

B) frightened by.

C) fascinated by.

D) oblivious to.

10

According to the passage, Mrs. Umney reacts to Washington's attempt to remove the stain with

A) awe, because the stain was said to be impossible to remove.

B) apprehension, because she believes in the legends surrounding the ghost.

C) dismay, because she knows that tragedy will soon befall the household.

D) joy, because Washington has liberated the house from the ghost.

Answer Key: CHAPTER TWO

Chapter 2.1
1. A
2. A
3. B
4. D
5. C
6. B
7. C
8. A
9. D
10. D

Chapter 2.2
1. D
2. A
3. D
4. D
5. C
6. A
7. A
8. A
9. D
10. B

Chapter 2.3
1. D
2. D
3. D
4. B
5. A
6. D
7. C
8. B
9. A
10. B

Chapter 2.4
1. B
2. D
3. C
4. C
5. C
6. A
7. C
8. D
9. D
10. A

Chapter 2.5
1. C
2. C
3. C
4. B
5. D
6. A
7. A
8. A
9. D
10. B

Answer Explanations

Chapter 2

Chapter 2.1 | *Kung I-Chi*

1) CORRECT ANSWER: A
The narrator spends the passage describing Kung I-Chi, a character who stood out for his good humor and his irresponsible ways: reflecting on Kung's jovial nature, the narrator declares that "That is why I still remember him" (line 17). A is the best answer, while B wrongly shifts focus away from Kung and onto the entire "clientele". C and D may seem appropriate to the episode at the end of the passage, but neglect the larger character sketch of Kung and should thus be eliminated.

2) CORRECT ANSWER: A
Towards the end of the passage, Kung asks about the narrator's "schooling" (line 74) and looks "most disappointed" (line 96) when the narrator does not take a lesson from him; this information, combined with Kung's own education, indicates that he values knowledge. Choose A and eliminate B and D, which refer to rather negative elements of Kung's character but wrongly indicate that he fully accepts them (since his outreach to the narrator may indicate the exact opposite, a desire to be more highly regarded). C is distorts an actual theme of the passage: the other customers find Kung lowly and humorous while he ACCEPTS their jesting.

3) CORRECT ANSWER: B
The relevant lines explain that some of the customers are watchful when wine is distributed; the narrator is assigned to "dilute the wine" (line 9) with water and these customers are suspicious that the wine is not pure. B is thus the best answer, while A and D wrongly apply strong positives to the situation of the suspicious customers. C is problematic because only the short-coated customers are considered at length, so the relevant lines do not primarily provide a "comparison".

4) CORRECT ANSWER: D
In lines 78-79, the narrator responds to Kung's lesson by reflecting that he is about to be "tested by a beggar", Kung himself. This belittling or condescending attitude towards Kung justifies D and can be used to eliminate A (positive) and C (neutral). B is a trap answer: Kung's character may intrigue the reader, but the narrator is well aware of Kung's habits and personality and thus cannot be intrigued or mystified by him.

5) CORRECT ANSWER: C
See above for the explanation of the correct answer. A indicates that the narrator remembers Kung as a source of laughter, B indicates that Kung had specific personality flaws, and D indicates that the narrator was indifferent to Kung's lesson (NOT to Kung

himself). Make sure not to wrongly take B as evidence for Question 4 D (since the line reference does not define how the narrator felt about Kung's failings beyond basic negativity) or D as evidence for Question 4 C.

6) CORRECT ANSWER: B
In lines 65-68, the narrator explains that, in response to questions from the other tavern-goers, the agitated Kung would utter "unintelligible classical expressions" and cause "the whole tavern" to be merry. Kung is thus provoked into entertaining the tavern, justifying B and eliminating answers A and C, which indicate considerable hostility. However, Kung is a disreputable man and is not entirely accepted by the tavern or the narrator: D is thus too positive to be correct.

7) CORRECT ANSWER: C
See above for the explanation of the correct answer. A describes Kung's response to an accusation (NOT a question), B indicates that Kung is bothered by a question (but not WHY the question was posed), and D indicates that the tavern-keeper provoked Kung for his amusement. D is a trap answer: the line reference refers to the master but does not DIRECTLY consider the motives of the customers.

8) CORRECT ANSWER: A
In the relevant lines, it is explained that Kung "liked drinking and was lazy" (line 46) and that he was not a trustworthy copyist; however, within the tavern "his behavior was exemplary" (line 52). This contrast supports A and can be used to eliminate B (which focuses only on one detail from the discussion, Kung's calligraphy). C wrongly indicates that Kung is a beggar (when in fact he is a thief), while D wrongly indicates that Kung's thieving is well-known or notorious (when in fact he mostly pilfers) and that he has "underlying" integrity (when in fact his integrity relates almost entirely to the tavern).

9) CORRECT ANSWER: D
In his work as a copyist, Kung "would invariably disappear" (line 47) and take various items with him. He thus cannot be trusted, so that D is an effective answer. Kung is in fact lazy, but this flaw is not what undermines his copyist employment (eliminating A). Instead of "manipulating" his employers he simply disappears (eliminating B), and despite his unreliability he is in fact skilled (lines 44-45, eliminating C).

10) CORRECT ANSWER: D
The word "settle" occurs to what Kung must do to have his name removed from the board that "listed debtors" (line 55); he thus eliminates his debt or pays his dues, making D the best answer. A, B, and C all assume that Kung is interacting or negotiating with those to whom he owes money, rather than simply paying up as indicated in line 53, and must thus be eliminated as out of context.

Chapter 2.2 | *Paul's Case*

1) CORRECT ANSWER: D
The first paragraph indicates that Paul has been called to account for his "various misdemeanors" (lines 2-3), then goes on to explain how his way of dressing gave him "something of the dandy about him" (line 9). This shift from the reason for his presence to his appearance is captured in D. A is incorrect because the characterization of and

observations about Paul occur simultaneously, B is incorrect because it treats the father and the faculty members (NOT Paul) as central to the paragraph, and C is incorrect because it is not clear why exactly Paul has been suspended, only that he has committed general "misdemeanors".

2) CORRECT ANSWER: A

The phrase "appear before" describes what Paul will do in terms of the faculty and his misdemeanors: he will meet with the faculty and account for his conduct, or "face" the faculty. A is the best answer. B indicates that Paul will physically move closer to the faculty (and does not indicate that he will need to account for himself), while C and D both treat the faculty as a body that Paul intends to oppose, when in fact he seems unbothered by the need to face them.

3) CORRECT ANSWER: D

In lines 11-14, the faculty members judge that Paul's carnation "was not properly significant" or was not appropriate to the harsh academic circumstances that Paul is facing. D is thus the best answer, while A and C introduce inappropriate positives. B, though negative, criticizes the wrong aspect of Paul's appearance: "the collar of his open overcoat" (lines 7-8) is untidy or worn, though other parts of his outfit are well-maintained.

4) CORRECT ANSWER: D

See above for the explanation of the correct answer. A describes Paul's entry, B describes the somewhat worn and untidy state of Paul's outfit, and C introduces the red carnation. Keep in mind that A and B do not explicitly describe the red carnation in any way, while C does not explain how the faculty members feel about the red carnation, as demanded by the previous question.

5) CORRECT ANSWER: C

Paul's eyes are described as "conscious", "theatrical", and "offensive" in their effect: they communicate a strong personality but not in a positive way, so that they convey a bold or "impudent" personality on Paul's part. Choose C and eliminate positives such as A and B. D involves a misreading of the references to the hysterical, addictive associations of Paul's eyes: though hysteria and addiction can make people "unstable", Paul's personality is in fact "stable" as one of boldness and theatricality.

6) CORRECT ANSWER: A

Most of the relevant paragraph is devoted to the "respective charges" (line 28) against Paul, which include his defiant manner and his physical aversion to the teachers themselves. A is thus the best answer, while the fact that the paragraph is delivered largely from the teachers' perspectives can be used to eliminate B. C is inaccurate because Paul's classroom conduct, though offensive, is not actually dishonest and genuinely reflects his aversion; D is problematic because the relationship between Paul (who does not want to come back to school) and his teachers is CONSISTENTLY antagonistic and does not really change.

7) CORRECT ANSWER: A

In lines 28-30, the different teachers are clearly shown to be united by sentiments of "rancor and aggrievedness" towards Paul: they thus dislike him strongly, so that A is an effective answer and C (which is somewhat positive) and D (which assumes that they do NOT know what to think) can be readily eliminated. B is a trap answer: Paul exhibits physical revulsion towards his teachers, but they in fact try to approach him and are not "revolted" in a similar way.

8) CORRECT ANSWER: A

See above for the explanation of the correct answer. B indicates that the teachers have trouble describing their problem with Paul, C indicates that one teacher was especially wounded by Paul's conduct, and D indicates that Paul has a physical aversion to the teachers (NOT that they return this sentiment). Make sure not to wrongly take B as evidence for Question 7 D, C as evidence for Question 7 C, or D as evidence for Question 7 B.

9) CORRECT ANSWER: D

The paragraph calls attention to "nervous trembling" (line 61) and "jerking" (line 63) motions that Paul cannot control, but contrasts these motions with the "conscious expression" (line 66) of smiling watchfulness that Paul assumes. This information supports D. The paragraph focuses on how Paul is perceived (NOT on how he perceives others, eliminating A) and indicates that he might feel and show discomfort (not that he is entirely "cheerful and confident" or "indifferent", eliminating B and C).

10) CORRECT ANSWER: B

The passage states that Paul is meeting with the teachers to "account for his various misdemeanors" (lines 2-3) for the alleged purpose of ending his suspension and coming "back to school" (line 25). In short, the goal of the meeting is to appeal Paul's suspension, making B the best choice. A (expulsion) may result from future "misdemeanors" but is never mentioned as an option here: C (venting frustration) and D (correcting Paul) may be positive side effects of the meeting, but neither is the primary reason for bringing Paul before the faculty.

Chapter 2.3 | *A Memoir* (Dina Peone)

1) CORRECT ANSWER: D

The passage as a whole closely describes the events that take place after the narrator "first spotted Serena" (line 1) and then "made plans for her to visit" (line 41). A detailed depiction of the visit itself takes up the later stages of the narrative, making D the best choice. A is too positive to fit the context of the nervous, physically injured narrator, B neglects the narrator's strong presence and the emphasis on significant events, and C places too much emphasis on the passage's darker content (which by no means overwhelms the narrator's positive impressions of Serena).

2) CORRECT ANSWER: D

In the first two paragraphs, the narrator lists Serena's precise physical appearance, at one point even re-positioning to "get a better view" (line 10) of Serena's face. This information supports D, while B (neutrality or "detachment") does not capture the narrator's strong positive impression and C is a mild negative that implies mockery. A is a trap answer: the narrator fails to catch Serena's attention because Serena does not notice the narrator, NOT because the narrator is being wary or extremely cautious. In fact, the narrator WANTS to be noticed by Serena.

3) CORRECT ANSWER: D
In lines 20-21, the narrator explains that she "almost forgot my own body" (particularly her amputations) in Serena's presence. D is thus the best answer, while A and B wrongly consider Serena's beauty from the perspective of individuals OTHER than the narrator (and are beyond the scope of the passage). C wrongly indicates that the narrator (whose impressions of Serena are almost entirely positive) has strongly negative or resentful feelings.

4) CORRECT ANSWER: B
See above for the explanation of the correct answer. A indicates that the narrator envied or wanted an aspect of Serena's beauty for herself, C indicates that the narrator found Serena beautiful even in difficult circumstances, and D records some of the narrator's reflections on Serena's beautiful and troubled nature. Make sure not to take A as evidence for Question 3 C: the narrator does not mostly RESENT Serena, but simply wishes that she could have some of Serena's apparent beauty for herself.

5) CORRECT ANSWER: A
In the first parenthetical statement, the narrator indicates that Serena may be feeling not "despair" but "reluctance" (line 40); in the second, the narrator expresses uncertainty as to whether Serena is "tipsy" or "nervous" (line 48). The narrator is thus unsure, in each case, which interpretation of Serena's actions and sentiments is best: A is the best answer. The parenthetical statements do not indicate concern about Serena (whom the narrator views with desire, eliminating B) or serve to criticize the narrator herself (eliminating C). D is a trap answer: Serena is hard to interpret in only two SPECIFIC instances, but this evidence should not indicate that she is unpredictable OVERALL.

6) CORRECT ANSWER: D
In lines 49-50, the narrator calls attention to Serena's "flawless" hair (which has been coordinated to look messy) and her makeup which appears to have been done "professionally". Serena has thus given her own appearance considerable attention, a fact which justifies D. A, B, and C all call attention to Serena's idiosyncratic appearance, but do not directly address the possibility that she "is mindful" of it (since she may be choosing her hair color or wardrobe with little forethought in these cases) in the manner of D.

7) CORRECT ANSWER: C
The word "weakness" refers to Serena's habit of drinking from her "flask" (line 52) of liquor: the narrator, who has seen Serena as ideal up to this point, sees this activity as an indication that Serena is human or vulnerable. C is the best answer. A and B both indicate that Serena is an obsessed or committed drinker (a critical possibility that the passage never analyzes, since she is only seen drinking on one occasion). D is clearly and inaccurately critical of Serena as a personal liability; however, the narrator continues to desire Serena even after discovering that Serena wants to drink.

8) CORRECT ANSWER: B

During their time in the later stages of the passage, the narrator explains her various mishaps while Serena continues to drink. The narrator explains that as she talked "the more relaxed I felt" (lines 86-87) and that as Serena drank "the sadder she got" (lines 89-90). This information supports B, while the boyfriend is a minor and briefly-mentioned topic (eliminating A) and Serena's main sentiments are unease and sadness (not "confidence", eliminating C). D is a trap answer: while Serena does speak positively about the narrator's pursuits, there is no indication that the narrator has lost interest in music, only that her injuries have made the pursuit of music difficult.

9) CORRECT ANSWER: A

In line 80, the narrator explains that a spontaneous voice (later identifiable as Serena's) "oozed, uncontainable" on a recording that Serena has located. This information supports A. Other answers misrepresent the emotions that the narrator locates in Serena's singing (lines 78-83). The image of a Barbie doll actually indicates injury and madness (eliminating B), the deathbed moans actually indicate high energy (eliminating C), and the shrieks are depicted by the narrator as one of the appealing features of Serena's music (eliminating D).

10) CORRECT ANSWER: B

The last sentence of the passage indicates that Serena was "also at war with herself" (line 93); the narrator is the only other primary character in the passage, so the narrator would logically "also" be the other character at war with herself. The sentence thus indicates a connection, making B an appropriate choice and eliminating negative or critical answers such as C and D. A is a trap answer: the narrator indicates pity or compassion in the PREVIOUS sentences (lines 89-92) but mainly uses this sentence to indicate that she and Serena are similar.

Chapter 2.4 | *Therese Raquin*

1) CORRECT ANSWER: B

Early in the passage, Madame Raquin considers that Camille's decision has "upset her way of living" (line 13); in response to this threat to her routine, she finds new premises that will allow her to maintain her role as a shopkeeper. This information supports B. A is inaccurate because Camille's marriage (NOT a career change) prompts changes in his family's lifestyle. C is inaccurate because Madame Raquin does give Camille independence (even if his resolution to move to Paris unsettles her), and because the passage focuses on Madame Raquin's preparations for the family's move to Paris, not the move itself. D is inaccurate because Madame Raquin finds an existing shop but does not actually CREATE a business over the course of the passage.

2) CORRECT ANSWER: D

The author describes how Madame Raquin "had arranged a plan for a new life" (lines 21-22) and then energetically "went straight to the Arcade of the Pont Neuf" (lines 46-47) to put her plan in motion. These indications of her assertive yet adaptive personality support D and can be used to eliminate B. A and C overstate her virtues; she takes over an existing business to support her family, but does not have the grand, creative business ambitions that "overachieving" or "entrepreneurial" would indicate.

3) CORRECT ANSWER: C

The narrator explains that Camille is leaving Vernon for Paris in order "to find a post in some important administration" (lines 34-35). This information supports C. A is inaccurate because a new family life may be a RESULT of Camille's primary desire for a career, B is incorrect because Madame Raquin will be accompanying her son, and D is a distortion of the passage's content. Camille wants a post in an "important" administration, but it is not clear that the post will pay well, only that it will be respectable.

4) CORRECT ANSWER: C

In lines 28-30, Madame Raquin concludes a description of her plans by informing Camille that he "will act as [he likes]". This information indicates her indifference to what he does, justifying C. A describes Camille's resolution (not Madame Raquin's sentiments), B indicates that Madame Raquin is upset (NOT that she wants to overlook Camille's role), and D describes Camille's motives (not Madame Raquin's).

5) CORRECT ANSWER: C

The relevant paragraph describes how Madame Raquin "sought to arrange another existence for herself and the married couple" (lines 14-15) and thus developed a "plan" (line 21) for managing the move. C is thus the best answer, while A (which refers to Madame Raquin's broad values, not to the more narrow and specific conflict that is the primary focus) is out of scope. B wrongly focuses on the couple (not Madame Raquin) and D is problematic because the paragraph does not definitively indicate what Madame Raquin's "course of action" will be, only that she has decided on a course.

6) CORRECT ANSWER: A

In lines 39-41, the narrator explains that Therese "was not consulted" in the move and displays "passive obedience" as a main personality trait. This information supports A and can be used to eliminate B (which wrongly assumes that her role is positive and assertive) and D (which wrongly assumes that the other characters view Therese negatively). If Therese can be disregarded in important decisions, it is also unlikely that she is central to the "emotional stability" of the family; C can be eliminated according to this logic.

7) CORRECT ANSWER: C

See above for the explanation of the correct answer. A explains that Madame Raquin wants Therese to have gainful employment, B indicates that Therese is meant to work alongside Madame Raquin, and D records one of Madame Raquin's attempts to appeal to Therese. Note that these line references involve only Therese and Madame Raquin, not the "family members" (including Camille) required by the previous question.

8) CORRECT ANSWER: D

The word "idiotic" refers to Camille's "ambition" (line 33) to find a post "in some important administration" (line 35). Camille's "ambition" results in a change of lifestyle and grand visions of himself, or is driven by "whims." D is thus the best answer; A, B, and C all indicate that finding an administrative post would be a strange or completely unreasonable maneuver. In fact, finding such a post is a relatively normal idea that has simply struck Camille's fancy.

9) CORRECT ANSWER: D

The factor that caused Madame Raquin to "make up her mind" (line 59) to buy the shop was its low price; it is also evident that the shop will make a profit and help her to meet daily expenses. This information justifies D. A, B, and C all indicate aspects of the shop that are appealing (as listed in lines 49-69), but not (as demanded by the question) the reason that "ultimately" prompted Madame Raquin to buy the shop.

10) CORRECT ANSWER: A

The word "palace" indicates how Madame Raquin remembered and "pictured . . . to herself" (line 75) the shop that she had found; from a distance, she is making the "damp, obscure shop" (line 74) seem better than it is. She thus romanticizes the shop, so that A is an effective answer. Madame Raquin is already "beaming with pleasure" (line 70) over the shop and thus does not need to convince herself that her decision was right (eliminating B). As a "palace" that promises comfort and stability, the shop represents psychological benefits that extend well beyond "social mobility" (eliminating C). And since Therese is not a major figure in the family's decisions (lines 39-41), it is unlikely that Madame Raquin has a strong interest in persuading Therese (eliminating D).

Chapter 2.5 | *The Canterville Ghost*

1) CORRECT ANSWER: C

Early in the passage, Mr. Otis tells Lord Canterville that "there is no such thing, sir, as a ghost" (lines 37-38); later, the unconcerned Otis family arrives at the Canterville estate and Washington Otis declares that the supernatural superstitions are "nonsense" (line 95). This information supports C and can be used to eliminate A and D, which wrongly indicate that the family has become more convinced of the ghost's existence. B is problematic because the issue of whether the ghost is real or fake is not resolved in the passage: the Otis family may not be in any danger if the ghost proves not to be real.

2) CORRECT ANSWER: C

Mr. Otis speaks offhandedly about the ghost, states that he comes from a "modern country" (line 23), and envisions a situation that would take place "if there were such a thing as a ghost in Europe" (lines 26-27). He thus believes that there is no such thing as a ghost present, so that this information justifies C and can be used to eliminate A and B (which assume that he DOES believe in the ghost). D is problematic for similar reasons: because the only possible danger would be the ghost, which Mr. Otis disregards as a fantasy, Mr. Otis would not see himself as being in danger.

3) CORRECT ANSWER: C

In lines 4-7, Lord Canterville is described as a "man of most punctilious honor" who sees a warning regarding the ghostly presence as his "duty". This information supports C, while Lord Canterville's main objective of selling the property logically eliminates A. B is inaccurate because Lord Canterville only mentions the ghost to one person (and is thus not mainly interested in spreading its reputation or notoriety), while D is flawed because Lord Canterville, by acknowledging that he is selling a haunted property, could easily become the TARGET of blame if the ghost proves dangerous. At best, avoiding blame would be an ulterior or subconscious motive, while Lord Canterville's main motive (observing his duty) is clearly stated.

4) CORRECT ANSWER: B

See above for the explanation of the correct answer. A indicates Mr. Otis's possible foolishness (and does not mention Lord Canterville at all), C indicates that the ghost has been a problem for previous residents, and D indicates Lord Canterville's acceptance of Mr. Otis's wishes. Make sure not to wrongly take C as evidence for Question 3 B or D as evidence for Question 3 D.

5) CORRECT ANSWER: D

In lines 37-39, Otis opposes the "laws of Nature" (which apparently argue against the presence of ghosts) to the "British aristocracy" and its belief in the supernatural. D thus indicates his scientific perspective, which prioritizes natural facts over opinions. A indicates Otis's lack of concern about the ghost, B indicates that his national background is modern and prosperous (but NOT necessarily that it is scientific), and C indicates that Americans would treat a ghost as an interesting attraction (but not, again, that Americans have a scientific perspective).

6) CORRECT ANSWER: A

Lord Canterville states that the ghost "always makes its appearance" (lines 33-34) before the death of a family member; Otis notes that the more commonplace family doctor does the same thing, indicating through such deflating mockery that he does not take the ghost seriously. A is the best answer, while Otis has been unconcerned and dismissive throughout the exchange (not serious regarding the ghost, eliminating B). Keep in mind that Otis is insulting Lord Canterville, not trying to appeal to him or make a needed observation: for these reasons, C and D can be eliminated.

7) CORRECT ANSWER: A

While the paragraph begins with a description of a "lovely July evening" (line 48), the sky becomes "suddenly overcast with clouds" (line 57) once the Otis family enters the grounds of Canterville Chase. A effectively reflects this shift. B should be eliminated because the surroundings in the first half of the paragraph are never specified to be of the Otis family's former home, C wrongly focuses on the family's perceptions (not on descriptions recorded from the perspective of the NARRATOR), and D wrongly signifies a considerable change in time (when in fact all of the events recorded take place during the evening).

8) CORRECT ANSWER: A

The narrator states that Mrs. Umley kept her position as a result of "Lady Canterville's earnest request" (line 65) that she stay on to serve the Otis family. This information supports A. Although Mrs. Umley may be able to educate the Otises about the ghost and protect them from it, her direct reason for staying on is not related to these factors (eliminating B and D). C is a slight but erroneous misstatement of the passage's content: Mrs. Umley responds primarily to Lady Canterville's request, not to Mrs. Otis's.

9) CORRECT ANSWER: D

The phrase "unconscious of" is used to describe the "dull red stain" (line 76) that Mrs. Otis is seeing for the first time: because she assumes that it is a spill stain (not a blood stain) she is unaware of or oblivious to what the stain signifies. D appropriately captures the context. A is a trap answer: Mrs. Otis seems sure or confident at first that the stain is a spill stain (even though this belief is in error). B wrongly identifies her sentiments as strongly negative, while C is an inappropriate positive that overstates the degree of her interest in the stain.

10) CORRECT ANSWER: B

Mrs. Umley indicates in lines 86-94 that she takes to heart the legends surrounding the stain; she is "terrified" (line 98) when Washington goes to remove the stain and unsuccessfully tries to interfere. This negative tone and sense of Mrs. Umley's belief in the lore surrounding the stain support B, and can be used to eliminate positive answers such as A and D. C is a trap: Mrs. Umley may be fearful of the consequences of removing the stain, but whether tragedy DOES befall the Otises is a question that is beyond the scope of the passage.

CHAPTER THREE

Questions 1-10 are based on the following passage.
Chapter 3.1
The following is an excerpt from *Thais* (1890) by Anatole France.

Thais was born of free, but poor, parents who were idolaters. When she was a very little girl, her father kept, at Alexandria, near the Gate of the Moon, an inn,
Line which was frequented by sailors. She still retained
5 some vivid, but disconnected, memories of her early youth. She remembered her father, seated at the corner of the hearth with his legs crossed—tall, formidable, and quiet, like one of those old Pharaohs who are celebrated in the ballads sung by blind men at the
10 street corners. She remembered also her thin, wretched mother, wandering like a hungry cat about the house, which she filled with the tones of her sharp voice, and the glitter of her phosphorescent eyes. They said in the neighborhood that she was a witch, and changed
15 into an owl at night, and flew to see her lovers. It was a lie. Thais knew well, having often watched her, that her mother practiced no magic arts, but that she was eaten up with avarice, and counted all night the gains of the day. The idle father and the greedy mother let
20 the child live as best it could, like one of the fowls in the poultry-yard. She became very clever in extracting, one by one, the oboli from the belt of some drunken sailor, and in amusing the drinkers with artless songs and obscene words, the meaning of which she did
25 not know. She passed from knee to knee, in a room reeking with the odors of fermented drinks and resiny wine-skins; then, her cheeks sticky with beer and pricked by rough beards, she escaped, clutching the oboli in her little hand, and ran to buy honey-cakes
30 from an old woman who crouched behind her baskets under the Gate of the Moon. Every day the same scenes were repeated, the sailors relating their perilous adventures, then playing at dice or knuckle-bones, and blaspheming the gods, amid their shouting for the best
35 beer of Cilicia.

Every night the child was awakened by the quarrels of the drunkards. Oyster-shells would fly across the tables, cutting the heads of those they hit, and the uproar was terrible. Sometimes she saw, by the
40 light of the smoky lamps, the knives glitter, and the blood flow.

It humiliated her to think that the only person who showed her any human kindness in her young days was the mild and gentle Ahmes. Ahmes, the house-slave,
45 a Nubian, blacker than the pot he gravely skimmed, was as good as a long night's sleep. Often he would take Thais on his knee, and tell her old tales about underground treasure-houses constructed for avaricious kings, who put to death the masons and architects.
50 There were also tales about clever thieves who married kings' daughters, and courtesans who built pyramids. Little Thais loved Ahmes like a father, like a mother, like a nurse, and like a dog. She followed the slave into the cellar when he went to fill the amphorae, and
55 into the poultry-yard amongst the scraggy and ragged fowls, all beak, claws, and feathers, who flew swifter than eagles before the knife of the black cook. Often at night, on the straw, instead of sleeping, he built for Thais little water-mills, and ships no bigger than his
60 hand, with all their rigging.

He had been badly treated by his masters; one of his ears was torn, and his body covered with scars. Yet his features always wore an air of joyous peace. And no one ever asked him whence he drew the consolation
65 in his soul, and the peace in his heart. He was as simple as a child. As he performed his heavy tasks, he sang, in a harsh voice, hymns which made the child tremble and dream.

The child, unloved and uncared for by its selfish
70 parents, had no bed in the house. She slept in a corner of the stable amongst the domestic animals, and there Ahmes came to her every night secretly. He gently approached the mat on which she lay, and sat down on his heels, his legs bent and his body straight. His
75 face and his body, which was clothed in black, were invisible in the darkness; but his big white eyes shone out, and there came from them a light like a ray of dawn through the chinks of a door. He spoke in a husky, monotonous tone, with a slight nasal twang
80 that gave it the soft melody of music heard at night in the streets. Sometimes the breathing of an ass, or the soft lowing of an ox, accompanied, like a chorus of invisible spirits, the voice of the slave as he recited the gospels. His words flowed gently in the darkness,
85 which they filled with zeal, mercy, and hope; and the neophyte, her hand in that of Ahmes, lulled by the monotonous sounds, and the vague visions in her mind, slept calm and smiling, amid the harmonies of the dark night and the holy mysteries, gazed down on by a star,
90 which twinkled between the joists of the stable-roof.

CONTINUE

1

Which choice best describes a major theme of the passage?

A) The healing power of companionship

B) The moral purity of young children

C) The grave consequences of child neglect

D) The destructive influence of greed

2

Over the course of the passage, Thais is characterized as

A) neglected yet unscathed.

B) resourceful yet fragile.

C) unscrupulous yet supportive.

D) downtrodden yet hopeful.

3

Over the course of the first paragraph, the main focus shifts from

A) a characterization of Thais's parents to an illustration of Thais's life as a result of her unusual upbringing.

B) a tale about the hardships of Thais's childhood to an analysis of the effects those hardships had on her character.

C) an anecdote illustrating the lifestyle that Thais's parents led to a commentary on how Thais adapted to her circumstances.

D) a narration of Thais's childhood memories to a reflection on those memories by Thais as an adult.

4

Which choice best describes a technique the narrator uses to represent Ahmes's character?

A) The narrator illustrates Ahmes's hopefulness by comparing his eyes to a single ray of sunlight shining through the darkness of a door.

B) The narrator reveals Ahmes's complexity by listing the various facets through which Thais forms a connection to him.

C) The narrator emphasizes Ahmes's purity by contrasting the former abuse he received with his unwavering gentle disposition.

D) The narrator highlights Ahmes's creativity by depicting the words of his stories as inspiring strong emotions in Thais.

5

The narrator uses the phrase "one of the fowls in the poultry-yard" (lines 20-21) to suggest that Thais's parents

A) valued Thais's freedom.

B) encouraged Thais's independence.

C) abandoned Thais to fend for herself.

D) deprived Thais of her humanity.

6

According to the passage, Thais is able to procure food for herself by

A) stealing from the drunken customers at her parents' inn.

B) receiving charitable donations from those she entertained.

C) begging in the streets of Alexandria.

D) depending on the kindness of Ahmes.

7

Which choice provides the best evidence for the answer to the previous question?

A) Lines 21-25 ("She became...know")

B) Lines 25-27 ("She passed...wine-skins")

C) Lines 44-46 ("Ahmes, the...sleep")

D) Lines 53-57 ("She followed...cook")

8

Which choice provides the best evidence for the conclusion that at times, Ahmes prioritized Thais's happiness over his own needs?

A) Lines 46-49 ("Often he...architects")

B) Lines 57-60 ("Often at...rigging")

C) Lines 61-63 ("He had...peace")

D) Lines 70-72 ("She slept...secretly")

73

CONTINUE

9

In describing the quality of Ahmes's voice, the narrator points to a harmony between

A) the somber tone of his melodies and the protective cover of the night sky.

B) the uplifting subjects of his songs and the brightness of the stars above.

C) his soothing effect on Thais and the calming content of his songs.

D) his intonation and the surrounding sounds of nature.

10

As used in line 72, "secretly" most nearly means

A) unseen.

B) quietly.

C) covertly.

D) incognito.

CONTINUE

Questions 1-10 are based on the following passage.
Chapter 3.2
The following is an excerpt from *Indian Boyhood*
(1902) by Ohiyesa.

What boy would not be an Indian when he thinks
of the freest life in the world? This life was mine.
Every day there was a real hunt. There was real game.
Line Occasionally there was a medicine dance away off in
5 the woods where no one could disturb us, in which
the boys impersonated their elders. They painted and
imitated their fathers and grandfathers to the minutest
detail, and accurately too, because they had seen the
real thing all their lives.
10 We were not only good mimics but we were close
students of nature. We studied the habits of animals
just as you study your books. We watched the men
of our people and represented them in our play; then
learned to emulate them in our lives. We could smell as
15 well as hear and see. We could feel and taste as well as
we could see and hear. Nowhere has the memory been
more fully developed than in the wild life, and I can
still see wherein I owe much to my early training.
I was so unfortunate as to be the youngest of
20 five children, and I had to bear the humiliating name
"Hakadah," meaning "the pitiful last." My mother was
dangerously ill. She held me tightly to her bosom upon
her death-bed, while she whispered a few words to her
mother-in-law. She said: "I give you this boy for your
25 own. I cannot trust my own mother with him; she will
neglect him and he will surely die."
The woman to whom these words were spoken
was remarkably active for her age and possessed of as
much goodness as intelligence. My mother's judgment
30 concerning her own mother was well founded, for soon
after her death that old lady appeared, and declared
that Hakadah was too young to live without a mother.
She offered to keep me until I died, and then she
would put me in my mother's grave. Of course my
35 other grandmother denounced the suggestion as a very
wicked one, and refused to give me up.
This grandmother, who had already lived through
sixty years of hardships, showed no less enthusiasm
over Hakadah than she had done when she held her
40 first-born, the boy's father, in her arms. Every little
attention that is due to a loved child she performed
with much skill and devotion. She made all my scanty
garments and my tiny moccasins with a great deal of
taste. It was said by all that I could not have had more
45 attention had my mother been living.
The Dakota women were wont to cut and bring

their fuel from the woods. Very often my grandmother
carried me with her on these excursions; and while
she worked it was her habit to suspend me from a wild
50 grape vine or a springy bough, so that the least breeze
would swing the cradle to and fro. She has told me
that when I had grown old enough to take notice, I was
apparently capable of holding extended conversations
in an unknown dialect with birds and red squirrels.
55 Once I fell asleep in my cradle while Uncheedah was
some distance away. A squirrel had found it convenient
to come upon the bow of my cradle and nibble his
hickory nut, until he awoke me by dropping the crumbs
of his meal. My disapproval of his intrusion was so
60 decided that he had to take a sudden and quick flight to
another bough, and from there he began to pour out his
wrath upon me, while I continued my objections to his
presence so audibly that Uncheedah soon came to my
rescue, and compelled the bold intruder to go away.
65 She then began calling my attention to natural
objects. Whenever I heard the song of a bird, she
would tell me what bird it came from:
"Hakadah, listen to Shechoka (the robin) calling
his mate. He says he has just found something good
70 to eat." Or "Listen to Oopehanska (the thrush); he is
singing for his little wife. He will sing his best."
In my infancy it was my grandmother's custom
to put me to sleep, as she said, with the birds, and to
waken me with them, until it became a habit. She did
75 this with an object in view. An Indian must always rise
early. In the first place, as a hunter, he finds his game
best at daybreak. Secondly, other tribes, when on the
war-path, usually make their attack very early in the
morning.
80 After all, my babyhood was full of interest and the
beginnings of life's realities. The spirit of daring was
already whispered into my ears. The value of the eagle
feather as worn by the warrior had caught my eye. One
day, when I was left alone, at scarcely two years of
85 age, I took my uncle's war bonnet and plucked out all
its eagle feathers to decorate my dog and myself. So
soon the life that was about me had made its impress,
and already I desired intensely to comply with all of its
demands.

CONTINUE

1

Which choice best describes what happens in the passage?

A) A character reflects on his early influences.

B) A character contrasts his two grandmothers.

C) A character romanticizes his childhood experiences.

D) A character analyzes the effects of a significant event.

2

Hakadah suggests which of the following about the influence of nature on him and his peers?

A) Life in nature provided the framework for their education.

B) Life in nature helped them understand their role in the world.

C) Life in nature instilled in them the values of their society.

D) Life in nature offered to them a means of self-sufficiency.

3

Hakadah indicates that the ways of his people are mainly transmitted through a process of

A) instruction and mentorship.

B) performance and illustration.

C) storytelling and memorization.

D) observation and simulation.

4

Which choice provides the best evidence for the answer to the previous question?

A) Lines 4-5 ("Occasionally there...us")

B) Lines 11-12 ("We studied...books")

C) Lines 12-14 ("We watched...lives")

D) Lines 16-18 ("Nowhere has...training")

5

The mother gave Hakadah to the paternal grandmother so that he would

A) survive past infancy.

B) escape a life of abuse.

C) avoid an unusual upbringing.

D) learn to respect his elders.

6

In context of the passage as a whole, Hakadah's encounter with the squirrel in lines 55-64 ("Once I... away") primarily serves to convey his

A) annoyance with wildlife.

B) mischievous personality.

C) early fascination with nature.

D) vivid imagination as a child.

7

As used in line 60, "decided" most nearly means

A) definite.

B) resounding.

C) determined.

D) conclusive.

8

It can be reasonably inferred that Hakadah's grandmother favors a form of child rearing that emphasizes the

A) importance of good health.

B) development of survival skills.

C) interdependence of the natural world.

D) admirable lifestyle of a warrior.

CONTINUE

9

Which choice provides the best evidence for the answer to the previous question?

A) Lines 47-51 ("Very often...fro")

B) Lines 68-71 ("Hakadah, listen...best")

C) Lines 75-79 ("An Indian...morning")

D) Lines 80-83 ("After all...eye")

10

The main idea of the last paragraph is that Hakadah

A) was an adventurous and courageous child.

B) was a particularly impressionable child.

C) developed the skills suitable for the life of a warrior.

D) acquired an early passion for the life of a warrior.

CONTINUE

Questions 1-10 are based on the following passage.

Chapter 3.3

Adapted from Stendhal, *The Red and the Black* (1830).

Julien Sorel had purple cheeks and downcast eyes. He was a young man of eighteen to nineteen years old, and of puny appearance, with irregular but
Line delicate features, and an aquiline nose. The big black
5 eyes which betokened in their tranquil moments a temperament at once fiery and reflective were at the present moment animated by an expression of the most ferocious hate. . . His air of extreme pensiveness and his great pallor had given his father the idea that
10 he would not live beyond his childhood, or that if he did, it would only be to be a burden to his family. The butt of the whole house, he hated his brothers and his father. He was regularly beaten in the Sunday sports in the public square.
15 A little less than a year ago his pretty face had begun to win him some sympathy among the young girls. Universally despised as a weakling, Julien had adored the old Surgeon-Major, a local man of learning, who had one day dared to talk to the mayor on the
20 subject of the plane trees.
This Surgeon had sometimes paid Old Sorel for taking his son for a day, and had taught him Latin and History, that is to say the 1796 Campaign in Italy, which was all the history he knew. When he died, he
25 had bequeathed his Cross of the Legion of Honour, his arrears of half pay, and thirty or forty volumes, of which the most precious had just fallen into the public stream, which had been diverted owing to the influence of M. the Mayor. . .
30 "But I shall never get anything out of you, you cursed hypocrite," exclaimed Old Sorel one day, after Julien had returned from church. "As a matter of fact, I am going to get rid of you, and my sawmill will go all the better for it. . . Run along and pack your traps, and
35 I will take you to M. de Rênal's, where you are going to be tutor to his children."
"What shall I get for that?"
"Board, clothing, and three hundred francs salary."
"I do not want to be a servant."
40 "Who's talking of being a servant, you brute, do you think I want my son to be a servant?"
"But with whom shall I have my meals?"
This question discomforted Old Sorel, who felt he might possibly commit some imprudence if he went on
45 talking. He burst out against Julien, flung insult after insult at him, accused him of gluttony, and left him to

go and consult his other sons.
Julien saw them afterwards, each one leaning on his axe just outside the sawmill and holding counsel.
50 Having looked at them for a long time, Julien saw that he could find out nothing, and went and stationed himself on the other side of the saw in order to avoid being surprised. He wanted to think over this unexpected piece of news, which changed his whole
55 life, but he felt himself unable to consider the matter prudently, his imagination being concentrated in wondering what he would see in M. de Rênal's fine mansion.
"I must give all that up," he said to himself,
60 "rather than let myself be reduced to eating with the servants. My father would like to force me to it. I would rather die. I have fifteen francs and eight sous of savings. I will run away to-night; I will go across country by paths where there are no gendarmes to
65 be feared, and in two days I shall be at Besançon. I will enlist as a soldier there, and, if necessary, I will cross into Switzerland. But in that case, no more advancement, it will be all up with my being a priest, that fine career which may lead to anything."
70 This abhorrence of eating with the servants was not really natural to Julien; he would have done things quite, if not more, disagreeable in order to get on. He derived this repugnance from the Confessions of Rousseau. It was the only book by whose help his
75 imagination endeavoured to construct the world. The collection of the Bulletins of the Grand Army, and the Memorial of St. Helena completed his sacred texts. He would have died for these three works. He never believed in any other. To use a phrase of the old
80 Surgeon-Major, he regarded all the other books in the world as packs of lies, written by rogues in order to get on.
Julien possessed both a fiery soul and one of those astonishing memories which are so often combined
85 with stupidity.
. . . Sorel and his son avoided talking to each other for the rest of the day as though by mutual consent. In the evening Julien went to take his theology lesson at the curate's, but he did not consider that it was prudent
90 to say anything to him about the strange proposal which had been made to his father. "It is possibly a trap," he said to himself, "I must pretend that I have forgotten all about it."

CONTINUE

1

Which of the following best summarizes the passage?

A) A character's life is drastically changed when he receives news of a job opportunity.

B) A character plans and executes his escape from an abusive family situation.

C) A character contemplates his future after receiving disturbing news from his father.

D) A character falls out of favor among his family and is forcibly cast out of his home.

2

What function do the second and third paragraphs (lines 15-29) serve in the passage as a whole?

A) They provide information that is irrelevant to the developmental pattern of the narrative.

B) They present an argument for which no evidence is provided anywhere in the passage.

C) They introduce a character whose influence on Julien plays a significant role in his view on life.

D) They provide context helpful for understanding the hatred that Julien's family harbors towards him.

3

The passage indicates that Julien was viewed by his father as a burden primarily because

A) he was not able to contribute to the family business due to his weak disposition.

B) he was more interested in intellectual endeavors than in manual labor.

C) he was rebellious and acted out by associating with the Surgeon Major.

D) he was unpopular and did not get along with any of the residents in the village.

4

It can be reasonably inferred that the outburst by Julien's father described in lines 43-47 ("This question... sons") was most likely because

A) Julien had categorically refused to take the job that his father had secured for him.

B) Julien had responded to his father's instructions with an insolent remark.

C) Julien had pointed out an embarrassing detail that his father had overlooked.

D) Julien had denied his father's wishes with an apparently superficial justification.

5

In lines 48-58 ("Julien saw...mansion") the narrator mainly presents a contrast between

A) Julien's inner turmoil and the calm demeanor of his brothers.

B) Julien's fear of his brothers and their apparent indifference towards him.

C) the complicity of Julien's brothers and his own isolation from them.

D) the reluctance of Julien's brothers to talk and his pleas for advice.

6

During the reflection made by Julien in line 59 ("I must...up") "that" refers most likely to

A) a potential benefit in an otherwise unattractive job prospect.

B) a promising career path consistent with his intellectual needs.

C) a mundane yet comforting life to which he has become accustomed.

D) a pleasant detail in the plans his father has outlined for him.

CONTINUE

7

The passage suggests that Julien aspired towards a career in

A) public education.

B) religious services.

C) writing and publishing.

D) the armed forces.

8

Which choice provides the best evidence for the answer to the previous question?

A) Lines 17-19 ("Julien had...mayor")

B) Lines 65-67 ("I will...Switzerland")

C) Lines 67-69 ("But in...anything")

D) Lines 75-78 ("The collection...texts")

9

Which choice provides the best evidence for the claim that Julien is an overly suspicious person?

A) Lines 61-63 ("My father...savings")

B) Lines 63-65 ("I will run...Besançon")

C) Lines 70-72 ("This abhorrence...on")

D) Lines 80-82 ("he regarded...on")

10

As used in line 75, "construct" most nearly means

A) manage.

B) organize.

C) navigate.

D) perceive.

CONTINUE

Questions 1-10 are based on the following passage.
Chapter 3.4
Adapted from O. Henry, *A Service of Love* (1906).

Joe Larrabee came out of the post-oak flats of the Middle West pulsing with a genius for pictorial art. At six he drew a picture of the town pump with a
Line prominent citizen passing it hastily. This effort was
5 framed and hung in the drug store window by the side of the ear of corn with an uneven number of rows. At twenty he left for New York with a flowing necktie and a capital tied up somewhat closer.

Delia Caruthers did things in six octaves so
10 promisingly in a pine-tree village in the South that her relatives chipped in enough in her chip hat for her to go "North" and "finish." They could not see her f—, but that is our story.

Joe and Delia met in an atelier where a number
15 of art and music students had gathered to discuss chiaroscuro, Wagner, music, Rembrandt's works, pictures, Waldteufel, wall paper, Chopin and Oolong. Joe and Delia became enamoured one of the other, or each of the other, as you please, and in a short time
20 were married—for (see above), when one loves one's Art no service seems too hard.

Mr. and Mrs. Larrabee began housekeeping in a flat. It was a lonesome flat—something like the A sharp way down at the left-hand end of the keyboard.
25 And they were happy; for they had their Art, and they had each other. And my advice to the rich young man would be—sell all thou hast, and give it to the poor— janitor for the privilege of living in a flat with your Art and your Delia. . .
30 They were mighty happy as long as their money lasted. So is every—but I will not be cynical. Their aims were very clear and defined. Joe was to become capable very soon of turning out pictures that old gentlemen with thin side-whiskers and thick
35 pocketbooks would sandbag one another in his studio for the privilege of buying. Delia was to become familiar and then contemptuous with Music, so that when she saw the orchestra seats and boxes unsold she could have sore throat and lobster in a private dining-
40 room and refuse to go on the stage.

But the best, in my opinion, was the home life in the little flat—the ardent, voluble chats after the day's study; the cozy dinners and fresh, light breakfasts; the interchange of ambitions—ambitions interwoven each
45 with the other's or else inconsiderable—the mutual help and inspiration; and—overlook my artlessness—

stuffed olives and cheese sandwiches at 11 p.m.

But after a while Art flagged. It sometimes does, even if some switchman doesn't flag it. Everything
50 going out and nothing coming in, as the vulgarians say. Money was lacking to pay Mr. Magister (Joe's teacher and mentor) and Herr Rosenstock (Delia's own) their prices. When one loves one's Art no service seems too hard. So, Delia said she must give music lessons to
55 keep the chafing dish bubbling.

For two or three days she went out canvassing for pupils. One evening she came home elated.

"Joe, dear," she said, gleefully, "I've a pupil. And, oh, the loveliest people! General—General A. B.
60 Pinkney's daughter—on Seventy-first street. Such a splendid house, Joe—you ought to see the front door! Byzantine I think you would call it. And inside! Oh, Joe, I never saw anything like it before.

"My pupil is his daughter Clementina. I dearly
65 love her already. She's a delicate thing—dresses always in white; and the sweetest, simplest manners! Only eighteen years old. I'm to give three lessons a week; and, just think, Joe! $5 a lesson. I don't mind it a bit; for when I get two or three more pupils I
70 can resume my lessons with Herr Rosenstock. Now, smooth out that wrinkle between your brows, dear, and let's have a nice supper."

"That's all right for you, Dele," said Joe, attacking a can of peas with a carving knife and a hatchet, "but
75 how about me? Do you think I'm going to let you hustle for wages while I philander in the regions of high art? Not by the bones of Benvenuto Cellini! I guess I can sell papers or lay cobblestones, and bring in a dollar or two."
80 Delia came and hung about his neck.

"Joe, dear, you are silly. You must keep on at your studies. It is not as if I had quit my music and gone to work at something else. While I teach I learn. I am always with my music. And we can live as happily
85 as millionaires on $15 a week. You mustn't think of leaving Mr. Magister."

"All right," said Joe, reaching for the blue scalloped vegetable dish. "But I hate for you to be giving lessons. It isn't Art."

CONTINUE

1

Which of the following best describes the developmental pattern of the passage?

A) A couple facing financial challenges finds it necessary to adapt.

B) A couple moves to a large city to further their education in the arts.

C) Two characters pursuing social advancement meet and fall in love.

D) Two characters overcome financial hardship through the power of love.

2

Over the course of the passage, the primary focus shifts from

A) Joe and Delia's initially idyllic marriage to their eventual disharmony brought on by hardship.

B) Joe and Delia's expectations of their careers in art to the harsh realities that beset them.

C) Joe and Delia's lives as struggling artists to Delia's excitement about a career change.

D) Joe and Delia's interconnected ambitions to Delia's sudden quest for independence.

3

The main purpose of the first and second paragraphs is to

A) compare the accomplishments of two main characters.

B) introduce two characters by detailing their similar backgrounds.

C) set up the context for a discussion of the characters' finances.

D) analyze the personalities of the main characters.

4

As used in line 4, "effort" most nearly means

A) accomplishment.

B) attempt.

C) struggle.

D) task.

5

Which choice best supports the claim that Joe and Delia's marriage was characterized by long-term commitment?

A) Lines 25-26 ("And they...other")

B) Lines 27-29 ("sell all...Delia")

C) Lines 43-45 ("the interchange...inconsiderable")

D) Lines 53-54 ("When one...hard")

6

In context of the portrayal of Delia in lines 36-40, the narrator uses the phrase "contemptuous with music" to suggest that she aspires to become a

A) pop star.

B) diva.

C) prodigy.

D) critic.

7

The narrator suggests which of the following about the nature of the art industry?

A) It engenders false hope in those who are young and naive.

B) It offers success only to those who are born into privilege.

C) It only recognizes as credible those who have pursued a formal education.

D) It is subject to random fluctuations that are not tied to individual agency.

CONTINUE

8

According to the passage, Joe and Delia are dissimilar in that Joe

A) aims to pursue art long-term, whereas Delia plans to eventually become a teacher.

B) is uncomfortable with compromising his ideals, whereas Delia has a more pragmatic view.

C) sees art lessons as a waste of money, whereas Delia sees them as a good investment.

D) measures success in terms of money, whereas Delia views it in terms of fame.

9

It can be inferred from the passage that Delia rebuffs Joe's offer of getting a job most likely because she believes that

A) she could eventually earn enough money for the two of them.

B) he would feel unfulfilled and resentful at his new job.

C) he would eventually abandon his passion for the arts.

D) he as an artist should not work outside of his field.

10

Which choice provides the best evidence for the answer to the previous question?

A) Lines 67-68 ("I'm to...lesson")

B) Lines 70-72 ("Now smooth...supper")

C) Lines 82-83 ("It is...else")

D) Lines 84-85 ("And we...week")

CONTINUE

Questions 1-10 are based on the following passage.
Chapter 3.5
Adapted from the short story *The Bald Truth* (2013) by Chris Holliday.

When I was a kid, I used to hate going to the barber's for a haircut. It was torture having to balance on a couple of cushions so I was at just the right height
Line for the barber to deploy his clippers. I squirmed and
5 wriggled and jittered until the barber got irritated.

"If you don't keep still, I can't cut your hair. If you don't get your haircut regularly, one day, I promise you, it will all fall out!" I think I put my tongue out at him. What did that barber know about hair? All he did was
10 cut it. Later, as an independent teenager, if I did recall such moments of defiance, I would shrug my shoulders, fling back my flowing Mick Jagger locks and remind myself that no one in my family had ever gone bald.

Cut to Christmas, many years later. I was going
15 home for the holidays. In the spirit of generosity befitting the season, I went to the hair stylist for a trim. It would please my mum, at least. I no longer fidgeted in the chair: in fact, I was almost dozing off when the scissors stopped mid-snip. The stylist straightened
20 himself and looked at me through the mirror.

"Do you know, sir, that you have a bald spot, just here?" He pressed his finger against the nape of my neck. I sat up, verging on panic. "You shouldn't worry. It's probably a result of overwork and stress. Quite a few
25 of my clients have this from time to time, but perhaps you should see a doctor, just to be sure."

You bet I saw a doctor.

"Ah yes, Alopecia Nervosa," the doctor informed me smoothly. "Caused by iron deficiency and stress.
30 Quite common really."

I swallowed and then nodded in what I hoped was a nonchalant manner. "Is there anything I should do?"

He shook his head as he wrote out a prescription. "You should take one of these each day. And just relax
35 as much as possible. It will probably get worse before it gets better, though still, I wouldn't worry about it too much."

Not worry? I recalled that scene from my childhood, and felt as though that barber's curse had
40 come terribly true.

I spent Christmas watching my hair fall out faster than the Christmas tree shed its needles. Sure, I went to a few parties, but I soon tired of friends glancing quickly yet inquisitively at my hair, resolutely averting their
45 eyes, and smiling very determinedly at my chest. In the end, I forced my mother to shave my head completely.

She was very reluctant to do so, and with good reason. I discovered that, stripped of its hair, my head revealed an appalling affinity to the low dome of Neanderthal man.
50 I tried to avoid mirrors: I had never realized before how many there were in my mother's house.

Not the happiest Christmas season, indeed. I set off back to London, to work. It was quite chilly—as my head constantly reminded me—but at least the crowds
55 were thin, meaning that almost nobody would be around to notice my strange shorn scalp. I entered the nearest Tube station and descended to the platform below. The area was deserted, save for one other passenger, a young boy about eleven or twelve years old. He glanced at me
60 and then did a double-take. I set my shoulders square and walked farther down the platform. I was aware of the boy's constant stare, yet I was set on ignoring him.

"Mister!" I turned my head. The boy was now at my side, staring fixedly at my head. "Mister, are you a
65 Punk?"

I glared at him. His eyes were not hostile, only excited. I relaxed a little. I gave a half smile. "No, I'm sorry. I am not a Punk. I have been a bit ill and my hair had to be shaved off. But I am getting better now."

70 He moved back a step and looked away, his face flushed, embarrassed that he might have been rude. Then he hunched his shoulders, faced me head-on, and looked at me earnestly. "You know, I think you'd make a really good Punk."

75 I felt suddenly lighter in spirit. "Oh. Thank you very much!" I grinned confidingly at him. "I also hate going to the barber."

The boy gave a broad grin. "So do I!"

We shook hands solemnly as the train arrived. The
80 curse was broken.

CONTINUE

1

This passage can best be described as

A) a lighthearted recounting of a humorous situation.

B) a heartfelt reflection of a meaningful encounter.

C) a poignant narrative of an embarrassing affliction.

D) a conversational anecdote of an ill-timed misfortune.

2

The rhetorical question in line 9 primarily serves to

A) foreshadow the narrator's struggle with Alopecia Nervosa.

B) indicate the narrator's thought process as a child.

C) exemplify the irony of the barber's curse being fulfilled later in the narrator's life.

D) express the narrator's denial about his diagnosis of Alopecia Nervosa.

3

The narrator implies that he "no longer fidgeted" (line 17) while getting his hair cut because

A) he did not feel uncomfortable at the barber's anymore and had learned to find the experience engaging.

B) he had become fully confident in the durability and longevity of his hair, despite what his childhood barber had told him.

C) he had grown enough so that he no longer had to balance on pillows to allow the barber to reach his head.

D) he was so preoccupied with thoughts of the upcoming holidays that he barely registered what the barber was doing.

4

In paragraph 4 (lines 21-26) the author creates a contrast between

A) the stylist's nonchalant attitude and the narrator's alarmed reaction.

B) the narrator's previous confidence and his current state of panic.

C) the stylist's ignorance of the barber's curse and the narrator's realization of its fulfillment.

D) the narrator's inner turmoil and his outer composure.

5

As used in line 10, "independent" most nearly means

A) emancipated.

B) unconventional.

C) rebellious.

D) detached.

6

As used in line 48, "revealed" most nearly means

A) affirmed.

B) displayed.

C) proved.

D) disclosed.

7

According to the passage, the narrator's Alopecia affected his holidays in what way?

A) It caused him immense stress, which then led to the shedding of even more hair.

B) It caused him to avoid his family and immerse himself in his work as a means of coping.

C) It caused him to seek out deserted areas for fear of people noticing his baldness.

D) It caused him to feel uncomfortable at and progressively withdraw from social events.

8

Which choice provides the best evidence for the answer to the previous question?

A) Lines 34-36 ("just relax...better")

B) Lines 43-45 ("I soon...chest")

C) Lines 52-53 ("I set...work")

D) Lines 54-56 ("the crowds...scalp")

9

The "young boy" (line 58-59) initially expresses what at the sight of the narrator's bald head?

A) Confusion.

B) Wonder.

C) Solidarity.

D) Discomfort.

CONTINUE

10

Which choice provides the best evidence for the answer to the previous question?

A) Lines 64-67 ("Mister, are...excited")

B) Lines 70-71 ("He moved...rude")

C) Lines 71-73 ("Then he...earnestly")

D) Lines 76-77 ("I grinned...barber")

Answer Key: CHAPTER THREE

Chapter 3.1
1. A
2. B
3. A
4. C
5. C
6. A
7. A
8. B
9. D
10. C

Chapter 3.2
1. A
2. A
3. D
4. C
5. A
6. C
7. B
8. B
9. C
10. D

Chapter 3.3
1. C
2. C
3. A
4. C
5. C
6. A
7. B
8. C
9. D
10. D

Chapter 3.4
1. A
2. B
3. B
4. A
5. C
6. B
7. D
8. B
9. D
10. C

Chapter 3.5
1. D
2. B
3. C
4. A
5. C
6. B
7. D
8. B
9. B
10. A

Answer Explanations

Chapter 3

Chapter 3.3 | *Thais*

1) CORRECT ANSWER: A

The passage describes how young Thais is shown "human kindness" (line 43) by only one person, Ahmes, who himself has had a hard life yet expresses "zeal, mercy, and hope" (line 85) in the company of Thais. This information supports A, while B (too positive) and C (too negative) pass judgments on the troubled yet hopeful Thais while neglecting Ahmes entirely. D would be appropriate to the description of Thais's mother; however, she is a minor character, so that greed cannot justly be considered a "major" theme of the passage.

2) CORRECT ANSWER: B

As described in the passage, Thais is "very clever" (line 21) in finding resources and in navigating her parents' tavern; nonetheless, she is sensitive enough to be "awakened" (line 36) by quarrels and "humiliated" (line 42) by her circumstances. This combination of resourcefulness and vulnerability supports B and can be used to eliminate A (since Thais is negatively influenced or "scathed" by her circumstances). C and D wrongly attribute the virtues of the supportive and hopeful Ahmes to Thais herself, and should be eliminated as misreadings of the passage.

3) CORRECT ANSWER: A

The relevant paragraph begins by considering Thais's "tall, formidable, and quiet" (lines 7-8) father and her "thin, wretched" (line 10) mother, then considers how Thais would normally navigate her father's raucous tavern. This information supports A, while Thais's late maturation and adulthood are never considered in any specificity (beyond passing references to what Thais remembered, eliminating B and D). C is a trap answer: though described, Thais's parents are presented mostly through brief overviews of their personalities, not through well-defined episodes or "anecdotes".

4) CORRECT ANSWER: C

The narrator explains that although Ahmes had "been badly treated by his masters" (line 61) his features "always wore an air of joyous peace" (line 63). This contrast and the descriptions that substantiate it support C. A refers to an actual description (lines 74-78) of a scene, not to a description that the narrator treats as SYMBOLIC of hopefulness. B (complexity) and D (creativity) attribute the wrong virtues to Ahmes: he is a hopeful and reassuring man, but he is not necessarily a talented or sophisticated person in the manner that these answers assume.

5) CORRECT ANSWER: C

The reference to the "fowls" is used to explain how Thais lived as a result of the negligence of her "idle father" and "greedy mother" (line 19). This indication of the parents' indifference to Thais supports C and can be used to eliminate wrongly positive answers such as A and B. D is a trap answer: Thais lives under unpleasant conditions, but her parents' real failing is their neglect, not more determined or violent efforts that would "deprive" Thais of her humanity.

6) CORRECT ANSWER: A

In lines 21-25, Thais is described as deftly removing the "oboli" (a form of currency) from a sailor's belt; she later uses the oboli to "buy honey cakes for an old woman" (lines 29-30). Thus, Thais steals from the sailors to feed herself, making A the best answer. B and C wrongly indicate that the kind donations of others (NOT her own efforts) are Thais's source of food, while D is a trap answer: Ahmes offers Thais companionship, but at no point in the passage is depicted offering her food.

7) CORRECT ANSWER: A

See above for the explanation of the correct answer. B describes Thais's progress through the inn, C offers a description of Ahmes's appearance, and D indicates that Thais followed Ahmes as he performed specific tasks. Make sure not to take C or D as evidence for Question 6 D, since Ahmes is depicted handling food but not actually GIVING food to Thais.

8) CORRECT ANSWER: B

In lines 57-60, Ahmes is described as building toys for Thais "instead of sleeping"; because he performs many duties, he is sacrificing his own rest to do something pleasant for the young girl. B is thus the best answer. A references some of Ahmes's stories, C describes Ahmes's difficult background, and D indicates that Ahmes's visits were secret. Although Ahmes is depicted as a kind or praiseworthy man in each of these line references, in none of these cases does Ahmes clearly sacrifice his comfort for Thais.

9) CORRECT ANSWER: D

In the final paragraph, the narrator explains that the voice of Ahmes possesses "the soft melody of music heard at night in the streets" (lines 80-81), including the sounds made by animals. D is thus the best answer, while A is incorrect because it characterizes his energetic and hopeful voice (line 85) as "somber" or melancholy. B and C wrongly focus on the content of Ahmes's songs (when the real focus of the passage and the question itself is the STYLE of his voice) and should be eliminated as inappropriate to the required focus.

10) CORRECT ANSWER: C

The word "secretly" refers to how Ahmes visited Thais "every night" (line 72), which he does without the knowledge of Thais's negligent parents or of any other character. He thus visits Thais covertly, or without the knowledge of other people: choose C and eliminate A and B (since Thais HERSELF can see and hear the singing, bright-eyed Ahmes). D is a trap answer: "incognito" means in disguise, yet Ahmes visits Thais in a manner that makes him perfectly recognizable as himself.

Chapter 3.2 | *Indian Boyhood*

1) CORRECT ANSWER: A
In the course of the passage, the narrator explains how his paternal grandmother's "enthusiasm" (line 38) for caring for him was in important formative influence; later, he discusses his response to the "spirit of daring" (line 81) promoted by his culture. This emphasis on the narrator's important early influences supports A, while the narrator's other grandmother is at best a minor character (eliminating B). C is inaccurate because the narrator is not "romanticizing" (or positively exaggerating) what happens in this positive yet straightforward account; D is incorrect because no single event dominates the passage, which rather discusses various events and habits that impacted the narrator.

2) CORRECT ANSWER: A
The narrator explains that he and the other boys were "students of nature" (line 11), and that their contact with the natural world helped to form their abilities in terms of perception and memory. A is thus the best answer, while the boys understand social life by observing their own community, NOT nature (lines 5-9, eliminating B and C). D is incorrect because the boys still return to their communities and still interact with one another when they are in nature, and are thus not self-sufficient.

3) CORRECT ANSWER: D
In lines 12-14, Hakadah explains that the boys from his childhood observed their elders and "learned to emulate them in our lives", including play activities. This emphasis on observing and imitating supports D and can be used to eliminate A and C, which assume that the members of the older generation exert a much more direct influence and are not mainly objects of observation. B is a trap answer; the boys do not simply respond to artificial "performances" or entertainments by their elders but take on their elders' actual values.

4) CORRECT ANSWER: C
See above for the explanation of the correct answer. A describes a medicine dance (but does not directly raise the topic of how customs are transmitted), B contrasts two approaches to studying nature (NOT human customs), and D indicates that contact with nature can help to foster specific abilities. Make sure not to wrongly take D (which mentions memory) as evidence for Question 3 C.

5) CORRECT ANSWER: A
Hakadah's mother gives Hakadah to his paternal grandmother to keep Hakadah alive: if Hakadah were to be given to his maternal grandmother instead, "she will neglect him and he will surely die" (lines 25-26). A is thus the best answer, while B and C present the wrong negatives. D refers to a possible benefit of life with Hakadah's paternal grandmother, but not to the REASONING used by Hakadah's mother.

6) CORRECT ANSWER: C

In the relevant lines, Hakadah explains that he communicated with animals in an "unknown dialect" (lines 54) and that on one occasion he conveyed "disapproval" (line 59) to a squirrel. He thus interacts with nature in an impassioned and fascinated way, so that C is the best answer. A and B both attribute strong negatives to Hakadah himself or his relationship to wildlife OVERALL (not simply the one squirrel), while D is a trap answer. Hakadah is not imagining his communication: he DOES effectively convey a message to the squirrel and even his grandmother acknowledges the fact of his "dialect".

7) CORRECT ANSWER: B

The word "decided" refers to the narrator's "disapproval" (line 60) as expressed to the squirrel: the disapproval sends the squirrel away, since it is emphatic or "resounding" enough to carry a clear message. B is the best answer. A and D both focus on the validity or truthfulness of the narrator's disapproval (not on the primary context of its strong EFFECT), while C refers to a personality trait (not to a quality of an outcry or strong expression).

8) CORRECT ANSWER: B

In lines 75-79, the narrator explains his grandmother's motives for training him to rise early: he can deal with life "as a hunter" or with tribes "on the war-path" if he acquires this habit. The grandmother thus prioritizes survival, so that B is the best answer. A and D may be elements of survival in a community such as the narrator's but are not directly prioritized by the grandmother, while C is closest to the ideas about nature that the narrator addresses early in the passage, BEFORE the grandmother is introduced.

9) CORRECT ANSWER: C

See above for the explanation of the correct answer. A describes how the grandmother situated the narrator while she worked, B indicates that the grandmother taught the narrator the identities of birds, and D indicates that the narrator was inspired by influences OTHER than the grandmother. Make sure not to take B as evidence for Question 8 C: the grandmother refers to elements of nature by naming the birds, but does not (beyond pairing birds with their mates) argue that the elements of nature are "interdependent".

10) CORRECT ANSWER: D

The final paragraph describes how Hakadah "at scarcely two years of age" (lines 84-85) was attracted to the warrior lifestyle: he "desired intensely to comply with all of its demands" (lines 88-89). This information supports D and can be used to eliminate A and B, which omit the important topic of Hakadah's attraction to the possibility of life as a warrior. Despite his fascination, he is too young as depicted at this stage to BE a warrior, so that C is an incorrect reading of the paragraph's themes.

Chapter 3.3 | *The Red and the Black*

1) CORRECT ANSWER: C

In the passage, Julien is informed that he will be taking a new post, which he believes will reduce him to the position of a servant (line 39); the young man resolves to "run away to-night" (line 63) rather than accept his changed situation. This evidence supports C, while A and B wrongly assume that possible events such as Julien's taking his new post or Julien's running away have come to pass. Nor is Julien forcibly cast out of his home, since he still lives with his father but on extremely strained terms (eliminating D).

2) CORRECT ANSWER: C

The relevant paragraphs explain that Julien "adored the old Surgeon-Major" (line 18) and that the Surgeon-Major passed some of his learning on to Julien (along with his specific opinions, as indicated by lines 79-82). These indications of the Surgeon-Major's significant impact on Julien can be used to justify C and to eliminate A (which wrongly indicates that the description of the Surgeon-Major is a diversion) and B (which assumes that the author is making an argument or professing an opinion, not describing a character). D wrongly overstates the extent of the negativity between Julien and his family, since Julien is mostly disliked by his father, and assumes that the father disliked the Surgeon (rather than ALLOWING the Surgeon to educate his son).

3) CORRECT ANSWER: A

Julien's father believed that Julien "would not live beyond his childhood" (line 10) and is regarded as a burden to the operations of the family sawmill (lines 32-34), which depends on physical labor for its effective operation. A is thus the best answer, while B and C both list intellectual activities that the father in fact sanctions by allowing Julien to study with the Surgeon-Major. D overstates Julien's alienation: he is on uneasy terms with his family but does get along with OTHER residents, such as the Surgeon-Major and the "young girls" (lines 16-17).

4) CORRECT ANSWER: C

Julien's objection to taking the new post is that he will be treated as a servant: the question "discomforted" (line 43) Old Sorel because he cannot answer in a way that would separate Julien from the servants. He contradicts his own idea that Julien will not be treated as a servant because he has overlooked the detail about the meals (which Julien will presumably take with the servants), so that C is the best answer. Keep in mind that Julien has not refused the post ITSELF (only refused to be treated as a servant, eliminating A and D) and has simply asked his father questions (not directly insulted his father, eliminating B).

5) CORRECT ANSWER: C

While the brothers are depicted "holding counsel" (line 49) in the relevant line reference, Julien is depicted as set apart from them, since he goes to "the other side of the saw" (line 52) to contemplate his situation alone. These pieces of evidence justify C, while the brothers are not directly described as "calm" (only as holding a meeting that gives Julien little information, eliminating A). Keep in mind that Julien's brothers are considering his situation (and are thus not indifferent towards him, eliminating B) and that they are talking without any direct input from Julien (eliminating D).

6) CORRECT ANSWER: A

Julien's main objection to the proposed position is that he will eat with the servants; however, he is attracted to the prospect of "M. de Rênal's fine mansion" (lines 57-58). He would have to give up the appealing prospect of visiting the mansion if he were to flee from his position, so that A is an effective answer. B wrongly refers to a larger career path (while the mansion and its IMMEDIATE benefits are Julien's concerns), C wrongly indicates that Julien finds his current life appealing, and D is inappropriate because the "mansion" itself is not anywhere mentioned by Julien's father.

7) CORRECT ANSWER: B

In lines 67-68, Julien describes the priesthood as a "fine career" to which he aspires. This information supports B, as do lines 88-89, which describe Julien's "theology lesson at the curate's". A distorts the idea that Julien may be brought in to educate M. de Rênal's children, C distorts the idea that Julien has gotten an education and become devoted to specific texts (though he is NOT a writer himself), and D mistakes a career that Julien may enter if he flees for one that he prefers, or "aspires" to enter.

8) CORRECT ANSWER: C

See above for the explanation of the correct answer. A indicates Julien's respect for the Surgeon-Major, B indicates that Julien may be forced to enter the army, and D indicates that Julien is especially devoted to specific texts. Make sure not to wrongly take A as evidence for Question 7 A, B as evidence for Question 7 D, or D as evidence for Question 7 C.

9) CORRECT ANSWER: D

In lines 80-82, the narrator indicates that Julien regards almost all books in the world as "a pack of lies", or is thus extremely distrustful of a considerable range of people and their ideas. D is thus the best answer. A indicates Julien's aversion to his father's plan, B indicates how he intends to escape from his father's plan, and C indicates that his dislike of eating with the servants may be somewhat artificial. None of these line references indicates negative sentiments or suspicions towards a broad group (BEYOND Julien's father or the servants) in the manner of D.

10) CORRECT ANSWER: D

The word "construct" is used to explain the "world" (line 75) as Julien has learned to see and understand it, using primarily his imagination and a single book. He thus "perceives" the world with the help of that book, the Confessions of Rousseau, so that D is the best answer. A and B both wrongly indicate that Julien can alter the world as a manager or organizer, rather than simply SEE it in a specific way. C refers to a physical action, and is at best a looser, less accurate word for "perceive" and should be eliminated as an inferior answer.

Chapter 3.4 | *A Service of Love*

1) CORRECT ANSWER: A

The passage begins by describing the acquaintance and marriage of Joe and Delia, goes on to describe that "Money was lacking" (line 51) after the marriage, and indicates that Delia has begun giving lessons and that Joe is willing to find work. Such adaptation to address the couple's lack of money justifies A. B neglects the fact that Joe and Delia arrive in New York (the "large city") BEFORE they become a couple, C mistakes the couple's devotion to the arts for "social advancement", and D wrongly projects beyond the passage. It is not clear whether Joe and Delia successfully escape financial hardship, and in any case their efforts involve finding gainful employment, not "the power of love."

2) CORRECT ANSWER: B

Early in the passage, Joe and Delia have visions of success: "old gentlemen" (line 34) will flock to buy Joe's pictures, while Delia will become a famous opera singer (lines 36-40). Later, the narrator notes that "Art flagged" (line 48) and that the couple must turn to routine work to survive. This information supports B, while A and D both wrongly indicate that the couple's bond is dissolving (not that Delia and Joe are simply considering more practical side jobs). C misstates Delia's intentions; she wants to give music lessons to support herself WHILE pursuing an opera career, not to switch careers in any major way.

3) CORRECT ANSWER: B
The first and second paragraphs explain that both Joe (drawing) and Delia (music) had artistic background that they left their home communities (to go to "New York", line 7, or "North", line 12) to pursue. This information justifies B. A is incorrect because the characters' accomplishments are mentioned separately (NOT paired off or analyzed in a comparative way), while D is incorrect because the separate accomplishments (NOT the personalities of the characters) are mostly emphasized. Trap answer C is problematic because the information about Joe and Delia's talents sets up the context for their meeting and falling in love (they meet where a lot of art students gather). The discussion about their finances comes after, and their financial situation is not a result of their talents, but of the art industry being an unstable one.

4) CORRECT ANSWER: A
The "effort" refers to something that is "framed and hung" (line 5), or to the "picture" (line 3) that Joe drew and that his town celebrated. In context, the effort is one of Joe's artistic accomplishments; A is the best choice. B wrongly indicates that the picture was "attempted" but not completed, while C and D both refer to ongoing ACTIONS that involve challenge, not to a finished item.

5) CORRECT ANSWER: C
In lines 43-45, the union between Joe and Delia is described as involving "ambitions interwoven each with the other's or else inconsiderable"; the two artists, in other words, have shared ambitions and regard ambitions outside of these as insignificant. This indication of ongoing, interconnected ambitions supports C. A simply indicates that the two characters shared each other and their art (but does not indicate for HOW LONG), B praises Joe's commitment to Delia (but not HERS to him), and D describes Delia's devotion to her art (but does not directly discuss Joe's commitment to Delia).

6) CORRECT ANSWER: B
The idea of becoming "contemptuous with music" is linked to the discussion of Delia's training in respected music and her eventual popularity; a "diva" is a respected but at times temperamental performer, one who might "refuse to go on the stage" (line 40) if an audience is not sufficiently large. This information supports B. A wrongly understates Delia's interest in refined training and high culture (as opposed to merely "popular" music), C refers to a talented child (not an adult such as Delia), and D would only be appropriate for a non-performer or an observer of the arts.

7) CORRECT ANSWER: D
In lines 48-50, the author indicates that "Art flagged" as it occasionally or "sometimes" does even if nobody takes action to make it flag (as suggested by the metaphor of the "switchman"). This idea that art is beyond individual control justifies D. A and B are inaccurate because the passage does not record the end results of the careers of Joe and Delia (even though these characters are young, naive, and not born into privilege). C also distorts some of the passage's content: the two main characters do pursue artistic education, but it is not ever indicated that such education is the ONLY means of attaining artistic success.

8) CORRECT ANSWER: B

Near the end of the passage, when the two main characters must find new resources, Delia spends "two or three days" looking for pupils and is "elated" to find work (lines 56-57). Joe, in contrast, becomes agitated and then claims that Delia's project "isn't Art" (line 89). The difference between Delia's embrace of practical necessities and Joe's defensiveness over "Art" justifies B. Keep in mind that Delia does not intend to abandon her artistic ambitions in favor of teaching (only to bring in money, eliminating A), and that Joe continues to value artistic knowledge over financial success (eliminating C and D).

9) CORRECT ANSWER: D

In lines 82-83, Delia notes that her music lessons will keep her active inside her chosen artistic field; however, Joe's plans (which she rejects) would have him working outside his chosen fields in the visual arts. This justification for Delia's music lessons indicates that D is the best answer. Delia's plan is designed mainly to raise new funds for her artistic education (NOT Joe's, eliminating A); moreover, her main objection is that Joe's proposed employment would DISTRACT him from the arts, not that it would be distasteful itself (eliminating B) or turn him AGAINST the arts (eliminating C).

10) CORRECT ANSWER: C

See above for the explanation of the correct answer. A describes some of the conditions of Delia's new employment, B records comments designed to placate Joe, and D indicates Delia's willingness to live on relatively little. Keep in mind that A and B occur BEFORE Delia rebuffs Joe's offer, and can automatically be eliminated for this reason.

Chapter 3.5 | *The Bald Truth*

1) CORRECT ANSWER: D

The narrator uses a style marked by short sentences and non-technical vocabulary to describe his hair loss, which happens around Christmas and results in people glancing "quickly yet inquisitively" (lines 43-44) at him. It is unfortunate that his hair loss coincided with a number of social events, so that C is the best answer. A does not properly capture the narrator's negative reaction to the hair loss, B focuses only on the final stage of the passage (the meeting with the boy), and C ("poignant" or highly emotional) applies tones that are too strong and too negative to a passage about a somewhat everyday problem.

2) CORRECT ANSWER: B

The question occurs in the context of a discussion of the narrator's childhood encounters with a barber; the young narrator stuck his tongue out (line 8) and would naturally have derisive thoughts about the barber. B is the best answer. A is problematic because Alopecia Nervosa is not mentioned in any form in the line reference (and because the narrator struggles against it mostly on his own, not with a barber). C is problematic because the barber's curse about "all" the hair falling out does not in fact come true (since the narrator only loses SOME of his hair), while D is problematic because the narrator accepts the Alopecia Nervosa diagnosis as soon as it is given. C and D can also be eliminated because they are most relevant to lines other than line 9.

3) CORRECT ANSWER: C

The narrator explains in the first paragraph that he "used to hate going to the barber's" (lines 1-2) because the cushions that the barber used to adjust the young narrator's height were uncomfortable and made him move about. At an older age, the narrator would be tall enough that this discomfort or "fidgeting" would be eliminated; C is the best answer. A and D are incorrect because the narrator dozes off at the barber (and thus is not engaged by the experience or preoccupied with thoughts that would keep him awake). B is a trap answer: the narrator seems to have disregarded the childhood barber's curse even as a teenager (lines 10-11) and is at first uninterested in the state of his hair (not positively confident in its condition) in adulthood.

4) CORRECT ANSWER: A

In the relevant paragraph, the narrator "sat up" in "panic" (line 23); although his emotions are strong, the doctor is mostly unconcerned, noting that the narrator "shouldn't worry" (line 23) and that other clients have similar problems. This information supports A and can be used to eliminate D, since the narrator sits up in a manner that conveys discomposure. B and C both rely on line references from OTHER paragraphs (since the narrator's earlier demeanor and the barber's curse are not mentioned here) and should thus be eliminated as out of scope.

5) CORRECT ANSWER: C

The word "independent" describes the narrator as a "teenager" (line 10) who has disregarded his earlier obligations and qualms, or "rebelled" against them, to lead life as he pleases. C is the best answer. A indicates freedom from bondage (and is thus too extreme in its associations), B indicates that the narrator's lifestyle is strange or unusual (not that he has rebelled against earlier constraints), and D is problematic because the narrator is not entirely "detached" or unemotional. In fact, he seems confident and proud of his hair in a way that would make this answer problematic.

6) CORRECT ANSWER: B

The word "revealed" refers to the "affinity to the low dome of Neanderthal man" (line 49) that the narrator's head was found to show or display after his mother shaved his head. B is thus the best answer. A and C both indicate that the head is doing something correctly (not that it is manifesting an undesirable state), while D would best refer to the action of a person who is unveiling or "disclosing" a fact, not to an aspect of a person's appearance that "displays" itself.

7) CORRECT ANSWER: D

In lines 43-45, the narrator explains that he "soon tired" of his friends and their uncomfortable looks at his hair, indicating that he grew averse to the Christmas season parties. D is thus the best answer. Although the narrator does feel stress, this stress did not cause him to lose additional hair (eliminating A) or to cut his vacation short (eliminating B). C is a trap answer: while the narrator avoids his friends, he does not seek entirely deserted areas and in fact spends time with his family so that his mother can shave his head.

8) CORRECT ANSWER: B

See above for the explanation of the correct answer. A records the doctor's response to the narrator's Alopecia Nervosa (NOT the narrator's life over the holidays), C describes the narrator's return to work, and D describes the thin crowds in London. Make sure not to wrongly take C as evidence for Question 7 B (since the narrator returns to work but does NOT necessarily avoid his family) or D as evidence for Question 7 C (since London is rather sparsely populated, but not "deserted").

9) CORRECT ANSWER: B

In lines 64-67, the young boy is described as "staring fixedly" at the narrator's head and the young boy's eyes are described as "not hostile, only excited". The young boy also asks whether the narrator is a punk, so that the young boy's reaction can best be described as positive and wondering. B is the best answer, while the same evidence can be used to eliminate negative answers such as A and D. C is a trap answer: it expresses the boy's LATER reaction after learning that the narrator dislikes going to the barber, not his initial reaction.

10) CORRECT ANSWER: A

See above for the explanation of the correct answer. B describes the boy's discomfort and embarrassment after his initial inquiry, C describes the boy's attempt to respond positively to the news that the narrator is not a punk, and D indicates that the narrator dislikes going to the barber. All of these line references occur AFTER the boy first saw the narrator's bald head and reacted with fascination, and should thus be eliminated.

CHAPTER FOUR

Questions 1-10 are based on the following passage.
Chapter 4.1
Adapted from Maxim Gorky, *Mother* (1911).

Pavel tried to live like the rest. He did all a young lad from a factory town should do—bought himself an accordion, a shirt with a starched front, a loud-colored

Line necktie, overshoes, and a cane. Externally he became
5 like all the other youths of his age. He went to evening parties and learned to dance a quadrille and a polka. In the morning his head ached, he was tormented by heartburns, his face was pale and dull.

Once his mother asked him:
10 "Well, did you have a good time yesterday?"
He answered dismally and with irritation:
"Oh, dreary as a graveyard! Everybody is like a machine. I'd better go fishing or buy myself a gun."
He worked faithfully, without intermission and
15 without incurring fines. He was taciturn, and his eyes, blue and large like his mother's, looked out discontentedly. He did not buy a gun, nor did he go a-fishing; but he gradually began to avoid the beaten path trodden by all. His attendance at parties became
20 less and less frequent, and although he went out somewhere on holidays, he always returned home sober. His mother watched him unobtrusively but closely, and saw the tawny face of her son grow keener and keener, and his eyes more serious. She noticed that his
25 lips were compressed in a peculiar manner, imparting an odd expression of austerity to his face. It seemed as if he were always angry at something, or as if a canker gnawed at him. At first his friends came to visit him, but never finding him at home, they remained away.
30 The mother was glad to see her son turning out different from all the other factory youth; but a feeling of anxiety and apprehension stirred in her heart when she observed that he was obstinately and resolutely directing his life into obscure paths leading away from
35 the routine existence about him—that he turned in his career neither to the right nor the left.
He began to bring books home with him. At first he tried to escape attention when reading them; and after he had finished a book, he hid it. Sometimes he copied a
40 passage on a piece of paper, and hid that also.
"Aren't you well, Pavlusha?" the mother asked once.
"I'm all right," he answered.
"You are so thin," said the mother with a sigh.
45 He was silent.
They spoke infrequently, and saw each other very little. In the morning he drank tea in silence, and

went off to work; at noon he came for dinner, a few insignificant remarks were passed at the table, and he
50 again disappeared until the evening. And in the evening, the day's work ended, he washed himself, took supper, and then fell to his books, and read for a long time. On holidays he left home in the morning and returned late at night. She knew he went to the city and the theater; but
55 nobody from the city ever came to visit him. It seemed to her that with the lapse of time her son spoke less and less; and at the same time she noticed that occasionally and with increasing frequency he used new words unintelligible to her, and that the coarse, rude, and hard
60 expressions dropped from his speech. In his general conduct, also, certain traits appeared, forcing themselves upon his mother's attention. He ceased to affect the dandy, but became more attentive to the cleanliness of his body and dress, and moved more freely and alertly.
65 The increasing softness and simplicity of his manner aroused a disquieting interest in his mother.
Once he brought a picture and hung it on the wall. It represented three persons walking lightly and boldly, and conversing.
70 "This is Christ risen from the dead, and going to Emmaus," explained Pavel.
The mother liked the picture, but she thought:
"You respect Christ, and yet you do not go to church."
75 Then more pictures appeared on the walls, and the number of books increased on the shelves neatly made for him by one of his carpenter friends. The room began to look like a home. . .
But her uneasiness increased. Since her son's
80 strangeness was not clarified with time, her heart became more and more sharply troubled with a foreboding of something unusual. Every now and then she felt a certain dissatisfaction with him, and she thought: "All people are like people, and he is like a
85 monk. He is so stern. It's not according to his years."

CONTINUE ➡

1

Which choice best describes a major theme of the passage?

A) The satisfaction and harmony of a family life in pious devotion

B) A mother's quest to suppress the self-discovery of her son

C) The disquieting effect of one family member's unconventional life on another

D) The unconditional love between mother and child in the face of failed expectation

2

The main idea of the first paragraph is that

A) though Pavel tried hard to fit in, he was not suited for the lifestyle of his peers.

B) Pavel sought to emulate his peers whom he admired and befriended.

C) while Pavel behaved similarly to his peers, he was never fully accepted by them.

D) Pavel found enjoyment in dressing flamboyantly and socializing with his peers.

3

Pavel uses the word "machine" (line 13) to characterize the people at the party as

A) depressed.

B) inhuman.

C) serious.

D) uninteresting.

4

In context of the passage as a whole, lines 14-29 primarily serve to

A) emphasize Pavel's diligent work ethic.

B) depict the beginnings of Pavel's transformation.

C) analyze the source of Pavel's dissatisfaction.

D) describe the ways in which Pavel is unlike his peers.

5

Pavel's mother initially reacts to his changed lifestyle with

A) anxiety.

B) hope.

C) excitement.

D) ambivalence.

6

Which choice provides the best evidence for the answer to the previous question?

A) Lines 22-24 ("His mother...serious")

B) Lines 26-28 ("It seemed...him")

C) Lines 30-32 ("The mother...heart")

D) Lines 79-82 ("Since her...unusual")

7

In describing the progression of Pavel's character, the narrator juxtaposes

A) the hobbies of Pavel's peers and his own intellectual endeavors.

B) the internal contentment Pavel feels and his mother's increasing discomfort.

C) the jobs commonly available in Pavel's village and his career pursuits in the city.

D) the life that Pavel aspires to live and the harsh realities of his circumstances.

CONTINUE

8

Which choice best supports the conclusion that the relationship between Pavel and his mother is distant?

A) Lines 33-35 ("she observed...him")

B) Lines 37-39 ("At first...it")

C) Lines 47-50 ("In the...evening")

D) Lines 57-60 ("she noticed...speech")

9

The primary impression created by the narrator's description of Pavel in lines 55-64 ("It seemed... alertly") is that he has become more

A) comfortable and honest.

B) stern and bitter.

C) insensitive and selfish.

D) reserved and refined.

10

As used in line 62, "affect" most nearly means

A) portray.

B) influence.

C) represent.

D) parody.

CONTINUE

Questions 1-10 are based on the following passage.
Chapter 4.2
Adapted from Gustave Flaubert, *A Simple Soul* (1877). Felicite, one of the primary characters, is an elderly woman who has long served as the maid to Madame Aubain.

The parrot, a gift to Madame Aubain's household, was called Loulou. His body was green, his head blue, the tips of his wings were pink and his breast was
Line
5 golden.

But he had the tiresome tricks of biting his perch, pulling his feathers out, scattering rubbish and spilling the water of his bath. Madame Aubain grew tired of him and gave him to the maid Felicite for good.

She undertook his education, and soon he was
10 able to repeat: "Pretty boy! Your servant, sir! I salute you, Marie!" His perch was placed near the door and several persons were astonished that he did not answer to the name of "Jacquot," for every parrot is called Jacquot. They called him a goose and a log, and these
15 taunts were like so many dagger thrusts to Felicite. Strange stubbornness of the bird which would not talk when people watched him!

Nevertheless, he sought society; for on Sunday, when the ladies Rochefeuille, Monsieur
20 de Houppeville and the new habitues, Onfroy, the chemist, Monsieur Varin and Captain Mathieu, dropped in for their game of cards, he struck the window-panes with his wings and made such a racket that it was impossible to talk. . .
25 When he went downstairs, he rested his beak on the steps, lifted his right foot and then his left one; but his mistress feared that such feats would give him vertigo. He became ill and was unable to eat. There was a small growth under his tongue like those
30 chickens are sometimes afflicted with. Felicite pulled it off with her nails and cured him. . . Finally he got lost.

Felicite had put him on the grass to cool him and went away only for a second; when she returned, she found no parrot! She hunted among the bushes, on the
35 bank of the river, and on the roofs, without paying any attention to Madame Aubain who screamed at her: "Take care! you must be insane!" Then she searched every garden in Pont-l'Eveque and stopped the passers-by to inquire of them: "Haven't you perhaps seen my
40 parrot?" To those who had never seen the parrot, she described him minutely. Suddenly she thought she saw something green fluttering behind the mills at the foot of the hill. But when she was at the top of the hill she could not see it. A hod-carrier told her that

45 he had just seen the bird in Saint-Melaine, in Mother Simon's store. She rushed to the place. The people did not know what she was talking about. At last she came home, exhausted, with her slippers worn to shreds, and
50 despair in her heart. She sat down on the bench near Madame and was telling of her search when presently a light weight dropped on her shoulder—Loulou! What the deuce had he been doing? Perhaps he had just taken a little walk around the town!

55 She did not easily forget her scare; in fact, she never got over it. In consequence of a cold, she caught a sore throat; and some time later she had an earache. Three years later she was stone deaf, and spoke in a very loud voice even in church. Although her sins
60 might have been proclaimed throughout the diocese without any shame to herself, or ill effects to the community, the curate thought it advisable to receive her confession in the vestry-room.

Imaginary buzzings also added to her
65 bewilderment. Her mistress often said to her: "My goodness, how stupid you are!" and she would answer: "Yes, Madame," and look for something.

The narrow circle of her ideas grew more restricted than it already was; the bellowing of the
70 oxen, the chime of the bells no longer reached her intelligence. All things moved silently, like ghosts. Only one noise penetrated her ears; the parrot's voice.

As if to divert her mind, he reproduced for her the tick-tack of the spit in the kitchen, the shrill cry of
75 the fish-vendors, the saw of the carpenter who had a shop opposite, and when the door-bell rang, he would imitate Madame Aubain: "Felicite! go to the front door."

They held conversations together, Loulou
80 repeating the three phrases of his repertory over and over, Felicite replying by words that had no greater meaning, but in which she poured out her feelings. In her isolation, the parrot was almost a son, a love. He climbed upon her fingers, pecked at her lips, clung to
85 her shawl, and when she rocked her head to and fro like a nurse, the big wings of her cap and the wings of the bird flapped in unison.

CONTINUE

1

Over the course of the passage, the primary focus shifts from

A) Felicite's reservation about taking on Loulou to her eventual obsession with him.

B) the events leading up to Loulou's disappearance to the incident's effect on Felicite.

C) Felicite's purchasing of Loulou to the codependence that develops between them.

D) an objective description of Loulou to Felicite's inner thoughts about the parrot.

2

Which of the following choices best describes Felicite's care of Loulou?

A) Prudent

B) Neglectful

C) Attentive

D) Imaginative

3

According to the passage, Felicite's main duty in Madame Aubain's household is to

A) take care of and educate Loulou.

B) serve as a companion.

C) entertain guests with Loulou.

D) perform domestic chores.

4

The narrator uses the phrase "like so many dagger thrusts" (line 15) to portray Felicite as

A) having a soft spot for her parrot.

B) being aggressively defensive of her parrot.

C) being oblivious to her friends' jokes.

D) embarrassed by her parrot's rebelliousness.

5

As used in line 18, "society" most nearly means

A) acceptance.

B) amusement.

C) attention.

D) company.

6

Which choice provides the best evidence to support the claim that the narrator views Felicite as a woman of decent morals?

A) Lines 7-8 ("Madame Aubain...good")

B) Lines 34-37 ("She hunted...insane")

C) Lines 59-62 ("Although her...community")

D) Lines 65-67 ("Her mistress...something")

7

The narrator indicates which of the following about Felicite's search for Loulou?

A) It was unsuccessful even though Felicite looked for Loulou at length.

B) It was difficult because Loulou was actively trying to avoid Felicite.

C) It was easily preventable if not for Felicite's carelessness with Loulou.

D) It was futile since Loulou had never even left the vicinity of the town.

8

Which choice provides the best evidence for the answer to the previous question?

A) Lines 32-34 ("Felicite had...parrot")

B) Lines 41-44 ("Suddenly she...it")

C) Lines 48-50 ("At last...heart")

D) Lines 52-54 ("a light...town")

CONTINUE

9

The contrast depicted in lines 71-72 ("All things... voice") has the effect of

A) highlighting the singularity of the parrot in Felicite's world.

B) revealing the seriousness of Felicite's debilitating condition.

C) suggesting that the parrot is aware of Felicite's need for stimulus.

D) implying that Felicite has willfully isolated herself to focus on Loulou.

10

The last two paragraphs (lines 73-90) primarily serve to

A) characterize Felicite's parrot as gradually becoming more intelligent and empathetic.

B) suggest that Felicite and her parrot heal each other with emotional support.

C) show how Felicite and her parrot have eventually settled into a comforting routine.

D) indicate that Felicite wrongfully interprets her parrots' actions in a state of delusion.

CONTINUE

Questions 1-10 are based on the following passage.
Chapter 4.3
The following is an excerpt from *The Tale of the Third Century* (1856) by John Henry Newman.

Jucundus set out to see how the land lay with his nephew, and to do what he could to prosper the tillage. His way led him by the temple of Mercury,
Line which at that time subserved the purpose of a boy's
5 school. It cannot be said that our friend was any warm patron of literature or education, though he had not neglected the schooling of his nephews. Letters seemed to him in fact to unsettle the mind; and he had never known much good come of them.
10 Rhetoricians and philosophers did not know where they stood, or what were their bearings. They did not know what they held, and what they did not. He knew his own position perfectly well, and, though the words "belief" or "knowledge" did not come into his
15 vocabulary, he could at once, without hesitation, state what he professed and maintained. He stood upon the established order of things, on the traditions of Rome, and the laws of the empire.

As he passed the temple, the metal plate was
20 sounding as a signal for the termination of the school, and on looking towards the portico with an ill-natured curiosity, he saw a young acquaintance of his, Arnobius, a youth of about twenty, coming out of it.

"Whom are you attending here?" asked Jucundus,
25 drily.

Arnobius sighed, exasperated at the events that had just unfolded. "You are the only man in Sicca who needs to ask the question. Did you not feel the presence in Sicca of Polemo, the most celebrated,
30 the most intolerable of men? That, however, is not his title, but the 'godlike', or the 'oracular', or the 'portentous', or something else as impressive." He dragged out the syllables of the titles theatrically, rolling his eyes as he did so. "Everyone goes to him.
35 I should not have a chance of success if I could not say that I had attended his lectures. He comes to the schools in a litter of cedar, ornamented with silver and covered with a lion's skin, slaves carrying him, and a crowd of friends attending, with the state of a
40 proconsul. He is dressed in the most exact style; his pallium is of the finest wool, white, picked out with purple; his tresses flow with unguent, his fingers glitter with rings. As soon as he puts foot on earth, a great hubbub of congratulation and homage breaks forth. He
45 takes no notice; his favorite pupils form a circle around him, and conduct him into one of the stages, till the

dial shows the time for lecture. Here he sits in silence, looking at nothing, or at the wall opposite him, talking to himself, a hum of admiration filling the room.
50 Presently one of his pupils cries out, 'Hush, gentlemen, hush! the godlike'—no, it is not that. What is his title? 'The Bottomless,' that's it—'The Bottomless speaks.' A dead silence ensues; a clear voice and a measured elocution are the sure token that it is the outpouring
55 of the oracle. 'Pray,' says the little man, 'pray, which existed first, the egg or the chick? Did the chick lay the egg, or the egg hatch the chick?' Then there ensues a whispering, a disputing, and after a while a dead silence. At the end of a quarter of an hour or
60 so, his pupil speaks again, and this time to the oracle. 'Bottomless man,' he says, 'I have to represent to you that no one of the present company finds himself equal to answer the question, which your condescension has proposed to our consideration!' On this there is a fresh
65 silence, and at length a fresh pronouncement from the oracular: 'Which comes first, the egg or the chick? The egg comes first in relation to the causativity of the chick, and the chick comes first in relation to the causativity of the egg,' on which there is a burst of
70 applause; the ring of adorers is broken through, and the shrinking professor is carried in the arms or on the shoulders of the literary crowd to his chair in the lecture hall."

Much as there was in Arnobius's description
75 which gratified Jucundus's prejudices, he had suspicions of his young acquaintance, and was not in the humor to be pleased unreservedly with those who satirized anything whatever that was established, or was appointed by government, even affectation and
80 pretense. He said something about the wisdom of ages, the reverence due to authority, the institutions of Rome, and the magistrates of Sicca. "Do not go after novelties," he said to Arnobius. "make a daily libation to Jove, the preserver, and to the genius of the emperor,
85 and then let other things take their course."

"I don't believe in god or goddess, emperor or Rome, or in any philosophy, or in any religion at all," said Arnobius.

"What!" cried Jucundus. "You're not going to
90 desert the gods of your ancestors?"

"Ancestors?" said Arnobius. "I've no ancestors. I'm not African certainly, nor am I Punic. I'm half Greek, but what the other half is I don't know. My good old gaffer, you're one of the old world. I believe
95 nothing. Who can? There is such a racket and whirl of religions on all sides of me that I am sick of the subject."

"Ah, the rising generation!" groaned Jucundus.

CONTINUE

"You young men! I cannot prophesy what you will
100 become, when we old fellows are removed from the
scene."

1

Which choice best describes what happens in the passage?

A) One character relays the essence of a lecture to another character who is appreciative.

B) Two characters casually exchange views on the merits of an education in philosophy.

C) One character admonishes another character for his sarcastic description of an event.

D) One character praises the wisdom of a famous lecturer to a cynical acquaintance.

2

Which statement about Jucundus is best supported by the first paragraph?

A) Although he reveres the gods and ancestors of Rome, he dislikes Roman government.

B) Although he is suspicious of philosophers, he understands their role in society.

C) Although he is skeptical about belief, he is steadfast in his support of tradition.

D) Although he values education, he views philosophers as misleading.

3

It can be inferred from Arnobius' description of Polemo that Arnobius chose to attend the lecture most likely to

A) improve his own chances of success.

B) obtain insights from a wise man.

C) satisfy his curiosity about a celebrity.

D) satirize the proceedings of the event.

4

Which choice provides the best evidence for the answer to the previous question?

A) Lines 30-32 ("That, however...impressive")

B) Lines 34-36 ("Everyone goes...lectures")

C) Lines 43-44 ("As soon...forth")

D) Lines 64-66 ("On this...oracular")

5

In his description of Polemo, Arnobius' references to "The godlike" , "The oracular" and "The Bottomless" mainly have which effect?

A) They evoke Arnobius' sense of disbelief.

B) They reflect Arnobius' extreme adulation.

C) They capture Arnobius' expectations of wisdom.

D) They reveal Arnobius' sarcastic tone.

6

In context of Arnobius' description of the lecture, Polemo's answer to the question "Which comes first, the egg or the chick?" (line 66) has what effect?

A) It underscores the futility of the question.

B) It illustrates the gullibility of Polemo's students.

C) It illustrates the absurdity of philosophical inquiry.

D) It depicts Polemo as a profound thinker.

7

Which aspect of Arnobius' description of the lecture most offends Jucundus?

A) Arnobius' apparent disrespect of tradition.

B) Arnobius' excessive adoration of Polemo.

C) Arnobius' ambivalence towards philosophy.

D) Arnobius' inconclusive account of the lesson.

8

Which choice best supports the conclusion that Jucundus favors tradition over innovation?

A) Lines 8-9 ("Letters seemed...them")

B) Lines 82-85 ("Do not...course")

C) Lines 89-90 ("You're not...ancestors")

D) Lines 99-101 ("I cannot...scene")

CONTINUE

9

The main purpose of lines 91-97 is to

A) provide information about Arnobius' ethnicity.

B) point to the source of discord between Arnobius and Jucundus.

C) establish a link between Arnobius' beliefs and his identity.

D) comment on the state of religion during Arnobius' time.

10

As used in line 98, "rising" most nearly means

A) improving.

B) elevating.

C) soaring.

D) new.

CONTINUE

Questions 1-10 are based on the following passage.
Chapter 4.4
Adapted from Brett Harte, *Mliss* (1874).

"The Master," as he was known to his little flock, sat alone one night in his schoolhouse, with some open copybooks before him . . . when he heard a gentle
Line tapping. The woodpeckers had been busy about the
5 roof during the day, and the noise did not disturb his work. But the opening of the door, and the tapping continuing from the inside, caused him to look up. He was slightly startled by the figure of a young girl, dirty and shabbily clad. Still, her great black eyes, her
10 coarse, uncombed, lusterless black hair falling over her sunburned face, her red arms and feet streaked with the red soil, were all familiar to him. It was Melissa Smith—Smith's motherless child.
"What can she want here?" thought the master.
15 Everybody knew Melissa or "Mliss," as she was called, throughout the length and height of Red Mountain. Everybody knew her as an incorrigible girl. Her fierce, ungovernable disposition, her mad freaks and lawless character, were in their way as proverbial as the story
20 of her father's weaknesses, and as philosophically accepted by the townsfolk. She wrangled with and fought the schoolboys with keener invective and quite as powerful arm. She followed the trails with a woodman's craft, and the master had met her before,
25 miles away, shoeless, stockingless, and bareheaded on the mountain road. The miners' camps along the stream supplied her with subsistence during these voluntary pilgrimages, in freely offered alms. Not but that a larger protection had been previously extended
30 to Mliss. The Rev. Joshua McSnagley, "stated" preacher, had placed her in the hotel as servant, by way of preliminary refinement, and had introduced her to his scholars at Sunday school. But she threw plates occasionally at the landlord, and quickly retorted to
35 the cheap witticisms of the guests, and created in the Sabbath school a sensation that was so inimical to the orthodox dullness and placidity of that institution that, with a decent regard for the starched frocks and unblemished morals of the two pink-and-white-faced
40 children of the first families, the reverend gentleman had her ignominiously expelled. Such were the antecedents, and such the character of Mliss as she stood before the master. It was shown in the ragged dress, the unkempt hair, and bleeding feet, and asked
45 his pity. It flashed from her black, fearless eyes, and commanded his respect.
"I come here tonight," she said rapidly and boldly, keeping her hard glance on his, "because I knew you was alone. I wouldn't come here when them gals was
50 here. I hate them and they hate me. That's why. You keep school, don't you? I want to be taught!"
If to the shabbiness of her apparel and uncomeliness of her tangled hair and dirty face she had added the humility of tears, the master would
55 have extended to her the usual moiety of pity, and nothing more. But with the natural, though illogical, instincts of his species, her boldness awakened in him something of that respect which all original natures pay unconsciously to one another in any grade. And
60 he gazed at her the more fixedly as she went on still rapidly, her hand on that door latch and her eyes on his:
"My name's Mliss—Mliss Smith! You can bet your life on that. My father's Old Smith—Old Bummer Smith—that's what's the matter with him. Mliss
65 Smith—and I'm coming to school!"
"Well?" said the master.
Accustomed to be thwarted and opposed, often wantonly and cruelly, for no other purpose than to excite the violent impulses of her nature, the master's
70 complacency evidently took her by surprise. She stopped; she began to twist a lock of her hair between her fingers; and the rigid line of upper lip, drawn over the wicked little teeth, relaxed and quivered slightly. Then her eyes dropped, and something like a blush
75 struggled up to her cheek and tried to assert itself through the splashes of redder soil, and the sunburn of years. Suddenly she threw herself forward, calling on heaven to strike her dead, and fell quite weak and helpless, with her face on the master's desk, crying and
80 sobbing as if her heart would break. . . . "
The master laughed. It was a hearty laugh, and echoed so oddly in the little schoolhouse, and seemed so inconsistent and discordant with the sighing of the pines without, that he shortly corrected himself with a
85 sigh. The sigh was quite as sincere in its way, however, and after a moment of serious silence he asked about her father.
Her father? What father? Whose father? What had he ever done for her? Why did the girls hate her? . . .
90 The schoolmaster, raising her to her feet, wrapped his shawl around her, and, bidding her come early in the morning, he walked with her down the road. There he bade her "good night." The moon shone brightly on the narrow path before them. He stood and watched
95 the bent little figure as it staggered down the road, and waited until it had passed the little graveyard and reached the curve of the hill, where it turned and stood for a moment, a mere atom of suffering outlined against the far-off patient stars.

1

The main purpose of the first paragraph is to

A) describe the moment when the master meets Mliss for the first time.

B) characterize the master as inattentive and neglectful towards others.

C) provide context for the conversation between Mliss and the master.

D) introduce the character of the master by showing his nightly habits.

2

The narrator uses the phrase "philosophically accepted" in lines 20-21 to suggest that

A) Mliss's aggressive temperament cannot be changed.

B) Mliss is as a bad example to the other children of the town.

C) the master believed Mliss's behavior resulted from her unusual upbringing.

D) the townsfolk have grown to tolerate Mliss's actions as part of the normal course of life.

3

As used in line 22, "keener" most nearly means

A) fiercer.

B) livelier.

C) more astute.

D) more enthusiastic.

4

What function do lines 41-46 ("Such were...respect") serve in the passage as a whole?

A) They reveal that the master was aware of Mliss's history.

B) They return the narrative to a point earlier in the passage.

C) They show the disarming effects of Mliss's words on the master.

D) They foreshadow a shift that occurs later in the passage.

5

Over the course of the encounter between Mliss and the master, Mliss's demeanor shifts from

A) one of confidence to one of humility.

B) one of bravado to one of vulnerability.

C) one of heedlessness to one of desperation.

D) one of belligerence to one of despair.

6

The passage indicates that Mliss visited the schoolhouse at night because she

A) wanted the master to teach her alone.

B) knew the master was there every night.

C) was at Sunday school during the day.

D) wanted to avoid the other schoolgirls.

7

Mliss's attitude towards her father can best be characterized as one of

A) resentment.

B) hostility.

C) indifference.

D) pride.

8

Which choice provides the best evidence for the answer to the previous question?

A) Lines 18-20 ("her mad...weaknesses")

B) Lines 62-64 ("My name's...him")

C) Lines 77-78 ("Suddenly she...dead")

D) Lines 88-89 ("Her father...for her")

CONTINUE

9

Which choice best describes the master's reaction towards Mliss's initial request that she be taught?

A) He felt pity for Mliss and wished to help improve her circumstances.

B) He felt intrigued by Mliss but doubted her sincerity in wanting an education.

C) He felt irrationally but intuitively captivated by Mliss's assertiveness.

D) He felt the urge to protect and nurture Mliss by allowing her to attend school.

10

Which choice provides the best evidence for the conclusion that the master had accepted Mliss's demand to attend his school?

A) Lines 67-70 ("Accustomed to...surprise")

B) Lines 77-80 ("Suddenly she...break")

C) Lines 85-87 ("The sigh...father")

D) Lines 90-92 ("The schoolmaster...road")

CONTINUE

Questions 1-10 are based on the following passage.
Chapter 4.5
The following is an excerpt from *A Mere Formality* (2017) by Chris Holliday.

Joan parked the car tight up against the curb. She sat for a moment, her hands gripping the wheel. She inhaled deeply, holding in her breath to the count
Line of ten before exhaling. She examined her face in the
5 driving mirror before picking up her handbag from the passenger's seat and exiting the vehicle. She shut the door, turned and paused. She cast a sly glance up and down the street, then lifted her head and gazed at the house. She held the pose for a moment before pushing
10 open the gate and moving along the path towards the house.

Once upon a time, the front door would have been flung open; he would have run half way down the path, calling out to her. There would be hugs and laughter
15 and questions about the child and an insistence that she must come and see the roses in the back garden for they were the best ever. Now there was nothing but silence. She glanced at the front bay windows. The curtains were still drawn.
20 She flung back her head, pushed open the gate and moved towards the door. On cue, it opened. The woman standing in the doorway was nervously breathless.

"Oh, Joan, dear. I was just dusting through and
25 taking the cleaner over the carpets—ready for when you were coming. I meant to have drawn back the curtains in the front before you got here—make things a bit more cheering. You are a bit earlier than I expected. Still, nothing has changed since you were
30 last here. Everything left as he liked it. Now, I've got the kettle on the go in the kitchen. You'd like a cup of tea, I expect. It must all feel a bit difficult for you at the moment."

Joan regarded her coolly. "In fact, I am somewhat
35 later than I intended to be... I only flew into London last night. I would have come earlier; but the studio needed me for more close-ups."

"Well, just fancy! You would think they could have waited, considering the situation. Your dad would
40 have had a thing or two to say about that, if he had been here."

"Yes, I remember that side of him only too well. Perhaps, in this case, it's just as well he couldn't. Time costs money in Hollywood." She looked around the
45 kitchen with the air of reminiscence. "How strange. Nothing seems to have changed since I was last here.

Look, there's the cuckoo clock, still on the wall." She moved to look at it. "Oh! it seems to have stopped."

"Yes. He was in one of his tempers. He dropped
50 it. It was in pieces. He put it all back together again." She smiled at the memory. "It took him weeks, and he could never get the mechanism to work again."

Joan gave a tight smile. "That sounds just like him: all emotion and no sense. You can never put
55 something back to what it was once it has shattered. He should just have replaced it with a new one and moved on. What's done is done. It's what I would do."

"Yes. I remember, just after her funeral when you made your grand exit—vowing never to return—he
60 said something like that about you. But the clock was something your mother always treasured: it was the first present he ever gave to her. He wanted to put everything back together again. Sadly, sometimes, you can't."

65 Joan looked away. The other woman poured out the tea and sat down at the table. There was a long silence. Eventually, Joan turned back to the table and sat. The two regarded each other. There was a long silence.

70 "My name is Florence."

"I know."

Florence nodded. "I know you know. It's just that you have not used it since you arrived."

Joan looked away. "It was my mother's name."

75 "Yes, I know it was, but it would be polite. He always liked to say that name." She sighed. "All these years. You and he, so stubborn. You should know that it was not until long after the funeral that he and I became friends. Just friends—nothing else. Whatever
80 you may have decided. That is the truth—I was just someone with a name he loved who he could talk to and watch TV with and, now and again, go to the cinema with, to see your latest film." Joan raised her eyebrows. "Oh, yes! Despite everything, he was proud
85 of you."

"How would I know? He never said it." A tear rolled down her cheek.

"Did you ever give him the chance? This is real life. Only Hollywood believes there is always a happy
90 ending."

Joan sighed. "Perhaps you are right."

Later, from the car, Joan waved goodbye as Florence closed the door. "Well, that's all done with." She put the car in gear and smiled into the mirror.
95 "Ready for my close-up, Mr. Director."

CONTINUE

1

Which choice best describes what happens in the passage?

A) One character attempts to repair her relationship with another character.

B) One character wistfully reflects on her relationship with her father.

C) Two characters reminisce about time spent with a mutual loved one.

D) Two characters have a strained meeting after the death of a mutual loved one.

2

The main purpose of the first paragraph is to

A) suggest that Joan is preparing herself for an emotionally difficult task.

B) convey Joan's reluctance to revisit unpleasant memories of her father.

C) show that Joan has a routine she performs before visiting her father.

D) indicate that Joan's presence in the house is supposed to be secret.

3

Over the course of the second paragraph, the narrator presents a contrast between

A) the noisiness of the neighborhood in the past and the quietness of it in the present day.

B) the liveliness of the house when Joan visited in the past and the dreariness of it in the present day.

C) the affection Joan's father displayed upon her arrival and Florence's indifferent reaction to her.

D) the loving relationship between Joan and her father during her childhood and their impersonal relationship as adults.

4

Which choice provides the best evidence for the conclusion that the death of Joan's father was recent?

A) Lines 17-19 ("Now there...drawn")

B) Lines 21-23 ("The woman...breathless")

C) Lines 24-26 ("I was...coming")

D) Lines 31-33 ("You'd like...moment")

5

As used in line 42, "side" most nearly means

A) characteristic.

B) opinion.

C) argument.

D) profile.

6

It can be reasonably inferred from the passage that in comparison to her father, Joan considers herself to be less

A) willing to seek forgiveness from others.

B) preoccupied with recreating the past.

C) prone to dwelling on her mistakes.

D) regretful about her past relationships.

7

Which choice provides the best evidence for the answer to the previous question?

A) Lines 53-54 ("Joan gave...sense")

B) Lines 54-57 ("You can...do")

C) Lines 60-62 ("But the...again")

D) Lines 84-87 ("Despite everything...cheek")

CONTINUE

8

The repetition of the phrase "there was a long silence" in lines 66-69 primarily serves to illustrate the

A) inability of Joan and Florence to express their emotions in words.

B) emptiness Joan and Florence feel following the death of Joan's father.

C) uncomfortable tension between Joan and Florence.

D) animosity Joan and Florence have towards each other.

9

According to the passage, Joan reacts to Florence's claim that her father watched her films with

A) surprise and sadness.

B) suspicion and disbelief.

C) skepticism and anger.

D) sorrow and regret.

10

Joan's remarks in the last paragraph (lines 92-95) imply that she

A) has finally found closure and is ready to move on.

B) is glad to finally see her father in a positive way.

C) is satisfied with the outcome of her visit.

D) has started to recover from her father's death.

Answer Key: CHAPTER FOUR

Chapter 4.1
1. C
2. A
3. D
4. B
5. D
6. C
7. B
8. C
9. D
10. A

Chapter 4.2
1. B
2. C
3. D
4. A
5. C
6. C
7. A
8. C
9. A
10. C

Chapter 4.3
1. C
2. C
3. A
4. B
5. D
6. A
7. A
8. B
9. C
10. D

Chapter 4.4
1. C
2. D
3. A
4. B
5. B
6. D
7. A
8. D
9. C
10. D

Chapter 4.5
1. D
2. A
3. B
4. D
5. A
6. C
7. B
8. C
9. A
10. A

Answer Explanations

Chapter 4

Chapter 4.1 | *Mother*

1) CORRECT ANSWER: C
While Pavel is hardworking, his habits and his tendency to bring home new books and items cause "anxiety and apprehension" (line 32) and increasing "uneasiness" (line 79) on the part of his mother. This evidence can be used to justify C, and can be used to eliminate answers that assume a more thoroughly positive relationship between Pavel and his mother (such as A and even D). B is problematic because, although the mother may find Pavel's activities unusual and unsettling, she does not make any effort to stop or "suppress" what he is doing.

2) CORRECT ANSWER: A
The relevant paragraph explains that Pavel followed the expected lifestyle of a "young lad from a factory town" (lines 1-2) but that he is not genuinely suited to the activities, since he emerges with physical pains and is "pale and dull" (line 8) in demeanor. This evidence supports A and can be used to eliminate B and D, which wrongly assume that Pavel's REACTION to his lifestyle is primarily positive. C misstates Pavel's problem; he is accepted by his peers, but does not HIMSELF accept the lifestyle he has chosen as desirable.

3) CORRECT ANSWER: D
Pavel describes the party as "dreary" (line 12) and would naturally use the image of a "machine" to make a similar complaint: he finds the party and the people in it dull or uninteresting, so that D is the best answer. A describes Pavel HIMSELF (since he is depressed by what he has seen), B is a much harsher criticism (unthinking or immoral) than the people at the party would warrant in context, and C can be taken as a term of praise and should be readily eliminated on this account.

4) CORRECT ANSWER: B
The relevant line reference explains how Pavel, after his disappointment with the typical diversions of young people his age, "gradually began to avoid the beaten path trodden by all" (lines 18-19); his demeanor changes and his friends cease to visit. This information supports B. A and D indicate some of Pavel's features (his diligence and his alienation from his peers) but avoid the PRIMARY topic of the change in Pavel. C wrongly references an issue (Pavel's dissatisfaction) that is primarily explained in the earlier paragraphs (lines 1-13).

5) CORRECT ANSWER: D

In lines 30-32, the narrator explains that Pavel's mother was initially "glad" that her son was becoming different but that she felt "anxiety and apprehension" as well: she has divided feelings or is "ambivalent". D is the best answer. A only captures her negative sentiments, B only captures her positive sentiments, and C assumes a much higher level of expression or emotion than the reserved mother manifests in the course of this passage.

6) CORRECT ANSWER: C

See above for the explanation of the correct answer. A indicates that the mother watches her son closely (but does not convey her emotions), B indicates the son's anger and estrangement from his friends (but not the mother's precise response), and D indicates that the son makes the mother uncomfortable. Keep in mind that D describes a LATER reaction to the son, not the "initial" reaction required by the previous question.

7) CORRECT ANSWER: B

In lines 65-66, the narrator explains that the "softness and simplicity" of Pavel's ways was accompanied by "a disquieting interest" on his mother's part, so that B effectively captures this juxtaposition. A is incorrect because Pavel's intellectual pursuits are not paired against or "juxtaposed" with the hobbies of his peers: the "hobbies" disappear from the narrative as Pavel's intellectual interests emerge. C wrongly indicates that Pavel is torn between professions (NOT that his use of leisure time is changing), while D wrongly identifies his mostly comfortable and peaceful life with his mother as a "harsh" reality.

8) CORRECT ANSWER: C

In lines 47-50, the narrator indicates that Pavel has little direct contact with his mother and that this contact primarily involves "silence" and "insignificant remarks", so that C effectively establishes the relationship as distant. A indicates the mother's awareness that Pavel is taking an unusual path in his ideas (NOT that their own relationship is distant), B indicates that Pavel is secretive about his books (but not about OTHER aspects of his relationship with his mother), and D describes the mother's incomprehension of Pavel's language (but not, in the manner of C, the fact that they do not communicate).

9) CORRECT ANSWER: D

In the relevant line reference, the narrator explains that Pavel has eliminated "coarse, rude, and hard" expressions from his way of speaking and that he observes superior standards of "cleanliness". He is becoming more refined, making D an effective answer and eliminating negative choices such as B and C. A is incorrect because Pavel was never especially dishonest, and because he is still not "comfortable" telling his mother about his new activities.

10) CORRECT ANSWER: A

The word "affect" refers to the "dandy" (line 63) that Pavel no longer puts on: he no longer presents or portrays himself to others as a dandy, so that A is the best answer. In context, B would indicate that Pavel is influencing ANOTHER dandy, C would wrongly indicate that he is showing someone another dandy (not trying to be one himself), and D would wrongly indicate that Pavel's original intent was to mock dandies (not to present himself as one).

Chapter 4.2 | *A Simple Soul*

1) CORRECT ANSWER: B
While the passage begins by describing Loulou's mischievous ways and his tendency to make dramatic scenes (lines 18-24), the author eventually transitions to Loulou's disappearance and to the fact that Felicite "did not easily forget her scare" (line 55) over this event. The final paragraphs describe the negative, lasting effects of Felicite's search for Loulou, so that B is the best answer. Note that Felicite is devoted to Loulou's "education" (line 9) from the start (eliminating A) and that Loulou is a "gift" (line 1) to the Aubain household (not a purchase by the servant Felicite, eliminating C). D wrongly neglects the centrality of the search to the passage, and overstates the importance of the brief description of Loulou at the beginning.

2) CORRECT ANSWER: C
The passage describes how Felicite trained Loulou (lines 9-11) and how she addressed his various problems (lines 25-31). She is thus caring or attentive, so that C is correct and B can be eliminated. Although Felicite cares about Loulou, she DOES make mistakes that get him into trouble (eliminating A, since "prudent" means extremely cautious). And although the author's descriptions of Loulou can seem idiosyncratic or imaginative, Felicite HERSELF is a simple and feeble woman (eliminating D).

3) CORRECT ANSWER: D
Felicite is designated as Madame Aubain's "maid" (line 8); Loulou also gives a sample of Felicite's common duties (answering the door) with his mimicry in lines 77-78. This information supports D. A describes one of Felicite's self-appointed duties, B is out of scope (since Madame Aubain and Felicite are not shown interacting at any length), and C distorts the idea that Loulou appeared among the guests (a habit of his, not a DUTY given to Felicite).

4) CORRECT ANSWER: A
The "dagger thrusts" are understood as the "taunts" directed at Loulou, whom Felicite trains and cares for. She is thus positively inclined towards Loulou and sensitive to insults directed at him, so that A is the best answer and D (with its negative tone towards Loulou) is automatically incorrect. B is problematic because Felicite never actually speaks up in Loulou's defense (even though she favors him), while C wrongly indicates that Felicite is "oblivious" to remarks that in fact hurt her.

5) CORRECT ANSWER: C
The word "society" refers to a condition desired by Loulou, who "made such a racket" (line 23) when certain guests appeared. He would naturally make noise to get their attention. C is the best answer, while A and D are inaccurate because the "racket" would in fact annoy or drive away the people who witness it. B relies on a faulty reading: the reader may be amused by Loulou's antics, but there is no clear indication that Loulou is HIMSELF amused.

6) CORRECT ANSWER: C

In lines 59-62, the author indicates that Felicite's sins could have been acknowledged publicly "without any shame to herself, or ill effects to the community". Sins of this sort would thus be extremely minor, so that Felicite's morals are generally good according to the line reference for C. A simply describes how Madame Aubain gave Loulou to Felicite, B describes Felicite's hunt for Loulou, and D indicates that Felicite is impervious to insults. Only C addresses her overall moral life.

7) CORRECT ANSWER: A

In lines 48-50, the narrator explains that Felicite "came home" without Loulou and found him only when he himself re-appeared. Her efforts were thus unsuccessful: A is the best answer, while B wrongly assumes a negative relationship between Loulou and Felicite and C wrongly criticizes Felicite as a caretaker. (In fact, according to line 33, she had turned away from Loulou "only for a second".) D is out of scope, since it is not known EXACTLY where Loulou had gone; he might have either left the town or stayed entirely within it.

8) CORRECT ANSWER: C

See above for the explanation of the correct answer. A describes events from before the search, B describes incidents from the course of the search itself, and D describes Loulou's re-appearance after the search. While A and D do not address the right series of events (the search itself), B should not be mistaken as evidence for Question 7 B. Loulou did not intersect with Felicite (as B indicates), but it is not clear that he was trying to AVOID her.

9) CORRECT ANSWER: A

According to the line reference, Felicite's world is silent with one exception: Loulou's voice. Loulou thus occupies a unique status in her perceptions, making A an effective answer. B avoids the important issue of Loulou's role in Felicite's life, C wrongly describes Loulou's own motives (when Felicite's consciousness is the focus), and D wrongly indicates that Felicite's isolation is "willful" (instead of being the product of her weakened health).

10) CORRECT ANSWER: C

The final two paragraphs describe the interactions between Loulou and the weakened Felicite: the two of them have fallen into a habit of holding "conversations" (line 79) that involve repetitions of "the three phrases" (line 80) that Loulou knows. Because this routine and its related gestures make Loulou seem "almost a son, a love" (line 83) for Felicite, C is the best answer. A and B focus on Loulou's inner life (NOT on Felicite's reactions to Loulou, the actual topic of the paragraphs), while D wrongly applies a faulty negative tone to Felicite, whose actions may seem strange to the READER but is not directly criticized by the author.

Chapter 4.3 | *The Tale of the Third Century*

1) CORRECT ANSWER: C
In the passage, a young man named Arnobius delivers a scathing and sarcastic account of recent lectures (lines 27-73) and is then warned against such an attitude by Jucundus, who prioritizes the "reverence due to authority" (line 81). This information supports C, while Anorbius's negative attitude towards the lectures can be used to eliminate D. A is incorrect because Jucundus, though uncomfortable with criticisms of authority, does not actually look positively on the intellectual CONTENT of the the lectures or show an appreciative stance. B is incorrect because the passage is dominated by a single account, NOT an exchange of views, and because the views exchanged deal with Arnobius, religion, and the rising generation (NOT philosophy).

2) CORRECT ANSWER: C
The relevant passage indicates that Jucundus "knew his own position perfectly well" (line 13) but did not accept such ideas as "belief" or "knowledge", or endorse abstract philosophical principles generally. This information supports C. A can be eliminated because Jucundus does in fact value the "laws of the empire" (line 18), while Jucundus's disregard of "Letters" (line 8) and low opinion of "philosophers" (line 10) can be used to eliminate positive answers B and D, respectively.

3) CORRECT ANSWER: A
In lines 34-36, Arnobius explains that his "chance of success" would have been hurt if he had not attended the lectures. This information supports A and can be used to eliminate C, which assumes that there was not a practical reason for attending the lectures. B wrongly applies a positive tone to Polemo (whom Arnobius mocks), while D is a trap answer: Arnobius's satire is the RESULT of attending the lecture, but his REASON for the lecture involves practical gain.

4) CORRECT ANSWER: B
See above for the explanation of the correct answer. A and C record the praise that other people (NOT Arnobius) have lavished on Polemo, and D records how Polemo's audience reacts to Polemo himself. Because these answers record reactions to Polemo but do NOT consider the motives of Arnobius, they should be systematically eliminated.

5) CORRECT ANSWER: D
The narrator indicates that Arnobius is "exasperated" (line 26) or moved to contempt and irritation by the praise lavished on Polemo; thus, any praise from Arnobius himself (such as the vocabulary designated by the question) should be understood as sarcastic, since Arnobius does not in fact respect Polemo. D is thus the best answer, while B and C both apply positives to Polemo (whom Arnobius despises). A is a trap answer: though he takes a negative stance, Arnobius fully accepts or "believes" what he has seen and simply finds it contemptible and ridiculous.

6) CORRECT ANSWER: A

The question regarding the chicken and the egg inspires useless deliberation until it is answered by Polemo (lines 66-69), whose answer is indirect and unclear yet terminates the debate. This sense that the inquiry leads nowhere meaningful justifies A and can be used to eliminate the positive answer D. B is problematic because the gullibility of the students would, at best, be indicated by OTHER aspects of the passage (such as their reaction to the question) while Polemo's answer mostly serves to characterize Polemo and his inquiry. C is problematic because Polemo's answer indicates the absurdity of Polemo's own philosophy only, not the absurdity of philosophy GENERALLY.

7) CORRECT ANSWER: A

The narrator explains that Jucundus is offended by Arnobius's description because Jucundus himself is uncomfortable with those who "satirized anything whatever that was established" (line 78). This information supports A, while Arnobius's contempt for Polemo can be used to eliminate B (wrongly positive). Arnobius's contempt for philosophy itself (line 87) can be used to eliminate C, while the fact that the story ends with a conclusive scene (Polemo being paraded out of the lecture hall, lines 71-73) can be used to eliminate D.

8) CORRECT ANSWER: B

In lines 82-85, Jucundus warns Arnobius not to "go after novelties," thus indicating a traditional mindset on his own part; his references to traditional authorities such as the gods and the emperor bolster this characterization. This information supports B. A records Jucundus's distaste for letters or learning, C indicates Jucundus's shock at Arnobius's distaste for tradition (but NOT Jucundus's own ideas about "innovation"), and D records Jucundus's dire prediction about the younger generation (but does not DIRECTLY link such negativity to his stances on tradition and innovation).

9) CORRECT ANSWER: C

Arnobius has already explained that he has no religious or ideological allegiances (lines 86-88); in lines 91-97, Arnobius further explains that he has "no ancestors" and is disoriented by religion. These lines thus provide reasons for his absence of belief and loyalty, thus justifying C. A and D refer to SUPPORTING information in the paragraph, not to the MAIN purpose of substantiating Arnobius's argument about himself. B is too negative (since Arnobius and Jucundus are ideologically different but still well-inclined towards one another) and wrongly indicates that Jucundus might be offended by Arnobius's ethnicity (not by the REAL cause of ideological difference, Arnobius's beliefs).

10) CORRECT ANSWER: D

The word "rising" refers to the "generation" (line 98) of men represented by Arnobius; these men are younger than Jucundus and would thus be a "new" generation from his perspective. D is the best answer. A applies a faulty positive (when in fact Jucundus is critical of the generation), while B and C both refer to literal or physical forms of "rising", not to a difference in age.

Chapter 4.4 | *Mliss*

1) CORRECT ANSWER: C
The first paragraph explains that the schoolmaster is "alone one night in his schoolhouse" (line 2) and that his visitor, Mliss, is "Smith's motherless child" (line 13). Information of this sort sets the context for the interactions that follow, so that C is the best answer. According to line 24, the master has clearly met Mliss before (eliminating A). The master is not described negatively (eliminating B) and is in fact described mostly so that the reader can understand how and why he reacts to Mliss on one specific night (not in terms of his OVERALL nightly habits, eliminating D).

2) CORRECT ANSWER: D
The townsfolk have "philosophically accepted" Mliss by allowing her to ramble about as she pleases, keeping her within their society despite her aggressive personality (as indicated by the examples that follow the line reference). This information supports D. Other answers approximate the content of the passage but do not fit the EXACT line reference: the townspeople have "philosophically accepted" Mliss's "ungovernable disposition" (line 18) and similar rebellious traits, not her influence on other children (eliminating B) or upbringing (eliminating C). Keep in mind also that Mliss's temperament, though strong and unpleasant, is not portrayed as "unchanging," so that A employs faulty reasoning.

3) CORRECT ANSWER: A
The word "keener" refers to the "invective" (line 22) or insulting language that Mliss employs in her conflicts with the schoolboys; she is thus stronger or "fiercer" in her language in an attempt to appear superior. A is the best choice, while B and D are positives (and are inappropriate to heated conflict) and C, "astute", indicates thoughtful or intelligent observation, NOT sheer aggression.

4) CORRECT ANSWER: B
In the lines immediately preceding the line reference, the narrator has departed from the scene in the schoolhouse and described flashback scenes from Mliss's life in the town; the line references itself returns to Mliss "as she stood before the master". B is thus the best answer, while it is revealed in line 15 that "Everybody" knew of Mliss's history (eliminating A). Mliss does not speak (eliminating C), and if anything her ragged state does NOT foreshadow her later desire to improve her situation (eliminating D).

5) CORRECT ANSWER: B
Soon after her appearance, Mliss speaks "rapidly and boldly" (line 47) and declares that she wants to be taught; later, she begins "crying and sobbing as if her heart would break" (lines 79-80). This shift is a transition from confidence (or bravado) to vulnerability, so that B is the best answer. Although she abandons her earlier assertiveness, Mliss is not humbled or ashamed of her conduct (eliminating B); nor does she indicate any conviction that the master will refuse to help her (making C and D much too negative in the emotions that they cite).

6) CORRECT ANSWER: D

In lines 49-50, Mliss reveals that she has visited the schoolhouse at night because she "wouldn't come here when them gals was here". She thus wants to avoid the female students, so that D is an effective answer. Mliss reveals in line 65 that she wants to come to school (not to be taught alone, eliminating A), does not appear to have extensive knowledge of the master's habits (though he is well aware of hers, eliminating B), and has been introduced to the "Sunday school" (line 33) but is not clearly there on the day of the narrative (eliminating C).

7) CORRECT ANSWER: A

In lines 88-89, the narrator paraphrases Mliss's thoughts about her father. It is indicated that he has been irresponsible and that he is linked, in Mliss's mind, to the hatred that the other girls have for her. A ("resentment") is thus the best answer, while C (neutral) and D (positive) introduce inappropriate tones. B is a trap answer: Mliss exhibits hostility or hatred towards the girls, while her stance towards her father is that he has wronged and neglected her.

8) CORRECT ANSWER: D

See above for the explanation of the correct answer. A indicates that Mliss and her father are both well known for different negative traits, B indicates that there is a problem with Mliss's father (but not that Mliss is strongly affected by this problem), and C records a strong negative reaction from Mliss (but does not directly relate to her father). Make sure not to wrongly take B as evidence for Question 7 A or Question 7 B.

9) CORRECT ANSWER: C

The schoolmaster responds to Mliss's request (itself in line 51) with the "natural, though illogical" (line 56) sentiment of "respect" (line 58) in the presence of another original and distinctive individual. This evidence supports C, while A and D describe the kind of "pity" (line 55) that is a possible and expected reaction but is NOT the master's. B is wrongly negative towards Mliss; make sure not to misinterpret the master's inquiries about Mliss as "doubts" that Mliss is sincere.

10) CORRECT ANSWER: D

In lines 90-92, the schoolmaster sees Mliss off by "bidding her come early in the morning". He thus expects her to attend the school, so that D is an effective choice. A indicates that Mliss is surprised by the schoolmaster's good nature (but does NOT definitively indicate that he wants her in the school), B records one of Mliss's dramatic reactions, and C transitions into an inquiry about Mliss's father.

Chapter 4.5 | *A Mere Formality*

1) CORRECT ANSWER: D
In the passage, the conversation that takes place between Joan and Florence is accompanied by moments of "long silence" (line 66-67) and by doubts, on Joan's part, about her father's regard for her (lines 86-87). This evidence supports D. Joan and Florence do not have a strong personal relationship (even though Florence knew Joan's father, eliminating A), while Joan is often critical of her relationship with her father (not yearning or "wistful", eliminating B). The distance between the two women and the evident tension between them make C (mutual "reminiscence" or remembrance of a more placid kind) a problematic answer.

2) CORRECT ANSWER: A
The first paragraph describes gestures ("gripping the wheel," inhaling "deeply") that indicate tension; Joan is preparing herself for what proves to be the psychologically taxing task of visiting her deceased father's home. This information supports A. Joan's real reluctance is to revisit the house (NOT to revisit the memories that quickly emerge in the next paragraph, eliminating B). She is not visiting her father (since he is dead, eliminating C), and is expected by Florence (who opens the door "On cue" in line 21, thus indicating that Joan's trip is not a secret and eliminating D).

3) CORRECT ANSWER: B
In the relevant paragraph, the author contrasts the joyful state of the house "Once upon a time" with the present condition: "Now there was nothing but silence". This information supports B. The house is the sole focus (not the entire "neighborhood," eliminating A), Florence has not yet appeared in any capacity (eliminating C), and Joan's father is ONLY depicted as warm and welcoming (eliminating D).

4) CORRECT ANSWER: D
In lines 31-33, Florence indicates that the death of Joan's father must "feel a bit difficult"; it is indicated that Joan is still trying to process the death and that her father's passing would thus be a recent occurrence. D is the best answer, while A simply describes the state of the house without indicating how recent the changes were, B describes Florence's appearance (but not the reason for her nervousness), and C describes Florence's cleaning (but does not provide a time signature for the father's death).

5) CORRECT ANSWER: A
The word "side" refers to a somewhat opinionated aspect of the father's personality; "characteristic", A, is an appropriate choice. B ("opinion") and C ("argument") refer to statements or viewpoints that could be attributed to the father, not to the PERSONALITY that would motive his actions. D, "profile", would refer to the father's ENTIRE personality, not to the one element or "side" that is here under consideration.

6) CORRECT ANSWER: C
In lines 54-57, Joan voices the idea that, unlike her father, she is not interested in making efforts to reverse the past: he should have just moved on and disregarded the broken clock, instead of attempting to fix it. This information supports C. Joan and her father never repaired their relationship (indicating that both were unforgiving and eliminating A), while Joan spends important portions of the passage mentally re-creating the past (eliminating B) and does in fact regret the course that her relationship with her father took (eliminating D).

7) CORRECT ANSWER: B

See above for the explanation of the correct answer. A describes Joan's father (but does not indicate a comparison to Joan in the manner of B), C explains the special status of the clock, and D indicates that Joan's father did not communicate his pride to Joan. Make sure not to take D as evidence for Question 6 A; Joan seems to want forgiveness, but the line reference does not explicitly indicate that her father did not want forgiveness himself.

8) CORRECT ANSWER: C

Earlier in the passage, Joan regards Florence "coolly" (line 34); the repeated phrase shows that the contact between the two women remains tense, as it would given Florence's role in the break between Joan and her father. This information supports C, while Florence in fact has ease expressing her emotions elsewhere in the passage (eliminating A) and does not herself express the "emptiness" that characterizes Joan's thoughts (eliminating B). It is also not clear that Florence feels animosity or extreme dislike regarding Joan (although Joan HERSELF has reacted harshly to the relationship between Florence and the father), so that D is an inaccurate choice.

9) CORRECT ANSWER: A

Towards the end of the passage, Joan learns that her father would go to see her films; she first "raised her eyebrows" (lines 83-84, indicating surprise), and then "A tear rolled down her cheek" (lines 86-87, indicating sadness). This information supports A. Both B and C indicate that Joan would find the news strange or unpleasant (when in fact she accepts Florence's testimony quickly and feels herself moved by it), while D neglects her first reaction (surprise) and focuses entirely on her sad and negative sentiments.

10) CORRECT ANSWER: A

Joan's final remarks indicate that she is "all done" with visiting the house and perhaps with revisiting her memories; the reference to "Mr. Director" shows that she is ready to return to her life as a film actress. This information supports A. The possible positive tones in the relevant lines concern Joan's ability to move on, not her father (who is not mentioned directly, eliminating B) or the visit (which she seems ready to put behind her, eliminating C). The finality of Joan's remarks also indicates that she has recovered COMPLETELY from her father's death, not that the process has simply "started" (eliminating D).

CHAPTER FIVE

Questions 1-10 are based on the following passage.
Chapter 5.1
Adapted from Stephen Crane, *The Pace of Youth* (1898).

Stimson stood in a corner and glowered. He was a fierce man and had indomitable whiskers, albeit he was very small.

Line
5 "That young tarrier," he whispered to himself. "He wants to quit makin' eyes at Lizzie. This is too much of a good thing. First thing you know, he'll get fired."

His brow creased in a frown, he strode over to the huge open doors and looked at a sign. "Stimson's Mammoth Merry-Go-Round," it read, and the glory of
10 it was great. Stimson stood and contemplated the sign. It was an enormous affair; the letters were as large as men. The glow of it, the grandeur of it was very apparent to Stimson. At the end of his contemplation, he shook his head thoughtfully, determinedly. "No,
15 no," he muttered. "This is too much of a good thing. First thing you know, he'll get fired."

A soft booming sound of surf, mingled with the cries of bathers, came from the beach. There was a vista of sand and sky and sea that drew to a mystic
20 point far away in the northward. In the mighty angle, a girl in a red dress was crawling slowly like some kind of a spider on the fabric of nature. A few flags hung lazily above where the bathhouses were marshalled in compact squares. Upon the edge of the sea stood a ship
25 with its shadowy sails painted dimly upon the sky, and high overhead in the still, sun-shot air a great hawk swung and drifted slowly.

Within the Merry-Go-Round there was a whirling circle of ornamental lions, giraffes, camels, ponies,
30 goats, glittering with varnish and metal that caught swift reflections from windows high above them. . .
Over in a corner, a man in a white apron and behind a counter roared above the tumult: "Popcorn! Popcorn!"

A young man stood upon a small, raised platform,
35 erected in a manner of a pulpit, and just without the line of the circling figures. It was his duty to manipulate the wooden arm and affix the rings, special features of the Merry-Go-Round. When all were gone into the hands of the triumphant children, he held forth
40 a basket, into which they returned all save the coveted brass one, which meant another ride free and made the holder very illustrious. The young man stood all day upon his narrow platform, affixing rings or holding forth the basket. He was a sort of general squire in
45 these lists of childhood. He was very busy.

And yet Stimson, the astute, had noticed that the young man frequently found time to twist about on his platform and smile at a girl who shyly sold tickets behind a silvered netting. This, indeed, was the
50 great reason of Stimson's glowering. The young man upon the raised platform had no manner of license to smile at the girl behind the silvered netting. It was a most gigantic insolence. Stimson was amazed at it. "By Jiminy," he said to himself again, "that fellow is
55 smiling at my daughter." Even in this tone of great wrath it could be discerned that Stimson was filled with wonder that any youth should dare smile at the daughter in the presence of the august father.

Often the dark-eyed girl peered between the
60 shining wires, and, upon being detected by the young man, she usually turned her head quickly to prove to him that she was not interested. At other times, however, her eyes seemed filled with a tender fear lest he should fall from that exceedingly dangerous
65 platform. As for the young man, it was plain that these glances filled him with valor, and he stood carelessly upon his perch, as if he deemed it of no consequence that he might fall from it. In all the complexities of his daily life and duties he found opportunity to gaze
70 ardently at the vision behind the netting.

This silent courtship was conducted over the heads of the crowd who thronged about the bright machine. The swift eloquent glances of the young man went noiselessly and unseen with their message. There had
75 finally become established between the two in this manner a subtle understanding and companionship. They communicated accurately all that they felt. The boy told his love, his reverence, his hope in the changes of the future. The girl told him that she loved
80 him, and she did not love him, that she did not know if she loved him. Sometimes a little sign, saying "cashier" in gold letters, and hanging upon the silvered netting, got directly in range and interfered with the tender message. . .

85 "This has got to stop," Stimson had said to himself, as he stood and watched them. They had grown careless of the light world that clattered about them; they were become so engrossed in their personal drama that the language of their eyes was almost as
90 obvious as gestures.

CONTINUE

1

Which choice best describes what happens in the passage?

A) Two characters find a way to express their mutual affection without being detected.

B) A father is disturbed when an employee begins a courtship with his daughter.

C) A young man expresses his affection for, and is rebuffed by, a young girl.

D) A father contemplates firing a young man for advancing on his daughter.

2

The description of the sign in lines 11-13 ("It was... Stimson") mainly emphasizes that Stimson feels which of the following about his Merry-Go-Round?

A) Pride.

B) Optimism.

C) Nostalgia.

D) Obsession.

3

The fourth paragraph (lines 17-27) is notable for its use of

A) sensory description.

B) personal anecdote.

C) extended analogy.

D) memorable language.

4

The passage indicates that Stimson reacts in which of the following ways when he notices the young man smiling at his daughter?

A) He is disapproving yet amused by the triviality of what he shrugs off as a fling.

B) He is initially unconcerned yet becomes worried when his daughter reciprocates.

C) He is pleased yet feels that the young man is overeager.

D) He is outraged yet astonished at the young man's gall.

5

Which choice provides the best evidence for the answer to the previous question?

A) Lines 4-6 ("That young...thing")

B) Lines 50-52 ("The young...netting")

C) Lines 55-58 ("Even in...father")

D) Lines 59-62 ("Often the...interested")

6

The narrator indicates that the young man "was very busy" (line 45) in order to point out

A) the complexity of managing a merry-go-round.

B) the hectic nature of his daily schedule.

C) the inappropriateness of his diverted attentions.

D) the admirable work ethic he possessed.

7

As used in line 68, "complexities" most nearly means

A) complications.

B) intricacies.

C) responsibilities.

D) struggles.

8

In context of the passage as a whole, lines 71-84 ("This silent...message") primarily serve to

A) reveal that the young man's feelings for Lizzie are unrequited.

B) convey Lizzie's contradictory feelings towards the young man.

C) highlight the extent of the connection between two characters.

D) foreshadow Stimson's intervention in a budding relationship.

CONTINUE

9

According to the passage, one consequence of the youngsters' communications is that

A) they are unable to perform their duties properly.

B) they have made their desires apparent to others.

C) they have become reckless in their actions.

D) they prompt Stimson to confront them.

10

Which choice provides the best evidence for the answer to the previous question?

A) Lines 77-79 ("They communicated...future")

B) Lines 85-86 ("This has...them")

C) Lines 86-88 ("They had...them")

D) Lines 88-90 ("they were...gestures")

CONTINUE

Questions 1-10 are based on the following passage.

Chapter 5.2

Adapted from Alexandre Dumas, *The Count of Monte Cristo* (1845). The setting of this passage is a forbidding French prison, the Château d'If.

A visit was made by the inspector-general of prisons. Dantès in his cell heard the noise of preparation,—sounds that at the depth where he lay
Line would have been inaudible to any but the ear of a
5 prisoner, who could hear the splash of the drop of water that every hour fell from the roof of his dungeon. He guessed something uncommon was passing among the living; but he had so long ceased to have any intercourse with the world, that he looked upon himself
10 as dead.

The inspector visited, one after another, the cells and dungeons of several of the prisoners, whose good behavior or stupidity recommended them to the clemency of the government. He inquired how they
15 were fed, and if they had any request to make. The universal response was, that the fare was detestable, and that they wanted to be set free.

The inspector asked if they had anything else to ask for. They shook their heads. What could they desire
20 beyond their liberty? The inspector turned smilingly to the governor.

"I do not know what reason government can assign for these useless visits; when you see one prisoner, you see all,—always the same thing,—ill fed
25 and innocent. Are there any others?"

"Yes; the dangerous and mad prisoners are in the dungeons."

"Let us visit them," said the inspector with an air of fatigue. "We must play the farce to the end. Let us
30 see the dungeons."

. . . At the sound of the key turning in the lock, and the creaking of the hinges, Dantès, who was crouched in a corner of the dungeon, whence he could see the ray of light that came through a narrow iron grating
35 above, raised his head. Seeing a stranger, escorted by two turnkeys holding torches and accompanied by two soldiers, and to whom the governor spoke bareheaded, Dantès, who guessed the truth, and that the moment to address himself to the superior authorities was come,
40 sprang forward with clasped hands.

The soldiers interposed their bayonets, for they thought that he was about to attack the inspector, and the latter recoiled two or three steps. Dantès saw that he was looked upon as dangerous. Then, infusing all
45 the humility he possessed into his eyes and voice, he

addressed the inspector, and sought to inspire him with pity.

The inspector listened attentively; then, turning to the governor, observed, "He will become religious—
50 he is already more gentle; he is afraid, and retreated before the bayonets—madmen are not afraid of anything; I made some curious observations on this at Charenton." Then, turning to the prisoner, "What is it you want?" said he.
55 "I want to know what crime I have committed—to be tried; and if I am guilty, to be shot; if innocent, to be set at liberty."

"Are you well fed?" said the inspector.

"I believe so; I don't know; it's of no consequence.
60 What matters really, not only to me, but to officers of justice and the king, is that an innocent man should languish in prison, the victim of an infamous denunciation, to die here cursing his executioners."

"You are very humble today," remarked the
65 governor; "you are not so always; the other day, for instance, when you tried to kill the turnkey."

"It is true, sir, and I beg his pardon, for he has always been very good to me, but I was mad."

"And you are not so any longer?"
70 "No; captivity has subdued me—I have been here so long."

"So long?—when were you arrested, then?" asked the inspector.

"The 28th of February, 1815, at half-past two in
75 the afternoon."

"Today is the 30th of July, 1816,—why, it is but seventeen months."

"Only seventeen months," replied Dantès. "Oh, you do not know what is seventeen months
80 in prison!—seventeen ages rather, especially to a man who, like me, had arrived at the summit of his ambition—to a man, who, like me, was on the point of marrying a woman he adored, who saw an honorable career opened before him, and who loses all in an
85 instant—who sees his prospects destroyed, and is ignorant of the fate of his affianced wife, and whether his aged father be still living! Seventeen months' captivity to a sailor accustomed to the boundless ocean, is a worse punishment than human crime ever
90 merited. Have pity on me, then, and ask for me, not intelligence, but a trial; not pardon, but a verdict—a trial, sir, I ask only for a trial; that, surely, cannot be denied to one who is accused!"

"We shall see," said the inspector; then, turning to
95 the governor, "On my word, the poor devil touches me. You must show me the proofs against him."

"Certainly; but you will find terrible charges."

"Monsieur," continued Dantès, "I know it is not in your power to release me; but you can plead for me—
100 you can have me tried—and that is all I ask. Let me know my crime, and the reason why I was condemned. Uncertainty is worse than all."

1

The primary function of the first paragraph is to

A) characterize Dantès as uncomfortable with his surroundings.

B) foreshadow an event that occurs later in the passage.

C) provide context for Dantès's encounter with the inspector.

D) contrast the life of a prisoner to the life of a citizen.

2

As used in line 9, "intercourse with" most nearly means

A) awareness of.

B) correspondence with.

C) influence on.

D) interaction with.

3

The inspector uses the phrase "ill fed and innocent" (lines 24-25) to suggest that he

A) no longer feels pity for the prisoners.

B) believes in the innocence of the prisoners.

C) anticipates no variation in the prisoners' responses.

D) doubts the validity of the prisoners' responses.

4

According to the passage, the inspector initially reacts to Dantès with

A) intrigue.

B) sympathy.

C) disgust.

D) alarm.

5

According to the passage, which of the following is Dantès's chief complaint to the inspector?

A) He has been wrongfully imprisoned.

B) His sentence is too severe for his crime.

C) He has been denied the reasons for his imprisonment.

D) His treatment in the prison is inhumane.

6

Which choice best supports the claim that Dantès believes in the fairness of justice?

A) Lines 11-14 ("The inspector...government")

B) Lines 44-47 ("Then, infusing...pity")

C) Lines 60-62 ("What matters...prison")

D) Lines 91-93 ("a trial...accused")

7

The passage indicates that over the course of his seventeen months in prison, Dantès has changed in which of the following ways?

A) He has become less violent in nature.

B) He has become resigned to his circumstances.

C) He has grown to see himself as a social outcast.

D) He has learned to appreciate his freedom while it lasted.

8

Which choice provides the best evidence for the answer to the previous question?

A) Lines 8-10 ("he had...dead")

B) Lines 51-53 ("madmen...Charenton")

C) Lines 70-71 ("No: captivity...long")

D) Lines 87-90 ("Seventeen months'...merited")

CONTINUE

9

It can be reasonably inferred from the passage that Dantès pleads to the inspector mainly because he believes that the inspector

A) will be able to help set him free.

B) has the power to grant him a trial.

C) is aware of the charges against him.

D) possesses the same values as he does.

10

In the context of the conversation between Dantès and the inspector, Dantès's comments in lines 78-90 ("Only seventeen...merited") mainly serve to

A) present the reasons for his desire to leave the prison.

B) depict himself as a righteous and honorable citizen.

C) emphasize the harshness of his conditions by contrasting them with his former life.

D) highlight the injustice of his arrest by stating that he has done nothing unlawful.

CONTINUE

Questions 1-10 are based on the following passage.
Chapter 5.3
Adapted from Charlotte Perkins Gilman, *What Diantha Did* (1912).

There was no dust nor smell of dust in Diantha Bell's home; no grease spots, no litter anywhere. In the dead quiet of the afternoon Diantha and her mother
Line sat there sewing. The sun poured down through the
5 dangling eucalyptus leaves. The dry air, rich with flower odors, flowed softly in, pushing the white sash curtains a steady inch or two. Ee-errr!—Ee-errr!—came the faint whine of the windmill.

To the older woman rocking in her small splint
10 chair by the rose-draped window, her thoughts dwelling on long dark green grass, the shade of elms, and cows knee-deep in river-shallows; this was California—hot, arid, tedious in endless sunlight—a place of exile.

To the younger, the long seam of the turned sheet
15 pinned tightly to her knee, her needle flying firmly and steadily, and her thoughts full of pouring moonlight through acacia boughs, it was California—rich, warm, full of sweet bloom and fruit, of boundless vitality, promise, and power—home!

20 Mrs. Bell drew a long weary sigh, and laid down her work for a moment.

"Why don't you stop it Mother dear? There's surely no hurry about these things."

"No—not particularly," her mother answered, "but
25 there's plenty else to do." And she went on with the long neat hemming. Diantha did the "over and over seam" up the middle.

"What do you do it for anyway, Mother—I always hated this job—and you don't seem to like it."

30 "They wear almost twice as long, child, you know. The middle gets worn and the edges don't. Now they're reversed. As to liking it—" She gave a little smile, a smile that was too tired to be sarcastic, but which certainly did not indicate pleasure.

35 "What kind of work do you like best—really?" her daughter inquired suddenly, after a silent moment or two.

"Why—I don't know," said her mother. "I never thought of it. I never tried any but teaching. I didn't
40 like that. Neither did your Aunt Esther, but she's still teaching."

"Didn't you like any of it?" pursued Diantha.

"I liked arithmetic best. I always loved arithmetic, when I went to school—used to stand highest in that."

45 "And what part of housework do you like best?" the girl persisted.

Mrs. Bell smiled again, wanly. "Seems to me sometimes as if I couldn't tell sometimes what part I like least!" she answered. Then with sudden heat—"O my
50 Child! Don't you marry till your husband can afford at least one girl for you!"

Diantha put her small, strong hands behind her head and leaned back in her chair. "I'll have to wait some time for that I fancy," she said. "But, Mother,
55 there is one part you like—keeping accounts! I never saw anything like the way you manage the money, and I believe you've got every bill since you were married."

"Yes—I do love accounts," Mrs. Bell admitted. "And I can keep run of things. I've often thought your
60 Father'd have done better if he'd let me run that end of his business."

Diantha gave a fierce little laugh. She admired her father in some ways, enjoyed him in some ways, loved him as a child does if not ill-treated; but she loved her
65 mother with a sort of passionate pity mixed with pride; feeling always nobler power in her than had ever had a fair chance to grow. It seemed to her an interminable dull tragedy; this graceful, eager, black-eyed woman, spending what to the girl was literally a lifetime, in the
70 conscientious performance of duties she did not love.

She knew her mother's idea of duty, knew the clear head, the steady will, the active intelligence holding her relentlessly to the task; the chafe and fret of seeing her husband constantly attempting against her judgment,
75 and failing for lack of the help he scorned. Young as she was, she realized that the nervous breakdown of these later years was wholly due to that common misery of "the square man in the round hole."

She folded her finished sheet in accurate lines and
80 laid it away—taking her mother's also. "Now you sit still for once, Mother dear, read or lie down. Don't you stir till supper's ready."

CONTINUE

1

Which choice best describes a major theme of the passage?

A) The desolation of fulfilled dreams

B) The satisfaction from housework

C) The power of a sense of duty

D) The neglect of paternal love

2

Over the course of the first three paragraphs, the focus of the narrative shifts from

A) an objective depiction of a scene to its contrasting effects on the main characters.

B) a description of a common task performed by two characters to a contrast in their approaches.

C) a serene and idyllic illustration of a home to the anxiety felt by its inhabitants.

D) an introduction of the work of two characters to an overview of the characters' personalities.

3

It can reasonably be inferred from the second paragraph that Mrs. Bell dislikes California because

A) she associates the state with her current oppressive lifestyle.

B) she had recently moved to the state and feels like an outsider.

C) she finds the weather to be tiring and unconducive to hard work.

D) she still feels a nostalgic connection to a different region.

4

Which choice provides the best evidence for the claim that Mrs. Bell considered steadfastness to be a core attribute of duty?

A) Lines 14-16 ("the long...steadily")

B) Lines 30-32 ("They wear...reversed")

C) Lines 55-57 ("I never...married")

D) Lines 71-73 ("She knew...task")

5

The description of Mrs. Bell's smile in lines 32-34 ("As to...pleasure") is used to portray her as

A) candid about her feelings.

B) resigned to her duties.

C) weary from the conversation.

D) optimistic despite her circumstances.

6

In context of the passage as a whole, lines 47-51 ("Mrs. Bell....you") primarily serve to

A) indicate for the first time that Mrs. Bell does not enjoy her responsibilities at home.

B) reveal that Diantha often wished for a maid to help her with her housework.

C) illustrate the true intensity of Mrs. Bell's emotions towards being a housewife.

D) describe the moment Diantha realizes Mrs. Bell's true feelings of Mr. Bell.

7

According to the narrator, one consequence of Mrs. Bell's designated role in the household is that

A) she felt obligated to give up her dream of running a business.

B) she was unable to continue with her career as a schoolteacher.

C) her husband might be worse off financially without her guidance.

D) her daughter was driven to pursue a different path than she did.

CONTINUE

8

Which choice provides the best evidence for the answer to the previous question?

A) Lines 39-41 ("I never...teaching")

B) Lines 59-61 ("I've often...business")

C) Lines 68-70 ("this graceful...love")

D) Lines 75-77 ("Young as...misery")

9

As used in line 66, "nobler power" most nearly means

A) higher aspirations.

B) greater potential.

C) more persistence.

D) more integrity.

10

The narrator uses the phrase "square man in the round hole" (line 78) to suggest that Diantha's father was

A) too closed-minded to be positively influenced by his wife.

B) too individualistic to be fully accepted by society.

C) too argumentative to manage his business efficiently.

D) too stubborn to form connections with his family.

CONTINUE

Questions 1-10 are based on the following passage.

Chapter 5.4

Adapted from Nikolai Gogol, *The Mysterious Portrait* (1835).

The young painter, Tchartkoff, paused involuntarily as he passed the shop. His old cloak and plain attire showed him to be a man who was devoted
Line to his art with self-denying zeal, and who had no time
5 to trouble himself about his clothes. He halted in front of the little shop, and at first enjoyed an inward laugh over the monstrosities in the shape of pictures.

At length he sank unconsciously into a reverie, and began to ponder as to what sort of people wanted
10 these productions? It did not seem remarkable to him that the Russian populace should gaze with rapture upon "Eruslanoff Lazarevitch," on "The Glutton" and "The Carouser," on "Thoma and Erema." The delineations of these subjects were easily intelligible to
15 the masses. But where were there purchases for those streaky, dirty oil-paintings? Who needed those Flemish boors, those red and blue landscapes, which put forth some claims to a higher stage of art, but which really expressed the depths of its degradation? . . .
20 Meanwhile the proprietor of the shop, a little grey man, in a frieze cloak, with a beard which had not been shaved since Sunday, had been urging him to buy for some time, naming prices, without even knowing what pleased him or what he wanted. "Here, I'll take a
25 silver piece for these peasants and this little landscape. What painting! It fairly dazzles one; only just received from the factory; the varnish isn't dry yet. Or here is a winter scene—take the winter scene; fifteen rubles; the frame alone is worth it. What a winter scene!" Here
30 the merchant gave a slight fillip to the canvas, as if to demonstrate all the merits of the winter scene. "Pray have them put up and sent to your house. Where do you live? Here, boy, give me some string!"

"Hold, not so fast!" said the painter, coming
35 to himself, and perceiving that the brisk dealer was beginning in earnest to pack some pictures up. He was rather ashamed not to take anything after standing so long in front of the shop; so saying, "Here, stop! I will see if there is anything I want here!" he stooped
40 and began to pick up from the floor, where they were thrown in a heap, some worn, dusty old paintings. There were old family portraits, whose descendants, probably could not be found on earth; with torn canvas and frames minus their gilding; in short, trash. But the
45 painter began his search, thinking to himself, "Perhaps I may come across something." He had heard stories

about pictures of the great masters having been found among the rubbish in cheap print-sellers' shops.

The dealer, perceiving what he was about, ceased
50 his importunities, and took up his post again at the door, hailing the passers-by with, "Hither, friends, here are pictures; step in, step in; just received from the makers!" He shouted his fill, and generally in vain, had a long talk with a rag-merchant, standing opposite,
55 at the door of his shop; and finally, recollecting that he had a customer in his shop, turned his back on the public and went inside. "Well, friend, have you chosen anything?" said he. But the painter had already been standing motionless for some time before a portrait in
60 a large and originally magnificent frame, upon which, however, hardly a trace of gilding now remained.

It represented an old man, with a thin, bronzed face and high cheek-bones; the features seemingly depicted in a moment of convulsive agitation. He wore
65 a flowing Asiatic costume. Dusty and defaced as the portrait was, Tchartkoff saw, when he had succeeded in removing the dirt from the face, traces of the work of a great artist. The portrait appeared to be unfinished, but the power of the handling was striking. The eyes
70 were the most remarkable feature of all: it seemed as though the full power of the artist's brush had been lavished upon them. They fairly gazed out of the portrait, destroying its harmony with their strange liveliness. When he carried the portrait to the door, the
75 eyes gleamed even more penetratingly. They produced nearly the same impression on the public. A woman standing behind him exclaimed, "He is looking, he is looking!" and jumped back. Tchartkoff experienced an unpleasant feeling, inexplicable even to himself, and
80 placed the portrait on the floor.

"Well, will you take the portrait?" said the dealer.

"How much is it?" said the painter.

"Why worry? give me seventy-five kopeks."

"No."

85 "Well, how much will you give?"

"Twenty kopeks," said the painter, preparing to go.

"What a price! Why, you couldn't buy the frame for that! Perhaps you will decide to purchase to-morrow. Sir, sir, turn back! Add ten kopeks. Take
90 it, take it! give me twenty kopeks. To tell the truth, you are my only customer to-day, and that's the only reason."

Thus Tchartkoff quite unexpectedly became the purchaser of the old portrait, and at the same time
95 reflected, "Why have I bought it? What is it to me?" But there was nothing to be done. He pulled a twenty-kopek piece from his pocket, gave it to the merchant, took the portrait under his arm, and carried it home.

CONTINUE

1

Which choice best describes the developmental pattern of the passage?

A) A character unmoved by the paintings on display in an art shop is struck by a portrait.

B) A man disillusioned with the art world comes across an unexpected source of inspiration.

C) A customer negotiates and purchases a painting that had been discarded by an art dealer.

D) An artist's perception of contemporary art changes when an art dealer shows him a moving painting.

2

The main purpose of the second paragraph is to

A) draw a distinction between two types of art.

B) describe the genre of paintings favored by Tchartkoff.

C) list examples of contemporary Russian art.

D) depict Tchartkoff as more informed than the average client of the art shop.

3

Which of the following would Tchartkoff most likely agree is the reason the art dealer does not have any customers?

A) He is overly pushy in selling to potential customers.

B) He demands unreasonably high prices for his art.

C) His art is not sufficiently accessible to artists.

D) His art is mass produced by unknown painters.

4

Which choice provides the best evidence for the answer to the previous question?

A) Lines 13-16 ("The delineations...paintings")

B) Lines 22-24 ("had...wanted")

C) Lines 24-27 ("Here, I'll...yet")

D) Lines 87-88 ("What a...that")

5

In context of the passage, lines 45-48 ("Perhaps I... shops") primarily serves to

A) foreshadow that the painting Tchartkoff eventually finds is one of the great masters'.

B) indicate that Tchartkoff had entered the shop with a specific goal in mind.

C) characterize Tchartkoff as extremely frugal in matters of art.

D) reveal the justification Tchartkoff gives himself for staying in the store.

6

The narrator uses the phrase "perceiving what he was about" (line 49) to indicate that the art dealer leaves the shop because he

A) understands that Tchartkoff is not likely to accept his recommendation.

B) observes that Tchartkoff is only interested in high art.

C) wants to give Tchartkoff time and room to find the piece that he is looking for.

D) knows Tchartkoff is poor and allows him to save face by pretending to browse.

CONTINUE

7

According to the passage, which quality of the portrait distinguished it from the other paintings in the shop?

A) its intriguingly faded frame.

B) the foreign origin of its artist.

C) its distinctively greater value.

D) the skill with which it was done.

8

Which choice provides the best evidence for the answer to the previous question?

A) Lines 58-61 ("But the...remained")

B) Lines 62-65 ("It represented...costume")

C) Lines 65-69 ("Dusty and...striking")

D) Lines 75-78 ("They produced...back")

9

As used in line 70, "feature" most nearly means

A) portrait.

B) aspect.

C) vision.

D) representation.

10

In context of the final paragraph, the questions in line 95 ("Why have...me?") suggest that

A) Tchartkoff still harbored doubts about the dealer's recommendations.

B) Tchartkoff suddenly realized that he had been manipulated by the art dealer.

C) Tchartkoff was searching for a motive behind his decision.

D) Tchartkoff felt regretful about buying a painting.

CONTINUE

Questions 1-10 are based on the following passage.
Chapter 5.5
The following is an excerpt from *A Yankee Cophetua* (2017) by Khalid Khashoggi.

Marcus stood by the window watching the dusk descend. He switched on the desk lamp. Turning back to draw the curtains, his hand caught a photo frame,

Line which fell to the floor. He picked it up and ran his
5 fingers slowly and lovingly across the picture of a woman smiling. "Sorry, my dear. Twenty years later, and I still manage to knock you down."

The door opened. "Is that you, Jolene?" he called.

10 "Nope! Wrong age, wrong gender, and wrong profession. It's your ageing money-minder, not your youthful girlfriend."

Marcus grinned. "Never mind. Come in, Albert. What brings you here? Don't tell me that I am finally
15 bankrupt. Help yourself to a drink."

"Not quite; not yet. Yes, please. Shall I pour you one too?" Marcus shook his head. "My goodness, Marcus! Are you sick? We've been drinking together since our teens. This is no time to stop." Albert glanced
20 at the photo that Marcus was holding. "Ah, I see: old memories of a very rich widower."

Marcus crossed the room to the fireplace. "The nights are drawing in. I will need to light the fire later." He placed the photo on the shelf above the hearth, then
25 turned back to Albert. "I was never worthy of her."

The other laughed. "What sentimental nonsense! You gave her everything: the trips around the world, the private jet, the villa in the south of France, this mansion."

30 "I wasn't always there for her."

"You were creating and building the business to what it is now. Money doesn't grow on trees."

"No, and it doesn't build a relationship."

"No, but it certainly helps. I am sure Jolene would
35 agree with that."

Marcus looked up sharply. "What do you mean by that?"

Albert took a deep breath. "Look, Marcus... the truth is that I didn't pass by here just to have a drink
40 with my oldest friend. It is a more serious matter that brings me. I am not sure how to say this..."

"Go on," instructed Marcus.

"I don't mean to be a sneak, but ... well, we both know what the real world is like." Albert paused long
45 enough to finish his drink. "It's about Jolene. I saw her today. On Madison Avenue."

"Of course you did. She went shopping." Marcus smiled. "She loves shopping on Madison Avenue."

Albert, feeling his courage stirred by the alcohol,
50 said defiantly: "She wasn't in a shop, Marcus! She was having lunch. She was with a young man! They were very lively together...very familiar...well, overly familiar...almost intimate."

Marcus, seemingly unperturbed, said nothing.

55 "You know I know her background. It's always worried me that you picked her up from nowhere. All those years after your wife's death, you never looked at another woman. Then, a year ago, you meet this girl from the Bronx who sells flowers at a corner store and
60 suddenly all is changed for you – and for her. Maybe, having reached this dizzying height, she wants to prepare for the future with someone younger?"

Marcus regarded him solemnly. Then he looked askance. "You know nothing about this guy she was
65 with?"

"Oh, but I do!" Albert seemed embarrassed. "When he left her, I followed him to his office. His name is Peter Nessuno. He is a high-level executive at Mackenzie Bank. That's all I found out." There was a
70 silence. "I am sorry. I thought you should know. We've been best friends since we were kids."

Marcus nodded. "Yes, I see. It's good to know you are still looking out for me." He paused. "I will deal with it from here. I think I will have that drink now."

75 After Albert had left, Marcus lit the fire in the hearth and sat in his armchair, regarding the flames. He heard the car crunch on the gravel outside, followed by the slamming of car doors and then the front door. A cheerful voice rang out "Marcus, darling! I'm home!"

80 "In the library!"

Jolene brought energy and several carrier bags into the room. Her face was flushed and her smile was broad. "Did you miss me? I hope so! What a day! I need a drink....no, don't get up. I'll do it. Do you want
85 another?"

He shook his head. "Come and show me what you bought today."

She carried her drink and the day's treasures across the room and sat herself down on the rug in
90 front of him. "Ooh, a lovely warm fire! My fingers are frozen!" She stretched her hands out and watched the jewels on her fingers flicker in the firelight. Marcus leaned forward and, taking her hand, gently guided her up and onto his lap.

95 With a soft voice he said, "They are beautiful, indeed. Now, Jolene, tell me all about Peter."

She lowered her eyes. Her smile vanished. She contemplated her rings quietly for a minute

CONTINUE ➤

and then, in a low stern voice, "Peter is fine. He sends
100 his love and, as always, he thanks you for all the
support you have given him over the years." Then,
turning her head to face Marcus, she lifted her pitch
and said, "But, darling, you have to understand. He
is not complete. He so much wants to meet you.
105 After all these years of waiting patiently, he feels the
time has come; he needs to know his father. It is so
important—for him—as it is for you. Isn't it time you
acknowledged him as your son? You can't keep him a
secret forever, you know." She looked up at the photo
110 on the shelf. "Surely by now, she could forgive you?"
      He nodded and squeezed her hand gently. "Yes,
you are right: the relationship is all."

1

Which choice best describes a major theme of the
passage?

A) The corrupting influence of material wealth

B) The destructive consequences of infidelity

C) The role of honesty in a successful marriage

D) The complications that arise from family secrets

2

Which choice best describes what happens in the passage?

A) One character argues with another character about a
potentially destructive relationship.

B) One character wrongfully reports the actions of another
character to his employer, who becomes concerned.

C) One character, motivated by resentment, unjustifiably
attempts to raise suspicion of another character.

D) One character, who knows the truth, remains
unperturbed when another character warns him about
an interaction.

3

With which of the following statements about Marcus's
previous relationship would Albert most likely agree?

A) It was secondary to Marcus's business ventures.

B) It lasted mostly because of Marcus's wealthy
lifestyle.

C) It ultimately caused Marcus to make irrational
decisions.

D) It was successful regardless of Marcus's emotional
distance.

4

Which choice provides the best evidence for the answer
to the previous question?

A) Lines 20-21 ("Ah, I...widower")

B) Lines 27-29 ("You gave...mansion")

C) Lines 31-32 ("You were...trees")

D) Lines 56-58 ("All those...woman")

5

In the passage, Albert addresses Marcus with

A) candor but not complete honesty.

B) patience but not unconditional acceptance.

C) respect but not utter deference.

D) partiality but not extreme bias.

6

As used in line 50, "defiantly" most nearly means

A) boldly.

B) contentiously.

C) rebelliously.

D) loudly.

CONTINUE

7

The primary impression created by Jolene's actions and dialogue within the passage is that she is

A) materialistic and pampered.

B) considerate and sincere.

C) diplomatic and mediating.

D) contemplative and serious.

8

Why does Jolene say that Peter is "not complete" (line 104)?

A) She fears that Peter will soon give up all attempts to know the identity of his father.

B) She worries that Peter will never accomplish his goals in life without more assistance from his father.

C) She believes that Peter is unsatisfied with the status of his relationship with his father.

D) She knows that Peter has feelings for her and cannot proceed on them without his father's approval.

9

Which of the following best describes Marcus's relationship with Peter?

A) Marcus refuses to meet Peter due to feelings of guilt towards his previous wife.

B) Marcus has kept his identity hidden from Peter while supporting him anonymously.

C) Marcus is ambivalent about reaching out to Peter, who is unaware of his existence.

D) Marcus only contacts Peter through Jolene, and was initially reluctant to do so.

10

Which choice provides the best evidence for the answer to the previous question?

A) Lines 95-97 ("With a...vanished")

B) Lines 99-101 ("Peter is...years")

C) Lines 104-106 ("He so...father")

D) Lines 108-110 ("You can't...you")

Answer Key: CHAPTER FIVE

Chapter 5.1
1. B
2. A
3. A
4. D
5. C
6. C
7. C
8. C
9. B
10. D

Chapter 5.2
1. B
2. D
3. C
4. D
5. C
6. D
7. A
8. C
9. B
10. C

Chapter 5.3
1. C
2. A
3. D
4. D
5. B
6. C
7. C
8. B
9. B
10. A

Chapter 5.4
1. A
2. A
3. A
4. B
5. D
6. A
7. D
8. C
9. B
10. C

Chapter 5.5
1. D
2. D
3. A
4. C
5. C
6. A
7. B
8. C
9. A
10. D

Answer Explanations

Chapter 5

Chapter 5.1 | *The Pace of Youth*

1) CORRECT ANSWER: B
In the passage, Stimson observes the man who operates the Merry-Go-Round and realizes that "that fellow is staring at my daughter" (lines 54-55); the young man and Stimson's daughter have struck up a flirtation, as the final few paragraphs indicate. B is the best answer, while A is incorrect because Lizzie and the young man's communications have been "detected" and observed by Stimson. C wrongly assumes that Stimson's daughter (as opposed to Stimson himself) has a somewhat negative response to the young man, while D wrongly indicates that the young man has made an advance (instead of communicating silently and from a distance).

2) CORRECT ANSWER: A
In the relevant lines Stimson reflects on the "grandeur" or impressive appearance of his own Merry-Go-Round; he is thus proud of this possession, so that A is an appropriate answer. While positive, B wrongly indicates thoughts about the future and C wrongly indicates thoughts about the past (not about the PRESENT state of the Merry-Go-Round). D is wrongly negative (or critical of Stimson as obsessive) and should be eliminated for this reason.

3) CORRECT ANSWER: A
The relevant paragraph begins with a reference to "A soft booming sound of surf" (line 17) and continues on to present the visual appearances of the girl in the red dress, the flags, the bathhouse, the ship, and the hawk. Thus, the paragraph is notable for its sensory descriptions: choose A and eliminate B (since the person describing the scene is never designated) and C (since the paragraph frequently switches focus, rather than indulging in a single "extended" analogy). D is problematic because there are no patterns of speech (such as prominent repetition) that would call unmistakable attention to the style or language; instead, the "sensory descriptions" of the aspects of the scene itself are memorable.

4) CORRECT ANSWER: D
In lines 55-58, Stimson feels both "wrath" and "wonder" regarding the young man; these emotions support D, an answer that appropriately captures the strength of Stimson's negative sentiments. A wrongly indicates that Stimson is not bothered by the young man's activity, B confuses his strong "wrath" with the much less vivid emotion of "worry," and C is inappropriately positive.

5) CORRECT ANSWER: C

See above for the explanation of the correct answer. A records Stimson's critical belief that the young man will get into trouble (but does not align with any of the answers to the previous question), B indicates the reasoning behind Stimson's reaction to the young man (but not the reaction itself), and D neglects Stimson entirely to explain how Lizzie reacts to the young man.

6) CORRECT ANSWER: C

The line reference in the question occurs after a description of the young man's various duties; Stimson, however, notices that the young man "frequently found time to twist about" (line 47) and look at Lizzie. This shift in attention is greeted with Stimson's disapproval, so that C is an effective answer. The young man's activities are not complex (since they can be described in a single paragraph, eliminating A) and are not hectic (since they are predictable and do give him time for mild diversion, eliminating B). Keep in mind also that the narrator does not take the young man's side or call attention to qualities such as diligence or ambition; D is thus too positive for the context.

7) CORRECT ANSWER: C

The word "complexities" is mentioned alongside the young man's "duties" (line 69) and is similar in meaning; the young man must attend to specific "responsibilities" as he goes about his life, but finds a pleasant diversion in looking at Lizzie. C is thus an effective answer. Both A and B wrongly indicate that the young man's life is difficult or confusing (when in fact his major responsibility is a somewhat predictable job), while D applies an overly negative tone to the simple, at times untroubled matter of the young man's day-to-day existence.

8) CORRECT ANSWER: C

In the relevant lines, the narrator explains how the "silent courtship" (line 71) operated, with the two young people finding ways to communicate specific feelings (devotion on the young man's part, flirtatious ambivalence on Lizzie's). This information supports C. A is inaccurate because the two young people do communicate warmly (and thus share some requited or mutual feelings). B wrongly focuses on Lizzie's feelings only, while D mentions Stimson, who is not in fact discussed anywhere in the paragraph.

9) CORRECT ANSWER: B

In lines 88-90, the narrator explains that the looks exchanged by the young people have become "almost as obvious as gestures"; pedestrians, or at least Stimson, could discern what the young people are communicating to one another. This information supports B. Nowhere does the author indicate that the young people's communication has hampered them by undermining their jobs (eliminating A) or by placing them in peril (eliminating C). At most, they have earned the disapproval of Stimson, but he has not in fact confronted them (eliminating D).

10) CORRECT ANSWER: D

See above for the explanation of the correct answer. A indicates that the two young people can communicate in detail without speaking, B indicates that Stimson disapproves of the young people's communication, and D indicates that the young people are indifferent to the world around them (but not that they or their jobs are in danger). Make sure not to take B as evidence for Question 9 D or C as evidence for Question 9 A or Question 9 C.

Chapter 5.2 | *The Count of Monte Cristo*

1) CORRECT ANSWER: B

In the first paragraph, the narrator mentions that the "inspector-general of prisons" is making a visit and is heard by Dantes; the author thus sets up the conditions of the eventual encounter between Dantes and the inspector-general, or "foreshadows" a meeting. B is thus the best answer, while Dantes has in fact become accustomed to his surroundings (eliminating A). C (context, addressed mainly in lines 1-2) and D (citizens, line 8-9) raise secondary topics and do not accurately reflect the PRIMARY function of the paragraph: to indicate that Dantes and the inspector will soon meet.

2) CORRECT ANSWER: D

The phrase "intercourse with" is used in describing the imprisoned and isolated Dantes, who does not have any contact or interaction "with the world" (line 9) to the point that he sees himself "as dead" (line 10). D is thus the best answer. A implies that Dantes is unaware that there is a world around him, which is contradicted by Dantes' vivid memories of his life before prison in lines 79-90, while B (communication) and C (actions) might be true but are not the main focus of the sentence.

3) CORRECT ANSWER: C

The phrase "ill fed and innocent" indicates a staple response ("always the same thing", line 24) that the inspector has come to expect from the prisoners. C thus captures his expectation that the responses will be unvarying, while his direct feelings toward the prisoners (as opposed to his boredom with their responses) is not a clear focus here. This fact can be used to eliminate both A and B, while D offers the wrong critique of the responses: they are consistent and uninteresting to the inspector, but not necessarily INVALID.

4) CORRECT ANSWER: D

Upon first meeting Dantes, the inspector "recoiled [or backed away] two or three steps" (line 43); Dantes for his part sees that he "was looked upon as dangerous" (line 44). This information indicates that the inspector is alarmed or concerned by the presence of Dantes, making D an effective answer and eliminating positive choices such as A and B. C, "disgust", is appropriately negative but attributes the wrong motive (distaste for Dantes, not alarm for his own safety) to the inspector's response.

5) CORRECT ANSWER: C

In the final paragraph, Dantes indicates that he does not know his crime and declares that "Uncertainty is worse than all" (line 102). His uncertainty about the crime that he has committed is thus the "worst" element of his imprisonment, so that C is the best answer. A and B wrongly indicate that Dantes DOES know his crime and can thus assess the fairness of his present condition, while D may be true but is not cited as the worst aspect or "chief complaint" that Dantes harbors.

6) CORRECT ANSWER: D

In lines 91-93, Dantes requests that he be put on trial; instead of asking to be released, he asks to be judged for his crimes and thus indicates that the verdict will be valid in his mind. D is the best answer. A describes the prisoners generally (not Dantes's specific ideas), B describes Dantes's attempt to inspire the inspector's pity (not his ideas about legal justice), and C indicates that Dantes may be innocent or unjustly accused (but not that Dantes accepts the judicial system as a source of "fairness").

7) CORRECT ANSWER: A

In lines 70-71, Dantes declares that he has been "subdued" (made more mellow or less violent) by his captivity. A is thus the best answer, while Dantes's desire to be put on trial contradicts the tone of resignation or complete acceptance indicated in B. Dantes does not see himself as a social "outcast" but as a man who has NO relation to society in his present condition (eliminating C); he also values liberty, but there is no sign that he did NOT value his liberty before being imprisoned and thus learn to value it only during his ordeal (eliminating D).

8) CORRECT ANSWER: C

See above for the explanation of the correct answer. A indicates that Dantes has been shut off from the world, B records some of the inspector's speculations, and D indicates (using a comparison) that Dantes finds his imprisonment to be a harrowing departure from his earlier state of liberty. Make sure not to take A as evidence for Question 7 B or C, or D as evidence for Question 7 D.

9) CORRECT ANSWER: B

Dantes's main request is that the inspector grant him "a trial; not pardon, but a verdict" (line 91); this information supports B and can be used to eliminate A, since Dantes seeks a trial (with a verdict of either guilty or innocent) rather than automatic freedom from the inspector's influence. C and D are problematic because Dantes wants the inspector to take practical action on his behalf, but not because he has the same knowledge as the inspector or shares the inspector's values. These other factors may, at most, lead to the trial that Dantes desires.

10) CORRECT ANSWER: C

In the relevant lines, Dantes describes his opportunities before he was imprisoned (his career and his marriage) and explains that a man in his position "loses all in an instant" through being cut off from the world. This information in his changed and now negative conditions supports C. Dantes may wish to leave the prison (A) and may be an honorable man (B), but he does not directly voice these sentiments here; moreover, he indicates that a trial (not his self-regard) will vindicate him. Moreover, while Dantes may in fact be innocent, he does not claim that he has done nothing unlawful in the relevant lines, and does not even seem to be aware of his exact crime (eliminating D).

Chapter 5.3 | *What Diantha Did*

1) CORRECT ANSWER: C

The passage explains the various household tasks that Diantha's mother regularly performs, and comments on this woman's "conscientious performance of duties she did not love" (line 70). This information supports C and can in fact be used to to eliminate the wrongly positive B. The passage focuses on an older woman who has resigned herself to her lifestyle (and does NOT feel fulfilled in her limited and repetitive responsibilities, eliminating A. The passage also reserves most of its discussion of Diantha's father for the end, and presents him mainly to accentuate the traits of Diantha's mother (eliminating D, which at best describes a minor theme).

2) CORRECT ANSWER: A

While the first paragraph describes the physical condition of "Diantha Bell's home" (lines 1-2), the second explains how Diantha's mother sees the home as a "a place of exile" (line 13), and the third describes how Diantha sees it as a site of "boundless vitality, promise, and power" (lines 18-19). This shift from objective description to personal reactions supports A. Diantha and her mother differ in their emotions (not in how they sew, eliminating B), do not BOTH view the home negatively (eliminating C), and are presented only in terms of how they react to their specific circumstances (not in terms of more general personality traits, eliminating D).

3) CORRECT ANSWER: D

The second paragraph contrasts the mellow, rural atmosphere that Mrs. Bell remembers and desires to the "hot, arid, tedious" nature of California. She dislikes her new setting, especially in comparison to a setting that she had known previously; D is thus the best answer, while A raises a theme (dissatisfaction with a way of living, as opposed to a climate) that occurs only later in the passage. B refers to other people (while the paragraph focuses entirely on Mrs. Bell), while C rightly applies a negative tone to the weather but wrongly indicates that the weather keeps Mrs. Bell from working effectively.

4) CORRECT ANSWER: D

In lines 71-73, Mrs. Bell's "idea of duty" is described as a version of "relentlessly" completing a specific task; this information indicates that Mrs. Bell values "steadfastness" and justifies D. A describes Diantha (not Mrs. Bell), B describes only a specific task (not a GENERAL conception of duty as required by the prompt), and C indicates that Diana finds her mother's way of managing money to be intensive and unique (but does not characterize Mrs. Bell's idea of "duty" overall).

5) CORRECT ANSWER: B

Mrs. Bell's smile is described as "tired" without sarcasm and clearly does not "indicate pleasure" (lines 32-34). Since the smile accompanies a description of one of her household tasks, it indicates that she accepts this task without joy or is "resigned" to it. Choose B and eliminate the positive D. A offers a broader characterization of Mrs. Bell as honest and is out of scope, while C wrongly indicates that the "conversation" (NOT a task) explains Mrs. Bell's somewhat negative sentiments.

6) CORRECT ANSWER: C

For much of the passage, Mrs. Bell appears to have accepted her role as a housewife; however, in the line reference, she indicates how little she enjoys housework and, in an agitated manner, advises her daughter not to marry without hiring a "girl" to perform housework. This revelation of her intense emotions supports C. Mrs. Bell's dislike for her duties is indicated earlier (line 34, eliminating A), the "girl" or maid is linked to Mrs. Bell's desires (not Diantha's, eliminating B), and Mr. Bell only emerges as a subject of analysis later (line 59, eliminating D).

7) CORRECT ANSWER: C

In lines 59-61, Mrs. Bell indicates that she can effectively keep accounts and that her skills, as applied in this way, have potential to further her husband's prosperity. Because she is already responsible for the household accounting, it can be reasonably inferred that her skills are what keeps her husband financially stable. C is the best answer. Though skilled in business, Mrs. Bell never actually says that she wanted her own business (eliminating A). She gave up her career as a schoolteacher because she disliked it (lines 39-40, eliminating B for faulty reasoning) and her daughter has the potential to pursue a different career but does not necessarily feel "driven" to do so (eliminating D).

8) CORRECT ANSWER: B

See above for the explanation of the correct answer. A describes Mrs. Bell's dislike for teaching, C indicates that Mrs. Bell has misspent her lifetime (according to Diantha), and D applies a negative tone to Mr. Bell's endeavors. Make sure not to wrongly take A as evidence for Question 7 B.

9) CORRECT ANSWER: B

The phrase "nobler power" refers to a capacity of Diantha's mother, Mrs. Bell, that was not given "a fair chance to grow" (line 67). This power is best understood as unrealized potential to advance in life, so that B is the best answer. A is illogical: Mrs. Bell could FORMULATE "higher aspirations" in her imagination, but did not FULFILL them. C and D both refer to qualities that Mrs. Bell does not appear to lack; the "nobler power", in contrast, is something that has not developed.

10) CORRECT ANSWER: A

Rather than accepting the aid of Diantha's mother, Diantha's father fails "for lack of the help he scorned" (line 75). This evidence explains why he is in a negative and alienating situation as a "square man in a round hole". A is thus the best answer. Mr. Bell's problems involve his wife and his business, so that B (society) raises a false topic. However, his problem is that he does not take constructive advice, not that he is aggressive or argumentative (eliminating C) or that he is not in contact with his wife (eliminating D). He simply receives her advice and chooses not to follow it.

Chapter 5.4 | *The Mysterious Portrait*

1) CORRECT ANSWER: A

Early in the passage, the young painter Tchartkoff critically examines the "monstrosities in the shape of pictures" (line 7) in the shop; later, Tchartkoff finds himself "standing motionless" (line 59) before a single painting that captures his attention. This evidence justifies A. B wrongly judges Tchartkoff's reaction to the painting; he is not prompted ("inspired") by the portrait to paint, but is mostly stunned and mystified by it. C is inaccurate in context since Tchartkoff does not make much effort to negotiate, and since the art dealer possesses the painting and in fact has not "discarded" it. D wrongly assumes that the "portrait" (line 68) was painted recently (contemporary), while the origins and time period of the portrait are unknown.

2) CORRECT ANSWER: A

The second paragraph begins with a discussion of paintings with subjects "easily intelligible to the masses" (lines 14-15), then moves on to consider paintings that "put forth some claims to a higher stage of art" (lines 17-18) but are in their own way unimpressive. This contrast between two artistic modes supports A, while the fact that neither form strongly appeals to Tchartkoff can be used to eliminate B. Examples of Russian art are only used to support the MAIN consideration of the paragraph (the comparison, eliminating C), while the main difference between Tchartkoff and other visitors to the shop involves matters of taste (not how much they know about art, eliminating D).

3) CORRECT ANSWER: A

In lines 22-24, the narrator explains that the art dealer has been energetically trying to persuade Tchartkoff to buy, but without consulting Tchartkoff. This pushy approach does not win Tchartkoff over, so that A is an effective answer. The art dealer does not demand unreasonable prices (since he accommodates Tchartkoff's price at the end, eliminating B) and his selection is in fact accessible to an artist such as Tchartkoff (eliminating C). D distorts lines 13-15, since some of the art is understandable to "the masses" of people, and wrongly indicates that the creators of such are "unknown" rather than unimpressive.

4) CORRECT ANSWER: B

See above for the explanation of the correct answer. A explains the kind of paintings that the shop has in stock (and indicates that some are in fact appealing to customers), C records the art dealer's talk (but does not indicate why such talk may be unappealing), and D indicates an initial (and temporary) rejection of Tchartkoff's price range. Make sure not to take A as evidence for Question 3 D or D as evidence for Question 3 B or C.

5) CORRECT ANSWER: D

In the relevant line reference, Tchartkoff decides to stay in the shop in the hope that he will find something, since there are tales of "pictures of the great masters" surfacing in unimpressive contexts. This information explains his motives and supports D. The precise origins of the painting that Tchartkoff buys are never explained in the passage (eliminating A) and Tchartkoff initially spends his time browsing without a clear goal (eliminating B). Tchartkoff's handling of money is not a central topic of the line reference, so that C raises a false topic.

6) CORRECT ANSWER: A

After trying to persuade Tchartkoff to make a purchase (lines 20-33), the art dealer goes to the door of the shop and encourages new customers to "step in" (line 52) from the street. In other words, the art dealer has perceived that Tchartkoff is not interested in making a purchase. A is the best answer. Both C and D wrongly assume a positive or sympathetic shift in the art dealer's attitude towards Tchartkoff, while trap answer B may indicate a genuine aspect of Tchartkoff's character (an interest in high art) but neglects the MATERIALISTIC reason for the shopkeeper's shift in approach.

7) CORRECT ANSWER: D

In lines 65-69, the narrator explains that the painting bears signs of "the work of a great artist" and is notable for "the power" of how its creator handled the subject depicted. The other paintings in the shop, in contrast, are described as unimpressive mass-produced pieces or as pretentious, failed approximations of real art. Thus, the painting stands out on account of its skillful execution: choose D and eliminate A (since the frames of the other, mass-marketed paintings are never analyzed) and B (since the origin of the artist is never DEFINITIVELY determined). C is a trap answer: the painting is artistically superior, but may be of little value as a commercial item and is in fact given to Tchartkoff at a low price.

8) CORRECT ANSWER: C
See above for the explanation of the correct answer. A indicates that the frame of the picture was once impressive, B describes the appearance of the subject of the picture, and D indicates the powerfully lifelike presence of the picture's subject. Make sure not to take A as evidence for Question 7 A or B as evidence for Question 7 D.

9) CORRECT ANSWER: B
The word "picture" refers to "eyes" (line 69), a part or aspect of the portrait-like image that Tchartkoff has found. Choose B and eliminate A (which would refer to the ENTIRE portrait, not simply the eyes) and C (which suggests that the eyes are an immaterial vision or illusion, not part of a real picture). D is out of scope; little is known about the picture, so it is impossible to say whether the "eyes" were part of the "representation" of an actual person or were simply a feature that the painter created through sheer imagination.

10) CORRECT ANSWER: C
The questions in the relevant line reference relate to Tchartkoff's purchase of the picture, which occurred "unexpectedly" (line 93) and which he is trying to explain to himself. This information supports C. The designated line reference refers mainly to the picture, NOT to the art dealer (eliminating A and B). Moreover, Tchartkoff does not try to give the picture back or feel strong negative emotions about his purchase, making D an inaccurate choice.

Chapter 5.5 | *A Yankee Cophetua*

1) CORRECT ANSWER: D
The passage introduces first a misunderstanding between Marcus and Albert, then a somewhat tense scene involving Marcus and Jolene. These events in the narrative arise because Marcus is keeping the nature of the relationship between him and his son, Peter, a secret (lines 105-110). This information supports D, while A is incorrect because Marcus (though not poor by any means) has not been corrupted by material prosperity. B misrepresents the content of the passage (since Jolene is NOT actually unfaithful to Marcus, proving Albert's supposition about her infidelity incorrect), while C wrongly indicates that Jolene is Marcus's wife (not his girlfriend).

2) CORRECT ANSWER: D
When Albert breaks the potentially scandalous news that Jolene has been seen with a young man, Marcus, "seemingly unperturbed, said nothing" (line 54). This unbothered reaction can be explained by Marcus's knowledge that Jolene, rather than being disloyal to him, is in fact talking with his own son. D is the best answer, while Marcus's composed reactions throughout the passage eliminate A and B (both of which assume that he had a strongly negative reaction to Albert). C is inaccurate because Albert reports the meeting between Jolene and the young man in order to assist his friend, NOT because he is motivated by resentment.

3) CORRECT ANSWER: A

In lines 31-32, Albert indicates that Marcus was "creating and building the business to what it is now"; this obligation took precedence over Marcus's relationship with his wife, since he "wasn't always there for her" (line 30). A indicates that Marcus prioritized his business ventures and is an effective answer. B wrongly indicates that wealth was the main reason that the marriage was viable (not simply ONE reason), C criticizes Marcus on the wrong grounds (since he is in fact distant, not irrational), and D wrongly indicates that the marriage was successful (when in fact it could have carried on under unpleasant circumstances and would thus not be deemed a "success").

4) CORRECT ANSWER: C

See above for the explanation of the correct answer. A indicates that Marcus is rich (but does not clearly characterize his relationship), B indicates that Marcus lavished material wealth on his wife (NOT that such wealth helped the marriage to survive), and D indicates that Marcus's decision to start a relationship with Jolene (NOT his marriage) is a source of worry for Albert. Make sure not to wrongly take A or B as evidence for Question 3 B, or D as evidence for Question 3 C.

5) CORRECT ANSWER: C

In the passage, Albert both acknowledges the success of Marcus's business ventures and addresses Marcus as "my oldest friend" (line 40); Albert thus respects Marcus, but also jokes with him and tells him bluntly about Jolene's meeting. C is the best answer, while A indicates that Albert holds back information when in fact he does the exact opposite. B wrongly suggests that Albert must negatively endure (or be "patient") with Marcus, while D wrongly UNDERSTATES how strongly biased Albert is in Marcus's favor, since he sides with Marcus even against Marcus's self-criticisms.

6) CORRECT ANSWER: A

The word "defiantly" refers to how Albert tells Marcus about Jolene's meeting: he feels "courage" (line 49) and delivers potentially unpleasant information in a direct manner. He thus acts boldly. A is the best answer, while B and C attribute the wrong motives to Albert (who wishes to help Marcus, not to rebel against or contend with his close friend). D is tempting but does not effectively fit the primary context of Albert's courage or passion; moreover, it is not clear why Albert would need to deliver several sentences of explanation in a "loud" voice when his friend is nearby.

7) CORRECT ANSWER: B

Jolene shows affectionate attention to Marcus, but also addresses him "in a low stern voice" (line 99) to convey her true sentiments about the situation with Peter. This combination of traits is accurately reflected in B, while A wrongly applies a critical tone to Jolene and C ("diplomatic") does not capture her candid and direct way of talking to Marcus. D, however, is inappropriate to the lively personality that Jolene manifests in lines 81-85, and should be eliminated for this reason.

8) CORRECT ANSWER: C

Jolene's description of Peter as "not complete" is followed by an explanation of why Peter "needs to know his father" (line 106); the status of this relationship would explain the sentiments that Jolene attributes to Peter. C is the best answer, while A is contradicted by Jolene's belief that Peter, despite his father's consistent absence, still wants to know his father. The possibility that Peter and Marcus will connect is Jolene's main concern, not Peter's life goals or level of assistance (eliminating B) or the relationship between Peter and Jolene (which the passage proves to be non-romantic, eliminating D).

9) CORRECT ANSWER: A

In lines 108-110, Jolene explains that Peter is being kept a "secret" and (upon looking at the photograph of Marcus's deceased wife) indicates that any transgression involving Peter can now be forgiven. Marcus thus harbors guilt (and needs forgiveness) where Peter is concerned, so that together these pieces of information justify A. It is indicated earlier that Peter is familiar enough with Marcus's identity to send his regards and thanks (eliminating both B and C). D rightly indicates that Jolene maintains contact between Marcus and Peter, but wrongly discusses Marcus's INITIAL response to the idea of helping Peter (a response that is never recorded in the passage).

10) CORRECT ANSWER: D

See above for the explanation of the correct answer. A records the change in Jolene's demeanor after Peter is mentioned, B shows how Jolene relays news of Peter to Marcus, and C indicates that Peter wants to meet Marcus. B can in fact be used as evidence AGAINST Question 9 B and Question 9 C, which assume that Peter has less information about Marcus than the passage indicates.

CHAPTER SIX

Questions 1-10 are based on the following passage.
Chapter 6.1
The following is an excerpt from *Corinne* (1807) by Madame De Stael.

I awoke in Rome. My first looks were saluted by the brilliancy of an Italian sun, and my soul was penetrated with a sentiment of love and gratitude
Line towards that Power which seemed manifested in
5 its resplendent beams. I heard the church bells; the firing of a cannon at intervals announced some great solemnity. I demanded the cause of it, and was informed that that morning was to be crowned, at the Capitol, the most celebrated woman in Italy: Corinne,
10 poetess, writer, and one of the greatest beauties of Rome. I made some enquiries respecting this ceremony and all the answers that I received strongly excited my curiosity.
I made my way to the public square, where I
15 heard everybody speaking of the genius and talents of Corinne. The streets through which she was to pass had been decorated; the people, who rarely assemble together except to pay their homage to fortune or power, were, upon this occasion, almost in a tumult
20 to behold a female whose mind was her only claim to distinction. In the actual state of the Italians the field of glory is only open to them in the fine arts, and they possess a sensibility for genius in that department. Everywhere I heard her name accompanied with some
25 anecdote, which implied the possession of all those talents that captivate the imagination. One said that her voice was the most touching in Italy; another, that nobody played tragedy like her; somebody else, that she danced like a nymph, and designed with as much
30 taste as invention: all said that nobody had ever written or improvised such fine verses, and that, in habitual conversation she possessed by turns, a grace and an eloquence which charmed every mind.
No one was acquainted with her family name. Her
35 first work had appeared five years before, and only bore the name of Corinne; nobody knew where she had lived, nor what she had been before that time: she was, however, nearly twenty-six years of age. This mystery and publicity both at the same time, this woman of
40 whom everybody spoke, but whose real name was known to nobody, appeared to me one of the wonders of the singular country I had just come to live in.
Very fine and brilliant music preceded the arrival of the triumphal procession. Any event, whatever
45 it may be, which is announced by music, always produces emotion. A way was made through the crowd

for the four white horses that drew the car of Corinne which was constructed upon an antique model; young girls, dressed in white, walked on each side of her.
50 Wherever she passed an abundance of perfumes was thrown into the air; the windows, decorated with flowers and scarlet tapestry, were crowded with spectators; everybody cried, "Long live Corinne!" "Long live Genius and Beauty!" The emotion was
55 general but I did not yet share it, until at last, I beheld Corinne.
She was dressed like the Sybil of Domenichino; her dress was white, with blue drapery from her bosom downwards, and her costume was very picturesque,
60 at the same time without departing so much from established modes as to savor of affectation. Her attitude on the car was noble and modest: it was easily perceived that she was pleased with being admired, but a sense of timidity was mingled with her joy, and
65 seemed to ask pardon for her triumph. The expression of her physiognomy, of her eyes, of her smile, interested all in her favor, and the first look made me her friend, even before that sentiment was subdued by a warmer impression. She gave at once the idea of a
70 priestess of Apollo advancing towards the temple of the Sun, and of a woman of perfect simplicity in the common relations of life.
The beauty of the sky, the enthusiasm of these Romans, and above all Corinne, electrified my
75 imagination. I had often, in my own country, seen statesmen carried in triumph by the people, but this was the first time I had been a witness of the honors paid to a woman—a woman illustrious only by the gifts of genius. Her chariot of victory was not
80 purchased at the cost of the tears of any human being, and no regret, no terror overshadowed that admiration which the highest endowments of nature, imagination, sentiment and mind, could not fail to excite.
It was at the foot of the flight of steps which leads
85 to the Capitol, that the car finally stopped. Corinne stepped out of the car and made a genuflection with so much nobleness and modesty, so much gentleness and dignity, that in that moment I felt my eyes moist with tears: I was astonished at my own tenderness, but in
90 the midst of all her pomp and triumph it seemed to me that Corinne had implored, by her looks, the protection of a friend—that protection which no woman, however superior, can dispense with; and how sweet, said I within myself, would it be to become the support of
95 her to whom sensibility alone renders that support necessary.

CONTINUE →

1

Over the course of the passage, the main focus shifts from

A) a general discussion of the narrator's surroundings to a specific detail.

B) a recounting of the narrator's anticipation of an event to the event's effect on him.

C) a portrayal of the narrator's idol to an analysis of her role in society.

D) a description of a tradition to an anecdote about a celebration of that tradition.

2

The narrator's description of Rome in the first paragraph primarily serves to

A) provide context for the purpose of the narrator's visit.

B) identify the nationality of a celebrated character.

C) establish a mood of anticipation and festivity.

D) characterize the narrator as naturally inquisitive.

3

Which choice best describes a technique the narrator uses to represent Corinne's character during the procession?

A) The narrator emphasizes the complexity of Corinne's character by describing the various paradoxes within her persona.

B) The narrator hints at the insecurity reflected in Corinne's character by depicting her as searching for the protection of a friend.

C) The narrator demonstrates the enigmatic nature of Corinne's character by referencing the mystery surrounding her identity.

D) The narrator underscores the unpretentious nature of Corinne's character by portraying her distaste for public attention.

4

The passage indicates that what makes the tribute to Corinne important to those in Italy is that she is celebrated

A) as a woman who has triumphed in a field dominated by men.

B) as a person with qualities of a purely artistic nature.

C) as an unassuming idol who is humble and accessible to her adorers.

D) as an artist who has accomplished more than others of her age.

5

It can be reasonably inferred from the passage that the narrator reacts to the frenzy preceding Corinne's appearance with

A) skepticism, but not complete disbelief.

B) intrigue, but not complete captivation.

C) excitement, but not complete abandon.

D) respect, but not complete worship.

6

Which choice provides the best evidence for the answer to the previous question?

A) Lines 11-13 ("I made...curiosity")

B) Lines 24-26 ("Everywhere I...imagination")

C) Lines 44-46 ("Any event...emotion")

D) Lines 54-56 ("The emotion...Corinne")

7

As used in line 23, "a sensibility" most nearly means

A) an awareness.

B) a sensitivity.

C) an intuition.

D) an affinity.

163

CONTINUE

8

As compared to other personalities whose triumphant celebrations have been witnessed by the narrator, Corinne is portrayed as

A) having more beauty.

B) deserving greater fame.

C) possessing less dignity.

D) arousing less fear.

9

Which choice provides the best evidence for the answer to the previous question?

A) Lines 57-59 ("She was...picturesque")

B) Lines 62-65 ("it was...triumph")

C) Lines 76-79 ("this was...genius")

D) Lines 79-81 ("Her chariot...admiration")

10

The main idea of the last paragraph is that

A) the celebration culminates in Corinne's greeting of the audience.

B) the narrator is encouraged by the connection between him and Corinne.

C) the narrator is moved by Corinne's display of virtue and vulnerability.

D) Corinne is overwhelmed by the tumultuous gathering around her.

CONTINUE

Questions 1-10 are based on the following passage.
Chapter 6.2
The following is an excerpt from *The Spaniard's Story* (1820) by Charles Maturin.

While I was yet unborn, my mother vowed that I should be devoted to religion. As the time drew near when I was to forsake the world and retire to a
Line monastery, I revolted in horror at the career before
5 me, and refused to take the vows. But my family were completely under the influence of a cunning and arrogant priest, who threatened God's curse upon me if I disobeyed; and ultimately, with a despairing heart, I consented.

10 The horror with which I had anticipated monastic life was nothing to my disgust and misery at the realization of its evils. The narrowness and littleness of it, the hypocrisies, all filled me with revolt; and it was only by brooding over possibilities of escape that I
15 could avoid utter despair. At length, a ray of hope came to me. My younger brother, a lad of spirit, who had quarreled with the priest who dominated our family, succeeded with great difficulty in communicating with me, and promised that a civil process should be
20 undertaken for the reclamation of my vows.

But presently my hopes were destroyed by the news that my civil process had failed. Of the desolation of mind into which this failure plunged me, I can give no account—despair has no diary. I remember that I
25 used to walk for hours in the garden, where alone I could avoid the neighborhood of the other monks. It happened that the fountain of the garden was out of repair, and the workmen engaged upon it had had to excavate a passage under the garden wall. But as this
30 was guarded by day and securely locked by night, it offered but a tantalizing image of escape and freedom.

One evening, as I sat gloomily by the door of the passage, I heard my name whispered. I answered eagerly, and a paper was thrust under the door. I
35 knew the handwriting—it was that of my brother Juan. From it I learned that Juan was still planning my escape, and had found a confederate within the monastery—a parricide who had turned monk to evade his punishment.
40 Juan had bribed him heavily, yet I feared to trust him until he confided to me that he himself also intended to escape. At length, our plans were completed; my companion had secured the key of a door in the chapel that led through the vaults to a trap-
45 door opening into the garden. A rope ladder flung by Juan over the wall would give us liberty.

At the darkest hour of the night we passed through the door, and crawled through the dreadful passages beneath the monastery. I reached the top of the ladder-a
50 lantern flashed in my eyes. I dropped down into my brother's arms.

We hurried away to where a carriage was waiting. I sprang into it.

"He is safe," cried Juan, following me.
55 "But are you?" answered a voice behind him. He staggered and fell back. I leapt down beside him. I was bathed in his blood. He was dead. One moment of wild, fearful agony, and I lost consciousness.

When I came to myself, I was lying in an
60 apartment not unlike my cell, but without a crucifix. Beside me stood my companion in flight.

"Where am I?" I asked.

"You are in the prison of the Inquisition," he replied, with a mocking laugh. He had betrayed me!
65 He had been all the while in league with the superior.

I was tried again and again by the Inquisition— charged not only with the crime of escaping from the convent and breaking my religious vows, but with the murder of my brother. My spirits sank with
70 each appearance before the judges. I foresaw myself doomed to die at the stake.

One night, and for several nights afterwards, a visitor presented himself to me. He came and went apparently without help or hindrance—as if he had
75 had a master-key to all the recesses of the prison. And yet he seemed no agent of the Inquisition—indeed, he denounced it with caustic satire and withering severity. But what struck me most of all was the preternatural glare of his eyes. I felt that I had never beheld such
80 eyes blazing in a mortal face. It was strange, too, that he constantly referred to events that must have happened long before his birth as if he had actually witnessed them.

On the night before my final trial, I awoke from a
85 hideous dream of burning alive to behold the stranger standing beside me. With an impulse, I flung myself before him and begged him to save me. He promised to do so—on one awful and incommunicable condition. My horror brought me courage; I refused, and he left
90 me.

Next day I was sentenced to death at the stake. But before my fearful doom could be accomplished, I was free—and by that very agency of fire that was to have destroyed me. The prison of the Inquisition was burned
95 to the ground, and in the confusion, I escaped.

CONTINUE

1

Which choice best describes what happens in the passage?

A) Two characters undertake a negotiation to secure the liberation of one of them from prison.

B) Two characters plot to deceive a third character, who holds the key to their freedom.

C) One character describes the circumstances surrounding his brother's untimely death.

D) One character recounts a series of events that led to his escape from two institutions.

2

In context of the passage as a whole, with which statement about himself would the narrator most likely agree?

A) Although he has strong morals, he is not completely above being corrupted.

B) Although he values his freedom, he would never attempt to incur the wrath of God.

C) He prefers to keep to himself, but is willing to work with others when necessary.

D) He usually complies with authority, unless he is facing unbearable despair.

3

Which choice provides the best evidence for the answer to the previous question?

A) Lines 5-9 ("But my...consented")

B) Lines 24-26 ("I remember...monks")

C) Lines 84-87 ("On the...me")

D) Lines 87-90 ("He promised...me")

4

The narrator indicates that his main objection with monastic life was that he found it to be

A) corrupt.

B) monotonous.

C) regimented.

D) immoral.

5

Which choice provides the best evidence for the claim that the narrator persevered in the monastery by retaining the hope of a life beyond its walls?

A) Lines 4-5 ("I revolted...vows")

B) Lines 13-15 ("it was...despair")

C) Lines 15-16 ("At length...me")

D) Lines 29-31 ("But as...freedom")

6

The narrator uses the phrase "despair has no diary" (line 24) to suggest that

A) His misery was so severe that he was unable to describe it with words.

B) His despair was such that he felt it too painful to document in a journal.

C) He abandoned all thoughts of escape after the outcome of the civil process.

D) He suppressed all traumatic memories of his experiences at the monastery.

7

As used in line 26, "neighborhood" most nearly means

A) residence.

B) territory.

C) company.

D) vicinity.

8

Prior to his escape from the monastery, the narrator's attitude towards the "confederate" (line 37) shifts from

A) confidence to apprehension.

B) suspicion to complicity.

C) bewilderment to understanding.

D) collaboration to hostility.

CONTINUE

9

The description of the visitor in lines 72-83 ("One night...them") mainly serves to

A) evoke an ominous and supernatural mood.

B) underscore the evil nature of the prison.

C) hint at the severity of the narrator's troubles.

D) present a key character in the outcome of the narrative.

10

In relating the events surrounding his escape from the prison of the Inquisition, the narrator presents which irony?

A) By turning down the visitor's offer, he succeeds in securing a path to freedom.

B) He is accused of crimes against religion by an institution without religious allegiances.

C) Although he was treated as a heretic, he had no intention of betraying the church.

D) The means of his intended punishment provided him with his eventual liberation.

CONTINUE

Questions 1-10 are based on the following passage.
Chapter 6.3
Adapted from Anton Chekhov, *Vanka* (1886).
As printed in the collection Best Russian Short
Stories, compiled and edited by Thomas Seltzer.

Nine-year-old Vanka Zhukov, who had been
apprentice to the shoemaker Aliakhin for three months,
did not go to bed the night before Christmas. He waited
Line till the master and mistress and the assistants had
5   gone out to an early church-service, to procure from
his employer's cupboard a small phial of ink and a
penholder with a rusty nib; then, spreading a crumpled
sheet of paper in front of him, he began to write.
Before, however, deciding to make the first letter,
10 he looked furtively at the door and at the window,
glanced several times at the sombre ikon, on either side
of which stretched shelves full of lasts, and heaved a
heart-rending sigh. The sheet of paper was spread on a
bench, and he himself was on his knees in front of it.
15 "Dear Grandfather Konstantin Makarych," he
wrote, "I am writing you a letter. I wish you a Happy
Christmas and all God's holy best. I have no mamma or
papa, you are all I have."
Vanka gave a look towards the window in which
20 shone the reflection of his candle, and vividly pictured to
himself his grandfather, Konstantin Makarych, who was
night-watchman at Messrs. Zhivarev. He was a small,
lean, unusually lively and active old man of sixty-five,
always smiling and blear-eyed. All day he slept in the
25 servants' kitchen or trifled with the cooks. At night,
enveloped in an ample sheep-skin coat, he strayed round
the domain tapping with his cudgel. Behind him, each
hanging its head, walked the old bitch Kashtanka, and
the dog Viun, so named because of his black coat and
30 long body and his resemblance to a loach. Viun was an
unusually civil and friendly dog, looking as kindly at a
stranger as at his masters, but he was not to be trusted.
Beneath his deference and humbleness was hid the most
inquisitorial maliciousness. No one knew better than he
35 how to sneak up and take a bite at a leg, or slip into the
larder or steal a muzhik's chicken. More than once they
had nearly broken his hind-legs, twice he had been hung
up, every week he was nearly flogged to death, but he
always recovered.
40 At this moment, for certain, Vanka's grandfather
must be standing at the gate, blinking his eyes at the
bright red windows of the village church, stamping his
feet in their high-felt boots, and jesting with the people
in the yard; his cudgel will be hanging from his belt, he
45 will be hugging himself with cold, giving a little dry, old

man's cough, and at times pinching a servant-girl or a
cook.
"Won't we take some snuff?" he asks, holding out
his snuff-box to the women. The women take a pinch of
50 snuff, and sneeze.
The old man goes into indescribable ecstasies,
breaks into loud laughter, and cries:
"Off with it, it will freeze to your nose!"
He gives his snuff to the dogs, too. Kashtanka
55 sneezes, twitches her nose, and walks away offended.
Viun deferentially refuses to sniff and wags his tail.
It is glorious weather, not a breath of wind, clear, and
frosty; it is a dark night, but the whole village, its white
roofs and streaks of smoke from the chimneys, the trees
60 silvered with hoar-frost, and the snowdrifts, you can see
it all. The sky scintillates with bright twinkling stars, and
the Milky Way stands out so clearly that it looks as if it
had been polished and rubbed over with snow for the
holidays…
65 Vanka sighs, dips his pen in the ink, and continues
to write.
"Last night I got punished, because, while I was
rocking his brat in its cradle, I unfortunately fell asleep.
And during the week, my mistress told me to clean a
70 herring, and I began by its tail, so she took the herring
and stuck its snout into my face. The assistants tease
me, send me to the tavern for vodka, make me steal
the master's cucumbers, and the master hits me with
whatever is handy. Food there is none; in the morning
75 it's bread, at dinner gruel, and in the evening bread
again. As for tea or sour-cabbage soup, the master and
the mistress themselves guzzle that. They make me
sleep in the vestibule, and when their brat cries, I don't
sleep at all, but have to rock the cradle. Dear Grandpapa,
80 for Heaven's sake, take me away from here, home to our
village.

CONTINUE

1

Over the course of the passage, the primary focus shifts from

A) an account of Vanka's actions to a description of his inner thoughts.
B) Vanka's experience writing a letter to a memory of his grandfather.
C) Vanka's relationship with his grandfather to his opinion of his employers.
D) the physical setting of the scene to the different characters' personality traits.

2

The main purpose of the second paragraph (lines 9-14) is to

A) outline the schedule of a typical day in Vanka's life.
B) indicate that Vanka planned to leave his apprenticeship.
C) characterize Vanka as an outcast among the shoemaker's assistants.
D) convey that Vanka's actions were unknown to his masters.

3

As used in line 25, "trifled with" most nearly means

A) annoyed.
B) socialized with.
C) played pranks on.
D) disrespected.

4

According to the passage, Vanka writes a letter specifically to his grandfather because

A) Vanka knew that Konstantin would help him leave the village.
B) Konstantin had taken care of him when his parents died.
C) Vanka had a particular affinity for him.
D) Konstantin is the only parental figure Vanka has left.

5

Which choice provides the best evidence for the answer to the previous question?

A) lines 16-17 ("I wish...best")
B) lines 17-18 ("I have...have")
C) lines 40-42 ("At this...church")
D) Lines 79-81 ("Dear Grandpapa...village")

6

Vanka's grandfather can best be described as

A) devious and scheming.
B) mischievous and animated.
C) loving and paternal.
D) untrustworthy and unpredictable.

7

The passage indicates which of the following about Vanka's work as an apprentice?

A) He was assigned to tasks that other employees had rejected.
B) He was a poor shoemaker and did not perform his duties well.
C) He was made to do jobs unrelated to his intended profession as shoemaker.
D) He was diligent but received no reward or acknowledgement from his master.

8

What function do lines 65-66 ("Vanka...write") serve in the passage as a whole?

A) It returns the narrative to a point earlier in the passage.
B) It reveals that Vanka was hallucinating the events with his grandfather.
C) It indicates that Konstantin's actions took place in the past.
D) It implies that Vanka understands the futility of his efforts to escape.

CONTINUE

9

Vanka pleads to be taken back to his village most likely because

A) he misses his grandfather and longs to be reunited with him.

B) the master and mistress mistreat their employees.

C) he is singled out and bullied by his employer and his employer's assistants.

D) he has lost interest in shoemaking and no longer wants to pursue the career.

10

Which choice provides the best evidence for the answer to the previous question?

A) lines 69-70 ("And during...a herring")

B) lines 71-74 ("The assistants...handy")

C) lines 74-76 ("Food there...again")

D) lines 76-77 ("As for...that")

CONTINUE

Questions 1-10 are based on the following passage.
Chapter 6.4
Adapted from L.M. Montgomery, "Akin to Love."
Reprinted in *Lucy Maude Montgomery Short Stories, 1909 to 1922*.

David Hartley had dropped in to pay a neighbourly call on Josephine Elliott. It was well along in the afternoon, and outside, in the clear crispness of
Line a Canadian winter, the long blue shadows from the tall
5 firs behind the house were falling over the snow.

It was a frosty day, and all the windows of every room where there was no fire were covered with silver palms. But the big, bright kitchen was warm and cozy, and somehow seemed to David more tempting than
10 ever before, and that is saying a good deal. He had an uneasy feeling that he had stayed long enough and ought to go. Josephine was knitting at a long gray sock with doubly aggressive energy, and that was a sign that she was talked out. As long as Josephine had plenty
15 to say, her plump white fingers, where her mother's wedding ring was lost in dimples, moved slowly among her needles. When conversation flagged she fell to her work as furiously as if a husband and half a dozen sons were waiting for its completion. David
20 often wondered in his secret soul what Josephine did with all the interminable gray socks she knitted. Sometimes he concluded that she put them in the home missionary barrels; again, that she sold them to her hired man. At any rate, they were very warm and
25 comfortable looking, and David sighed as he thought of the deplorable state his own socks were generally in.

When David sighed Josephine took alarm. She was afraid David was going to have one of his attacks of foolishness. She must head him off someway, so
30 she rolled up the gray sock, stabbed the big pudgy ball with her needles, and said she guessed she'd get the tea.

David got up.

"Now, you're not going before tea?" said
35 Josephine hospitably. "I'll have it all ready in no time."

"I ought to go home, I suppose," said David, with the air and tone of a man dallying with a great temptation. "Zillah'll be waiting tea for me; and there's the stock to tend to."

40 "I guess Zillah won't wait long," said Josephine. She did not intend it at all, but there was a certain scornful ring in her voice. "You must stay. I've a fancy for company to tea."

David sat down again. He looked so pleased that
45 Josephine went down on her knees behind the stove, ostensibly to get a stick of firewood, but really to hide her smile.

"I suppose he's tickled to death to think of getting a good square meal, after the starvation rations Zillah
50 puts him on," she thought.

But Josephine misjudged David just as much as he misjudged her. She had really asked him to stay to tea out of pity, but David thought it was because she was lonesome, and he hailed that as an encouraging sign.
55 And he was not thinking about getting a good meal either, although his dinner had been such a one as only Zillah Hartley could get up. As he leaned back in his cushioned chair and watched Josephine bustling about the kitchen, he was glorying in the fact that he could
60 spend another hour with her, and sit opposite to her at the table while she poured his tea for him and passed him the biscuits, just as if—just as if—

Here Josephine looked straight at him with such intent and stern brown eyes that David felt she must
65 have read his thoughts, and he colored guiltily. But Josephine did not even notice that he was blushing. She had only paused to wonder whether she would bring out cherry or strawberry preserve; and, having decided on the cherry, took her piercing gaze from
70 David without having seen him at all. But he allowed his thoughts no more vagaries.

Josephine set the table with her mother's wedding china. She used it because it was the anniversary of her mother's wedding day, but David thought it was out
75 of compliment to him. And, as he knew quite well that Josephine prized that china beyond all her other earthly possessions, he stroked his smooth-shaven, dimpled chin with the air of a man to whom is offered a very subtly sweet homage.

80 Josephine whisked in and out of the pantry, and up and down cellar, and with every whisk a new dainty was added to the table. Josephine, as everybody in Meadowby admitted, was past mistress in the noble art of cookery. Once upon a time rash matrons and
85 ambitious young wives had aspired to rival her, but they had long ago realised the vanity of such efforts and dropped comfortably back to second place.

CONTINUE

1

The passage can best be described as

A) an improbable romance between two characters.

B) a description of two characters' daily lives.

C) a somber account of a character's mistake.

D) a misunderstanding between two characters.

2

Throughout the passage, the narrator primarily draws a contrast between

A) David's relationship with Josephine and his relationship with Zillah.

B) David's pursuit of Josephine and Josephine's denial of his endeavors.

C) David and Josephine's assumptions and the reality of their situations.

D) David's observation of the cold weather and Josephine's warm personality.

3

Which of the following provides the best evidence for the answer to the previous question?

A) Lines 6-8 ("It was….cozy")

B) Lines 36-39 ("I ought...to")

C) Lines 65-68 ("But Josephine...preserve")

D) Lines 72-75 ("Josephine set...him")

4

According to the narrator, the relationship between David and Josephine is portrayed as

A) new friends who were recently introduced to each other.

B) friends who are romantically attracted to each other.

C) acquaintances who have previously met occasionally.

D) neighbors who are familiar and sociable with each other.

5

The main purpose of the third paragraph is to

A) indicate that Josephine is familiar with the meanings of David's behaviors.

B) imply that Josephine is aware of David's romantic feelings towards her.

C) suggest that Josephine wants David to leave her house and return to Zillah.

D) hint that Josephine fears David will attempt to begin a relationship with her.

6

It can be reasonably inferred from the passage that Josephine asks David to stay for tea mainly because

A) she feels that it is her responsibility to make sure David is well fed.

B) she is beginning to feel romantically interested in David.

C) she feels guilty for being the object of David's unrequited feelings.

D) she is happy to have a guest who will be impressed by her cooking skills.

7

Which of the following provides the best evidence for the answer to the previous question?

A) Lines 40-42 ("I guess...voice")

B) Lines 48-50 ("I suppose...thought")

C) Lines 52-54 ("She had...lonesome")

D) Lines 82-84 ("Josephine as...cookery")

CONTINUE

8

In line 54, "encouraging" most nearly means
A) reassuring.
B) cheerful.
C) beneficial.
D) welcoming.

9

The final paragraph (lines 80-87) serves primarily to
A) reinforce David's admiration of Josephine.
B) characterize Josephine as exceptionally skilled.
C) describe the foods Josephine cooks for David.
D) show Josephine's competitive nature.

10

As used in line 86, "vanity" most nearly means
A) frivolousness.
B) arrogance.
C) futility.
D) redundancy.

CONTINUE

Questions 1-10 are based on the following passage.

Chapter 6.5

Adapted from Joseph Conrad, *Typhoon* (1902). In this passage, the Nan-Shan is the ship on which Jukes and Captain MacWhirr are serving.

Jukes was as ready a man as any half-dozen young mates that may be caught by casting a net upon the waters; and though he had been somewhat taken
Line aback by the startling viciousness of the first squall, he
5 had pulled himself together on the instant, had called out the hands and had rushed them along to secure such openings about the deck as had not been already battened down earlier in the evening. Shouting in his fresh, stentorian voice, "Jump, boys, and bear a hand!"
10 he led in the work, telling himself the while that he had "just expected this."

But at the same time he was growing aware that this was rather more than he had expected. From the first stir of the air felt on his cheek the gale seemed
15 to take upon itself the accumulated impetus of an avalanche. Heavy sprays enveloped the Nan-Shan from stem to stern, and instantly in the midst of her regular rolling she began to jerk and plunge as though she had gone mad with fright.

20 Jukes thought, "This is no joke." While he was exchanging explanatory yells with his captain, a sudden lowering of the darkness came upon the night, falling before their vision like something palpable. It was as if the masked lights of the world had been
25 turned down. Jukes was uncritically glad to have his captain at hand. It relieved him as though that man had, by simply coming on deck, taken most of the gale's weight upon his shoulders. Such is the prestige, the privilege, and the burden of command.

30 Captain MacWhirr could expect no relief of that sort from any one on earth. Such is the loneliness of command. He was trying to see, with that watchful manner of a seaman who stares into the wind's eye as if into the eye of an adversary, to penetrate the hidden
35 intention and guess the aim and force of the thrust. The strong wind swept at him out of a vast obscurity; he felt under his feet the uneasiness of his ship, and he could not even discern the shadow of her shape. He wished it were not so; and very still he waited, feeling
40 stricken by a blind man's helplessness.

To be silent was natural to him, dark or shine. Jukes, at his elbow, made himself heard yelling cheerily in the gusts, "We must have got the worst of it at once, sir." A faint burst of lightning quivered all
45 round, as if flashed into a cavern—into a black and secret chamber of the sea, with a floor of foaming crests.

It unveiled for a sinister, fluttering moment a ragged mass of clouds hanging low, the lurch of the
50 long outlines of the ship, the black figures of men caught on the bridge, heads forward, as if petrified in the act of butting. The darkness palpitated down upon all this, and then the real thing came at last.

It was something formidable and swift, like
55 the sudden smashing of a vial of wrath. It seemed to explode all round the ship with an overpowering concussion and a rush of great waters, as if an immense dam had been blown up to windward. In an instant the men lost touch of each other. This is the disintegrating
60 power of a great wind: it isolates one from one's kind. An earthquake, a landslip, an avalanche, overtake a man incidentally, as it were—without passion. A furious gale attacks him like a personal enemy, tries to grasp his limbs, fastens upon his mind, seeks to rout
65 his very spirit out of him.

Jukes was driven away from his commander. He fancied himself whirled a great distance through the air. Everything disappeared—even, for a moment, his power of thinking; but his hand had found one
70 of the rail-stanchions. His distress was by no means alleviated by an inclination to disbelieve the reality of this experience. Though young, he had seen some bad weather, and had never doubted his ability to imagine the worst; but this was so much beyond his
75 powers of fancy that it appeared incompatible with the existence of any ship whatever. He would have been incredulous about himself in the same way, perhaps, had he not been so harassed by the necessity of exerting a wrestling effort against a force trying to tear
80 him away from his hold. Moreover, the conviction of not being utterly destroyed returned to him through the sensations of being half-drowned, bestially shaken, and partly choked.

It seemed to him he remained there precariously
85 alone with the stanchion for a long, long time. The rain poured on him, flowed, drove in sheets. He breathed in gasps; and sometimes the water he swallowed was fresh and sometimes it was salt. For the most part he kept his eyes shut tight, as if suspecting his sight might
90 be destroyed in the immense flurry of the elements. When he ventured to blink hastily, he derived some moral support from the green gleam of the starboard light shining feebly upon the flight of rain and sprays.

CONTINUE

1

Which choice best describes the developmental pattern of the passage?

A) A ship is completely destroyed in a storm, leaving a sole survivor adrift in the ocean.

B) Two crew members collaborate during an unexpected storm to bring their crew and ship to safety.

C) A ship's crew prepares for a building storm which sends one character overboard when it erupts.

D) An inexperienced officer loses control of a ship during a storm and is reassured by the captain of the ship.

2

The narrator uses the phrase "the loneliness of command" (lines 31-32) to present the captain as

A) pessimistic by nature.

B) isolated in his work.

C) requiring no assistance.

D) ultimately accountable.

3

The narrator uses the image of the "blind man" (line 40) most likely to

A) emphasize the captain's inability to gauge the characteristics of the storm.

B) suggest that even the Captain had lost all hope of surviving the storm.

C) highlight the fact that the storm struck in the middle of the night.

D) foreshadow the fate of the ship and its crew members.

4

In describing the effect of the building storm, the narrator draws a comparison between the ship and

A) a panicking creature.

B) an evil spirit.

C) a broken dam.

D) a shattered vessel.

5

Which choice provides the best evidence for the answer to the previous question?

A) Lines 16-19 ("Heavy sprays...fright")

B) Lines 36-38 ("The strong...shape")

C) Lines 54-55 ("It was...wrath")

D) Lines 55-58 ("It seemed...windward")

6

As used in line 59, "disintegrating" most nearly means

A) alienating.

B) dissolving.

C) destructive.

D) separating.

7

In context of the passage as a whole, the seventh paragraph (lines 54-65) primarily serves to

A) differentiate the storm from other natural disasters by portraying it as random.

B) indicate a transition from the anticipation of a storm to its culmination.

C) explain the psychological state of the crew during the worst moments of the storm.

D) illustrate through figurative language the destructive nature of the storm.

CONTINUE

8

Which choice best supports the statement that the storm occurring in the passage was the most severe that Jukes had ever experienced?

A) Lines 8-11 ("Shouting in...this")
B) Lines 12-13 ("But at...expected")
C) Lines 55-58 ("It seemed...windward")
D) Lines 74-76 ("this was...whatever")

9

In lines 66-83, the passage signals a shift from Jukes'

A) state of powerless shock to his urgent struggle for survival.
B) perseverance in battling the storm to his ultimate resignation.
C) panic at being separated from his captain to his assuming of a position of authority.
D) denial of the severity of the storm to his panic as he realizes his imminent death.

10

As used in line 78, "harassed by" most nearly means

A) hurt by.
B) distracted by.
C) annoyed with.
D) preoccupied with.

Answer Key: CHAPTER SIX

SAT

Chapter 6.1
1. B
2. C
3. A
4. B
5. B
6. D
7. D
8. D
9. D
10. C

Chapter 6.2
1. D
2. D
3. D
4. A
5. B
6. A
7. C
8. B
9. A
10. D

Chapter 6.3
1. A
2. D
3. B
4. D
5. B
6. B
7. C
8. A
9. C
10. B

Chapter 6.4
1. D
2. C
3. D
4. D
5. A
6. A
7. B
8. D
9. B
10. C

Chapter 6.5
1. C
2. D
3. A
4. A
5. A
6. D
7. D
8. D
9. A
10. D

Answer Explanations

Chapter 6

Chapter 6.1 | *Corrine*

1) CORRECT ANSWER: B
Early in the passage, the narrator becomes aware that Corinne, "the most celebrated woman in Italy" (line 9), is making her way through Rome for a ceremony; later, the narrator comes across Corinne's "triumphal procession" (line 44) and sees Corinne herself. This shift from the anticipated event to the actual event supports B and can be used to eliminate A, since the narrator's surroundings CHANGE as he comes across Corinne. C is problematic because Corinne is idolized by the narrator (as opposed to the people of Rome) only after he sees her, while D distorts the purpose of Corinne's procession: it is a new and remarkable event, not an expected "tradition".

2) CORRECT ANSWER: C
The first paragraph explains that Corinne "was to be crowned" (line 8) for her exceptional accomplishments, and that the narrator's growing information about this event "strongly excited" (line 12) his curiosity. This information supports C as the best answer, while neither the reason for the narrator's visit (eliminating A) nor Corinne's nationality (eliminating B) are identified. It is only known that both characters are simply in Rome at the same time, and that the narrator is preoccupied with the pleasant events before him, not that he is inquiring or curious OVERALL or as a matter of personality (eliminating D).

3) CORRECT ANSWER: A
In lines 61-65, the narrator explains that Corinne was both "pleased with being admired" and distinguished by her "timidity"; later, in lines 69-72, he indicates that Corinne's presence simultaneously appeared to be both mythic and ordinary. Such paradoxes support A as the best answer, while Corinne's pleasure with being admired can be used to eliminate D. B wrongly refers to the themes of protection and friendship mentioned in the final paragraph, AFTER the procession has run its course, while C wrongly indicates that Corinne's identity (which is well defined in the first paragraph) remains in question.

4) CORRECT ANSWER: B
The narrator explains that Corinne is a writer (line 10) and that, rather than winning recognition through fortune or power, Corinne possessed a mind that was "her only claim to distinction" (lines 20-21). This information on Corinne's artistic prowess supports B, while she is praised for her accomplishments regardless of factors such as gender (eliminating A) or age (eliminating D). C is a trap answer: Corinne may have an appealing personality, but she is "celebrated" for her work in the arts, not for her demeanor.

5) CORRECT ANSWER: B

In lines 54-56, the narrator indicates that he "did not yet share" the jubilant emotions surrounding Corinne, at least until Corinne herself appeared. The narrator has already established that Corinne interests him (lines 11-13), so that B is the best answer. A ("skepticism" or critical disbelief) is too strongly negative, C ("excitement") is too strongly positive, and D wrongly assumes that the narrator, who is mostly asking questions about Corinne, is more decidedly committed to a positive "respectful" approach.

6) CORRECT ANSWER: D

See above for the explanation of the correct answer. A indicates the narrator's curiosity (but does not qualify it as demanded by the previous question), B indicates how highly Corinne is regarded in Rome (but does not mention the narrator's opinion), and D indicates that the procession (NOT Corinne herself) was accompanied by strong emotion.

7) CORRECT ANSWER: D

The "sensibility" is possessed by the Italians, who admire "genius" (line 23) in the arts or thus exhibit an attraction to or "affinity for" it. D is the best answer. A, B, and C all indicate that the Italians are AWARE of artistic genius, but do not indicate that they RESPECT artistic genius in the manner demanded by the narrator's discussion of Corinne's celebrated accomplishments.

8) CORRECT ANSWER: D

In lines 79-81, the narrator explains that Corinne's procession was not in any way the result of "tears", "regret", or "terror": other processions, however, are premised on exactly these negative sentiments. D is thus the best answer, while B and C are negative answers that wrongly critique the procession as deficient in beauty and recognition. A is a trap answer: Corinne's procession is indeed beautiful, but the narrator does not explicitly compare its beauty to the beauty of OTHER processions that he has witnessed.

9) CORRECT ANSWER: D

See above for the explanation of the correct answer. A describes Corinne's impressive appearance, B describes Corinne's demeanor, and C indicates that the narrator has only seen men celebrated in triumphal processions in his own country. Only C compares Corinne's procession to another procession, yet its themes (gender, artistic genius) do not align with an answer to the previous question.

10) CORRECT ANSWER: C

In the final paragraph, the narrator explains that Corinne's virtues of "nobleness and modesty" (line 87) move him to tears, and that Corinne appears to be in need of a friend and protector. Such evidence supports C, while A and D both neglect the important topic of the narrator's strong reaction to Corinne. B is a trap answer: the narrator apparently WANTS to form a connection with Corinne, but does not ACTUALLY form a connection with her in the relevant stage of the narrative.

Chapter 6.2 | *The Spaniard's Story*

1) CORRECT ANSWER: D

After explaining how he entered monastic life, the narrator explains how he obtained "liberty" (line 46) from his monastery; this escape led to his captivity under the Inquisition, which he in turn escaped when "the Inquisition was burned to the ground" (lines 94-95). This information supports D, while A neglects the fact that negotiation proves futile in the narrator's attempt to escape from the monastery. B wrongly refers to two characters deceiving a third (when in fact two characters, the narrator and his brother, are DECEIVED by a third). C also distorts content from the passage: the narrator's brother does die, but this event is only one occurrence in a narrative that has other significant stages.

2) CORRECT ANSWER: D

In lines 87-90, when the strange figure appears, the narrator refuses to go along with the "awful and incommunicable condition" put forward by the mysterious figure, or only goes against an authority figure when the circumstances are as bad as possible. This information (along with the narrator's tolerance of religious authority until his circumstances become unbearable) justifies D. A wrongly indicates that the narrator has been corrupted, while B wrongly emphasizes the narrator's religious life (when the real emphasis of the passage is the narrator's desire to escape oppressive circumstances REGARDLESS of his religious values). C misinterprets a situation described by the narrator; he keeps to himself in the monastery because of his sadness about the results of his civil process, but it is not indicated that he prefers to be alone IN GENERAL.

3) CORRECT ANSWER: D

See above for the explanation of the correct answer. A indicates that the narrator was unable to oppose his family (NOT that he agreed with the priest), B indicates that the narrator disliked the other monks, and C explains that the narrator tried to obtain the assistance of the stranger. Make sure not to wrongly take A as evidence for Question 2 A or B as evidence for Question 2 C.

4) CORRECT ANSWER: A

In lines 10-13, the narrator explains that he objects to monastic life on account of its "evils" and its "narrowness and littleness". He thus finds monastic life hypocritical and corrupt, so that A is the best answer. B and C may in fact be true of a lifestyle that is austere and predictable, but are not EXPLICITLY cited by the narrator as objections. D is a trap answer: the narrator's main complaint regarding the monks is not that they are completely "immoral", but that they pretend not to be so.

5) CORRECT ANSWER: B

In lines 13-15, the narrator explains that he avoids complete despair by brooding over (or thinking over) "possibilities of escape". This information supports the idea that the narrator preserved hope by contemplating life beyond the monastery, justifying B as the best answer. A describes the narrator's aversion to monastic life (and avoids the theme of hope), C indicates that the narrator became hopeful (but not explicitly WHY), and D simply indicates that the narrator desired freedom (not that his HOPE for freedom sustained him during a difficult time).

6) CORRECT ANSWER: A

The phrase "despair has no diary" is used to explain the narrator's sense that he can "give no account" (lines 23-24) that truly captures his negative feelings: A is thus the best answer, while B wrongly refers to a literal "diary" instead of taking the phrase metaphorically. C is problematic because the narrator DOES attempt escape, while D is illogical because the narrator does relate events from his time at the monastery (but cannot capture the negativity that they inspired in him).

7) CORRECT ANSWER: C

The word "neighborhood" refers to the narrator's situation regarding the "other monks" (line 26), whom he wanted to avoid. He thus did not want to socialize or associate with them, since he would stay alone or avoid their "company". C is the best answer. A, B, and D are illogical because the narrator and the other monks are in the same PLACE as residents of the monastery: they are physically close, but the narrator does not want to talk with or spend time with the other monks around him.

8) CORRECT ANSWER: B

In describing the "confederate", the narrator explains that he initially "feared to trust" (lines 40-41) this fellow monk, but then worked with him in order to escape. This information supports the shift described in B, and can be used to eliminate the positive to negative shifts in A and D. C is problematic because the narrator does have a strong initial opinion (distrust) that is then replaced with cooperation or "complicity" in escaping.

9) CORRECT ANSWER: A

In the relevant lines, the narrator explains that the stranger has eyes he has never seen "blazing in a mortal face" (line 80) and that the stranger makes familiar references to events that apparently "happened long before his birth" (line 82): the stranger is meant to seem supernatural and mencing, so that A is the best answer. B (prison) and C (the narrator himself) shift emphasis away from the central topic of the stranger, while D wrongly indicates that the stranger is responsible for the outcome of the narrative. In fact, the fire that sets the narrator free apparently has nothing to do with the stranger himself.

10) CORRECT ANSWER: D

In the final paragraph, the narrator (who was sentenced to be burned at the stake) observes that he was set free "by that very agency of fire which was to have destroyed me" (lines 93-94). This information supports D. A is incorrect because the stranger plays no evident or explicit part in the narrator's release by means of the fire. B is problematic because the Institution, while apparently hypocritical, IS linked directly to the church, while C is incorrect because the narrator DOES betray the church by escaping from a monastery.

Chapter 6.3 | *Vanka*

1) CORRECT ANSWER: A

In the first two paragraphs, the narrator describes Vanka's physical actions in preparation for writing a letter to his grandfather (lines 1-14); as the passage proceeds, the narrator explains how Vanka "vividly pictured to himself " (lines 20-21) his grandfather under a few different circumstances. This shift from actions to thoughts supports A, while the passage as a WHOLE involves the writing of the letter (eliminating B) and Vanka considers his grandfather and his employers alongside one another (lines 67-81, eliminating C). D is incorrect because Vanka describes specific scenes and the characters who inhabit them simultaneously, rather than focusing on scenery in the opening of the passage and personalities only in later portions.

2) CORRECT ANSWER: D

In the relevant paragraph, Vanka looks "furtively [or secretively] at the door" (line 10); in light of his harsh treatment from his superiors, he is naturally afraid that he will be discovered writing a letter that criticizes them. D is the best answer, since Vanka has so far kept his actions secret. A is incorrect because the paragraph only considers one isolated event (not a whole day), while B and C refer to Vanka's unpleasant situation in his apprenticeship, a topic that is NOT directly addressed in this paragraph.

3) CORRECT ANSWER: B

The word "trifled with" refers to an action performed by Vanka's grandfather, a "lively and active" (line 23) old man who is spending time with the cooks for most of the day. As a good-natured and energetic man, he would socialize with them, so that B is the best answer. A, C, and D all apply inappropriate negatives to the grandfather (whom the cooks do not reject) and should thus be eliminated.

4) CORRECT ANSWER: D

In lines 17-18, Vanka informs his grandfather that, since Vanka's parents have died, "you are all I have". Vanka thus has no other older figure within his family who can play a parental role, so that D is the best answer. A is problematic because Vanka wants Konstantin to help him but does not KNOW for certain that Konstantin will (and wants to leave the shoemaker, not a village). B wrongly states that Konstantin has taken care of Vanka (not that Vanka wants his care) and C wrongly indicates that friendly feelings (NOT a desire for care and assistance) are the primary motivation behind Vanka's letter.

5) CORRECT ANSWER: B

See above for the explanation of the correct answer. A records Vanka's positive greeting at the beginning of the letter (but not his MOTIVE for writing), C records one of Vanka's memories of the grandfather, and D indicates that Vanka wants his grandfather's assistance. Make sure not to take D as evidence for Question 4 A; the line reference only states that Vanka wants Konstantin's assistance, not that he definitively "knew" that Konstantin would help.

6) CORRECT ANSWER: B

Vanka's grandfather is described as "lively and active" (line 23); later, Vanka remembers that Konstantin would engage in small pieces of mischief by getting the attention of women and offering them snuff (lines 48-53). This evidence supports B, while A and D are both too strongly negative (since the small mischief that Konstantin provokes does not warrant harsh punishment or criticism from those around him). C is inaccurate because Vanka WANTS the aid and affection of his grandfather, but has not yet clearly RECEIVED these sentiments as he, Vanka, is depicted in the passage.

7) CORRECT ANSWER: C

In lines 67-71, Vanka explains that he has been assigned tasks such as looking after a baby and cleaning a herring; these tasks are not clearly related to the profession of shoemaking, so that C is an effective answer. A distorts the passage's description of the "assistants" (line 71), who make Vanka run casual errands that have nothing to do with their employment (and are thus not "rejected" assignments); B and D are both rightly negative, but wrongly judge Vanka's performance in shoemaking, which the passage avoids.

8) CORRECT ANSWER: A

The relevant line reference describes how Vanka continues the writing process, which is detailed in lines 9-18 but is then interrupted by extended scenes involving Vanka's grandfather. A is thus the best answer. B is incorrect because the line reference deals simply with physical actions (not with questions of reliability or authority) and C wrongly refers to Konstantin (who is NOT in fact mentioned in the relevant lines). D is a tempting answer (on account of Vanka's sigh) but is ultimately illogical: there would be no reason for Vanka to continue writing if he understands that his efforts are futile.

9) CORRECT ANSWER: C

In lines 71-74, Vanka explains that the assistants "tease" him and that the master "hits" him; this rough treatment would explain why he wants to leave his position, thus justifying C. A relies on a misinterpretation of the passage: Vanka remembers the grandfather vividly, but writes to the grandfather PRIMARILY as a means of escape from his negative circumstances. B wrongly states that the shoemaker mistreats all of the employees (not just Vanka) and D reflects on Vanka's career as a shoemaker (a topic that Vanka himself never analyzes).

10) CORRECT ANSWER: B

See above for the explanation of the correct answer. A explains that Vanka was given an unusual task (but does not define cleaning the herring as unpleasant), C indicates that Vanka is unhappy with the food that he is given, and D indicates that the master and mistress indulge in specific foods that Vanka is not given. Both C and D describe negatives, but should be eliminated because the topics of food and health are not raised in the answers to the previous question.

Chapter 6.4 | *Akin to Love*

1) CORRECT ANSWER: D

In explaining the situation involving David and Josephine, the narrator notes that "Josephine misjudged David just as much as he misjudged her" (lines 51-52); the passage thus centers on a misunderstanding between two characters, so that D is the best answer. The passage describes a "neighbourly call" (line 2, not a fulfilled "romance" as indicated in A), focuses on a single event (not on the entire "daily lives" of the two characters, eliminating B), and addresses casual events in a manner that is not serious or "somber" in tone (eliminating C).

2) CORRECT ANSWER: C

In lines 72-75, the narrator explains a difference in understanding between the characters: Josephine is using the china to mark an anniversary, but David assumes that the use of the china is "a compliment to him". This manifestation of how the characters "misjudged" (lines 51-52) one another supports C. Zillah is mentioned as waiting for David (not as a rival to Josephine, eliminating A), and David enjoys Josephine's company but does not aggressively "pursue" her (and is in any case welcomed into her household, eliminating B). And although the weather is cold, the narrator never directly contrasts this condition with Josphine's personal warmth (and in fact portrays Josephine as somewhat misunderstanding and distant, eliminating D).

3) CORRECT ANSWER: D
See above for the explanation of the correct answer. A describes the weather, B indicates David's willingness to stay around despite his obligations at home, and C indicates that Josephine does not fully perceive David's condition. Make sure not to pair A with Question 2 D, B with question 2 A, and C with Question 2 B.

4) CORRECT ANSWER: D
The passage as a whole describes a "neighbourly call" (line 2) that David pays to Josephine; he is on his way home to his wife Zillah, but feels comfortable with Josephine's hospitality and conversation. This information supports D. A and C both wrongly assume that the two characters have a weaker relationship involving less regular contact, while B relies on a misreading of the passage: the kind of contact that Josephine and David have is common in romantic attractions, but there are no textual clues that clearly argue for a shared romantic attraction between them, since Josephine is most interested in her housekeeping.

5) CORRECT ANSWER: A
In the third paragraph, Josephine fears that the sighing David will "have one of his attacks of foolishness" (lines 28-29); she is thus aware of his habits and takes measures to deal with him. This information supports A. Keep in mind that David sighs in reaction to the socks Josephine is handling, and that the exact course of the attack of "foolishness" is never explained: answers that indicate romance (B and D) are thus out of context. C is inaccurate because Josephine, in response to David's actions, begins to accommodate David in a manner that encourages him to spend time in her house.

6) CORRECT ANSWER: A
In lines 48-50, Josephine expresses her desire to give David a "good square meal" because his own wife, Zillah, does not feed him adequately. A thus explains why she invites David to stay. B and C wrongly introduce the topic of romance between the two; David may harbor some romantic or at least yearning feelings for Josephine, but she does not share his sentiments. Josephine is also an accomplished cook, but pride in this accomplishment is not her MAIN motive for keeping David for tea.

7) CORRECT ANSWER: B
See above for the explanation of the correct answer. A indicates Josephine's scorn towards David's wife (but not her attraction towards David), C indicates a difference in David's and Josephine's perceptions, and D indicates Josephine's skill as a cook. Make sure not to wrongly take D as evidence for Question 6 D.

8) CORRECT ANSWER: D
The word "encouraging" refers to a "sign" (line 54) that Josephine gives to David in inviting him to tea. She thus welcomes him to spend time with her, so that D is the best answer. A would assume that she is offering him comfort or support (not simply

hospitality), B wrongly characterizes the "sign" itself as having a cheerful personality, and trap answer C wrongly indicates that the "sign" (NOT its effect of welcoming David to a good meal) will be beneficial on its own.

9) CORRECT ANSWER: B
In the final paragraph, the narrator explains that Josephine is adept in "the noble art of cookery" (lines 83-84) and that no woman who has seen her skill can successfully "rival her" (line 85). This information supports B. David is not in any way a direct focus of this paragraph (eliminating A and C), while Josephine does not actually compete with other women (eliminating D). Instead, they compete against HER and Josephine's reaction to such efforts is not directly recorded.

10) CORRECT ANSWER: C
The word "vanity" is used in relation to the "efforts" (line 86) of women who have tried to rival Josephine as a cook, but whose inferior efforts only occupy second place compared to hers. These efforts are thus unsuccessful or "futile," so that C is the best answer. A and B would characterize or criticize the women THEMSELVES (not their "efforts"), while trap answer D is in fact illogical. "Redundancy" involves virtually identical repetition, yet the women's inferior efforts are NOT virtually identical to the Josephine's superior demonstrations of cooking.

Chapter 6.5 | *Typhoon*

1) CORRECT ANSWER: C
The passage begins with a description of the "startling viciousness of the first squall" (line 4) and goes on to portray Jukes, the captain, and the other members of the crew as the storm intensifies: eventually, Jukes is "driven away from his commander" (line 66) and engulfed with water when the storm reaches its full power. This information supports C, while the passage ends with the ship still afloat (eliminating A) and with the storm still raging (eliminating B). D is a faulty overstatement: Jukes is thrown off guard by the storm, but the ship ITSELF remains under the control of the captain.

2) CORRECT ANSWER: D
Before the relevant line reference, the narrator indicates that Jukes could depend on the captain but that the captain must deal with "the prestige, the privilege, the burden of command" (lines 28-29). Unlike a subordinate such as Jukes, the captain is primarily responsible for the ship's fate, so that D is the best answer and A (which criticizes the captain's personality rather than describing his role) is overly negative. B and C are both incorrect because the captain DOES have people who work with him; however, the failure or success of a voyage will be attributed to him, not to them.

3) CORRECT ANSWER: A
In the sentences before the line reference, Captain MacWhirr tries to understand the situation that the growing storm has created but cannot "even discern the shadow" (line 38) of his own ship's shape. The image of a blind man beset by "helplessness" reflects the captain's limited perception as the storm sets in. A is the best answer, while B and D apply ominous and negative tones to the ENTIRE fate of the ship (not to the smaller, actual issue of the captain's sensory perceptions). C reflects the nighttime setting of the passage but does not fit the line reference, since it does not apply the needed negative tone to Captain MacWhirr's perceptions.

4) CORRECT ANSWER: A

In lines 16-19, the narrator refers to the ship as an animate being ("her") that has "gone mad with fright". This evidence supports A, while B wrongly indicates that the ship is compared to a CAUSE of evil influences (not to a being AFFECTED by such influences). Keep in mind that some of the other figurative descriptions refer to the action of the storm, which calls to mind a breaking dam (eliminating C) or a breaking vessel (eliminating D).

5) CORRECT ANSWER: A

See above for the explanation of the correct answer. B personifies the ship (but does not attach any emotion to it as demanded by the answer to the previous question), C describes a burst of the storm (not the ship), and D also describes the storm using the image of a dam. Make sure not to wrongly take C as evidence for Question 4 D or D as evidence for Question 4 C.

6) CORRECT ANSWER: D

The word "disintegrating" refers to the "power of a great wind" (line 60) such as the wind which drove the members of the crew apart. The wind thus separated them with its force, so that D is the best answer. A wrongly refers to making people hostile or suspicious (not separating them in physical space), while B and C both assume that a substance is being broken down or destroyed, not that men are being forced apart.

7) CORRECT ANSWER: D

The relevant paragraph describes the power of the storm using a variety of comparisons: "the sudden smashing of a vial of wrath" (line 55), the explosion of "an immense dam" (lines 57-58), and an attack from "a personal enemy" (line 63). This paragraph thus relies on figurative language, so that D is the best answer. A (other natural disasters) and C (the crew) wrongly focus on topics other than the storm itself, while trap answer B indicates the wrong time signature. Instead of providing a transition, the paragraph is ENTIRELY devoted to the "culmination" of the storm, since the preceding paragraph ends with the statement that "the real thing came at last" (line 53).

8) CORRECT ANSWER: D

In lines 74-77, the narrator explains that the storm was beyond Jukes's "powers of fancy", while the immediately preceding lines indicate that Jukes has seen bad weather and can easily imagine negative circumstances. This evidence indicates that Jukes has never seen a more severe storm, thus justifying D. A simply describes Jukes's efforts, B describes that the storm is worse than he had expected (not that it is the WORST storm he had witnessed), and C describes the power of the storm (but does NOT provide a comparison or evaluation that is directly from Jukes's perspective).

9) CORRECT ANSWER: A

Early in the paragraph, the narrator notes that Jukes is so disoriented that he loses even "his power of thinking" (line 69); however, he soon realizes the "the necessity of exerting a wrestling effort" (lines 78-79) in order to survive in perilous and weakening conditions. A is the best answer, while Jukes's assertive final response to the storm can be used to eliminate both B and D. Keep in mind also that he has been driven away from the other members of the crew, and thus could not assume a position of "authority" as wrongly noted in C.

10) CORRECT ANSWER: D

The word "harassed" refers to the "necessity" (line 78) of making an effort to survive, which drives Jukes's determined struggle against the elements. He is thus preoccupied with the necessity of survival, so that D is the best answer. A, B, and C are wrongly negative: Jukes may be harmed by the storm, but he WANTS to survive and the appropriate answer should indicate a positive desire.

CHAPTER SEVEN

Questions 1-10 are based on the following passage.
Chapter 7.1
Adapted from John Galsworthy, *The Inn of Tranquility* (1912).

I knew him from the days of my extreme youth, because he made my father's boots; inhabiting with his elder brother two little shops let into one, in a small by-street—now no more, but then most fashionably placed in the West End.

That tenement had a certain quiet distinction; there was no sign upon its face that he made for any of the Royal Family—merely his own German name of Gessler Brothers: and in the window a few pairs of boots. I remember that it always troubled me to account for those unvarying boots in the window, for he made only what was ordered, reaching nothing down, and it seemed so inconceivable that what he made could ever have failed to fit. Had he bought them to put there?

That, too, seemed inconceivable. He would never have tolerated in his house leather on which he had not worked himself. Besides, they were too beautiful—the pair of pumps, so inexpressibly slim, the patent leathers with cloth tops, making water come into one's mouth, the tall brown riding boots with marvellous sooty glow, as if, though new, they had been worn a hundred years. Those pairs could only have been made by one who saw before him the Soul of Boot—so truly were they prototypes incarnating the very spirit of all foot-gear. These thoughts, of course, came to me later, though even when I was promoted to him, at the age of perhaps fourteen, some inkling haunted me of the dignity of himself and brother. For to make boots—such boots as he made—seemed to me then, and still seems to me, mysterious and wonderful.

I remember well my shy remark, one day, while stretching out to him my youthful foot:

"Isn't it awfully hard to do, Mr. Gessler?"

And his answer, given with a sudden smile from out of the sardonic redness of his beard: "Id is an Ardt!"

Himself, he was a little as if made from leather, with his yellow crinkly face, and crinkly reddish hair and beard, and neat folds slanting down his cheeks to the corners of his mouth, and his guttural and one-toned voice; for leather is a sardonic substance, and stiff and slow of purpose. And that was the character of his face, save that his eyes, which were gray-blue, had in them the simple gravity of one secretly possessed by the Ideal. His elder brother was so very like him—though watery, paler in every way, with a great industry—that sometimes in early days I was not quite sure of him until the interview was over. Then I knew that it was he, if the words, "I will ask my brudder," had not been spoken; and that, if they had, it was his elder brother.

When one grew old and wild and ran up bills, one somehow never ran them up with Gessler Brothers. It would not have seemed becoming to go in there and stretch out one's foot to that blue iron- spectacled glance, owing him for more than—say—two pairs, just the comfortable reassurance that one was still his client.

For it was not possible to go to him very often—his boots lasted terribly, having something beyond the temporary—some, as it were, essence of boot stitched into them.

One went in, not as into most shops, in the mood of: "Please serve me, and let me go!" but restfully, as one enters a church; and, sitting on the single wooden chair, waited—for there was never anybody there. Soon, over the top edge of that sort of well— rather dark, and smelling soothingly of leather—which formed the shop, there would be seen his face, or that of his elder brother, peering down. A guttural sound, and the tip-tap of bast slippers beating the narrow wooden stairs, and he would stand before one without coat, a little bent, in leather apron, with sleeves turned back, blinking—as if awakened from some dream of boots, or like an owl surprised in daylight and annoyed at this interruption.

And I would say: "How do you do, Mr. Gessler? Could you make me a pair of Russia leather boots?"

CONTINUE

1

Which choice best describes the developmental pattern of the passage?

A) A lighthearted story of a childhood incident

B) A wistful retelling of an influential experience

C) A nostalgic reflection on a remarkable place

D) A thoughtful depiction of a mysterious character

2

In context of the passage as a whole, the second paragraph primarily serves to

A) portray the particular moment the narrator saw Mr. Gessler's boots for the first time.

B) underscore the narrator's fascination with the boots in Mr. Gessler's store.

C) characterize Mr. Gessler as humble despite having achieved relative success.

D) illustrate the narrator's assumptions about the boots in Mr. Gessler's store.

3

It can be reasonably inferred from the passage that what captivated the narrator about Mr. Gessler's boots was their

A) mystical quality.

B) overwhelming beauty.

C) unclear origin.

D) outstanding durability.

4

Which choice provides the best evidence for the answer to the previous question?

A) Lines 10-11 ("I remember...window")

B) Lines 14-15 ("Had he...inconceivable")

C) Lines 22-23 ("Those pairs...Boot")

D) Lines 57-58 ("his boots...temporary")

5

As used in line 26, "promoted to" most nearly means

A) working for.

B) mentored by.

C) introduced to.

D) told about.

6

The narrator indicates which of the following about his admiration for Mr. Gessler's boots?

A) He was not able to fully realize it until he became older.

B) He was always too shy to communicate it to Mr. Gessler.

C) He only recognized it when Mr. Gessler's shop closed.

D) He conveyed it to Mr. Gessler through his patronage.

7

Which choice provides the best evidence for the answer to the previous question?

A) Lines 17-21 ("Besides, they...years")

B) Lines 25-28 ("These thoughts...brother")

C) Lines 31-35 ("I remember...Ardt")

D) Lines 41-44 ("And that...Ideal")

8

The narrator uses the word "prototypes" in line 24 to suggest that he considered the boots in Mr. Gessler's window to be

A) of questionable quality.

B) created before the rest.

C) those all others were modeled after.

D) embodiments of the perfect boots.

CONTINUE

9

In describing his experiences with Mr. Gessler, the narrator draws a connection between

A) the qualities of leather and Mr. Gessler's physical features.

B) his polite demeanor at church and his respect for Mr. Gessler.

C) Mr. Gessler's patience with customers and the longevity of his boots.

D) Mr. Gessler's soothing personality and the comforting scent of leather.

10

The repeated use of the word "would" in lines 63-74 ("Soon, over...boots") primarily has which effect?

A) It implies that the narrator will visit in the near future.

B) It indicates that the narrator frequently visited the shop.

C) It depicts the event as following a predictable sequence.

D) It reveals that the narrator's visit to the shop is hypothetical.

CONTINUE

Questions 1-10 are based on the following passage.

Chapter 7.2

Adapted from P.D. Wodehouse, "Bill the Bloodhound." Published in *The Man with Two Left Feet and Other Stories* (1917).

There's a divinity that shapes our ends. Consider the case of Henry Pifield Rice, detective.

I must explain Henry early, to avoid
Line disappointment. If I simply said he was a detective,
5 and let it go at that, I should be obtaining the reader's interest under false pretences. He was really only a sort of detective, a species of sleuth. At Stafford's International Investigation Bureau, in the Strand, where he was employed, they did not require him to solve
10 mysteries which had baffled the police. He had never measured a footprint in his life, and what he did not know about bloodstains would have filled a library. The sort of job they gave Henry was to stand outside a restaurant in the rain, and note what time someone
15 inside left it. In short, it is not "Pifield Rice, Investigator. No. 1.—The Adventure of the Maharajah's Ruby" that I submit to your notice, but the unsensational doings of a quite commonplace young man, variously known to his comrades at the Bureau as "Fathead," "That blighter
20 what's-his-name," and "Here, you!"

Henry lived in a boarding-house in Guildford Street. One day a new girl came to the boarding-house, and sat next to Henry at meals. Her name was Alice Weston. She was small and quiet, and rather pretty. They
25 got on splendidly. Their conversation, at first confined to the weather and the moving-pictures, rapidly became more intimate. Henry was surprised to find that she was on the stage, in the chorus. Previous chorus-girls at the boarding-house had been of a more pronounced type—
30 good girls, but noisy, and apt to wear beauty-spots. Alice Weston was different.

"I'm rehearsing at present," she said. "I'm going out on tour next month in *The Girl From Brighton*. What do you do, Mr Rice?"
35 Henry paused for a moment before replying. He knew how sensational he was going to be.

"I'm a detective."

Usually, when he told girls his profession, squeaks of amazed admiration greeted him. Now he was
40 chagrined to perceive in the brown eyes that met his distinct disapproval.

"What's the matter?" he said, a little anxiously, for even at this early stage in their acquaintance he was conscious of a strong desire to win her approval. "Don't
45 you like detectives?"

"I don't know. Somehow I shouldn't have thought you were one."

This restored Henry's equanimity somewhat. Naturally a detective does not want to look like a
50 detective and give the whole thing away right at the start.

"I think—you won't be offended?"

"Go on."

"I've always looked on it as rather a *sneaky* job."
55 "Sneaky!" moaned Henry.

"Well, creeping about, spying on people."

Henry was appalled. She had defined his own trade to a nicety. There might be detectives whose work was above this reproach, but he was a confirmed creeper,
60 and he knew it. It wasn't his fault. The boss told him to creep, and he crept. If he declined to creep, he would be sacked *instanter*. It was hard, and yet he felt the sting of her words, and in his bosom the first seeds of dissatisfaction with his occupation took root.
65 You might have thought that this frankness on the girl's part would have kept Henry from falling in love with her. Certainly the dignified thing would have been to change his seat at table, and take his meals next to someone who appreciated the romance of detective
70 work a little more. But no, he remained where he was, and presently Cupid, who never shoots with a surer aim than through the steam of boarding-house hash, sniped him where he sat.

He proposed to Alice Weston. She refused him.
75 "It's not because I'm not fond of you. I think you're the nicest man I ever met.' A good deal of assiduous attention had enabled Henry to win this place in her affections. He had worked patiently and well before actually putting his fortune to the test. 'I'd marry you
80 tomorrow if things were different. But I'm on the stage, and I mean to stick there. Most of the girls want to get off it, but not me. And one thing I'll never do is marry someone who isn't in the profession. . ."

It seemed final, but Henry did not wholly despair.
85 He was a resolute young man. You have to be to wait outside restaurants in the rain for any length of time.

CONTINUE

1

Which choice best describes a major theme of the passage?

A) The power of personal conviction

B) The futility of individual goals in a world dictated by fate

C) The unpredictability of personal relationships

D) The prevailing nature of logic over emotion

2

The main purpose of the second paragraph (lines 3-20) is to

A) point out that Henry did not have much experience as a detective.

B) differentiate between the various types of detectives.

C) show that Henry was bullied by his coworkers at the Bureau.

D) indicate that Henry's job consisted of menial and mundane tasks.

3

Over the course of the passage, it is revealed that Alice is unlike other chorus girls in that she

A) intends to continue her job long-term.

B) has a quiet and unassuming personality.

C) works hard and takes her job seriously.

D) does not hold detectives in high regard.

4

As used in line 36, "sensational" most nearly means

A) respectable.

B) impressive.

C) romantic.

D) unique.

5

According to the passage, Henry begins to feel dissatisfied with his job because

A) he found that Alice perceived detective work negatively.

B) he saw that girls no longer considered it attractive.

C) he was forced to creep with the threat lest he be fired.

D) he realized that he had been romanticizing his work.

6

Which choice provides the best evidence for the answer to the previous question?

A) Lines 39-41 ("Now he...disapproval")

B) Lines 43-44 ("even at...approval")

C) Lines 49-51 ("Naturally a...start")

D) Lines 61-62 ("If he...instanter")

7

The passage states which of the following about Henry's proposal of marriage to Alice?

A) It was delayed because he worked to gain her trust and friendship beforehand.

B) It was ill-timed because Alice had just criticized his detective work.

C) It was declined because he proposed too quickly after meeting.

D) It was spontaneous because he had rapidly developed romantic feelings for Alice.

CONTINUE

8

It can reasonably be inferred from the passage that Alice refuses Henry's proposal mainly because

A) she did not have romantic feelings towards him.

B) she did not respect his career as a detective.

C) she wanted to marry someone with a job in entertainment.

D) she was suspicious about his morals and his character.

9

In describing the relationship between Henry and Alice, the narrator draws a connection between Henry's

A) unhappiness with his job and Alice's fulfillment with show business.

B) patience applied to his detective work and his dedication to Alice.

C) growing unrequited feelings and Alice's brutal honesty.

D) firm conviction about his love and his ambivalence about his profession.

10

Which choice provides the best evidence for the answer to the previous question?

A) Lines 25-27 ("Their conversation...intimate")

B) Lines 65-67 ("You might...her")

C) Lines 79-81 ("I'd marry...there")

D) Lines 84-86 ("It seemed...time")

CONTINUE

Questions 1-10 are based on the following passage.

Chapter 7.3

Adapted from Rabindranath Tagore "The Castaway." Published in *Mashi and Other Stories* (1918).

Towards evening the storm was at its height. From the terrific downpour of rain, the crash of thunder, and the repeated flashes of lightning, you might think
Line that a battle of the gods and demons was raging in the
5 skies. Black clouds waved like the Flags of Doom. The Ganges was lashed into a fury, and the trees of the gardens on either bank swayed from side to side with sighs and groans.

In a closed room of one of the riverside houses at
10 Chandernagore, a husband and his wife were seated on a bed spread on the floor, intently discussing. An earthen lamp burned beside them.

The husband, Sharat, was saying: 'I wish you would stay on a few days more; you would then be
15 able to return home quite strong again.'

The wife, Kiran, was saying: 'I have quite recovered already. It will not, cannot possibly, do me any harm to go home now.'

Every married person will at once understand
20 that the conversation was not quite so brief as I have reported it. The matter was not difficult, but the arguments for and against did not advance it towards a solution. . .

25 What had happened was this: Kiran was a universal favourite with her family and neighbours, so that, when she fell seriously ill, they were all anxious. The village wiseacres thought it shameless for her husband to make so much fuss about a mere wife and
30 even to suggest a change of air, and asked if Sharat supposed that no woman had ever been ill before, or whether he had found out that the folk of the place to which he meant to take her were immortal. Did he imagine that the writ of Fate did not run there?
35 But Sharat and his mother turned a deaf ear to them, thinking that the little life of their darling was of greater importance than the united wisdom of a village. People are wont to reason thus when danger threatens their loved ones. So Sharat went to Chandernagore,
40 and Kiran recovered, though she was still very weak. There was a pinched look on her face which filled the beholder with pity, and made his heart tremble, as he thought how narrowly she had escaped death.

Kiran was fond of society and amusement; the
45 loneliness of her riverside villa did not suit her at all.

There was nothing to do, there were no interesting neighbours, and she hated to be busy all day with medicine and dieting. There was no fun in measuring doses and making fomentations. Such was the subject
50 discussed in their closed room on this stormy evening.

So long as Kiran deigned to argue, there was a chance of a fair fight. When she ceased to reply, and with a toss of her head disconsolately looked the other way, the poor man was disarmed. He was on the
55 point of surrendering unconditionally when a servant shouted a message through the shut door.

Sharat got up, and, opening the door, learnt that a boat had been upset in the storm, and that one of the occupants, a young Brahmin boy, had succeeded in
60 swimming ashore in their garden.

Kiran was at once her own sweet self, and set to work to get out some dry clothes for the boy. She then warmed a cup of milk, and invited him to her room.

The boy had long curly hair, big expressive eyes,
65 and no sign yet of hair on the face. Kiran, after getting him to drink some milk, asked him all about himself.

He told her that his name was Nilkanta, and that he belonged to a theatrical troupe. They were coming to play in a neighbouring villa when the boat
70 had suddenly foundered in the storm. He had no idea what had become of his companions. He was a good swimmer, and had just managed to reach the shore.

The boy stayed with them. His narrow escape from a terrible death made Kiran take a warm interest
75 in him. Sharat thought the boy's appearance at this moment rather a good thing, as his wife would now have something to amuse her, and might be persuaded to stay on for some time longer. . . But in a short while Sharat and his mother changed their opinion,
80 and longed for his departure. The boy found a secret pleasure in smoking Sharat's hookas; he would calmly go off in pouring rain with Sharat's best silk umbrella for a stroll through the village, and make friends with all whom he met. Moreover, he had got hold of
85 a mongrel village dog which he petted so recklessly that it came indoors with muddy paws, and left tokens of its visit on Sharat's spotless bed. Then he gathered about him a devoted band of boys of all sorts and sizes, and the result was that not a solitary mango in the
90 neighbourhood had a chance of ripening that season. There is no doubt that Kiran had a hand in spoiling the boy. Sharat often warned her about it, but she would not listen to him. She made a dandy of him with Sharat's cast-off clothes, and gave him new ones too.

CONTINUE ➤

1

It can be inferred that over the course of the passage, the narrative reveals a significant shift in

A) Sharat's influence over Kiran.
B) Sharat's perspective of Kiran's health.
C) Kiran's stance on leaving Chandernagore.
D) Kiran's motives behind her decision to stay.

2

The exchanges between Sharat and Kiran are best characterized as

A) at odds because Kiran repeatedly ignores Sharat's wishes.
B) tense because the boy's presence has caused animosity between them.
C) mutually affectionate because Kiran's illness has made their marriage stronger.
D) harmonious because they respect each other's role in the household.

3

The narrator suggests that Kiran's true motive for wanting to leave Chandernagore was that she

A) felt that she was cured of her illness and was ready to go home.
B) wanted to distance herself from Sharat and reunite with her family.
C) craved a distraction that would take her mind off her daily routine.
D) doubted the effectiveness of the medical treatment provided there.

4

Which choice provides the best evidence for the answer to the previous question?

A) Lines 16-18 ("I have...now")
B) Lines 25-27 ("Kiran was...anxious")
C) Lines 41-43 ("There was...death")
D) Lines 46-48 ("There was...dieting")

5

As used in line 28, "shameless" most nearly means

A) foolish.
B) scandalous.
C) defiant.
D) impractical.

6

The "village wiseacres" (line 28) most likely believed that Kiran

A) would fall victim to charlatans posing as medicine men in Chandernagore.
B) could not be helped in Chandernagore anymore than in her own village.
C) could be cured by the wiseacres as her illness was common in their village.
D) was not in mortal danger and that Sharat had exaggerated the severity of her illness.

7

Sharat's decision to ignore the wiseacres' comments about Chandernagore can best be explained by which of the following?

A) He was angered because they had denigrated his wife.
B) He thought that they were short-sighted and overly conservative.
C) He prioritized his wife's well-being above everything else.
D) He wanted to take his chances with a nontraditional cure.

CONTINUE

8

Which choice best describes Sharat's initial reaction to the boy's arrival?

A) Grateful, because there is a possibility that Kiran will stay.

B) Resentful, because Kiran immediately dotes on the boy.

C) Relieved, because the boy is lucky to have survived the storm.

D) Delighted, because the boy brings out Kiran's compassionate nature.

9

Which choice provides the best evidence for the answer to the previous question?

A) Lines 61-63 ("Kiran was...room")

B) Lines 73-75 ("The boy...him")

C) Lines 75-78 ("Sharat thought...longer")

D) Lines 91-94 ("There is...too")

10

According to the passage, Sharat's opinion of the Brahmin boy changes mainly because the boy

A) takes Kiran's affection away from him.

B) has become too popular within the neighborhood.

C) disturbs the household and the neighborhood.

D) prevents him from taking care of Kiran.

CONTINUE

Questions 1-10 are based on the following passage.
Chapter 7.4
Adapted from Charlotte Bronte, *Villette* (1853). The narrator, Lucy Snowe, is a well-bred but disadvantaged young woman who finds herself in need of employment.

Miss Marchmont was a woman of fortune, and lived in a handsome residence; but she was a rheumatic cripple, impotent, foot and hand, and had been so for

Line 5 twenty years. She always sat upstairs: her drawing-room adjoined her bed-room. I had often heard of Miss Marchmont, and of her peculiarities (she had the character of being very eccentric), but till now had never seen her. I found her a furrowed, grey-haired woman, grave with solitude, stern with long affliction,

10 irritable also, and perhaps exacting. It seemed that a maid, or rather companion, who had waited on her for some years, was about to be married; and she, hearing of my bereaved lot, had sent for me, with the idea that I might supply this person's place. She made the

15 proposal to me after tea, as she and I sat alone by her fireside.

"It will not be an easy life;" said she candidly, "for I require a good deal of attention, and you will be much confined; yet, perhaps, contrasted with the

20 existence you have lately led, it may appear tolerable."

I reflected. Of course it ought to appear tolerable, I argued inwardly; but somehow, by some strange fatality, it would not. To live here, in this close room, the watcher of suffering—sometimes, perhaps, the butt

25 of temper—through all that was to come of my youth; while all that was gone had passed, to say the least, not blissfully! My heart sunk one moment, then it revived; for though I forced myself to realise evils, I think I was too prosaic to idealise, and consequently to exaggerate

30 them.

"My doubt is whether I should have strength for the undertaking," I observed.

"That is my own scruple," said she; "for you look a worn-out creature."

35 So I did. I saw myself in the glass, in my mourning-dress, a faded, hollow-eyed vision. Yet I thought little of the wan spectacle. The blight, I believed, was chiefly external: I still felt life at life's sources.

40 . . . Two hot, close rooms thus became my world; and a crippled old woman, my mistress, my friend, my all. Her service was my duty—her pain, my suffering—her relief, my hope—her anger, my punishment—her regard, my reward. I forgot that there

45 were fields, woods, rivers, seas, an ever-changing sky outside the steam-dimmed lattice of this sick chamber; I was almost content to forget it. All within me became narrowed to my lot. Tame and still by habit, disciplined by destiny, I demanded no walks in the fresh air; my

50 appetite needed no more than the tiny messes served for the invalid. In addition, she gave me the originality of her character to study: the steadiness of her virtues, I will add, the power of her passions, to admire; the truth of her feelings to trust. All these things she had, and for

55 these things I clung to her.

For these things I would have crawled on with her for twenty years, if for twenty years longer her life of endurance had been protracted. But another decree was written. It seemed I must be stimulated into action. I

60 must be goaded, driven, stung, forced to energy. My little morsel of human affection, which I prized as if it were a solid pearl, must melt in my fingers and slip thence like a dissolving hailstone. My small adopted duty must be snatched from my easily contented

65 conscience. I had wanted to compromise with Fate: to escape occasional great agonies by submitting to a whole life of privation and small pains. Fate would not so be pacified; nor would Providence sanction this shrinking sloth and cowardly indolence.

70 One February night—I remember it well—there came a voice near Miss Marchmont's house, heard by every inmate, but translated, perhaps, only by one. After a calm winter, storms were ushering in the spring. I had put Miss Marchmont to bed; I sat at the

75 fireside sewing. The wind was wailing at the windows; it had wailed all day; but, as night deepened, it took a new tone—an accent keen, piercing, almost articulate to the ear; a plaint, piteous and disconsolate to the nerves, trilled in every gust.

80 "Oh, hush! hush!" I said in my disturbed mind, dropping my work, and making a vain effort to stop my ears against that subtle, searching cry. I had heard that very voice ere this, and compulsory observation had forced on me a theory as to what it boded. Three

85 times in the course of my life, events had taught me that these strange accents in the storm—this restless, hopeless cry—denote a coming state of the atmosphere unpropitious to life. Epidemic diseases, I believed, were often heralded by such a gasping, sobbing,

90 tormented, long-lamenting east wind. . .

I listened and trembled; Miss Marchmont slept.

CONTINUE

1

Which choice best summarizes the passage?

A) One character's perspective on life is changed by an unexpected encounter.

B) One character beset by tragedy finds fulfillment in a new and unusual job.

C) One character reflects on the acquiring and consequences of a significant job.

D) One character befriends an invalid but eccentric and interesting old woman.

2

As used in line 7, "character" most nearly means

A) impression.

B) demeanor.

C) reputation.

D) personality.

3

According to the passage, Lucy was sent for by Miss Marchmont most likely because

A) Miss Marchmont understood that the hardship Lucy faced would make her grateful for the position.

B) Miss Marchmont felt sympathy for Lucy in her state of grief and aimed to alleviate her suffering.

C) Miss Marchmont believed that Lucy, due to her circumstances, would not find the job unbearable.

D) Miss Marchmont knew that Lucy had the required credentials and qualifications to be a suitable aide.

4

Which choice provides the best evidence for the answer to the previous question?

A) Lines 2-4 ("she was...years")

B) Lines 12-14 ("she, hearing...place")

C) Lines 19-20 ("yet, perhaps...tolerable")

D) Lines 35-36 ("I saw...vision")

5

The author uses the phrase "I still felt life at life's sources" (lines 38-39) to present Lucy as

A) resilient in spite of her outer appearance.

B) optimistic regardless of her personal loss.

C) decisive when faced with an important choice.

D) in denial of her true physical condition.

6

Which statement best describes a technique the author uses to represent Lucy's growing sense of duty as she bonds with Miss Marchmont?

A) The author provides examples of experiences Lucy shares with Miss Marchmont that solidify their growing friendship and trust.

B) The author emphasizes certain aspects of Miss Marchmont's mindset which Lucy willfully adopts as her own.

C) The author highlights the sacrifice Lucy undertakes for Miss Marchmont by depicting Lucy's deprivation of a life outdoors.

D) The author depicts Lucy's decreasing materialism as she becomes accustomed to a life of economic hardship.

7

Which choice provides the best evidence for the answer to the previous question?

A) Lines 42-44 ("Her service...reward")

B) Lines 44-47 ("I forgot...it")

C) Lines 49-51 ("I demanded...invalid")

D) Lines 51-54 ("In addition...trust")

CONTINUE

8

According to the passage, Lucy accepted a life in an environment of austerity because she believed that such a life would

A) allow her to better understand Miss Marchmont.

B) offer her lifelong fulfillment and friendship.

C) adequately prepare her for her old age.

D) immunize her against major disappointments.

9

What function does the eighth paragraph (lines 56-69) serve in the passage as a whole?

A) It reveals Lucy's feelings about her employment with Miss Marchmont.

B) It indicates that fate bars Lucy from living life on her own terms.

C) It foreshadows an event that occurs later in the passage.

D) It deviates from the narrative to reflect on the nature of fate.

10

The narration creates a sense of doom within Lucy's recounting of the "February night" (line 70) by

A) juxtaposing Lucy's panicked screams with Miss Marchmont's peaceful sleep.

B) using vivid imagery to depict the wind as an inescapable voice.

C) making a prediction about the fate of Miss Marchmont.

D) describing the wind as having a supernatural origin.

CONTINUE

Questions 1-10 are based on the following passage.
Chapter 7.5
Adapted from James Joyce, "Counterparts," published in the collection of linked short stories *Dubliners* (1914).

The bell rang furiously and, when Miss Parker went to the tube, a furious voice called out in a piercing North of Ireland accent:

Line
5

"Send Farrington here!"

Miss Parker returned to her machine, saying to a man who was writing at a desk:

"Mr. Alleyne wants you upstairs."

The man muttered "Blast him!" under his breath and pushed back his chair to stand up. When he stood up he was tall and of great bulk. He had a hanging face, dark wine-coloured, with fair eyebrows and moustache: his eyes bulged forward slightly and the whites of them were dirty. He lifted up the counter and, passing by the clients, went out of the office with a heavy step.

He went heavily upstairs until he came to the second landing, where a door bore a brass plate with the inscription Mr.. Alleyne. Here he halted, puffing with labour and vexation, and knocked. The shrill voice cried:

"Come in!"

The man entered Mr. Alleyne's room. Simultaneously Mr. Alleyne, a little man wearing gold-rimmed glasses on a clean-shaven face, shot his head up over a pile of documents. The head itself was so pink and hairless it seemed like a large egg reposing on the papers. Mr. Alleyne did not lose a moment:

"Farrington? What is the meaning of this? Why have I always to complain of you? May I ask you why you haven't made a copy of that contract between Bodley and Kirwan? I told you it must be ready by four o'clock."

"But Mr. Shelley said, sir——"

"Mr. Shelley said, sir.... Kindly attend to what I say and not to what Mr. Shelley says, sir. You have always some excuse or another for shirking work. Let me tell you that if the contract is not copied before this evening I'll lay the matter before Mr. Crosbie.... Do you hear me now?"

"Yes, sir."

"Do you hear me now?... Ay and another little matter! I might as well be talking to the wall as talking to you. Understand once for all that you get a half an hour for your lunch and not an hour and a half. How many courses do you want, I'd like to know.... Do you

mind me, now?"

"Yes, sir."

Mr. Alleyne bent his head again upon his pile of papers. The man stared fixedly at the polished skull which directed the affairs of Crosbie & Alleyne, gauging its fragility. A spasm of rage gripped his throat for a few moments and then passed, leaving after it a sharp sensation of thirst. The man recognised the sensation and felt that he must have a good night's drinking. The middle of the month was passed and, if he could get the copy done in time, Mr. Alleyne might give him an order on the cashier. He stood still, gazing fixedly at the head upon the pile of papers. Suddenly Mr. Alleyne began to upset all the papers, searching for something. Then, as if he had been unaware of the man's presence till that moment, he shot up his head again, saying:

"Eh? Are you going to stand there all day? Upon my word, Farrington, you take things easy!"

"I was waiting to see...."

"Very good, you needn't wait to see. Go downstairs and do your work."

The man walked heavily towards the door and, as he went out of the room, he heard Mr. Alleyne cry after him that if the contract was not copied by evening Mr. Crosbie would hear of the matter.

He returned to his desk in the lower office and counted the sheets which remained to be copied. He took up his pen and dipped it in the ink but he continued to stare stupidly at the last words he had written: In no case shall the said Bernard Bodley be.... The evening was falling and in a few minutes they would be lighting the gas: then he could write. He felt that he must slake the thirst in his throat. He stood up from his desk and, lifting the counter as before, passed out of the office. As he was passing out the chief clerk looked at him inquiringly.

"It's all right, Mr. Shelley," said the man, pointing with his finger to indicate the objective of his journey.

The chief clerk glanced at the hat-rack but, seeing the row complete, offered no remark. As soon as he was on the landing the man pulled a shepherd's plaid cap out of his pocket, put it on his head and ran quickly down the rickety stairs. From the street door he walked on furtively on the inner side of the path towards the corner and all at once dived into a doorway. He was now safe in the dark snug of O'Neill's shop.

1

Which of the following best summarizes the passage?

A) A character reluctant to undertake the task assigned to him comes to accept his duty.

B) A character reacts to being reprimanded by his employer by going into a fit of rage.

C) A character suppresses his frustration at work with a distraction.

D) A character faced with impossible expectations experiences a nervous breakdown at work.

2

Over the course of the passage, the narrative shifts from

A) the main character's outspoken feelings to his inner thoughts.

B) the depiction of one character's actions to an analysis of his motives.

C) the presentation of a character's problem to his formulation of a solution.

D) the objective description of an encounter to a character's subjective reaction.

3

The description of Farrington in lines 8-15 mainly creates which effect?

A) It portrays Farrington as a weary and unhappy employee.

B) It illustrates the effect the work environment has on its employees.

C) It foreshadows the ill fate about to befall the main character.

D) It reveals the inner workings of Farrington's mindset.

4

According to the passage, Mr. Alleyne's primary concern about Farrington is that he is

A) a drunkard.

B) an idiot.

C) a burden.

D) a slacker.

5

Which choice provides the best evidence for the answer to the previous question?

A) Lines 28-29 ("Why have...you")

B) Lines 35-36 ("You have...work")

C) Lines 41-43 ("Do you...you")

D) Lines 53-55 ("The man...drinking")

6

It can be reasonably inferred from the passage that if Farrington did not complete his contract by the deadline that was given to him by Mr. Alleyne

A) he would face punishment meted out by Mr. Alleyne.

B) his misconducts would be disclosed to Mr. Alleyne's partner.

C) he would be terminated from his position by Mr. Alleyne.

D) his behavior would be reported to Mr. Alleyne's supervisor.

7

The passage suggests which of the following about the relationship between Mr. Shelley and Farrington?

A) Mr. Shelley is aware of and familiar with Farrington's habits.

B) Mr. Shelley is an accomplice in Farrington's misdemeanors.

C) Mr. Shelley is sympathetic towards Farrington's actions.

D) Mr. Shelley is suspicious about Farrington's whereabouts.

CONTINUE

8

Which choice best supports the conclusion that Farrington intends to complete his work after having stepped out?

A) Lines 72-73 ("He returned...copied")

B) Lines 77-78 ("The evening...write")

C) Lines 79-82 ("He stood...inquiringly")

D) Lines 83-86 ("It's all...remark")

9

As used in line 75, "stupidly" most nearly means

A) blankly.

B) confusedly.

C) unintelligently.

D) carelessly.

10

What function does the last paragraph serve in the passage as a whole?

A) It highlights the urgency of Farrington's pursuit of relief.

B) It depicts Farrington's destination as obvious and expected.

C) It juxtaposes Farrington's discomfort at work to his feeling of accomplishment at O'Neill's.

D) It implies that Farrington's urge to drink is uncontrollable but not destructive.

Answer Key: CHAPTER SEVEN

Chapter 7.1
1. C
2. B
3. A
4. C
5. C
6. A
7. B
8. D
9. A
10. C

Chapter 7.2
1. A
2. D
3. A
4. B
5. A
6. A
7. A
8. C
9. B
10. D

Chapter 7.3
1. C
2. A
3. C
4. D
5. A
6. B
7. C
8. A
9. C
10. C

Chapter 7.4
1. C
2. C
3. C
4. C
5. A
6. B
7. A
8. D
9. B
10. B

Chapter 7.5
1. C
2. D
3. A
4. D
5. B
6. B
7. A
8. B
9. A
10. A

Answer Explanations

Chapter 7

Chapter 7.1 | *The Inn of Tranquility*

1) CORRECT ANSWER: C
In this passage, the narrator prominently uses the phrase "I remember" (lines 10 and 31) to clarify his observations: these observations concern a boot shop which is different from "most shops" (line 60) in its mood. This information supports C as the best answer, while the fact that the narrator (though respectful) is at some stages an adult interacting with a bootmaker eliminates A. B is problematic because the narrator is impressed (but not clearly influenced or CHANGED) by the shop, while D wrongly identifies Gessler (whose skills and background are well known to the narrator) as "mysterious".

2) CORRECT ANSWER: B
In the relevant paragraph, the narrator notes that he is "troubled . . . to account" (line 10) for the boots in Gessler's window, and after reflecting at length on these boots declares bootmaking itself "mysterious and wonderful" (line 30). This information indicates the narrator's fascination with Gessler's work: choose B and eliminate C, since the boots (not Gessler himself) are the focus here. A wrongly discusses the narrator's first encounter (as opposed to the narrator's RECURRING yet memorable contact with the boots), while D wrongly indicates that the narrator has made specific assumptions or conclusions (not that he is fascinated and TRYING to understand the boots).

3) CORRECT ANSWER: A
In lines 22-23, the narrator states that the boots in the window were so remarkable that their maker must have seen "the Soul of Boot": there is thus something transcendent or mystical about the boots. A is the best answer, while B and D both refer to assets that may be traits of remarkable boots but that the narrator does not EXPLICITLY link to his fascination or captivation. C is problematic because the passage suggests that the exceptional boots were made by Gessler himself, and were thus not of "unclear origin".

4) CORRECT ANSWER: C
See above for the explanation of the correct answer. A and B indicate that the narrator was unsettled or intrigued by the presence of the boots (though it later becomes apparent that they were Gessler's creations), while D indicates that Gessler's boots were long-lasting. Make sure not to take D as evidence for Question 3 D: the durability of the boots is impressive, but does not necessarily "captivate" or intrigue the narrator.

5) CORRECT ANSWER: C

The phrase "promoted to" describes the narrator at the age of fourteen, when the narrator met Mr. Gessler and had positive inklings (or impressions) regarding "himself and brother" (line 28). The narrator thus first met Mr. Gessler at this age and found that his thoughts about Gessler developed over time: C, "introduced to", is the best answer. A and B wrongly indicate that the narrator was in Gessler's industry (NOT that he was a customer), while D neglects the fact that the narrator had contact with the boots (and thus with Mr. Gessler) when Mr. Gessler made his father's boots.

6) CORRECT ANSWER: A

In lines 25-28, the narrator explains that his fully-formulated admiring thoughts about Gessler's craft came with age, but that "some inkling haunted" him as a youth regarding Gessler's boots. A is the best answer, since it indicates the formation of the narrator's thoughts over time. B wrongly indicates that the narrator never communicated his admiration (which he in fact does in line 33), C wrongly indicates that Gessler's shop has disappeared (a possibility that the narrative does not directly address), and D attributes the wrong motive (conveying admiration, not obtaining footwear) to the narrator's patronage of the shop.

7) CORRECT ANSWER: B

See above for the explanation of the correct answer. A indicates the narrator's admiration for the beauty of the boots (but does not align with an answer to the previous question), C records a time when the narrator conveyed his admiration, and D indicates that Gessler was committed to the art of bootmaking. Keep in mind that C can in fact be used to eliminate Question 6 B.

8) CORRECT ANSWER: D

The word "prototypes" refers to the remarkable boot "pairs" (line 22) in Gessler's window, beautiful specimens crafted by a man who must have seen "the Soul of Boot" (line 23). The prototypes are thus exceptional or even perfect, justifying D and eliminating the negative answer A. B and C raise the issue of WHEN the boots were crafted (not of HOW well crafted they were, the narrator's primary concern) and should thus be eliminated as out of context.

9) CORRECT ANSWER: A

In lines 40-41, the narrator explains that "leather is a sardonic substance" and connects the properties of leather to the "character" of Mr. Gessler's face. This information supports A. B wrongly takes the narrator's figurative comparison between the shop and a church (line 62) for a reference to actual church-going. C and D both ascribe faulty positives: Gessler's personality as he deals with other people is a minor point in the narrative and thus should be eliminated.

10) CORRECT ANSWER: C

The narrator prefaces the designated line references by noting that "there was never anybody" (line 63) in Mr. Gessler's shop; he then describes what happens under these expected circumstances, so that the use of "would" indicates predictability. C is the best answer, while the fact that the narrator is dealing with repeated PAST events can be used to eliminate A (future) and D (hypothetical). B is a trap answer: the narrator's visits to the shop are predictable in their events, but the narrator never indicates that these visits are "frequent" (only that they are clearly remembered).

Chapter 7.2 | *Bill the Bloodhound*

1) CORRECT ANSWER: A
The passage describes two characters: Henry Pitfield Rice, a detective who is committed to his job and is set on marrying, and Alice Weston, who objects to him on professional grounds and whose refusal to marry him "seemed final" (line 84). Both characters have strong personal convictions. A is the best choice, while the fact that Alice wants to determine her own way of life eliminates B. The characters do have set ideas (and may thus act strongly yet predictably, eliminating C) and act based on emotional attachments to their jobs and to specific plans (such as Henry's desire for Alice, eliminating D).

2) CORRECT ANSWER: D
The relevant paragraph indicates that Henry's job is to stand outside places (not to solve exciting mysteries) and refers to his occupation as "the unsensational doings of a quite commonplace young man" (lines 17-18). This information makes D an effective description of the paragraph. The real negative about Henry's job is that it is not glamorous or eventful, not that he lacks experience (eliminating A). B focuses on broad groups of detectives WITHOUT considering Henry's role (the real main topic), while C focuses only on lines 19-20 and neglects the fact that the recorded remarks are offhand comments (not systematic bullying).

3) CORRECT ANSWER: A
In lines 80-82, Alice explains that she is "on the stage, and [means] to stick there", in contrast to the other girls who want to leave life on the stage behind. A is thus the best answer, while B and D distort content from the third paragraph (which explains Henry's impressions of a few chorus girls, not chorus girls as a LARGER group). C is problematic because, although Alice does seem to take her job seriously, there is no clear indication that other chorus girls are lazy and uncommitted in contrast.

4) CORRECT ANSWER: B
The word "sensational" refers to Henry's assumption that the disclosure of his profession will be impressive: girls who hear that he is a detective usually greet him with "amazed admiration" (line 39). This information supports B. A and C both introduce themes from ELSEWHERE in the passage: Henry is a respectable man with romantic inclinations, but his disclosure is not ITSELF respectable or romantic. D is a trap: though positive, this answer illogically indicates that there are no OTHER detectives (when in fact such men are mentioned in the second paragraph).

5) CORRECT ANSWER: A
In lines 39-41, Henry is "chagrined" or disappointed because Alice regards detective work with "distinct disapproval"; this information supports A. Keep in mind that Alice is the ONLY one in Henry's experience to dislike his work (eliminating B) and that he fully accepts duties such as "creeping" until Alice disapproves of them (eliminating C). D is problematic because READERS run the danger of romanticizing Henry's work (according to the second paragraph), not Henry himself.

6) CORRECT ANSWER: A
See above for the explanation of the correct answer. B indicates that Henry wants Alice's approval (but does not directly mention his detective work), C indicates that Henry wants to veil his role (not make it seem better than it really is) because a detective is naturally

drawn to concealment, and D indicates that Henry must perform specific duties to keep his job. Make sure not to wrongly take B as evidence for Question 5 B, C as evidence for Question 5 D, or D as evidence for Question 5 C.

7) CORRECT ANSWER: A

Regarding Henry's proposal to Alice, the narrator notes that Henry "worked patiently and well before actually putting his fortune to the test" (lines 78-79) or tried to gain her trust before taking action and actually making the proposal. A is the best answer, while the length of time between Henry's early acquaintance with Alice and his actual proposal can be used to eliminate B, C, and D, which all indicate that he moved much more quickly.

8) CORRECT ANSWER: C

Alice has a profession on the stage as a chorus girl; referring to her own line of work, she informs Henry that "one thing I'll never do is marry someone who isn't in the profession" (lines 82-83). Alice also says that she'd marry Henry if his profession were different (lines 79-80, eliminating A) and does not object to his company. At most, she has somewhat negative questions about his job (eliminating B and D as both too negative).

9) CORRECT ANSWER: B

In lines 84-86, the narrator explains that Henry "did not wholly despair" and was resolute in pursuing Alice, just as he was resolute in waiting outside restaurants for his detective work. This information supports B. Henry does not express a desire to leave his profession (unpleasant though some aspects of it may be, eliminating A and D), while his feelings ARE to some extent requited because Alice is also "fond" (line 75) of him (eliminating C).

10) CORRECT ANSWER: D

See above for the explanation of the correct answer. A describes the growing bond between Henry and Alice, B indicates the possibility that Henry's affection for Alice will weaken, and C indicates that Alice would willingly marry Henry under other professional circumstances. Use A and C to eliminate NEGATIVE answers to the previous question, and makes sure not to wrongly take B (which describes an unfulfilled potentiality ONLY) as evidence for Question 9 C.

Chapter 7.3 | *Castaway*

1) CORRECT ANSWER: C

Early in the passage, Kiran expresses the belief that it would not do her "any harm to go home now" (line 18), though later it is clear that she has settled in to take care of Nilkanta and "might be persuaded to stay on for some time longer" (lines 77-78). This information supports C and eliminates D, since Kiran's attitude towards staying ITSELF (not the motive behind a stable decision) is what changes. A is problematic because Kiran seems consistently willful (rather than growing more or less submissive to Sharat), while B is problematic because, even though Kiran's state of health has changed (lines 39-40), Sharat's "perspective" on this issue does not change over the course of the passage.

2) CORRECT ANSWER: A

Kiran opposes Sharat's wish that she stay on at the village (lines 13-18), continues to "argue" (line 51) with him, and refuses to listen to his warnings against spoiling Nilkanta (lines 92-93). This information supports A and can be used to eliminate strongly positive answers such as C and D. B is problematic because the boy's presence has not caused or created animosity: it has simply intensified a state of tension that already existed.

3) CORRECT ANSWER: C

In lines 46-48, the narrator explains that the normally lively and sociable Kiran disliked her surroundings because "There was nothing to do, there were no interesting neighbours" and because her life is confined to medicine and dieting. C is the best answer, while Kiran's MAIN objection to the medical treatment is its impact on her lifestyle (not to its perceived effectiveness or ineffectiveness, eliminating both A and D). B is a trap answer; although Kiran is liked by her family, there is no sign that she wants exclusively to be reunited with them: she wants company GENERALLY, whether provided by her family or by other people.

4) CORRECT ANSWER: D

See above for the explanation of the correct answer. A indicates Kiran's belief that she has been cured, B indicates that Kiran is liked by her family, and C indicates that Kiran is still quite weak. Make sure not to wrongly take A as evidence for Question 3 A (which at best decribes a questionable argument or secondary motive), B as evidence for Question 3 B, or C as evidence for Question 3 D.

5) CORRECT ANSWER: A

The word "shameless" describes the "fuss" (line 29) that Sharat has made on Kiran's account; his actions are seen by the town wiseacres as based on ridiculous, over-sensitive premises, or are "foolish". A is the best answer, while B wrongly indicates that Sharat is acting immorally and C wrongly indicates that he is rebelling (NOT trying to help his wife). D is a trap answer: staying in a town is not itself an unlikely or "impractical" idea, though Kiran's reasoning for doing so (as indicated in A) is deemed foolish.

6) CORRECT ANSWER: B

The "wiseacres" are critical of Sharat's idea that his wife needs "a change of air" (30) and mock him through exaggeration, flippantly suggesting that "the folk of the place to which he meant to take her were immortal" (lines 32-33). The find the idea of locating away from Chandernagore needless and pointless, so that B is the best answer. Keep in mind that the wiseacres criticize Sharat's methods, not the methods of medical "charlatans" (eliminating A) or the perceptions of Kiran's illness (which is in fact severe, eliminating D). The wiseacres are critical commentators, not individuals who have any involvement in medical cures (eliminating C).

7) CORRECT ANSWER: C

The narrator explains that Sharat "turned a deaf ear" (line 35) to the critical wiseacres and prioritized Kiran's well-being over the opinions of the community (lines 36-37). This information supports C, while Sharat primarily acts to help Kiran (not to go against the wiseacres, eliminating A and B). Beyond re-location and rest, the narrator never explains what exactly Kiran's cure entails (so that D, with its description of a "nontraditional" cure, raises a topic that is never addressed in the passage).

8) CORRECT ANSWER: A

In lines 75-78, Sharat judges that the boy's arrival is "rather a good thing" because this turn of events may cause his wife to stay longer: A is an effective answer, while B is wrongly negative. Although the boy does survive the storm, Sharat is not explicitly described displaying "gratitude" or any other reaction to the boy's feat (eliminating C). And although the boy may bring out Kiran's compassion, Sharat's reaction to his wife's show of compassion is not recorded in the text either (eliminating D).

9) CORRECT ANSWER: C

See above for the explanation of the correct answer. A describes how Kiran helped the boy after his arrival, B explains that Kiran became attached to the boy on account of his death-defying experience, and D indicates that Kiran went against Sharat's wishes in spoiling the boy. Do not wrongly take A as evidence for Question 8 D, B as evidence for Question 8 C, or D as evidence for Question 8 B.

10) CORRECT ANSWER: C

The narrator explains that Sharat and his mother "changed their opinion" (line 79) of the boy because the boy made inappropriate uses of Sharat's possessions and then gathered "a devoted band of boys" (line 88) who raided the village for fruit. C is the best answer, while A wrongly assumes that Kiran's growing affection for the boy corresponds to lessening affection for Sharat (a possibility that the narrative does not explicitly present). B overstates the boy's popularity (among other boys, NOT within the entire neighborhood, which he in fact disrupts), while D is inaccurate because the boy is a diversion who arguably HELPS Kiran to recover, not an impediment to Sharat's care for her.

Chapter 7.4 | *Villette*

1) CORRECT ANSWER: C

In the passage, the narrator "reflected" on the employment that Miss Marchmont has proposed to her and finds that her emotions change from positive to negative (lines 21-30), then explains that she might have "crawled on with [Miss Marchmont] for twenty years (lines 56-57) had not a new chain of events been set in motion. This information supports C, while the rather formal encounter with Miss Marchmont is not unexpected or surprising (eliminating A) and the job is limiting (not fulfilling, eliminating B). D refers only to evidence from a single, confined portion of the passage (lines 40-55, which also contain NEGATIVE sentiments) and should thus be eliminated as too narrow to fulfill the question.

2) CORRECT ANSWER: C

The word "character" refers to Miss Marchmont, of whom the narrator has heard and who is reputed to be "eccentric" (line 7). Since the word "character" occurs in the contexts of reports and reputation, C is the best answer. A, B, and D already assume that the narrator is familiar with Miss Marchmont BEFOREHAND; in contrast, the narrator is meeting Miss Marchmont for the first time, and so would have no way to judge Miss Marchmont's impression, demeanor, or personality previously. These answers can also be eliminated because they do not directly reflect the context of what the narrator has "heard" (line 5).

3) CORRECT ANSWER: C

In line 19-20, Miss Marchmont tells Lucy that the job "may appear tolerable" in contrast to Lucy's recent circumstances, or may have some measure of appeal. This information supports C. Keep in mind that Miss Marchmont is described as irritable and exacting (line 10) and summons Lucy for pragmatic reasons: this evidence eliminates the strong positives in A and B. D is a trap answer: it is not clear that ANY credentials or qualifications are necessary for the position, though Miss Marchmont does seem to require a patient and attentive employee.

4) CORRECT ANSWER: C

See above for the explanation of the correct answer. A explains Miss Marchmont's condition, B explains that Miss Marchmont sent for Lucy for practical reasons (a theme that none of the answers to the previous question address), and D indicates that Lucy perceives her own tired state. Make sure not to wrongly take B or D as evidence for Question 3 A or question 3 B: Miss Marchmont is aware that Lucy is in a bad state, but is NOT actually offering her the job on this account.

5) CORRECT ANSWER: A

The line reference is used to explain Lucy's idea that her depleted state is "chiefly external" (line 38); she still feels inward life or power despite apparent hardship. Choose A as an effective choice and eliminate D, which wrongly indicates that Lucy is not aware of her external state. B (optimism or hopefulness) and C (decisiveness or assertiveness) do in fact raise positive qualities, but NOT the qualities of vitality and resilience that are needed to fit the context.

6) CORRECT ANSWER: B

In lines 42-44, Lucy lists various positive and negative responses from Miss Marchmont, and then explains that she greeted each of Miss Marchmont's moods or circumstances with a concordant positive or negative on her end. This information supports B, while A wrongly construes the relationship as mostly positive and C wrongly construes the relationship as mostly negative (when in fact it combines strong positives with strong negatives). D applies an inappropriate negative to the relationship: Lucy is deprived of the word outside Miss Marchmont's household, but Miss Marchmont's household ITSELF is stable because she is "a woman of fortune" (line 1).

7) CORRECT ANSWER: A

See above for the explanation of the correct answer. B indicates Lucy's isolation from the outside world, C indicates that Lucy is adopting aspects of Miss Marchmont's own lifestyle, and D indicates that Lucy found specific aspects of Miss Marchmont's personality admirable and beneficial. Make sure not to align B with Question 6 C, C with Question 6 D, or D with Question 6 A.

8) CORRECT ANSWER: D

Lucy explains that she wanted "to escape occasional great agonies" (line 66) by living a life of "privation and small pains" (line 67); in other words, she wants to prevent hardship in her own life by adjusting her lifestyle, so that D is the best answer. A and B refer to side effects of Lucy's chosen lifestyle (and are mostly products of her contact with Miss Marchmont, not of "austerity" itself), while C distorts a theme of the passage: Lucy becomes like the aged Miss Marchmont, but is not TRYING to prepare herself for old age.

9) CORRECT ANSWER: B

In the relevant paragraph, Lucy explains that despite the "human affection" (line 61) that her situation entails, Fate and Providence would not allow her to continue in this lifestyle: she faces a change from the way of living that she has come to accept, so that B is the best answer. Keep in mind that Lucy's feelings about Miss Marchmont are mainly revealed in the PREVIOUS paragraph (eliminating A) and that no specific allusions to the nighttime event that follows are made (eliminating C, since the real change in Lucy's situation will presumably occur AFTER the event). D is a trap answer: the reflection on fate is not a "deviation", but a means of explaining how Lucy's life will eventually unfold.

10) CORRECT ANSWER: B

In the description of the February night, Lucy mentions a melancholy "wailing" (line 75) wind that makes a "plaint, piteous and disconsolate" (line 78). This imagery of sadness and suffering creates an ominous mood, so that B is an effective answer. Although Lucy feels INWARD turmoil, she does not scream (eliminating A) and does not in fact make a specific prediction about what will happen to Miss Marchmont (even though the IMAGERY indicates a possible negative fate, eliminating C). D is a faulty answer because the wind is simply made to SEEM supernatural through personification; it does not have an ACTUAL supernatural origin.

Chapter 7.5 | *Counterparts*

1) CORRECT ANSWER: C

In the passage, Farrington feels "vexation" (line 19) and "A spasm of rage" (line 51) in relation to how he is treated at work, but stifles these emotions and eventually escapes to the refuge of "O'Neill's shop" (line 92). This information supports C and can be used to eliminate A (which implies that Farrington is able to overcome his frustration). B and D both wrongly assume that Farrington lets his strong negative emotions lead to dramatic action, and should thus be eliminated as inaccurate.

2) CORRECT ANSWER: D

While the early stages of the narrative focus on Farrington's appearance and movements (lines 8-15) and record his exchange with Mr. Alleyne, the later stages focus on Farrington's private emotions and impulses, such as his "spasm of rage" (line 51) and his "sharp sensation of thirst (line 53). This information supports D. Keep in mind that Farrington suppresses many of his negative feelings towards Mr. Alleyne (making "outspoken" in A inaccurate) and that the "motives" for his earlier actions at work are less of an emphasis than his intense dislike and his desire to escape (making B problematic). C employs faulty logic: Farrington does not necessarily SOLVE his problems at work by leaving, and instead simply DISREGARDS them for the time being.

3) CORRECT ANSWER: A

In the relevant lines, the large Farrington mutters a negative comment and moves about the office "with a heavy step"; he is not energetic and clearly does not enjoy his present situation, making A an effective choice. Farrington is the sole focus here (not OTHER employees as well, eliminating B) and neither his fate nor the precise content of Mr. Alleyne's reason for seeing Farrington is clearly indicated in these lines (eliminating C). These lines are also an EXTERNAL description of Farrington's features, size, and movements, so that D ("inner workings") introduces the wrong focus.

4) CORRECT ANSWER: D

In lines 35-36, Mr. Alleyne accuses Farrington of always having "some excuse or other for shirking [or avoiding] work". This evidence supports D as an appropriate answer. A introduces a tempting criticism (considering Farrington's growing desire to get a drink), but not a criticism that Mr. Alleyne himself directs at Farrington. B and C indicate character flaws that Mr. Alleyne would most likely attribute to Farrington, but that are secondary in light of Mr. Alleyne's PRIMARY concern with Farrington's poor work ethic.

5) CORRECT ANSWER: B

See above for the explanation of the correct answer. A indicates that Mr. Alleyne feels negative sentiments regarding Farrington (but does not specify WHY), C indicates that Mr. Alleyne finds Farrington uncomprehending, and D indicates Farrington's own inclination to drink (but does not clearly record Mr. Alleyne's ideas). C is a trap answer; it gives a secondary reason (Farrington's uncomprehending nature) for Mr. Farrington's dislike, which is premised PRIMARILY on Farrington's poor work.

6) CORRECT ANSWER: B

Mr. Alleyne threatens to alert Mr. Crosbie to Farrington's relatively poor work on the contract (lines 38 and 70-71); it is indicated in lines 49-51 that Crosbie shares control of the company with Alleyne, or is his business partner. B is an effective answer. A wrongly neglects the role of Mr. Crosbie, C indicates a form of punishment that the critical Mr. Alleyne might want to administer (but does not actually mention), and D wrongly characterizes Mr. Crosbie as Mr. Alleyne's superior, not as his partner.

7) CORRECT ANSWER: A

While stepping out of the office, Farrington passes Mr. Shelley and points "with his finger to indicate the objective of his journey" (line 84). Mr. Shelley is aware of the significance of this gesture without any further explanation, and is thus aware of Farrington's usual destinations or habits. A is the best answer. Although Mr. Shelley allows Farrington to leave the office, it is not clear that he is motivated to do so by loyalty or sympathy (eliminating overly positive answers such as B and C). If anything, Mr. Shelley seems somewhat indifferent to Farrington and accommodates his work, not "suspicious" (eliminating D).

8) CORRECT ANSWER: B

In lines 77-78, Farrington muses that in a few minutes the gas lamps will be lighted and that "then he could write". He intends to start work after a short delay, so that B is an effective answer. A simply indicates that Farrington is determining the amount of work that remains (NOT that he will soon complete the work), C indicates that Farrington is leaving the office, and D indicates that he is going to an allowed destination but NOT that he will finish his work when he returns.

9) CORRECT ANSWER: A

The word "stupidly" describes how Farrington stares at "the last words he had written" (lines 75-76). He cannot continue with his work, so that his demeanor would be best described as without meaningful activity or emotion, or as "blank". A is the best answer. B is out of scope (since Farrington's problem is that he does not feel like continuing the work, NOT that he does not understand the work); C and D are both critical words that Mr. Alleyne might apply to Farrington, but that are not directly appropriate to Farrington's uninspired or "blank" state here.

10) CORRECT ANSWER: A

In the final paragraph, Farrington is described as seeking relief in a dramatic and energetic fashion: he "ran quickly" from the office and "dived" into a new location that made him feel "now safe". This information supports A. B is inaccurate because the exact destination (O'Neill's shop) has not been mentioned before in the passage, C distorts the positive implications of O'Neill's shop (where Farrington simply feels "safe", not "accomplished"), and D raises the issue of Farrington's drinking habits (which are NOT discussed, even though he may in fact drink at his destination).

CHAPTER EIGHT

Questions 1-10 are based on the following passage.
Chapter 8.1

The following is an excerpt from *Mothwise* (1904) by Knut Hamsun.

The priest was not a rich man, far from it. It was only his poor little wife who was full of thoughtless, luxurious fancies she had been brought up with, and
Line wanted a host of servants and such. There was nothing
5 for her to do herself in the house; they had no children, and she had never learned housekeeping, and that was why she was forever hatching childish ideas out of her little head. A sweet and lovely torment in the house she was.
10 Heavens alive, how the good priest had fought his comical battles with his wife again and again, trying to teach her a scrap of sense and thought and order! He picked up threads and bits of paper from the floor, put odds and ends of things in their proper places, closed
15 the door after her, tended the stoves, and screwed the ventilators as was needed. When his wife went out, he would make a tour of the rooms and see the state she had left them in: hairpins here, there, and everywhere; combs full of combings; handkerchiefs lying about;
20 chairs piled up with garments. And he shuddered and put things straight again.

He had scolded and entreated at first, with some effect; his wife admitted he was right, and promised to improve. And then she would get up early the next
25 morning and set about putting things in order, like a child in a sudden fit of earnestness, playing "grown-up peoples." But the fit never lasted; a few days after all was as before. It never occurred to her to wonder at the disorder when it appeared once more; on the contrary,
30 she could not understand why her husband should begin again with his constant discontent. "I knocked over that dish and it smashed," she would say. "It was only a cheap thing, so it doesn't matter."—"But the pieces have been lying about ever since this morning,"
35 he answered.

After a time, the priest grew hardened to it all, and gave up his daily protest; he still went on setting in order and putting things straight, but it was with compressed lips and as few words as might be. He felt
40 at times that she was to be pitied. There she was, going about so pleasantly, a trifle thin, and poorly dressed, yet never uttering a sigh at her poverty, though she had been brought up to lack for nothing. She would sit and sew, altering her dresses that had been altered so many
45 times already, humming over her work as cheerfully as a young girl. Then suddenly she would throw down

her work, leave everything strewed as it fell, and go off for a walk. And chairs and tables might be left for days strewn with tacked sleeves and unpicked skirts.
50 It was an old habit of hers from her youth at home to go fluttering about among the shops; she delighted in buying things. She could always find some use for remnants of material, bits of ribbon, combs and perfumes and toilet trifles, odd little metal things,
55 matchboxes, and the like. Much better buy a big thing and have done with it, thought her husband; never mind if it were expensive and brought him into debt. He might try to write a book, a popular Church history, or something, and pay for it that way.
60 And so the years passed. There were frequent little quarrels, but the two were fond of each other none the less, as long as the priest did not interfere too much. But yesterday he had noticed a couple of blankets left out in the rain. Should he tell someone? Then
65 suddenly he saw his wife coming back from her walk. She would notice them herself, no doubt. But she went straight up to her room, so he went out himself and brought the blankets in.

And so the matter might have passed off, and no
70 more said. But the priest could not keep his peace. In the evening his wife asked for the blankets. They were brought. "They're wet," said she. "They would have been wetter if I hadn't fetched them in out of the rain," said her husband.
75 But his wife was offended. Was there any need to make such a fuss about a drop of rain or so? "Oh, but you're unreasonable," she said; "always bothering about all sorts of things."

"I wish I were not obliged to bother about such
80 things," said he. "Just look at your washing-basin now; what's it doing on the bed?"

"I put it there because there was no room anywhere else."

"If you had another wash-stand, it would be all the
85 same," said he. "You'd have that loaded up with other things too in no time."

Then she lost patience: "Oh, how can you be so unreasonable; really, I think you must be ill. I can't bear any more of it, I can't!"
90 But a moment after it was all forgotten, and her kind heart forgave him. Careless and happy she was; it was her nature.

CONTINUE

1

The passage as a whole presents the priest's wife as the type of person who

A) prioritizes her own well-being above that of others.

B) is demanding and spoiled due to her wealthy upbringing.

C) is ignorant of the troubles within her marriage.

D) tends to justify her behavior by trivializing the issue.

2

According to the passage, the marriage between the priest and his wife can best be described as

A) romantically fulfilling.

B) fundamentally strong.

C) strained by hardship.

D) fraught with hostility.

3

The main purpose of the first paragraph is to

A) depict the priest and his wife as struggling financially.

B) provide context for why the priest's wife is a nuisance.

C) portray the priest's wife as bored with her household duties.

D) characterize the priest's wife as prone to irrational impulses.

4

As used in line 11, "comical" most nearly means

A) playful.

B) absurd.

C) humorous.

D) petty.

5

Which statement best describes a technique the narrator uses to represent the effect the wife's clutter has on the priest?

A) The narrator underscores the overwhelming nature of the clutter by listing the abundance of chores the priest must habitually undertake.

B) The narrator emphasizes the nonchalant attitude of the priest towards the clutter by depicting his cleaning routine as effortless.

C) The narrator highlights the priest's bewilderment with the clutter by describing the state of the house as illogical and senseless.

D) The narrator reveals the priest's unhealthy fixation with the clutter by portraying him as becoming increasingly obsessed with tidiness.

6

Over the course of the third and fourth paragraphs (lines 22-59) the priest's attitude shifts from

A) persistence to resignation.

B) denial to acceptance.

C) optimism to disappointment.

D) annoyance to resentment.

7

Which choice provides the best evidence for the claim that the wife perceives her husband as a nitpicker?

A) Lines 28-29 ("It never...more")

B) Lines 32-33 ("It was...matter")

C) Lines 75-76 ("Was there...so")

D) Lines 87-88 ("Oh, how...ill")

CONTINUE

8

With which of the following statements about his wife's shopping habits would the priest most likely agree?

A) Her shopping impulses are reflective of an emotional emptiness resulting from an unfulfilling marriage.

B) Her extravagant spending habits cannot be helped as they are rooted in her privileged upbringing.

C) She need not shop so frugally since he is willing to make the necessary sacrifices to meet her needs.

D) She is an impractical spender since she wastes money on items that have no significant value to him.

9

Which choice provides the best evidence for the answer to the previous question?

A) Lines 39-43 ("He felt...nothing")

B) Lines 50-52 ("It was...things")

C) Lines 52-55 ("She could...like")

D) Lines 55-59 ("Much better...way")

10

In context of the passage as a whole, the conversation between the priest and his wife concerning the wet blankets primarily serves to

A) suggest that the priest and his wife have irreconcilable differences.

B) hint at the wife's underlying unhappiness with her marriage.

C) illustrate the occasional flare-up in an otherwise settled matter.

D) highlight the contentious nature of the priest's accusations.

CONTINUE

Questions 1-10 are based on the following passage.
Chapter 8.2
Adapted from Edith Wharton, *Mrs. Manstey's View* (1891).

Left to herself, old Mrs. Manstey turned once more to the window. How lovely the view was that day! The blue sky with its round clouds shed a
Line brightness over everything; the ailanthus had put on a
5 tinge of yellow-green, the hyacinths were budding, the magnolia flowers looked more than ever like rosettes carved in alabaster. Soon the wistaria would bloom, then the horse-chestnut; but not for her. Between her eyes and them a barrier of brick and mortar would
10 swiftly rise; presently even the spire would disappear, and all her radiant world be blotted out. . .

Early the next day she was up and at the window. It was raining, but even through the slanting gray gauze the scene had its charm—and then the rain was
15 so good for the trees. She had noticed the day before that the ailanthus was growing dusty.

"Of course I might move," said Mrs. Manstey aloud, and turning from the window she looked about her room. She might move, of course; so might she be
20 flayed alive; but she was not likely to survive either operation. The room, though far less important to her happiness than the view, was as much a part of her existence. She had lived in it seventeen years. She knew every stain on the wall-paper, every rent in the
25 carpet; the light fell in a certain way on her engravings, her books had grown shabby on their shelves, her bulbs and ivy were used to their window and knew which way to lean to the sun. "We are all too old to move," she said. . .

30 On Sunday afternoon a card was brought to Mrs. Black, as she was engaged in gathering up the fragments of the boarders' dinner in the basement. The card, black-edged, bore Mrs. Manstey's name.

"One of Mrs. Sampson's boarders; wants to move,
35 I suppose. Well, I can give her a room next year in the extension. Dinah," said Mrs. Black, "tell the lady I'll be upstairs in a minute."

Mrs. Black found Mrs. Manstey standing in the long parlor garnished with statuettes and
40 antimacassars; in that house she could not sit down.

Stooping hurriedly to open the register, which let out a cloud of dust, Mrs. Black advanced on her visitor.

"I'm happy to meet you, Mrs. Manstey; take a seat, please," the landlady remarked in her prosperous
45 voice, the voice of a woman who can afford to build extensions. There was no help for it; Mrs. Manstey sat

down.

"Is there anything I can do for you, ma'am?" Mrs. Black continued. "My house is full at present, but I am
50 going to build an extension, and—"

"It is about the extension that I wish to speak," said Mrs. Manstey, suddenly. "I am a poor woman, Mrs. Black, and I have never been a happy one. I shall have to talk about myself first to—to make you
55 understand."

Mrs. Black, astonished but imperturbable, bowed at this parenthesis.

"I never had what I wanted," Mrs. Manstey continued. "It was always one disappointment after
60 another. For years I wanted to live in the country. I dreamed and dreamed about it; but we never could manage it. There was no sunny window in our house, and so all my plants died. . . I have grown a little infirm, as you see, and I don't get out often; only
65 on fine days, if I am feeling very well. So you can understand my sitting a great deal in my window—the back window on the third floor—"

"Well, Mrs. Manstey," said Mrs. Black, liberally, "I could give you a back room, I dare say; one of the
70 new rooms in the ex—"

"But I don't want to move; I can't move," said Mrs. Manstey, almost with a scream. "And I came to tell you that if you build that extension I shall have no view from my window—no view! Do you
75 understand?"

Mrs. Black thought herself face to face with a lunatic, and she had always heard that lunatics must be humored.

"Dear me, dear me," she remarked, pushing her
80 chair back a little way, "that is too bad, isn't it? Why, I never thought of that. To be sure, the extension WILL interfere with your view, Mrs. Manstey."

"You do understand?" Mrs. Manstey gasped.

"Of course I do. And I'm real sorry about it, too.
85 But there, don't you worry, Mrs. Manstey. I guess we can fix that all right."

Mrs. Manstey rose from her seat, and Mrs. Black slipped toward the door.

"What do you mean by fixing it? Do you mean
90 that I can induce you to change your mind about the extension? Oh, Mrs. Black, listen to me. I have two thousand dollars in the bank and I could manage, I know I could manage, to give you a thousand if—" Mrs. Manstey paused; the tears were rolling down her
95 cheeks.

"There, there, Mrs. Manstey, don't you worry," repeated Mrs. Black, soothingly. "I am sure we can settle it. I am sorry that I can't stay and talk about it

CONTINUE →

any longer, but this is such a busy time of day, with
100 supper to get—"

Her hand was on the door-knob, but with sudden
vigor Mrs. Manstey seized her wrist.

"You are not giving me a definite answer. Do you
mean to say that you accept my proposition?"
105   "Why, I'll think it over, Mrs. Manstey, certainly I
will. I wouldn't annoy you for the world—"

1

Over the course of the first paragraph, the primary focus
shifts from

A) the current view Mrs. Manstey enjoys to the future
alteration of that view.

B) the physical setting of the scene to Mrs. Manstey's
inner thoughts.

C) Mrs. Manstey's feeling of contentment to her growing
anxiety about a structure.

D) a depiction of a daily routine to a threatening disruption
to that routine.

2

The narrator mainly presents Mrs. Manstey as the type of
person who

A) is strong-willed and assertive.

B) has always faced dissatisfaction.

C) is unable to deal with change.

D) prefers to spend time outdoors.

3

Which choice provides the best evidence for the claim
that Mrs. Manstey notices the slightest change in her
surroundings?

A) Lines 14-16 ("then the...dusty")

B) Lines 23-25 ("She knew...carpet")

C) Lines 58-60 ("I never...another")

D) Lines 65-67 ("So you...floor")

4

In lines 23-28, ("She knew...sun") the description of
Mrs. Manstey's room supports the narrator's claim that
Mrs. Manstey found her room to be

A) hospitable and welcoming.

B) comforting and familiar.

C) decrepit and worn.

D) calming and relaxing.

5

Which of the following best characterizes Mrs. Black's
profession as a landlady?

A) It necessitates a fast-paced lifestyle and busy
schedule.

B) It affords her a degree of privacy and distance from
her clients.

C) It entails a significant amount of hands-on
involvement.

D) It requires empathy when dealing with unusual
requests from customers.

6

Which choice provides the best evidence for the answer
to the previous question?

A) Lines 30-32 ("On Sunday...basement")

B) Lines 44-46 ("the landlady...extensions")

C) Lines 56-57 ("Mrs. Black...parenthesis")

D) Lines 98-100 ("I am...get")

7

As used in line 42, "advanced on" most nearly means

A) approached.

B) greeted.

C) confronted.

D) encountered.

CONTINUE

8

Over the course of the conversation between Mrs. Manstey and Mrs. Black, the narrator presents a contrast between

A) Mrs. Manstey's earnest approach and Mrs. Black's evasive responses.

B) Mrs. Manstey's firm negotiation tactics and Mrs. Black's ambiguous answers.

C) Mrs. Manstey's respectful demeanor and Mrs. Black's patronizing attitude.

D) Mrs. Manstey's ardent pleas and Mrs. Black's flippant dismissal of those requests.

9

It can be inferred from the passage that Mrs. Manstey's tears are caused mainly by her

A) realization that her endeavors are misunderstood.

B) feelings of desperation to keep her view.

C) joy that Mrs. Black is considering her offer.

D) desire to elicit sympathy from Mrs. Black.

10

According to the passage, Mrs. Manstey seizes Mrs. Black's wrist primarily in order to

A) force Mrs. Black to accept her proposition.

B) prompt Mrs. Black to provide her with an answer.

C) show her commitment to resolving the matter.

D) prevent Mrs. Black from leaving the room.

CONTINUE

Questions 1-10 are based on the following passage.
Chapter 8.3
Adapted from Anton Chekhov, *An Upheaval* (1886). Translated by Constance Garnett.

Mashenka Pavletsky, a young girl who had only just finished her studies at a boarding school, returning from a walk to the house of the Kushkins, with whom
Line she was living as a governess, found the household in a
5 terrible turmoil. . .

"Madame Kushkin is in a fit, most likely, or else she has quarrelled with her husband," thought Mashenka.

In the hall and in the corridor she met maid-
10 servants. One of them was crying. Then Mashenka saw, running out of her room, the master of the house himself, Nikolay Sergeitch, a little man with a flabby face and a bald head, though he was not old. He was red in the face and twitching all over. He passed the
15 governess without noticing her, and throwing up his arms, exclaimed:

"Oh, how horrible it is! How tactless! How stupid! How barbarous! Abominable!"

Mashenka went into her room, and then, for the
20 first time in her life, it was her lot to experience in all its acuteness the feeling that is so familiar to persons in dependent positions, who eat the bread of the rich and powerful, and cannot speak their minds. There was a search going on in her room. The lady of the house,
25 Fedosya Vassilyevna, a stout, broad-shouldered, uncouth woman with thick black eyebrows, a faintly perceptible moustache, and red hands, who was exactly like a plain, illiterate cook in face and manners, was standing, without her cap on, at the table, putting back into
30 Mashenka's workbag balls of wool, scraps of materials, and bits of paper.... Evidently the governess's arrival took her by surprise, since, on looking round and seeing the girl's pale and astonished face, she was a little taken aback, and muttered:

35 "Pardon. I ... I upset it accidentally.... My sleeve caught in it ..."

And saying something more, Madame Kushkin rustled her long skirts and went out. Mashenka looked round her room with wondering eyes, and, unable to
40 understand it, not knowing what to think, shrugged her shoulders, and turned cold with dismay. . . The whatnot with her books on it, the things on the table, the bed—all bore fresh traces of a search. Her linen-basket, too. The linen had been carefully folded, but it was not in the
45 same order as Mashenka had left it when she went out. So the search had been thorough, most thorough. But

what was it for? Why? What had happened? Mashenka remembered the excited porter, the general turmoil which was still going on, the weeping servant-girl;
50 had it not all some connection with the search that had just been made in her room? Was not she mixed up in something dreadful? Mashenka turned pale, and feeling cold all over, sank on to her linen-basket.

A maid-servant came into the room.
55 "Liza, you don't know why they have been rummaging in my room?" the governess asked her.

"Mistress has lost a brooch worth two thousand," said Liza.

"Yes, but why have they been rummaging in my
60 room?"

"They've been searching every one, miss. They've searched all my things, too. They stripped us all naked and searched us.... God knows, miss, I never went near her toilet-table, let alone touching the brooch. I shall say
65 the same at the police-station."

"But ... why have they been rummaging here?" the governess still wondered.

"A brooch has been stolen, I tell you. The mistress has been rummaging in everything with her own hands.
70 She even searched Mihailo, the porter, herself. It's a perfect disgrace! Nikolay Sergeitch simply looks on and cackles like a hen. But you've no need to tremble like that, miss. They found nothing here. You've nothing to be afraid of if you didn't take the brooch."

75 "But, Liza, it's vile ... it's insulting," said Mashenka, breathless with indignation. "It's so mean, so low! What right had she to suspect me and to rummage in my things?"

"You are living with strangers, miss," sighed Liza.
80 "Though you are a young lady, still you are ... as it were ... a servant.... It's not like living with your papa and mamma."

Mashenka threw herself on the bed and sobbed bitterly. Never in her life had she been subjected to such
85 an outrage, never had she been so deeply insulted.... She, well-educated, refined, the daughter of a teacher, was suspected of theft; she had been searched like a street-walker! She could not imagine a greater insult. And to this feeling of resentment was added an oppressive
90 dread of what would come next.

CONTINUE ▶

1

Which choice best summarizes the passage?

A) One character feels degraded after learning she had been a subject of a search.

B) One character is unexpectedly and unfairly accused of a crime by her employers.

C) One character is confronted with a dilemma soon after beginning her first job.

D) One character feels overwhelmed when she misunderstands a series of events.

2

Which of the following statements best describes the role of the narrator in the passage?

A) The narrator conveys Mashenka's reactions to the search and the effects it has on her.

B) The narrator contrasts Mashenka's assumptions with the true nature of her situation.

C) The narrator evokes sympathy by justifying Mashenka's thoughts and comments on the search.

D) The narrator reveals Mashenka's true perceptions of her employers as inconsistent with her actions.

3

The passage as a whole presents Mashenka as the type of person who

A) has been sheltered by her parents.

B) imposes her values on others.

C) is inexperienced and naive.

D) is guided by a strong sense of morality.

4

Which choice provides the best evidence for the claim that in the search, Mashenka was experiencing an unprecedented sense of oppression?

A) Lines 1-5 ("Mashenka Pavletsky...turmoil")

B) Lines 19-23 ("Mashenka went...minds")

C) Lines 80-82 ("Though you... mamma")

D) Lines 83-85 ("Mashenka threw...insulted")

5

As used in line 35, "upset" most nearly means

A) annoyed.

B) neglected.

C) overturned.

D) agitated.

6

In lines 37-53 ("And saying...linen-basket") the narrative presents Mashenka as undergoing a transition from feeling

A) indifference to panic.

B) confusion to distress.

C) shock to embarrassment.

D) self-assurance to paranoia.

7

In the exchange between Mashenka and Liza (lines 55-82), the passage primarily draws a contrast between

A) Mashenka's belief that she is the sole target of the search and Liza's understanding that Madame Kushkin was not discriminatory in her actions.

B) Mashenka's panic when confronted with an accusation and Liza's composure when she reassures Mashenka that her fears are unfounded.

C) Mashenka's feelings of superiority within the hierarchy of the staff and Liza's humility regarding her role in the household.

D) Mashenka's disbelief of the circumstances surrounding the search and Liza's acceptance of those circumstances as standard practice.

CONTINUE

8

It can reasonably be inferred that unlike Madame Kushkin, Nikolay Sergeitch

A) has not been searching for the missing brooch.

B) sympathizes with the staff's indignation at being searched.

C) found the frenzy of the search to be amusing.

D) believes that all members of his household are above suspicion.

9

Which choice provides the best evidence for the answer to the previous question?

A) Lines 13-14 ("He was...over")

B) Lines 17-18 ("Oh, how...Abominable")

C) Lines 63-64 ("God knows...brooch")

D) Lines 71-72 ("Nikolay Sergeitch...hen")

10

Which function does the last paragraph (lines 83-90) serve in the passage as a whole?

A) It characterizes Mashenka as reacting in an overly sensitive and dramatic way in the face of an otherwise routine event.

B) It presents the particular moment at which Mashenka realizes that she is regarded as nothing more than a servant.

C) It reveals a change in Mashenka's perception of her employers by highlighting her growing distrust of them.

D) It underscores Mashenka's hypocrisy when being subjected to the same treatment that her peers were going through.

CONTINUE

Questions 1-10 are based on the following passage.
Chapter 8.4
The following passage is a Chris Holliday adaptation of *The Pardoner's Tale* (1478) by Geoffrey Chaucer.

The church clock struck the half-hour. Josh swore—then took a quick look round. There was no one in the street to hear him. Not that he cared, but
Line best that one of the neighbors wasn't about or they
5 would tell his mum and then there would be hell to pay when he got home. He grinned. Get home, indeed. He wasn't going home, not for a long while. This was the fourteenth century and he was damned if he was going to spend his life as a penniless, cheerless peasant.
10 He swaggered into the tavern. The pot-boy nodded. "They're down there," he said, pointing to the dark area at the back of the room. Josh, grinning, went to join his two older buddies. He had met them a while ago. Rough, rude, and notorious in the village for
15 bullying, petty theft and being drunk most of the time, they possessed a loud independence that Josh envied. They had welcomed him like a new plaything.
"At last! Wouldn't she let you go this morning?" Josh grinned at their guffaws. "Get a tankard of beer
20 down you and start the day properly!"
From the street outside, the tolling of a bell could be heard. "What's that noise?" the ringleader asked.
"It's a coffin, being taken to the church," the pot-boy answered. "An old buddy of yours. Last night he
25 was sitting there in his seat, drinking deep. That villain, Death, came in, stole his life and went on his way. You need to be wary of him. He has slain many others in this pestilence. You never know when he will strike you...or any other of your gang."
30 The oldest and the leader of the three spluttered into his beer. "Not on my patch! I will seek him out. And you guys can help me. We will find and slay this false traitor, Death."
Knocking over their stools, the three cheered and
35 set off, swearing oaths, through the village and out into the countryside.
They had not gone far before they met with an old, poor man, plodding along the lane with the aid of his staff. He greeted them, "Good-morrow, lords. God sees
40 you."
"Old man, how come you are so old and still alive?"
"You may well ask. I wander the world in search of a young man that will exchange his age for mine.
45 I call to Death, but he ignores me. I strike the earth

with my staff and cry "sweet mother, let me in! To no avail."
"We want words with this villain, Death. Old man, tell us where we may find him."
50 "Easily. You will find him under the oak tree in that grove. God save you."
The three ran to the grove. They found the tree. Piled amongst its roots, there lay a fortune of shining golden florins.
55 They gazed at it. Then their leader spoke. "Clearly, this money is for us. But there's a problem. If we cart all this home in broad daylight, people will think we are thieves and get us hanged. We must wait till night. Let's cut straws to see who goes to the village
60 for bread and wine whilst the other two guard our gift from Fortune."
Josh got the short straw. He felt really important. The other two waved as he ran off to the village.
"You know," said the older of the two. "It's a lot
65 of money shared between three. Between two, it would be even more." The other nodded. "When Josh returns, start play-fighting with him and grab his arms. I will use this dagger. Are you agreed?" The other was.
Josh was having similar thoughts. "If all that
70 money were mine, what could I do with it? Be someone important for the rest of my life."
He went to the apothecary. "My place is plagued with rats. You have some suitable poison?"
"Oh yes, young sir. This poison will kill any living
75 creature in the world..."
Josh bought fresh bread and three bottles of wine. He put the poison into two of them and set off back to the tree of gold.
There is nothing more to tell. The game was
80 played. Once Josh was dead, the other two sat with their backs against the oak and ate the bread and quaffed the wine. The victory was Death's.

CONTINUE

1

Which choice best describes a major theme of the passage?

A) The wisdom of older generations

B) The corrupting influence of greed

C) The rebellious nature of adolescents

D) The inevitability of death

2

Josh's character can best be described as

A) clever and ambitious.

B) careless and naive.

C) unsatisfied with his lot.

D) actively seeking validation.

3

Which choice provides the best evidence for the answer to the previous question?

A) Lines 6-7 ("He grinned...while")

B) Lines 7-9 ("This was...peasant")

C) Lines 62-63 ("Josh got...village")

D) Lines 76-78 ("Josh bought...gold")

4

The author indicates that the relationship between Josh and the two boys was

A) superficial and rooted in mischief.

B) genuine and long-standing.

C) newly-forged and driven by hatred.

D) harmful and disapproved of by his mother.

5

In the first two paragraphs (lines 1-17), the author mainly draws a contrast between Josh's

A) nervousness about sneaking out and his friends' nonchalant attitudes.

B) fear of his mother and the consequences of his disobedient actions.

C) restriction by his mother and his friends' uninhibited behavior.

D) past dependence on his mother and his current freedom.

6

As used in line 16, "loud" most nearly means

A) noisy.

B) apparent.

C) coveted.

D) blaring.

7

As used in line 28, "strike" most nearly means

A) assault.

B) influence.

C) beat.

D) target.

CONTINUE

8

According to the passage, the boys' "old buddy" (line 24) had recently died from

A) contracting a deadly disease.

B) excessive alcohol consumption.

C) being poisoned by a false friend.

D) getting involved in a bar fight.

9

In context of the whole passage, the boys' encounter with the old man (lines 37-51)

A) foreshadows the grave end of the boys.

B) contrasts the old and the young's opinion of Death.

C) characterizes the boys as reckless bullies.

D) introduces the old man as a representation of Death.

10

Which of the following provides the best evidence for the answer to the previous question?

A) Lines 26-29 ("You need...gang.")

B) Lines 30-33 ("The oldest...Death.")

C) Lines 43-45 ("You may...me.")

D) Lines 48-51 ("We want...you")

CONTINUE

Questions 1-10 are based on the following passage.
Chapter 8.5
Adapted from Wilkie Collins, *After Dark* (1856).

Shortly after my education at college was finished, I happened to be staying at Paris with an English friend. We were both young men then, and lived, I
Line am afraid, rather a wild life, in the delightful city
5 of our sojourn. One night we were idling about the neighborhood of the Palais Royal, doubtful to what amusement we should next betake ourselves. My friend proposed a visit to Frascati's; but his suggestion was not to my taste. I knew Frascati's, as the French
10 saying is, by heart; had lost and won plenty of five-franc pieces there, merely for amusement's sake, until it was amusement no longer, and was thoroughly tired, in fact, of all the ghastly respectabilities of such a social anomaly as a respectable gambling-
15 house. "For Heaven's sake," said I to my friend, "let us go somewhere where we can see a little genuine, blackguard*, poverty-stricken gaming with no false gingerbread glitter thrown over it all. Let us get away from fashionable Frascati's, to a house where they
20 don't mind letting in a man with a ragged coat, or a man with no coat, ragged or otherwise." "Very well," said my friend, "we needn't go out of the Palais Royal to find the sort of company you want. Here's the place just before us; as blackguard a place, by all report, as
25 you could possibly wish to see." In another minute we arrived at the door, and entered the house, the back of which you have drawn in your sketch.

When we got upstairs, and had left our hats and sticks with the doorkeeper, we were admitted into the
30 chief gambling-room. We did not find many people assembled there. But, few as the men were who looked up at us on our entrance, they were all types—lamentably true types—of their respective classes.

We had come to see blackguards; but these men
35 were something worse. There is a comic side, more or less appreciable, in all blackguardism—here there was nothing but tragedy—mute, weird tragedy. The quiet in the room was horrible. . . I soon found it necessary to take refuge in excitement from the depression of spirits
40 which was fast stealing on me. Unfortunately I sought the nearest excitement, by going to the table and beginning to play. Still more unfortunately, as the event will show, I won—won prodigiously; won incredibly; won at such a rate that the regular players at the table
45 crowded round me; and staring at my stakes with hungry, superstitious eyes, whispered to one another that the English stranger was going to break the

bank. . .
For the first time in my life, I felt what the passion
50 for play really was. My success first bewildered, and then, in the most literal meaning of the word, intoxicated me. Incredible as it may appear, it is nevertheless true, that I only lost when I attempted to estimate chances, and played according to previous
55 calculation. If I left everything to luck, and staked without any care or consideration, I was sure to win—to win in the face of every recognized probability in favor of the bank. At first some of the men present ventured their money safely enough on my color; but I
60 speedily increased my stakes to sums which they dared not risk. One after another they left off playing, and breathlessly looked on at my game. . .

But one man present preserved his self-possession, and that man was my friend. He came to my side, and
65 whispering in English, begged me to leave the place, satisfied with what I had already gained. I must do him the justice to say that he repeated his warnings and entreaties several times, and only left me and went away after I had rejected his advice . . .
70 Shortly after he had gone, a hoarse voice behind me cried: "Permit me, my dear sir—permit me to restore to their proper place two napoleons which you have dropped. Wonderful luck, sir! I pledge you my word of honor, as an old soldier, in the course of
75 my long experience in this sort of thing, I never saw such luck as yours—never! Go on, sir—Sacre mille bombes! Go on boldly, and break the bank!"

I turned round and saw, nodding and smiling at me with inveterate civility, a tall man, dressed in a frogged
80 and braided surtout.

If I had been in my senses, I should have considered him, personally, as being rather a suspicious specimen of an old soldier. He had goggling, bloodshot eyes, mangy mustaches, and a broken nose. His voice
85 betrayed a barrack-room intonation of the worst order, and he had the dirtiest pair of hands I ever saw—even in France. These little personal peculiarities exercised, however, no repelling influence on me. In the mad excitement, the reckless triumph of that moment, I was
90 ready to "fraternize" with anybody who encouraged me in my game.

*Blackguard: a coarse and dishonorable person

CONTINUE

1

Over the course of the passage, the narrator's attitude shifts from

A) doubt about his gambling skills to confidence in his possibilities of winning.

B) excitement about going to a gambling house to suspicion about a character there.

C) nonchalance about an establishment to utter absorption in a riveting game.

D) boredom with one neighborhood of a city to exhilaration with another.

2

The main purpose of the first paragraph is to

A) introduce the two main characters who will eventually have a disagreement.

B) recount the events and the motives that led the narrator to the gambling house.

C) contrast the pretentious atmosphere of Frascati's to that of the gambling house.

D) convey that the narrator and his friend have differing opinions about gambling.

3

The narrator uses the phrase "social anomaly" (line 14) to indicate that gambling houses like Frascati's are

A) refined.

B) uncommon.

C) dishonest.

D) contradictory.

4

The narrator indicates that he began to play in the gambling room because

A) he needed a way to pass the time after seeing the blackguards.

B) he became disinterested with Frascati's and thought it was insufficiently seedy.

C) he found its eclectic clientele to be refreshing compared to those of Frascati's.

D) he wanted to distract himself from the desperation of its clientele.

5

Which choice provides the best evidence for the answer to the previous question?

A) Lines 5-7 ("One night...ourselves")

B) Lines 15-18 ("let us...all")

C) Lines 37-40 ("The quiet...me")

D) Lines 43-45 ("I won...me")

6

As used in line 35, "comic" most nearly means

A) lively.

B) silly.

C) amusing.

D) ironic.

7

According to the passage, the narrator begins to feel thrilled by the games at the gambling house because

A) the money he won incited in him a craving for more.

B) the bad luck he had at Frascati's did not follow him here.

C) he was encouraged and cheered on by the other patrons.

D) he became the only player when his competitors dropped out.

CONTINUE

8

Which choice provides the best evidence for the answer to the previous question?

A) Lines 47-48 ("the English...bank")

B) Lines 50-52 ("My success...me")

C) Lines 61-62 ("One after...game")

D) Lines 89-91 ("I was...game")

9

It can be reasonably inferred from the passage that the narrator's friend thinks that the narrator has

A) fallen under the influence of a deceptive scheme.

B) succumbed to his own greed and ambition.

C) become infatuated with the allure of the criminal class.

D) been corrupted by the unscrupulous clientele.

10

In lines 70-91, the appearance of the old soldier mainly has the effect of

A) creating a sense of foreboding danger about to befall the narrator.

B) implying that the narrator has become the target of an impending scam.

C) commenting on the reckless and shortsighted behavior induced by gambling.

D) contrasting the naïveté of the narrator to the immorality of the establishment.

Answer Key: CHAPTER EIGHT

SAT

Chapter 8.1
1. D
2. B
3. B
4. B
5. A
6. A
7. C
8. D
9. D
10. C

Chapter 8.2
1. A
2. C
3. A
4. B
5. C
6. A
7. A
8. A
9. B
10. B

Chapter 8.3
1. A
2. A
3. C
4. B
5. C
6. B
7. D
8. C
9. D
10. B

Chapter 8.4
1. B
2. C
3. B
4. A
5. C
6. B
7. D
8. A
9. A
10. D

Chapter 8.5
1. C
2. B
3. D
4. D
5. C
6. A
7. A
8. B
9. B
10. A

Answer Explanations

Chapter 8

Chapter 8.1 | *Mothwise*

1) CORRECT ANSWER: D
In the passage, the priest's wife disregards the mess that she makes around the house and attempts to excuse specific instances of messiness (such as the dish in lines 31-35 and the blankets in lines 75-78). This information justifies D. Keep in mind that the wife is careless (but not especially greedy or destructive, eliminating A) and disregards problems (rather than making demands, eliminating B). C is a trap answer, and relies on a misreading of the fact that the wife quickly MOVES PAST problems: to do so, however, she needs to be AWARE of the problems themselves.

2) CORRECT ANSWER: B
Despite their differences in character, the priest and his wife have a marriage that is quite secure: they are "fond of each other none the less" (lines 61-62) and the wife with her "kind heart forgave" (line 91) the priest after their significant quarrel. This information supports B and can be used to eliminate more negative answers such as C and D. A overstates the positive tone applied to the marriage: the wife and the priest get along over a long period of time, but do not display the passion or intensity that would be signs of a fulfilling "romance".

3) CORRECT ANSWER: B
The first paragraph describes the background of the priest's wife, but also indicates that "she had never learned housekeeping" (line 6) and is something of a "torment" (line 8); the passage later explains that her carelessness makes her a mild torment to the priest. This information supports B. A distorts the content of the paragraph: the wife's lifestyle is not luxurious, but is not necessarily marked by struggle or deprivation. C (boredom) and D (irrational) attribute the wrong flaws to the wife, who is mostly immature and careless in how she handles her household space.

4) CORRECT ANSWER: B
The word "comical" refers to the "battles" (line 11) that the priest fights with his wife: he repeatedly tries to teach her to be sensible but finds that his efforts are futile, so that his battles are pointless or absurd. B is the best answer. A and C wrongly apply positive tones to the "battles", while D ("petty" or "unimportant") applies the wrong negative. The "battles" are important to the priest, but are criticized as time-wasting and unsuccessful in their results.

5) CORRECT ANSWER: A

In lines 16-21, the priest is described as touring his rooms and putting things straight in order to deal with the wife's clutter; later he attends to the blankets that have been left outside in a similar manner. These additional chores account for one of the priest's significant activities, so that A is an effective answer. B is incorrect because the priest is bothered by the clutter (not "nonchalant"), C is inaccurate because the priest understands his wife's tendencies and personality (and is not "bewildered" by the clutter), and D wrongly criticizes the priest (when in fact the clutter is a household problem, not an "unhealthy fixation" that undermines his life and marriage).

6) CORRECT ANSWER: A

Initially, the priest "scolded and entreated" (line 22) his wife about the clutter, but eventually "grew hardened to it all" (line 36) upon realizing that his wife's habits would not change. A accurately reflects this shift in attitude. B wrongly indicates that the priest did not acknowledge the clutter at first, while C wrongly indicates a shift from positive to negative regarding the clutter (rather than a shift from one negative stance to a different negative stance). D overstates the negativity of the priest's later attitude: he dislikes the clutter but does not in fact "resent" his wife, of whom he remains "fond" (line 61).

7) CORRECT ANSWER: C

In lines 75-76, the narrator explains the perspective of the wife, who believes that her husband is making a "fuss" about a "drop of rain or so". She sees him as someone who is upset by trifles or as a "nitpicker", so that C is the best answer. A indicates that the wife is not bothered by disorder, B indicates that the wife is not concerned about the plate, and D indicates that the wife finds the priest unreasonable. Only D mentions the priest, and criticizes him as irrational (not necessarily as obsessed with small things).

8) CORRECT ANSWER: D

In lines 55-59, the husband reflects that the wife's purchases are needless and that he would prefer to "buy a big thing" that would bring the process of irritating expenditures to an end. Ths information supports D. A is inaccurate because the husband and wife are in fact "fond" (line 61) of one another, B neglects the fact that the priest wants to change his wife's habits (and makes efforts to correct her), and C wrongly attributes a positive attitude (frugal and collaborative) regarding the spending habits to the priest.

9) CORRECT ANSWER: D

See above for the explanation of the correct answer. A records the priest's pity for his wife's appearance and endurance, B describes the wife's upbringing and tendency to make purchases (but does not describe the husband himself), and C considers the wife's perspective (but not her husband's). Make sure not to wrongly take A as evidence for Question 8 C, since the priest is favorably inclined towards his wife but DISLIKES her spending habits.

10) CORRECT ANSWER: C

The narrator explains that "the years passed" (line 60) after the husband accepted his wife's lapses in housekeeping; the incident involving the blankets, however, is a rare case of the wife's inattentiveness leading to conflict with the husband. C is an effective choice, while the differences between the wife and the priest are established EARLIER (and have in fact been reconciled in the course of their mostly peaceful marriage, eliminating A). B is contradicted by the final description of the wife as "Careless and happy" (line 91), while D is problematic because the priest's remarks are factual and calmly delivered (not meant to stir up emotions or "contentious").

Chapter 8.2 | *Mrs. Mantsey's View*

1) CORRECT ANSWER: A

Towards the beginning of the paragraph, Mrs. Manstey reflects on "How lovely the view was that day!" (lines 2-3). However, by the end of this portion of the text, her thoughts have shifted to "a barrier of brick and mortar" (line 9) that "would swiftly rise" (line 10) to block out the view. This information supports A. B distorts the actual structure of the paragraph, since Mrs. Manstey's inner thoughts are considered almost simultaneously with scenic details (NOT in a shift of emphasis). The second half of the paragraph focuses on the future structure itself, NOT on the feeling that structure inspires in Mrs. Manstey, eliminating C, and D wrongly indicates a "daily routine" (when in fact Mrs. Manstey's action of looking at the view is not defined as repeated, or linked to any larger habits).

2) CORRECT ANSWER: C

In lines 17-29, the author explains that Mrs. Manstey is incapable of leaving settled habits and that her room, like her view, is "a part of her existence". The rest of the passage depicts Mrs. Mastey's panic over the prospect of changing her living conditions, thus justifying C. A is too broad (since Mrs. Mastey is ONLY assertive when her room and view are threatened, not on any other occasions) while B overstates a theme from the passage (since Mrs. Manstey is clearly satisfied with her room and view in the early paragraphs). D is problematic because, in the passage, Mrs. Manstey is depicted enjoying her time indoors as opposed to spending, or even wanting to spend, time outdoors.

3) CORRECT ANSWER: A

In lines 14-16, Mrs. Manstey notices the increasingly "dusty" condition of a single plant, indicating that she pays close attention to her immediate surroundings. A is thus an effective choice, while B is a trap, since lines 23-25 list aspects of Mrs. Manstey's surroundings but not aspects that have CHANGED in any clearly recent way. C and D refer to Mrs. Manstey's general situation in life, not to small details that Mrs. Manstey notices, and should thus be eliminated.

4) CORRECT ANSWER: B

In lines 21-23, the narrator explains that Mrs. Manstey's room plays a role in providing her with happiness and that it is "a part of her existence"; the lines designated in the question indicate exactly how well Mrs Manstey knows her room. B is thus the best answer, since it captures Mrs. Manstey's sense of positive familiarity. A ("hospitable and welcoming") implies that Mrs. Manstey's room would be comforting to visitors, while the text focuses on how it affects her. C is strongly and incorrectly negative, while D makes an assumption that is not supported with text from the passage.

5) CORRECT ANSWER: C

In lines 30-32, Mrs. Black both receives a message and attends to the final stages of her boarders' meal. This information, along with Mrs. Black's direct involvement with Mrs. Manstey's situation, justifies C and can be used to eliminate B. Mrs. Black is clearly doing well as a landlady, but does not have a lifestyle that is entirely hectic or "fast-paced" on the basis of the passage (eliminating A). She also FAILS to show Mrs. Manstey empathy by regarding Mrs. Manstey as a "lunatic" (line 77), thus eliminating D.

6) CORRECT ANSWER: A

See above for the explanation of the correct answer. B lists some of Mrs. Black's pleasantries and indicates that she is "prosperous", C describes Mrs. Black's calm and determined demeanor, and D indicates that one time of the day (dinner) is "busy" for Mrs. Black. Make sure not to mistake B or D as evidence for Question 5 A.

7) CORRECT ANSWER: A

The phrase "advanced on" describes a physical action that Mrs. Black takes with regard to Mrs. Manstey. She thus moves towards or "approaches" Mrs. Manstey, making A the best answer. C implies a conflict or a negative tone (which only emerges LATER in the passage), while B and D involve the wrong time signatures. Mrs. Black greets Mrs. Manstey AFTER she advances, and encounters (meets) her BEFORE she advances.

8) CORRECT ANSWER: A

In the course of the discussion, Mrs. Manstey bluntly describes herself as a "poor woman" (line 52) and voices her strong opposition to moving. Mrs. Black, for her part, offers answers that are somewhat vague but designed to quickly negotiate around the issue ("I guess we can fix that all right", lines 85-86). This information supports A; B (negotiation) and C (respectful) mischaracterize Mrs. Manstey, who is moved to passion and at one point addresses Mrs. Black "almost with a scream" (line 72), not with respect. D subtly mischaracterizes Mrs. Black, who listens to the pleas but wants to address them QUICKLY, not to DISMISS them outright.

9) CORRECT ANSWER: B

Mrs. Manstey's "tears" (line 94) accompany her remarks about the "extension" (line 91) that will block a view that she desperately wants to keep. This information supports B, while the negative tone that accompanies the tears can be used to eliminate C and D (both positive). A distorts the content of the passage: Mrs. Black clearly understands what Mrs. Manstey wants, but resists giving in to Mrs. Manstey's request.

10) CORRECT ANSWER: B

In lines 101-104, Mrs. Manstey seizes Mrs. Black's wrist and then calls for a "definite answer" regarding the "proposition" involving her living situation. This information supports B. Keep in mind that Mrs. Manstey demands an answer (but not necessarily an AFFIRMATIVE one, eliminating A) and that her commitment to resolving the matter is ALREADY apparent (eliminating C). Choice D is incorrect because Mrs. Black is not trying to leave the room, but reaching for the handle to let Mrs. Manstey out of the room, as Mrs. Manstey is a visitor in Mrs. Black's house and would be the one leaving in this situation.

Chapter 8.3 | *An Upheaval*

1) CORRECT ANSWER: A

Early in the passage, the author explains that "there was a search going on" (lines 23-24) in Mashenka's room; as a result of this search, Mashenka reflects that "Never in her life had she beens subjected to such an outrage, never had she been so deeply insulted" (lines 84-85). This information supports A, while other answers distort actual content from the passage. The search ends with negative emotions for Mashenka, but not an actual accusation (B) or dilemma (C), since she is simply left alone with her thoughts. Nor does she completely misunderstand the events (eliminating D), since she expects that something negative has happened (and since Liza quickly clarifies the purpose of the search).

2) CORRECT ANSWER: A

Early in the passage, the narrator explains the acute "feeling" (line 21) that Mashenka experiences after discovering that she is being searched; later, the narrator uses questions (lines 46-52) to capture Mashenka's emotions and reflections. These line references support A, the idea that the narrator mostly reflects Mashenka's perspective. B and D would only be possible if the narrator had a critical or negative perspective OUTSIDE of Mashenka's, while C wrongly assumes that the narrator does more than accurately channel Mashenka's ideas and is instead opinionated or "justifying."

3) CORRECT ANSWER: C

Mashenka is described early in the passage as "a young girl who had only just finished her studies at a boarding school (lines 1-2); later, Liza tells Mashenka that living with employers is not "like living with your papa and mamma" (lines 81-82). This information indicates that Mashenka is new to settings outside school and family, or has little experience of the world. C is the best answer, while B and D wrongly indicate that Mashenka is more independent and assertive than these same line references reveal her to be. A is incorrect because Mashenka has been to "boarding school" and has thus left her parents in some capacity.

4) CORRECT ANSWER: B

In lines 19-23, the author explains that Mashenka is experiencing an acute feeling of oppression and helplessness "for the first time in her life". B thus describes a feeling of "unprecedented" oppression in a manner that effectively fits the prompt. A describes the household's "turmoil" (not Mashenka's), C records Liza's comments (not Mashenka's feelings) and D indicates that Mashenka feels "outraged" and "insulted", but not necessarily helpless and stifled or "oppressed".

5) CORRECT ANSWER: C

The word "upset" describes an item belonging to Mashenka (the "workbag", line 30) that the lady of the house, Madame Kushkin, is trying to put back in order after searching it. The lady of the house has emptied or "overturned" the workbag to get at its contents. C is the best answer, while A and D refer to emotions that humans would have (not to the situation of a possession). B contradicts the content, since Madame Kushkin has to in fact give the bag attention in order to search it.

6) CORRECT ANSWER: B

Early in the designated lines, Mashenka is described as "unable to understand" what is going on; later, she speculates that she may be mixed up in "something dreadful". This shift of sentiments is accurately described in B. A (which wrongly assumes that Mashenka is neutral at first) and D (which wrongly assumes that her earliest sentiments are positive) introduces inaccurate tones. Trap answer C properly uses two negatives, though the idea of "embarrassment" is inappropriate (since Mashenka is alone at the end of the line reference, not embarrassed in public) and is too weak a negative to capture her strong distress.

7) CORRECT ANSWER: D

While Mashenka asks questions about the search and feels "indignation" (line 76), Liza reminds Mashenka that she is "living with strangers" (line 79) who have the authority to conduct searches. This information (and the contrast between Mashenka's panic and Liza's accepting tone) justifies D. Other answers distort the content of the passage: Mashenka does not understand the purpose of the search at first and quickly realizes that she is not the only person being targeted (eliminating both A and B). Note also that Mashenka does not feel "superior" (and is instead trying to make sense of her place in unfamiliar events), thus eliminating C.

8) CORRECT ANSWER: C

In lines 71-72, it is explained that, during the search, Nikolai Sergeitch "simply looks on and cackles like a hen". He thus finds the search a humorous or amusing spectacle, so that C is the best answer. B is inaccurate, since it is unlikely that Nikolai Sergeitch would "cackle" at people he sympathizes with. Keep in mind that he is involved in the search (if only from a distance, eliminating A) and that he allows the search to go on (eliminating D, since there would be no need to search if all members of the household were "above suspicion").

9) CORRECT ANSWER: D

See above for the explanation of the correct answer. A and B both describe Nikolai Sergeitch's strong emotions, and C refers to Liza alone. Make sure not to wrongly take A or B as evidence for Question 8 B; Nikolai Sergeitch may in fact be worked up, but (considering his later amusement in the correct line reference) he may just be displaying mock "indignation".

10) CORRECT ANSWER: B

In the final paragraph, Mashenka reflects that "she could not imagine a greater insult" than being searched, a process that the entire household has had to endure. She now sees that her upbringing and education do not separate her from the other servants; this information supports B. A and D both wrongly assume that the narrator is criticizing Mashenka (rather than depicting a negative realization on her part), while C wrongly focuses on how Mashenka perceives her employers, not on the actual main topic: her self-perception.

Chapter 8.4 | *The Pardoner's Tale*

1) CORRECT ANSWER: B
The passage explains how Josh and his companions turn to murder (a worse deed than any that they have yet committed) after they discover "a fortune of shining gold florins" (lines 53-54). The idea that this fortune is corrupting supports B. Keep in mind that the old man is significant because he sets a trap (not because he is wise, eliminating A) and that Josh and his companions are led to their unfortunate ends through their greed, not through adolescent rebelliousness (eliminating C). Death is not inevitable in the story (eliminating D) since Josh and his companions could have avoided death by not reacting poorly to the fortune.

2) CORRECT ANSWER: C
In lines 7-9, Josh reflects that he does not want to spend his life as a "penniless, cheerless peasant": he comes from a peasant household, so that life as a "peasant" is a likely fate that he wants to avoid. This sense of dissatisfaction supports C. A is incorrect because Josh spends his time drinking with undesirable companions (rather than thinking up ingenious or ambitious plans for prosperity), while B is incorrect because Josh is simply more innocent than his companions (not completely experienced or "naive"). Keep in mind also that Josh wants to change his lifestyle with the help of his companions (not to "validate" his present one, eliminating D).

3) CORRECT ANSWER: B
See above for the explanation of the correct answer. A indicates that Josh does not intend to return home (but not WHY in the manner of B), C indicates that Josh feels important as the result of a single event (NOT validated overall), and D indicates that Josh has devised a single scheme (not that he is generally clever). Make sure not to wrongly take C as evidence for Question 2 D or D as evidence for Question 2 A.

4) CORRECT ANSWER: A
The narrator explains that Josh "envied" (line 16) the two other boys, who "welcomed him like a new plaything" (line 17) and brought him into their irresponsible, rowdy lifestyle; however, the discovery of the gold proves that these characters have so little regard for one another that they will kill one another for gain. A is thus the best answer, while the same evidence can be used to eliminate B (which is wrongly positive) and C (which identifies hatred, NOT envy or interest, as the motive). D mentions Josh's mother (who may punish Josh if he is discovered swearing, NOT on account of his companions) in a manner that points to the wrong source for her disapproval.

5) CORRECT ANSWER: C
In the first paragraph, Josh becomes self-conscious and realizes that "there would be hell to pay when he got home" (lines 5-6) if his mother learns that he has been swearing; the second paragraph, though, calls attention to the activities of his "Rough, rude" (line 14) elder buddies, who have no trouble disregarding authority. C properly captures this contrast, while A attributes the wrong cause to Josh's nervousness ("sneaking out") and B does not properly focus on Josh's friends (the main topic of the second paragraph). D wrongly indicates that Josh was only "dependent" on his mother in the past, when in fact he still lives at home and so is NOT yet "independent".

6) CORRECT ANSWER: B

The word "loud" refers to the "independence" (line 16) of Josh's two companions, an independence that Josh discerns and envies. The independence is thus clear or "apparent" to Josh, so that B is the best answer. A and D both refer to the boys themselves (not to the quality of their "independence", which cannot make noise of its own), while C wrongly indicates that people other than Josh might envy the boys' independence, a possibility that the text does not raise.

7) CORRECT ANSWER: D

The word "strike" refers to the activity of "Death" (line 26), which has already designated or "targeted" other people and may soon find new targets. D is the best answer. A and C both wrongly assume that Death's activity is violent (when in fact Death simply takes "a life and [goes] on his way", line 26). B is a trap answer: to be "influenced", a person must be alive over a period of time, yet the word "strike" is used in reference to people who are suddenly dead.

8) CORRECT ANSWER: A

The boys' "older buddy" was at one point healthy, but is mentioned by the pot-boy as an example of those whom Death has slain in "this pestilence" (line 28) or plague-like disease. A is the best answer, while B mentions a vice that the passage discusses in a critical manner (NOT a cause of death). C refers to Josh's own activity near the end of the passage, while D is a possible fate for Josh's rowdy lifestyle (not an actual cause of death mentioned by the narrator).

9) CORRECT ANSWER: A

In lines 48-51, the boys indicate that they want to find Death, and the old man indicates that Death can be found "in the old oak tree in that grove", which is in fact where Josh and his friends kill one another (lines 79-82). A is thus the best answer. B is incorrect because BOTH the young and the old characters want to find Death, C is inaccurate because the boys have ALREADY been characterized as reckless bullies (lines 14-17), and D distorts the passage's references (since the old man, who wants to FIND Death, cannot logically be Death himself).

10) CORRECT ANSWER: D

See above for the explanation of the correct answer. A records a dialogue with the pot-boy (NOT the old man), B records the remarks of one of the boys BEFORE encountering the old man, and C indicates that the old man is himself searching for Death. Make sure not to misread C as evidence for Question 9 D.

Chapter 8.5 | *After Dark*

1) CORRECT ANSWER: C
Early in the passage, the narrator is unemotional and unconcerned, and has apparently become "thoroughly tired" (lines 12-13) of respectable establishments; later, the narrator's attitude shifts to one of interest and absorption when he for the first time "felt what the passion of play really was" (lines 49-50). This shift from nonchalance to emotional involvement justifies C. A is incorrect because the narrator wins as soon as he starts to play (line 43), B wrongly identifies the narrator's initial sentiments as "excitement", and D wrongly indicates that the blackguard gambling-house and the Palais Royal are in different neighborhoods, while the narrator's friend recommends the blackguard gambling house because it was "just before us" (line 24).

2) CORRECT ANSWER: B
In the first paragraph, the narrator explains that one of his friend's suggestions is "not to [his] taste" (line 9) and indicates a preference instead for "blackguard, poverty-stricken gaming" (line 17); these are the narrator's motives for seeking out the gaming house described later in the passage, so that B is the best answer. The narrator and his friend in fact agree on a course of action (and the friend later leaves without having an argument with the narrator, eliminating A), while the new gaming house has not yet been described (eliminating C). D is problematic because the narrator and his friend differ over which gaming house they intend to visit, not over the issue of whether gambling ITSELF is acceptable or not.

3) CORRECT ANSWER: D
The narrator argues that gambling houses such as Frascati's are characterized by "ghastly respectabilities" (line 13); this oxymoronic phrase indicates that such gambling houses are "anomalies" because they involve contradictory or inappropriate values. D is the best answer, while the positive A can be eliminated. The narrator never explains whether such gambling houses are common or not (only that their principles are nonsensical, eliminating B) and does not characterize Frascati's as immoral (in contrast to the gambling house that he visits later, eliminating C).

4) CORRECT ANSWER: D
In lines 37-40, the narrator indicates his discomfort with the apparently tragic people around him and explains that he "found it necessary to take refuge in excitement" by beginning to gamble. This information supports D, while A understates the narrator's negative sentiments and B refers to a motive (disinterest regarding Frascati's) that is only considered earlier. C wrongly applies a positive tone to the "clientele" and should be eliminated on this account.

5) CORRECT ANSWER: C
See above for the explanation of the correct answer. A and B both refer to portions of the passage that concern events BEFORE the narrator even entered the gambling room, while D refers to the narrator's good fortune AFTER he has begun to gamble; naturally, none of these answers offer clear explanations for why the narrator began to play.

6) CORRECT ANSWER: A

The word "comic" is used to describe "blackguardism" (lines 36), which the narrator contrasts with the tragic, "mute", and "quiet" (line 37) state of the people that he has encountered in the gambling house. The people are thus not lively, so that the contrasting comedy of blackguardism involves liveliness: A is the best answer. B and C indicate that the narrator finds blackguardism absurd (not, as the context demands, energetic), while D points to a larger irony involved in the passage (that the narrator's expectations have been badly defeated) but does not fit the specific discussion of levels of energy or liveliness.

7) CORRECT ANSWER: A

In lines 50-52, the narrator explains that he was "bewildered" and then "intoxicated" with success; in other words, his triumphs at gambling encouraged him to continue playing despite an initial reaction of confusion. A is the best answer. B is incorrect because the narrator's real objection to Frascati's is that it is not sufficiently stimulating, C does not capture the nature of the mostly mute and tragic fellow attendees, and D refers to an event (the decision of other gamblers to leave the game) that occurs AFTER the narrator began to feel thrilled.

8) CORRECT ANSWER: B

See above for the explanation of the correct answer. A describes the perspective of those who are watching the narrator (not that of the narrator himself), and C and D describe the RESULTS of the narrator's enthusiastic and successful gambling (not how it originated). Make sure not to wrongly pair A with Question 7 D.

9) CORRECT ANSWER: B

The narrator explains that his friend begged him "to leave the place, satisfied with what [he] had already gained" (lines 65-66). While the narrator pursues greater winnings, the friend urgently wants the narrator to cease accumulating money and make an exit, so that B is the best answer. A wrongly indicates that the narrator is being fooled (not that he is helpless to deal with a vice), while C and D wrongly focus on the people around the narrator (whom the narrator in fact harshly criticizes) instead of on the game that is the narrator's real negative influence.

10) CORRECT ANSWER: A

The old soldier encourages the narrator to "Go on Boldly, and break the bank!" (line 77). In a departure from the friend's spirit of caution; the narrator himself is overcome by "mad excitement" (lines 88-89) and "reckless triumph" (89), qualities that may lead to his downfall now that he is on his own. A is thus the best answer, while the old soldier's motives, though suspicious, do not definitively indicate a trick or scam that will harm the narrator (eliminating B). C is problematic because the narrator is commenting on his case alone (not on gambling GENERALLY), while D is problematic because the narrator is reckless and shortsighted but not necessarily "naive" or inexperienced in the ways of the world (eliminating D).

CHAPTER NINE

Questions 1-10 are based on the following passage.
Chapter 9.1
This excerpt is from a Chris Holliday adaptation of *Pygmalion* (1913) by George Bernard Shaw.

Eliza stared along the silent, orderly middle-class gentility that defined the superiority of Wimpole Street. She felt like turning tail and fleeing all the way back to
Line the cheerful warmth of Covent Garden where everyone
5 laughed and yelled and wore their feelings on their sleeves.

Taking a deep breath, she mounted the steps to the front door of number 21 and peered at the discreet plaque beside the door: "Professor Higgins,
10 Phonetics." The last word defeated her; she didn't even know how to say it. She jangled the chain of the shining brass bell.

Mrs. Pearce opened the door and scrutinized Eliza from head to toe. "The door for tradespeople is down
15 the steps that lead to the kitchen."

"I'm come to see the professor," replied Eliza.

"Heavens! Professor Higgins certainly sees some very peculiar people. I can only think that he wants you to speak into one of his talking machines."

20 "Dunno. 'eel be pleased to see me. I saw 'im last night, in Covent Garden. 'ad a bit to drink, I think. 'e was with a mate."

"That would be Colonel Pickering. He is not a "mate"—as you call him—but a colleague visiting
25 from India and an expert in spoken Sanskrit. They are comparing notes. I doubt he will have time for the likes of you, but I will enquire. Wait here."

The door closed. Eliza shuffled a little on the top step. "Spoken Sanskrit? What's that when it's at
30 'ome?"

Mrs Pearce knocked and entered the study. Professor Higgins was volubly explaining his recording machine to Colonel Pickering, who was sitting in an armchair, looking a little exhausted.
35 "Excuse me, sir. There's a young girl outside—quite a common looking girl—from Covent Garden, who claims you will be pleased to see her."

"Really? Does she have an accent?"

"Oh, yes sir. Quite dreadful!"

40 "Wonderful! Bring her in, Mrs. Pearce." The housekeeper nodded and left the room. "This gives me a chance to show you exactly how this machine records different accents. It is so important we understand this. You see, an Englishman's way of speaking completely
45 classifies him, far beyond the rather generalised levels of Upper, Middle and Lower Class."

"Is that important?" asked Pickering.

"But, of course! It absolutely defines society: an Englishman's way of speaking classifies him
50 immediately." The study door re-opened and Mrs Pearce entered with a nervous Eliza in tow. Higgins took one glance and, waving a dismissive hand, protested, "Oh, she's no good. This is the flower girl we saw last night. I don't need any more of her!"

55 For a moment, Eliza was taken aback. Then, summoning her courage, she retorted loudly, "'Ere, you 'aven't 'eard what I come for yet. I come to do you a favour, and make you some money. You must need it 'cos you was throwing enough of it about last night!"

60 Professor Higgins turned to the colonel. "You see this creature with her kerb-stone English, Pickering? This is what will keep her in the gutter as a flower-girl for the rest of her life."

"Oh really, Higgins," rebuked Pickering. "That
65 is rather harsh, not to mention more than a little condescending." He turned to Eliza. "will you not sit down and tell us your name and the reason for your visit, please?"

"Thanks. Nice to see there is one gentleman 'ere."
70 Plumping herself into an armchair, Eliza continued, "It's like this: I want to be a lady in a flower shop— instead of just trying to sell flowers from a basket at the street corners. But a shop won't take me on, cos they say I don't talk proper. So I come 'ere to ask 'im
75 (nodding at Higgins) to give me lessons on 'ow to speak proper. I'm willing to pay."

"How much?" grinned Higgins.

"Oh, look 'oo's interested now! Well, I know what's fair and I know what's not. I got a friend 'oo
80 gets French lessons from a real Frenchman and she pays a shilling a lesson. Well, you wouldn't 'ave the nerve to charge the same for teaching me my own language—would you, now? So, I'll give you sixpence an hour. Take it or leave it!"

85 Colonel Pickering nodded. "What do you think, Higgins? It is a bit of a challenge. Are you up to it?"

Higgins, egged on by Pickering's remark, rose to his feet and puffed his chest. "Give me three months and I could pass off this draggle-tailed specimen as a
90 duchess in an Ambassador's garden party."

"I don't want to be a duchess!" interrupted Eliza. "I want to be a lady in a flower-shop!"

"Which probably demands better English than a duchess," Higgins swept on.

95 Noticing that the professor was circling the bait, Pickering decided to secure the situation. "Higgins, I will lay you a bet that you cannot succeed. What's more, I will pay all its costs for this young lady's

CONTINUE

elevation in society. Are you up to it?"
100   "Done, Pickering!"
        "Oh, Colonel! You're a real brick*!"
        Mrs Pearce shook her head in disbelief. "Oh,
Professor, what have you taken on!"

*Cockney for "one who is supportive."

1

Over the course of the passage, Eliza's demeanor shifts from

A) hesitant to confident.
B) assertive to amicable.
C) rebellious to accommodating.
D) poised to nonchalant.

2

As used in line 10, "defeated" most nearly means

A) overwhelmed.
B) confused.
C) frustrated.
D) disheartened.

3

In context of the passage as a whole, the interaction between Eliza and Mrs. Pearce (lines 13-27) serves to

A) emphasize the class differences between the residents of Covent Garden and those of Wimpole Street.
B) indicate the condescending attitude towards Eliza brought on by the manner of her speech.
C) introduce two of the passage's main characters by engaging them in a short conversation.
D) convey the passage's setting and the era in which it takes place by presenting period details.

4

Eliza's initial impression of Higgins is that he was

A) chauvinistic and rude.
B) intimidating and intelligent.
C) pretentious and egotistical.
D) intoxicated and reckless.

5

Which choice best supports the conclusion that Professor Higgins is overconfident about his own abilities?

A) lines 51-55 ("Higgins took...aback")
B) lines 60-63 ("You see...life")
C) lines 74-77 ("So I...Higgins")
D) lines 87-90 ("Higgins egged...party")

6

In the context of the passage, the conversation between Higgins and Pickering in lines 40-66 primarily serves to

A) explain the purpose and function of Higgins's talking machine.
B) convey Higgins's motivation behind his research.
C) give an overview on the distinctions between social classes.
D) highlight their differing treatments of people based on social hierarchy.

7

As compared to Higgins, Eliza is portrayed as being

A) less intelligent.
B) less respectful.
C) more pragmatic.
D) more calculating.

8

Which choice provides the best evidence for the answer to the previous question?

A) lines 29-30 ("Spoken Sanskrit...'ome")
B) lines 35-36 ("Excuse me...Covent Garden")
C) lines 91-92 ("I don't...flower-shop")
D) lines 102-103 ("Oh Professor...on")

CONTINUE

9

It can reasonably be inferred from the passage that Pickering offers to pay for Eliza's lessons mainly because

A) he knew she was unable to pay for the lessons herself.

B) he empathized with her situation and wanted to help her improve it.

C) he supported Higgins's research and was curious about the talking machine.

D) he predicted that Higgins would lose the bet Pickering had proposed.

10

Eliza's remark in line 101 ("Oh Colonel...brick") implies that

A) she is aware of Pickering's manipulation of Higgins into giving her lessons.

B) she is incapable of changing her accent and way of speaking.

C) she is grateful for Pickering's support and was previously bluffing about paying for lessons.

D) she is skeptical of Higgins's effectiveness as a teacher and prefers Pickering instead.

CONTINUE

Questions 1-10 are based on the following passage.
Chapter 9.2
Adapted from Katherine Mansfield, *Prelude*.
Originally published in 1918 and re-printed in
1920 in *Bliss and Other Stories*.

In the kitchen at the long deal table under the two
windows old Mrs. Fairfield was washing the breakfast
dishes. The kitchen window looked out on to a big
Line grass patch that led down to the vegetable garden and
5 the rhubarb beds. On one side the grass patch was
bordered by the scullery and wash-house and over
this whitewashed lean-to there grew a knotted vine.
She had noticed yesterday that a few tiny corkscrew
tendrils had come right through some cracks in the
10 scullery ceiling and all the windows of the lean-to had
a thick frill of ruffled green.

"I am very fond of a grape vine," declared Mrs.
Fairfield, "but I do not think that the grapes will ripen
here. It takes Tasmanian sun." And she remembered
15 how Beryl when she was a baby had been picking
some white grapes from the vine on the back verandah
of their Tasmanian house and she had been stung on
the leg by a huge red ant. She saw Beryl in a little
plaid dress with red ribbon tie-ups on the shoulders
20 screaming so dreadfully that half the street rushed in.
And how the child's leg had swelled! "T—t—t—t!"
Mrs. Fairfield caught her breath remembering. "Poor
child, how terrifying it was." And she set her lips
tight and went over to the stove for some more hot
25 water. The water frothed up in the big soapy bowl with
pink and blue bubbles on top of the foam. Old Mrs.
Fairfield's arms were bare to the elbow and stained a
bright pink. She wore a grey foulard dress patterned
with large purple pansies, a white linen apron and a
30 high cap shaped like a jelly mould of white muslin. At
her throat there was a silver crescent moon with five
little owls seated on it, and round her neck she wore a
watch guard made of black beads.

It was hard to believe that she had not been in that
35 kitchen for years; she was so much a part of it. She put
the crocks away with a sure, precise touch, moving
leisurely and ample from the stove to the dresser,
looking into the pantry and the larder as though there
were not an unfamiliar comer. When she had finished,
40 everything in the kitchen had become part of a series
of patterns. She stood in the middle of the room wiping
her hands on a check cloth; a smile beamed on her lips;
she thought it looked very nice, very satisfactory.

"Mother! Mother! Are you there?" called Beryl.
45 "Yes, dear. Do you want me?"

"No. I'm coming," and Beryl rushed in, very
flushed, dragging with her two big pictures.

"Mother, whatever can I do with these awful
hideous Chinese paintings that Chung Wah gave
50 Stanley when he went bankrupt? It's absurd to say that
they are valuable, because they were hanging in Chung
Wah's fruit shop for months before. I can't make out
why Stanley wants them kept. I'm sure he thinks
them just as hideous as we do, but it's because of the
55 frames," she said spitefully. "I suppose he thinks the
frames might fetch something some day or other."

"Why don't you hang them in the passage?"
suggested Mrs. Fairfield; "they would not be much
seen there."

60 "I can't. There is no room. I've hung all the
photographs of his office there before and after
building, and the signed photos of his business friends,
and that awful enlargement of Isabel lying on the mat
in her singlet." Her angry glance swept the placid
65 kitchen. "I know what I'll do. I'll hang them here. I
will tell Stanley they got a little damp in the moving so
I have put them in here for the time being."

She dragged a chair forward, jumped on it, took a
hammer and a big nail out of her pinafore pocket and
70 banged away.

"There! That is enough! Hand me the picture,
mother."

"One moment, child." Her mother was wiping
over the carved ebony frame.

75 "Oh, mother, really you need not dust them. It
would take years to dust all those little holes." And
she frowned at the top of her mother's head and bit her
lip with impatience. Mother's deliberate way of doing
things was simply maddening. It was old age, she
80 supposed, loftily.

CONTINUE →

1

Which choice best summarizes the passage?

A) One character reminisces about her past experiences as a young mother.

B) One character takes advantage of another character's kind and trusting nature.

C) One character revisits an old home and reflects on memories spent there.

D) One character is interrupted from her recollections by a sudden request.

2

Which statement best describes a technique the narrator uses to represent Mrs. Fairfield's character?

A) The narrator underscores Mrs. Fairfield's reluctance to move on from the past by indicating that she was inseparable from her Tasmanian home.

B) The narrator emphasizes Mrs. Fairfield's fulfillment in her work by depicting her tasks as fitting into an organized and harmonious system.

C) The narrator demonstrates Mrs. Fairfield's attention to detail by describing the various colors of objects surrounding her.

D) The narrator hints at Mrs. Fairfield's dependence on her daughter by contrasting Beryl's actions to Mrs. Fairfield's reaction to them.

3

As compared to her current home, Mrs. Fairfield's Tasmanian house is described as

A) a source of greater happiness.

B) being more dangerous.

C) receiving more sunlight.

D) being easier to clean.

4

As used in line 36, "sure" most nearly means

A) steadfast.

B) valid.

C) secure.

D) routine.

5

It can be inferred from the passage that Beryl came home with the intention to

A) seek consolation from her mother about a difficult situation.

B) get rid of the paintings in some way or another.

C) drop the paintings off for Mrs. Fairfield to clean.

D) hide the paintings from Stanley by keeping them in the kitchen.

6

Which choice provides the best evidence for the answer to the previous question?

A) Lines 48-50 ("Mother, whatever...bankrupt")

B) Lines 55-56 ("I suppose...other")

C) Lines 71-74 ("There! That...frame")

D) Lines 75-78 ("Oh mother...impatience")

7

In lines 57-67, the narrator primarily draws a contrast between

A) Mrs. Fairfield's suggestion and Beryl's offended reaction.

B) Stanley's office before and after it was built.

C) Beryl's frustration and the calm mood of Mrs. Fairfield's kitchen.

D) Beryl's and Stanley's feelings towards the accumulation of paintings.

8

Beryl's general attitude towards her mother can best be described as

A) condescending.

B) pitying.

C) appreciative.

D) indignant.

CONTINUE

9

Which choice provides the best evidence for the answer to the previous question?

A) Line 44 ("Mother! Mother...Beryl")

B) Lines 53-54 ("I'm sure...do")

C) Line 65 ("I know...here")

D) Lines 79-80 ("It was...loftily")

10

As used in line 78, "deliberate" most nearly means

A) thoughtful.

B) painstaking.

C) calculated.

D) tentative.

CONTINUE

Questions 1-10 are based on the following passage.
Chapter 9.3
Adapted from Leo Tolstoy, *The Forged Coupon* (1912).

Fedor Mihailovich Smokonikov, the president
of the local Income Tax Department, a man of
unswerving honesty—and proud of it, too—a gloomy
Line Liberal, a free-thinker, and an enemy to every
5 manifestation of religious feeling, which he thought a
relic of superstition, came home from his office feeling
very much annoyed. The Governor of the province
had sent him an extraordinarily stupid minute, almost
assuming that his dealings had been dishonest.
10 Fedor Mihailovich felt embittered, and wrote at
once a sharp answer. On his return home everything
seemed to go contrary to his wishes.
It was five minutes to five, and he expected the
dinner to be served at once, but he was told it was
15 not ready. He banged the door and went to his study.
Somebody knocked at the door. "Who the devil is
that?" he thought; and shouted,—"Who is there?"
The door opened and a boy of fifteen came in, the
son of Fedor Mihailovich, a pupil of the fifth class of
20 the local school.
"What do you want?"
"It is the first of the month to-day, father."
"Well! You want your money?"
It had been arranged that the father should pay his
25 son a monthly allowance of three roubles as pocket
money. Fedor Mihailovich frowned, took out of his
pocket-book a coupon of two roubles fifty kopeks
which he found among the bank-notes, and added to
it fifty kopeks in silver out of the loose change in his
30 purse. The boy kept silent, and did not take the money
his father proffered him.
"Father, please give me some more in advance."
"What?"
"I would not ask for it, but I have borrowed a
35 small sum from a friend, and promised upon my word
of honour to pay it off. My honour is dear to me, and
that is why I want another three roubles. I don't like
asking you; but, please, father, give me another three
roubles."
40 "I have told you—"
"I know, father, but just for once."
"You have an allowance of three roubles and you
ought to be content. I had not fifty kopeks when I was
your age."
45 "Now, all my comrades have much more. Petrov
and Ivanitsky have fifty roubles a month."

"And I tell you that if you behave like them you
will be a scoundrel. Mind that."
"What is there to mind? You never understand my
50 position. I shall be disgraced if I don't pay my debt. It
is all very well for you to speak as you do."
"Be off, you silly boy! Be off!"
Fedor Mihailovich jumped from his seat and
pounced upon his son. "Be off, I say!" he shouted.
55 "You deserve a good thrashing, all you boys!"
His son was at once frightened and embittered.
The bitterness was even greater than the fright. With
his head bent down he hastily turned to the door.
Fedor Mihailovich did not intend to strike him, but he
60 was glad to vent his wrath, and went on shouting and
abusing the boy till he had closed the door.
When the maid came in to announce that dinner
was ready, Fedor Mihailovich rose.
"At last!" he said. "I don't feel hungry any
65 longer."
He went to the dining-room with a sullen face.
At table his wife made some remark, but he gave
her such a short and angry answer that she abstained
from further speech. The son also did not lift his eyes
70 from his plate, and was silent all the time. The trio
finished their dinner in silence, rose from the table and
separated, without a word.
After dinner the boy went to his room, took the
coupon and the change out of his pocket, and threw the
75 money on the table. After that he took off his uniform
and put on a jacket.
He sat down to work, and began to study Latin
grammar out of a dog's-eared book. After a while he
rose, closed and bolted the door, shifted the money into
80 a drawer, took out some cigarette papers, rolled one up,
stuffed it with cotton wool, and began to smoke.
He spent nearly two hours over his grammar and
writing books without understanding a word of what
he saw before him; then he rose and began to stamp
85 up and down the room, trying to recollect all that his
father had said to him. All the abuse showered upon
him, and worst of all his father's angry face, were
as fresh in his memory as if he saw and heard them
all over again. "Silly boy! You ought to get a good
90 thrashing!" And the more he thought of it the angrier
he grew. He remembered also how his father said: "I
see what a scoundrel you will turn out. I know you
will. You are sure to become a cheat, if you go on like
that." He had certainly forgotten how he felt when he
95 was young!

CONTINUE

1

Which choice best summarizes the passage?

A) One character whose request is denied by another character becomes embittered.

B) One character negotiates a sum of money with another character.

C) One character falls out of favor with another character over a family matter.

D) One character becomes disheartened after a violent confrontation with another character.

2

The main purpose of lines 10-17 ("Fedor Mihailovich... there") is to

A) show that Fedor's mood is easily susceptible to change based on circumstances.

B) indicate that Fedor's reaction to the event that is about to occur is an unusual one.

C) provide context for understanding Fedor's excessively harsh treatment of his son.

D) reveal the exact incident that triggers a transformation in Fedor's temperament.

3

In lines 50-65, the narrator reveals that Fedor is the type of person who

A) has a strong system of values.

B) demands respect from his family.

C) refuses to let others speak their views.

D) is more vocal than physically violent.

4

Which choice provides the best evidence for the claim that Fedor had previously heard such a request from his son?

A) Lines 21-24 ("What do...money")

B) Lines 30-31 ("The boy...him")

C) Lines 40-43 ("I have...content")

D) Lines 47-48 ("And I...that")

5

In depicting the relationship between Fedor Mihailovich and his son, the narrator presents an explicit contrast between their perspectives on

A) the priority of paying back one's debt.

B) the harmful influence of one's friends.

C) the allowance that is considered fair.

D) the importance of keeping one's word.

6

In Fedor's denial of his son's request, there is a shift from his use of

A) personal anecdotes to abstract arguments.

B) feigned sympathy to assertion of authority.

C) logic to emotional appeal.

D) reason to intimidation.

7

It can be inferred from the passage that in asking for additional money, Fedor's son anticipates his father will

A) consent without difficulty, as they had made an agreement.

B) stubbornly resist, as he was unaccepting of views other than his own.

C) initially object, but comply once an argument was made.

D) vehemently refuse, as he was struggling to make ends meet.

8

Which choice provides the best evidence for the answer to the previous question?

A) Lines 24-26 ("It had...money")

B) Lines 34-36 ("I would...off")

C) Lines 49-51 ("What is...do")

D) Lines 56-58 ("His son...door")

CONTINUE

9

As used in line 72, "separated" most nearly means

A) split.

B) divided.

C) disconnected.

D) parted.

10

What function does the last paragraph (lines 82-91) serve in the context of the passage as a whole?

A) It illustrates the powerful effect Fedor's rant had on his son.

B) It reveals that Fedor's son has been struggling with his studies.

C) It highlights the severity of Fedor's anger towards his son.

D) It shows that Fedor's son is no longer concerned with his allowance.

CONTINUE

Questions 1-10 are based on the following passage.
Chapter 9.4
Adapted from Guy de Maupassant, *The Wrong House*. Published in Original Short Stories, Volume IV (1880).

Quartermaster Varajou had obtained a week's leave to go and visit his sister, Madame Padoie. Varajou, who was in garrison at Rennes and was
Line leading a pretty outlandish life, finding himself high
5 and dry, wrote to his sister saying that he would devote a week to her. It was not that he cared particularly for Mme. Padoie, a little moralist, a devotee, and always cross; but he needed money, needed it very badly, and he remembered that, of all his relations, the Padoies
10 were the only ones whom he had never approached on the subject. . .

Varajou, on leaving the train station in his sister's town, had someone direct him to the house of his brother-in-law, whom he found in his office arguing
15 with the Breton peasants of the neighborhood. Padoie rose from his seat, held out his hand across the table littered with papers, murmured, "Take a chair. I will be at liberty in a moment," sat down again and resumed his discussion.

20 The peasants did not understand his explanations, the collector did not understand their line of argument. He spoke French, they spoke Breton, and the clerk who acted as interpreter appeared not to understand either.

It lasted a long time, a very long time. Varajou
25 looked at his brother-in-law and thought: "What a fool!" Padoie must have been almost fifty. He was tall, thin, bony, slow, hairy, with heavy arched eyebrows. He wore a velvet skull cap with a gold cord vandyke design round it. His look was gentle, like his actions.
30 His speech, his gestures, his thoughts, all were soft. Varajou said to himself, "What a fool!"

He, himself, was one of those noisy roysterers for whom the greatest pleasures in life are the cafe and abandoned women. He understood nothing outside of
35 these conditions of existence.

A boisterous braggart, filled with contempt for the rest of the world, he despised the entire universe from the height of his ignorance. When he said: "Dear lord, what a spree!" he expressed the highest degree of
40 admiration of which his mind was capable.

Having finally got rid of his peasants, Padoie inquired:

"How are you?"

"Pretty well, as you see. And how are you?"

45 "Quite well, thank you. It is very kind of you to

have thought of coming to see us."

"Oh, I have been thinking of it for some time; but, you know, in the military profession one has not much freedom."

50 "Oh, I know, I know. All the same, it is very kind of you."

"And Josephine, is she well?"

"Yes, yes, thank you; you will see her presently."
"Where is she?"

55 "She is making some calls. We have a great many friends here; it is a very nice town."

"I thought so."

The door opened and Mme. Padoie appeared. She went over to her brother without any eagerness, held
60 her cheek for him to kiss, and asked:

"Have you been here long?"

"No, hardly half an hour."

"Oh, I thought the train would be late. Will you come into the parlor?"

65 They went into the adjoining room, leaving Padoie to his accounts and his taxpayers. As soon as they were alone, she said:

"I have heard nice things about you!"

"What have you heard?"

70 "It seems that you are behaving like a blackguard, getting drunk and contracting debts."

He appeared very much astonished.

"I! never in the world!"

"Oh, do not deny it, I know it."

75 He attempted to defend himself, but she gave him such a lecture that he could say nothing more.

She then resumed:

"We dine at six o'clock, and you can amuse yourself until then. I cannot entertain you, as I have so
80 many things to do."

When he was alone he hesitated as to whether he should sleep or take a walk. He looked first at the door leading to his room and then at the hall door, and decided to go out. He sauntered slowly through the
85 quiet Breton town, so sleepy, so calm, so dead, on the shores of its inland bay that is called "le Morbihan." He looked at the little gray houses, the occasional pedestrians, the empty stores, and he murmured:

"Vannes is certainly not gay, not lively. It was a
90 sad idea, my coming here."

He reached the harbor, the desolate harbor, walked back along a lonely, deserted boulevard, and got home before five o'clock. Then he threw himself on his bed to sleep till dinner time. The maid woke him, knocking
95 at the door.

"Dinner is ready, sir:"

He went downstairs. In the damp dining-room

CONTINUE

with the paper peeling from the walls near the floor, he saw a soup tureen on a round table without any table
100 cloth, on which were also three melancholy soup-plates.

M. and Mme. Padoie entered the room at the same time as Varajou. They all sat down to table, and the husband and wife crossed themselves over the pit of
105 their stomachs, after which Padoie helped the soup, a meat soup. It was the day for pot-roast.

After the soup, they had the beef, which was done to rags, melted, greasy, like pap. The officer ate slowly, with disgust, weariness and rage.

1

Which choice best describes a major theme of the passage?

A) The boredom and isolation of a life in the countryside
B) The disappointment within a family caused by opposing lifestyles
C) The enduring and sustaining benefits from a moral way of life
D) The corrupting influence of alcohol and gambling on a family

2

Which of the following best describes what happens in the passage?

A) A character seeks redemption with the help and guidance of a family member.
B) A character is affectionately welcomed by his close relatives during a long-overdue visit.
C) A character who harbors high expectations is disappointed when they are not met.
D) A character becomes dismayed as he realizes the futility of his visit to a relative's home.

3

In comparison to her brother, the narrator depicts Madame Padoie as

A) more pious.
B) more extravagant.
C) less content.
D) less independent.

4

The narrator implies that Varajou calls Padoie "a fool" mainly because

A) Varajou thinks that his brother-in-law dresses inappropriately for his age.
B) Varajou's wayward lifestyle limits his understanding of mundane interactions.
C) Varajou is frustrated at his brother-in-law's extended negotiations with the peasants.
D) Varajou considers Padoie's inability to communicate with the peasants to be a mark of stupidity.

5

Which choice provides the best evidence for the conclusion that Varajou's activities had not remained a secret?

A) Lines 3-6 ("Varajou, who...her")
B) Lines 32-35 ("He, himself...existence")
C) Lines 61-64 ("Have you...parlor")
D) Lines 68-71 ("I have...debts")

6

As used in line 38, "height" most nearly means

A) magnitude.
B) altitude.
C) peak.
D) severity.

7

It can be reasonably inferred from the passage that the true reason Varajou had not visited the Padoies recently is that

A) he held a position in the army that prevented him from taking multiple vacations.
B) he felt condescension towards his sister and thought it below himself to visit her.
C) he had approached other relatives for money before resorting to visit his sister.
D) he disliked spending time with his sister whose system of values was alien to him.

CONTINUE

8

Which choice provides the best evidence for the answer to the previous question?

A) Lines 6-8 ("It was...money")

B) Lines 9-11 ("of all...subject")

C) Lines 36-38 ("A boisterous...ignorance")

D) Lines 47-49 ("Oh, I...freedom")

9

Which of the following best describes the interchange between Madame Padoie and Varajou?

A) She greets him effusively and he reciprocates.

B) She boldly reprimands him and he is outraged.

C) She accuses him of immoral conduct and he is embarrassed.

D) She reports what is being said about him and he acts shocked.

10

In describing Varajou's visit to the Padoies' neighborhood, the narrator primarily creates a contrast between

A) the mood in the Padoie household and the atmosphere of the surrounding village.

B) Madame Padoie's impatience with Varajou's lack of religious devotion and her husband's tolerance of it.

C) Varajou's inner resentment towards his sister and his facade of respect for her.

D) the Padoies' positive perception of the village they reside in and Varajou's despairing reaction to it.

CONTINUE

Questions 1-10 are based on the following passage.
Chapter 9.5
The following is an excerpt from *The Vengeance of Felix* (1921) by José de Medeiros E Albuquerque.

Old Felix had followed his trade of digger in all the quarries that Rio de Janeiro possessed. He was a sort of Hercules with huge limbs, but stupid as a
Line post. His companions had nicknamed him Hardhead
5 because of his obstinate character. Once an idea had penetrated his skull it would stick there like a gimlet and the devil himself couldn't pull it out. But Felix, despite his vigorous and sanguine constitution, was by no means quick to anger nor immediately responsive
10 to injury; on the contrary he was exceedingly patient in his vindictiveness. His ruses were not of very great finesse and required very little talent; but by dint of considering and reconsidering the case, by dint of waiting patiently for the propitious opportunity to
15 present itself, he finally would play some evil trick upon his comrades.

Felix's wife survived just long enough to leave him a son and a daughter. The son became a notorious character, the daughter an impudent, cynical little
20 runabout who would fill their rickety abode with chatter about affairs concerning the "man" of so-and-so or such-and-such. And thus things were going when an excruciating rheumatism attacked both his legs, rendering him incapable of moving about, and
25 confining him to an old armchair.

Just about this time, the son attacked a peaceful citizen and, with a knife thrust in the stomach, despatched him to a better world. The old man was in the habit of reading his gazette religiously; thus he
30 learned the news of his son's conviction. This made him furious, not because of the sentence but because of a special circumstance. The policeman who had arrested his son was Bernardo, his own neighbor—the same chap who would greet him daily with the ironic
35 words: "How are things, Felix old boy? And when will you be ready for a waltz?"

From that moment hatred dominated Felix's existence and became the only power that could vanquish the ever-growing misery of his broken-down
40 body. The thought that he could not grow well, while Bernardo would continue to live in insolent impunity, was enough to give him convulsions of rage; he would concoct scheme upon scheme of vengeance, almost all of them impracticable, for he was chained to the spot
45 in stupid impotence.

Months rolled on. A plan had arisen in his brain, and slowly, ever since he had learned that his case was incurable, his project had absorbed his entire mental activity. He breathed only for his plan, for the sure,
50 propitious opportunity.

At last it came. At dusk his daughter had left. In the morning, his daughter returned, and with her came Jane, Bernardo's "friend". "You rotten thing!" Jane cried. "Trying to take away somebody else's
55 man." The two women came to blows, there was a whistle, the police arrived, and the women were taken to the lock-up. An anger only savage beasts can know overpowered Felix. What! His daughter, the mistress of Bernardo!

60 Bernardo returned, ignorant of the morning's events. He approached Felix, asking him the classic question: "Now then, how goes it?"

Felix said that he had something very serious to tell him. But first he insisted that Bernardo go and
65 bring his knife.

"All right, I'll get it," he replied. And he was back with the knife, which he gave to the invalid.

"Now," continued the latter, "go and close the door. Close it well, and turn the key."

70 Bernardo felt some mistrust at all this mystery, but knowing that the old man could do him no harm, he obeyed.

"Here, put this watch in your pocket." And Felix drew from his pocket a nickel watch.

75 "What am I to do with this, Felix?" asked Bernardo.

"Keep it," was the reply.

"The old duffer is crazy for sure," thought Bernardo, nevertheless doing as he was told.

80 Felix made a movement that caused his pain to increase anew, and he began to utter terrible cries. "I am dying! I am dying!"

Bernardo's mistrust grew, and, seeing that the old man still clutched the knife, he thought the invalid
85 would kill him if he should attempt to approach. He said, "I'll be back right away, Felix." and turned to leave.

Brusquely, Felix uncovered his own breast, and with a rapid movement, right over the heart, he thrust
90 in the blade with all his might.

Bernardo rushed to the door, called for help and returned to pull the knife from the wound, and to see whether it was yet possible to save the unfortunate man. Men and women ran up to the house crying
95 loudly, seeing Bernardo with a long knife whence the blood was dripping, and seeing the pierced breast of old Felix. Bernardo was punched and kicked and

CONTINUE

cudgelled from one infuriated person to the other, and led to the police-station.

100   Bernardo was sentenced to hard labor for life. Nobody would believe his story. Had he not been caught red-handed? The presence of the nickel-watch in his pocket indicated sufficiently that the motive of the crime was robbery. The vengeance of old Felix had

105 been well calculated: the old man had conquered.

1

Which choice best describes the developmental pattern of the passage?

A) A lighthearted retelling of a comical story

B) A candid portrayal of a tragic misunderstanding

C) A reflective account of an unfortunate event

D) A descriptive narrative of a series of events

2

In context of the passage as a whole, the description of Felix's daughter in lines 19-22 ("the daughter...such-and-such") primarily serves to

A) foreshadow an event that occurs later in the passage.

B) introduce a character that is central to the passage.

C) indicate that Felix's daughter is a neglectful caretaker.

D) point out a source of Felix's annoyance in his daily life.

3

The passage implies that Felix regards Bernardo as

A) fortunate.

B) sadistic.

C) meddlesome.

D) audacious.

4

Which choice provides the best evidence for the claim that Bernardo habitually taunts Felix?

A) Lines 22-25 ("And thus...armchair")

B) Lines 33-36 ("the same...waltz")

C) Lines 60-62 ("Bernardo returned...it")

D) Lines 78-79 ("The old...told")

5

According to the passage, one consequence of Felix's hatred for Bernardo was that

A) Felix's condition worsened as he continued to neglect his health.

B) Felix's condition improved as he began to feel that revenge was possible.

C) Felix was unable to contain his anger and lashed out at Bernardo.

D) Felix was empowered enough to overcome his unbearable suffering.

6

It can be reasonably inferred from the passage that the intensity of Felix's obsession over his plan was mainly caused by the

A) dismay that he felt when his son was incarcerated.

B) news that his disease was impossible to cure.

C) thought that Bernardo would never experience his pain.

D) realization that his daughter was Bernardo's mistress.

7

Which choice provides the best evidence for the answer to the previous question?

A) Lines 40-42 ("The thought...rage")

B) Lines 42-44 ("he would...impracticable")

C) Lines 47-49 ("slowly, ever...activity")

D) Lines 57-59 ("An anger...Bernardo")

CONTINUE

8

The narrator uses the phrase "stupid impotence" (line 45) to convey Felix's

A) manifestations of uncontrollable rage.

B) demonstrations of stubbornness.

C) feelings of utter powerlessness.

D) conception of a foolish plan.

9

As used in line 61, "classic" most nearly means

A) simple.

B) ordinary.

C) basic.

D) usual.

10

The narrator indicates that Felix gave Bernardo his watch primarily to

A) ensure that Felix's body is properly identified by the authorities.

B) plant evidence on Bernardo that identified him as Felix's killer.

C) distract Bernardo so Felix could take his knife from him.

D) reassure Bernardo that Felix was too crazy to be a threat to him.

Answer Key: CHAPTER NINE

Chapter 9.1
1. A
2. B
3. B
4. D
5. D
6. D
7. C
8. C
9. B
10. A

Chapter 9.2
1. D
2. B
3. C
4. D
5. B
6. A
7. C
8. A
9. D
10. B

Chapter 9.3
1. A
2. C
3. D
4. C
5. C
6. D
7. C
8. B
9. D
10. A

Chapter 9.4
1. B
2. D
3. A
4. B
5. D
6. A
7. C
8. B
9. D
10. D

Chapter 9.5
1. D
2. A
3. D
4. B
5. D
6. B
7. C
8. C
9. D
10. B

Answer Explanations

Chapter 9

Chapter 9.1 | *Pygmalion* (Chris Holliday Adaptation)

1) CORRECT ANSWER: A
Early in the passage, Eliza feels like "turning tail and fleeing" (line 3) to her home; however, by the final stages of the passage she has asserted herself, declaring that she wants "to be a lady in a flower-shop" (line 92). This information supports A and can be used to eliminate B and C (which wrongly assume that Eliza is strong-willed at the BEGINNING of the passage). D is problematic because the other characters would not regard Eliza as poised or refined in manner, and because she speaks brusquely and emphatically (not calmly or "nonchalantly") as the passage nears its end.

2) CORRECT ANSWER: B
The word "defeated" refers to Eliza's reaction to a word that she did not "even know how to say" (line 11); she is thus uncertain of or confused by how to say it, so that B is the best answer. Keep in mind that Eliza does not spend a long time regarding the word: A, C, and D all indicate lasting or overpowering negative reactions that would cause her to either linger or leave the premises, and should thus be eliminated.

3) CORRECT ANSWER: B
In the relevant lines, Mrs. Pearce assumes that Eliza is a tradesperson who does not deserve to enter by the front door, then criticizes Eliza as a "peculiar" (line 18) person whom Professor Higgins might not want to see. This negative attitude on Mrs. Pearce's part supports B. A is incorrect because the two characters (NOT the larger groups they represent) are the focus, C is incorrect because Mrs. Pearce soon takes a secondary role in the narrative, and D is incorrect because the era (or historical timeframe) of the passage is nowhere mentioned in these lines. It is suggested by Mrs. Pearce's attitude that the context is an era of social stratification, but WHICH era is never clarified.

4) CORRECT ANSWER: D
Eliza's first impression of Higgins is that he was "throwing" money about (lines 58-59) on the night before the events depicted in the passage: she thinks that he is an irresponsible man who needs more money, so that D is an effective answer. A, B, and C could refer to SECOND impressions that Eliza has on the day depicted in the passage (or to the reader's own impressions), but do not accurately reflect her first ideas about Higgins.

5) CORRECT ANSWER: D

In lines 87-90, Higgins predicts that he can radically improve Eliza's entire way of speaking in "three months"; his belief that he can accomplish this daunting feat (considering his low opinion of Eliza) and the short timespan that he gives both show that he is overconfident. D is thus the best answer. A indicates that Higgins has temporarily lost interest in Eliza, B indicates that Eliza's way of speaking is hurting her prospects in life, and C records Eliza's desire to learn from Higgins. These answers do not deal with the topic of how Higgins regards HIS OWN abilities and should thus be eliminated.

6) CORRECT ANSWER: D

The conversation begins with Higgins's claim that English speakers can be classified into "Upper, Middle and Lower Class" (line 46), a set of distinctions that Pickering does not find entirely important; as the conversation proceeds, Higgins insults Eliza on the basis of her lowly social status, in conduct that Pickering finds "condescending" (line 66). This information supports the difference of opinion indicated in D. A addresses a topic (the talking machine) that only occurs in one confined part of the conversation, B distorts a main topic (the methodology of Higgins's research, not WHY he undertook it), and C calls too much attention to a topic that only Higgins (NOT Pickering) finds important.

7) CORRECT ANSWER: C

In lines 91-92, Eliza claims that she wants to be "a lady in a flower-shop", a goal that is less grandiose and more pragmatic than Higgins's goal of passing off Eliza as a duchess. C is the best answer. A mistakenly indicates that Higgins is smarter (when in fact he is simply better educated), B wrongly identifies the condescending Higgins as respectful, and D introduces the possibility that Eliza has ulterior motives (when in fact she has straightforward desires and is not especially clever or "calculating" in this regard).

8) CORRECT ANSWER: C

See above for the explanation of the correct answer. A indicates Eliza's incomprehension of one of Higgins's topics of study, B records remarks from Mrs. Pearce, and D indicates that Eliza and Mrs. Pearce have differing reactions to Higgins's project. Make sure not to take A as evidence for Question 7 A; Eliza does not possess Higgins's specialized knowledge of language, but she may be smarter than he is in other ways.

9) CORRECT ANSWER: B

Throughout the passage, Pickering is at odds with Higgins's apparent bias against people from lower classes; he even scolds Higgins for treating Eliza harshly and speaks kindly to Eliza herself (lines 64-68). Pickering is thus sympathetic towards Eliza and is genuine in his desire to help her improve her life. B is the best answer. A wrongly assumes that Pickering is aware of Eliza's finances (a subject he never raises), while C wrongly assumes a positive tone towards parts of Higgins's research that involve class biases. D is a trap answer: Pickering bets that Henry CANNOT help Eliza, but does so MAINLY as a ploy to get Henry to take Eliza as a student and help Eliza improve her situation.

10) CORRECT ANSWER: A

Pickering has just made a bet that Higgins "cannot succeed" (line 97) with Eliza as a student; Eliza would not approve of this sentiment at face value, so, in praising Pickering, she must be aware of Pickering's ulterior motive of getting Higgins to take her on as a student. This information supports A and can be used to eliminate B (since Eliza does want to move forward with the lessons and the prospect of improvement) and D (since Eliza is still taking Higgins as a teacher). C is a trap answer; although Eliza may in fact have underestimated the cost of the lessons earlier (lines 78-84), she arrived at her estimate through her own chain of reasoning (not through deception or "bluffing").

Chapter 9.2 | Prelude

1) CORRECT ANSWER: D

The passage begins with Mrs. Fairfield's reflections on her daughter Beryl's childhood and her former kitchen, but then changes focus when the adult Beryl calls for her (line 44) and requests her help disposing of some pictures. This information supports D, while A is only applicable to the first major portion of the passage. B mischaracterizes the relationship between Mrs. Fairfield and Beryl (who does not "take advantage" of her mother but works with her to decide the fate of the pictures), while C misstates Mrs. Fairfield's situation (reflecting on an old home, not REVISITING it).

2) CORRECT ANSWER: B

In lines 40-41, the narrator calls attention to the "series of patterns" by which Mrs. Fairfield organizes her kitchen, which Mrs. Fairfield finds "very nice, very satisfactory" (line 43). This information supports B, while the passage's positive depiction of Mrs. Fairfield as satisfied and self-sufficient can be used to eliminate both A and D. C is a trap answer: the most prominent colors in the passage ("green" in line 11 and "red" in lines 18-19, for instance) occur in MEMORIES that Mrs. Fairfield has and thus do not actually describe the objects that "surround" her.

3) CORRECT ANSWER: C

Reflecting on her change in living situation, Mrs. Fairfield muses that "It takes Australian sun" (line 14) such as the the superior sunlight in her former house to ripen grapes; the Tasmanian house thus received more sunlight, so that C is the best answer. A and B are problematic because Mrs. Fairfield has fond impressions of BOTH houses. D is a trap answer: cleaning is in fact a major theme or topic of the passage, but Mrs. Fairfield does not focus on the issue of cleaning the Tasmanian house (only her present residence).

4) CORRECT ANSWER: D

The word "sure" is used to describe the everyday task of putting the crocks away, which Mrs. Fairfield executes in a "precise" (line 36) manner. She is adept at and accustomed to this task, which has become routine for her. D is the best answer, while other answers do not fit the exact context and line reference. A indicates a personality trait (determined or "holding fast"), B indicates that something is true, and C would refer to the crocks themselves (which are in secure positions) not to the TASK that Mrs. Fairfield is performing.

5) CORRECT ANSWER: B

In lines 48-50, Beryl (who is carrying two large pictures) asks her mother what she can do with "these awful hideous Chinese paintings". Her dislike of the pictures indicates that she wants to get rid of them in some way, so that B is the best answer. A neglects the fact that Beryl has a practical goal in mind (and overstates the negativity of her situation), C refers to an event (the cleaning) that happens towards the end of the passage and that Beryl did hope for, and D assumes that Stanley himself (NOT Beryl) dislikes the paintings and wants them out of sight.

6) CORRECT ANSWER: A

See above for the explanation of the correct answer. B indicates that Stanley thinks that the picture frames might be valuable, and C and D indicate Beryl's frustration with her mother's methods. All of these answers occur significantly far after Beryl makes her first appearance and indicates that she does not want the paintings.

7) CORRECT ANSWER: C

In the relevant lines, Beryl is described as directing an "angry glance" at her mother's "placid kitchen" (lines 64-65). This information supports C as the best answer. A wrongly indicates that Beryl (who simply rejects her mother's suggestion) is offended by Mrs. Fairfield's idea, while B and D both call attention to aspects not explicitly described in the passage (Stanley's office in its different stages and Stanley's emotions towards the accumulation of photographs).

8) CORRECT ANSWER: A

In lines 79-80, Beryl "loftily" attributes her mother's apparently vexing way of doing things to "old age"; she thus sees herself as above her mother, or is "condescending". A is the best answer, while the same evidence can be used to to eliminate positive choices such as B and C. D, "indignant", means strongly offended and can be eliminated as too negative for Beryl's emotions of frustration and superiority.

9) CORRECT ANSWER: D

See above for the explanation of the correct answer. A records Beryl's early question about what to do with the paintings, B indicates Beryl's (and presumably Stanley's and Mrs. Fairfield's) distaste for the paintings, and C indicates Beryl's intended course of action. Since these answers deal primarily with Beryl's approach to the paintings (not her ideas about her mother) they should be readily eliminated.

10) CORRECT ANSWER: B

The word "deliberate" refers to Mrs. Fairfield's "way of doing things" (lines 78-79), which (on the evidence of her cleaning habits) involves considerable or painstaking attention to detail. B is the best answer. A and C wrongly indicate that Mrs. Fairfield must think through or prepare her tasks (when in fact she begins cleaning the painting almost immediately), while D means "temporary" or "uncertain" and is thus inappropriate to Mrs. Fairfield's decisive habits.

Chapter 9.3 | *The Forged Coupon*

1) CORRECT ANSWER: A
In the passage, Fedor Mihailovich's son asks for "more in advance" (line 32) in terms of allowance; when Fedor Mihailovich denies the request, the son becomes "frightened and embittered" (line 56) and spends time sulking in his room. This evidence supports A, while B is inaccurate because Fedor quickly and emphatically refuses the request (rather than negotiating). C is inaccurate because the son wishes to obtain money for a school-related (not family) matter, while D wrongly characterizes the unpleasant confrontation between father and son as "violent", when in fact Fedor has no interest in striking his son.

2) CORRECT ANSWER: C
The relevant lines indicate that Fedor Mihailovich feels "embittered" and that "everything seemed to go contrary to his wishes"; this negative set of circumstances explain why he, in reaction, would treat his son negatively. Choose C and eliminate B, since it would be natural for a man in a negative mood to react negatively to new circumstances. A wrongly offers a broad assessment of Fedor's personality (rather than focusing on SPECIFIC events as the passage does), D is incorrect because Fedor's temperament has ALREADY changed to one of annoyance (line 7) by the end of the first paragraph.

3) CORRECT ANSWER: D
Fedor Mihailovich shouts at his son as a boy who deserves "a good thrashing" (line 55) but "did not intend to strike him" (line 59). This information supports D. Fedor's system of values is mainly the focus of the first paragraph (not the conversation with his son, eliminating A), while his exchange only involves his son (not the rest of his family as well, eliminating B). Moreover, Fedor has given his son a chance to speak his views, so that C is a faulty characterization of Fedor.

4) CORRECT ANSWER: C
In lines 40-43, Fedor responds to his son's request with the words "I have told you" and lays out a set of firm conditions, indicating that this information has been delivered before. C is thus the best answer. A and B indicate that Fedor and his son have a routine regarding the money, but NOT that the son has at some earlier point made a special request regarding the money. D records one of Fedor's criticisms of his son's companions, not a direct commentary on whether Fedor has ever received a request for more money than he usually gives.

5) CORRECT ANSWER: C
While the son sees an increase in the allowance as a justifiable matter of "honour" (line 36), Fedor Mihailovich believes the son "ought to be content" (line 43) and that a smaller amount is reasonable and just. C is thus the best answer. A and D record principles that the son uses to justify his actions (and that Fedor Mihailovich might concur with in OTHER scenarios), while B addresses one of the ideas that Fedor uses to argue against his son (and that the son, instead of opposing, disregards to argue that an increase is honorable).

6) CORRECT ANSWER: D

At first, Fedor calmly argues that his son's allowance is greater than was his own as a young man (line 43-44) and criticizes the influence of the son's friends (lines 47-48); he abandons this means of making fairly rational points to "vent his wrath" (line 60) and frighten the son off. This shift from reason to intimidating emotion justifies D. A wrongly indicates that he continues to make "arguments" rather than simply shouting, B wrongly mistakes Fedor's initial calmness for "feigned sympathy", and C wrongly assumes that he later tries to "appeal" to his son (rather than scaring the son away and terminating the argument)

7) CORRECT ANSWER: C

In lines 34-36, the son tells his father that he "would not ask" for the money but gives a justification (a matter of honor) that is intended to win the father over despite apparent reservations; this information supports C. A is inaccurate because the son DOES feel compelled to make an argument (rather than simply present the request and have it fulfilled), while B (which wrongly indicates that the father would not listen to the son's viewpoint) and D (which would make the son's entire task illogical if refusal is expected) should both be eliminated as too strongly negative. In addition, Fedor's financial situation and whether he is "struggling to make ends meet" (D) is not specified in the passage.

8) CORRECT ANSWER: B

See above for the explanation of the correct answer. A simply describes the arrangement between father and son, C records some of the son's objections to Fedor's arguments, and D records the son's response to Fedor's outburst. Only B, which unlike the other line references closely follows upon the original request for more money, clarifies the son's expectation of the final outcome.

9) CORRECT ANSWER: D

The word "separated" refers to the action of Fedor and his family members after they "finished their dinner" (line 71) and then left the table. They thus "parted" from one another; D is the best answer, while A and B would refer to a physical item that is being broken into pieces (not to people going off for different activities) and C would refer to a breakdown or interruption in communication (not to the end of a group event).

10) CORRECT ANSWER: A

The final paragraph records the distracted state of Fedor's son, who reflects on "All the abuse showered upon him" (line 86-87) and vividly remembers his father's words. A accurately reflects the strength of the son's reaction; B involves a misreading of lines 82-84 (which indicate that the angry scene has distracted the son from his studies, NOT that the son has difficulty in school). C wrongly focuses on Fedor (not the son), while D is inaccurate because the events surrounding the allowance still preoccupy the son, even though the son does not consider re-negotiating the allowance itself.

Chapter 9.4 | *The Wrong House*

1) CORRECT ANSWER: B

The passage centers on Varajou, who has been "leading a pretty outlandish life" (line 4), but finds himself filled with "disgust, weariness and rage" (line 109) after visiting his sister's quiet household and lonely town. This information supports B, while the narrator in fact criticizes Varajou (eliminating A, which wrongly assumes agreement with his emotions). C is inaccurate because the narrator does not apply a strong positive tone to Varajou's sister and brother-in-law (and even closely conveys Varajou's negative sentiments), while D is problematic because Varajou is still functional and because his wild lifestyle has not corrupted his very different sister.

2) CORRECT ANSWER: D

Early on, the narrator reveals that Varajou "needed money, needed it very badly" (line 8) and intends to ask the Padoies; unfortunately for him, his sister simply lectures him on his bad ways (lines 75-76) and does not show any clear inclination to help him financially. This information supports the idea in D that his visit is futile and can be used to eliminate A (since Varajou wants money, not a change in lifestyle) and B (since his sister is chastising in demeanor, not affectionate). C is problematic because it is not clear that Varajou's desired sum is "high" or indicative of "high expectations"; he may just need a modest sum to fulfill a pressing or time-sensitive obligation.

3) CORRECT ANSWER: A

While Varajou's pleasures involve "the cafe and abandoned women" (lines 33-34), Madame Padoie is a woman who professes high moral standards and religiously crosses herself (line 104) before eating. She is thus more "pious" than her brother; the evidence of the passage supports A and contradicts B. Though different, the two siblings BOTH seem content with their lifestyles and personalities (eliminating C), while Varajou's financial obligations may mean that he has LESS independence to do what he wants that his sister does (eliminating D).

4) CORRECT ANSWER: B

Varajou's description of Padoie as a "fool" (line 31) occurs after the narrator's description of Padoie's soft and gentle demeanor, which strongly contrasts with Varajou's wild nature; in fact, Varajou "understood nothing" (line 34) outside of his wild mode of existence. B is thus the best answer, while Padouie's attire (A) and his interactions with the peasants (C and D) are mentioned but are not the reason for Varajou's distaste, which has to do with Varajou's OWN character and the limits of his understanding.

5) CORRECT ANSWER: D

In lines 68-71, Varajou's sister tells Varajou that he has apparently "been behaving like a blackguard, getting drunk and contracting debts". She is thus aware that his lifestyle is, in fact, disreputable, making D a highly effective answer. A simply indicates that Varajou intends to visit his sister, B indicates Varajou's likings and the limits of his understanding, and C records pleasantries exchanged by Varajou and his sister. None of these answers name a SPECIFIC person who is aware of Varajou's lifestyle in the manner of D.

6) CORRECT ANSWER: A

The word "height" refers to Varajou's "ignorance" (line 38), which is so considerable in extent or magnitude that it leads him to despise the entire universe. Thus, "height" explains how considerable his ignorance is, making A the best answer. B and C wrongly refer to literal or physical "height", while D does not fit the line reference: Varajou himself may be "severe", but his "ignorance" is a trait and cannot, logically, have personality traits of its own, such as "severity".

7) CORRECT ANSWER: C

In lines 9-11, it is revealed that the Padoies are the "only ones" of Varajou's relations whom he has not approached for money: they are thus a last resort for him now that other options have been exhausted, so that C is the best answer. While Varajou is on leave, HOW MANY absences from the army he is allowed is never discussed (eliminating A). Keep in mind also that he has little respect for the lifestyle observed by his sister, but that his PRIMARY reason for staying away is that they were not financially useful to him for a time (eliminating B and D).

8) CORRECT ANSWER: B

See above for the explanation of the correct answer. A indicates that Varajou does not share his sister's moral code, C indicates that he despises other people, and D indicates that his military duties supposedly leave him with little freedom. Make sure not to wrongly take A as evidence for Question 7 B, C as evidence for Question 7 D, or D as evidence for Question 7 A.

9) CORRECT ANSWER: D

During the exchange between Madame Padoie and Varajou, Madame Padoie tells her brother of reports that he has been "behaving like a blackguard" (line 70); Varajou appeared "astonished" (line 72) and "attempted to defend himself" (line 75) even though he is fully aware that he is devoted to disreputable pleasures. D is the best answer. A is incorrect because the two characters greet in a strained manner and clearly have a difference of opinion; B (outrage) and C (embarrassment) do not capture the fact that Varajou defends his conduct, rather than lashing out at his sister or allowing her scolding to humble him.

10) CORRECT ANSWER: D

Padoie states that he lives in "a very nice town" (line 56) where he and his wife have many friends. In sharp contrast, Varajou finds the town "not gay, not lively" (line 89) because he dislikes its lonely and deserted state. D is thus an effective answer. A is incorrect because the same quiet mood prevails both throughout the town and when the Padoies sit down to dinner, B wrongly states that Padoie tolerates Varajou's lack of religiosity (when in fact the two men never raise the subject), and C wrongly indicates that Varajou pretends to respect his sister (when in fact he is more neutral and simply keeps his aversion to himself).

Chapter 9.5 | *The Vengeance of Felix*

1) CORRECT ANSWER: D

The passage describes Felix's character and family, then explains that after losing his mobility he concocted "scheme upon scheme" (line 43) of vengeance upon Bernardo; finally, Felix uses a trick to get Bernardo arrested. Such descriptions of the events make D the best answer. A wrongly identifies the story (which involves violence and murder) as "lighthearted", while B at best focuses on only PART of the passage (Bernardo's misunderstanding towards the end). C is problematic because the passage depicts a SERIES of unfortunate events, not only one as indicated by the question.

2) CORRECT ANSWER: A

In the relevant lines, the daughter is described as "a cynical little runabout" (lines 19-20) who is preoccupied with affairs; it is later revealed that Felix's daughter is involved in an "affair" herself as the "mistress of Bernardo" (lines 58-59). This information supports A, while the daughter is only mentioned prominently in these two short instances (eliminating B, since Felix and Bernardo are more important to the passage). C wrongly identifies the daughter as a caretaker of some sort (when in fact she seems indifferent to her father's welfare), while D indicates that the daughter constantly irritates Felix (when in fact he views her negatively, but might not have to endure the daily company of someone who "runs about").

3) CORRECT ANSWER: D

In lines 33-36, Bernardo asks Felix (who cannot walk) when he will "be ready for a waltz"; this question is seen as a boldly insulting commentary by Felix, who subsequently plots revenge against the "insolent" (line 41) Bernardo. D is the best answer, while A misdirects some of the content of the passage (since Felix has dealt with misfortune, but does not envy Bernardo's good fortune in contrast). B and C apply the wrong negatives to Bernardo, who is not unusually cruel and does not try to invade Felix's affairs. At most, Bernardo arrests Felix's son out of obligation (not because he is sadistic) and finds that Felix's daughter meddles in his (Bernardo's) household.

4) CORRECT ANSWER: B

In lines 33-36, the narrator explains that Bernardo would greet Felix "daily" by asking if Felix, who cannot walk, is "ready for a waltz". This repeated insult directed towards Felix's condition supports B. A does not mention Bernardo at all, C records a question that is apparently harmless, and D conveys Bernardo's idea that Felix is crazy (a criticism that occurs during a strange, catastrophic event and that is not repeated "habitually").

5) CORRECT ANSWER: D

In lines 37-40, the narrator explains that Felix's hatred of Bernardo inspired Felix to "vanquish the ever-growing misery of his broken-down body"; Felix in fact finds a way to kill Bernardo and, apparently, escape his physical misery. This information supports D, while Felix grows neither worse (eliminating A) nor better (eliminating B) but remains confined in the same position after his hatred of Bernardo emerges. C is a trap answer: Felix is in fact angry, but he does successfully contain his anger until the scheme against Bernardo has been set fully in motion.

6) CORRECT ANSWER: B

In lines 47-49, the narrator explains that Felix's determination to set his plan in motion against Bernardo is linked to the fact that Felix's "case was incurable". B is thus the best answer. Keep in mind that Felix does not object to his son's imprisonment (eliminating A), is mostly unconcerned with Bernardo's feelings and perspective (beyond resenting Bernardo, eliminating C), and becomes obsessed with vengeance BEFORE it is revealed that his daughter and Bernardo are having an affair (eliminating D).

7) CORRECT ANSWER: C

See above for the explanation of the correct answer. A discusses Felix's hatred for Bernardo, B indicates that Felix thought up multiple schemes against Bernardo, and D indicates that Felix was angered by Bernardo's affair with his daughter (but does not mention his plan against Bernardo). A and B are trap answers: they describe stages when Felix is still trying to develop a plan, not stages when he HAS arrived at the "plan" mentioned in the previous question.

8) CORRECT ANSWER: C

The phrase "stupid impotence" is used to explain the situation of Felix, who is "chained to the spot" (line 44) and thus cannot put in motion his desired schemes against Bernardo. He is physically powerless, so that C is the best answer and B and D (which criticize Felix's CHARACTER, not his position) are off-topic. A refers to a different part of the passage: Felix does in fact feel rage as described ELSEWHERE, but the reference to his "stupid impotence" conveys physical powerlessness, not strong emotion.

9) CORRECT ANSWER: D

The word "classic" refers to Bernardo's "question" (line 62) about how Felix is doing: because the two men are neighbors, such a question would be expected or usual on Bernardo's part (and in fact calls to mind the similar but more negative question in lines 35-36). D is the best answer. A, B, and C wrongly indicate that the question is uninteresting or without complexity, when in fact it may have interesting answers or lead to strange events, such as those that end the passage.

10) CORRECT ANSWER: B

The "nickel watch" that is first mentioned in lines 73-74 is later pointed to in Bernardo's situation as proof that "the motive of the crime was robbery" (lines 103-104); Felix, who wants vengeance on Bernardo, would naturally want to give Bernardo the watch to frame him in this manner. B is the best answer. A is incorrect because the watch is found on Bernardo (not on Felix as an identifier), C is incorrect because Felix simply gets Bernardo to give him the knife (and does not need a distraction), and D is incorrect because Bernardo feels that Felix is harmless in lines 70-72, BEFORE the watch is initially mentioned.

CHAPTER TEN

Questions 1-10 are based on the following passage.
Chapter 10.1
Adapted from Anne Bronte, *Agnes Grey* (1847).
The narrator is Agnes herself, a young woman
who has left her home to work as a governess*
for the Murray family.

At eighteen, Miss Murray was to emerge from
the quiet obscurity of the schoolroom into the full
blaze of the fashionable world—as much of it, at
Line least, as could be had out of London; for her papa
5 could not be persuaded to leave his rural pleasures
and pursuits, even for a few weeks' residence in town.
She was to make her début on the third of January, at a
magnificent ball, which her mamma proposed to give
to all the nobility and choice gentry of O--- and its
10 neighbourhood for twenty miles round. Of course, she
looked forward to it with the wildest impatience, and
the most extravagant anticipations of delight.
"Miss Grey," said she, one evening, a month
before the all-important day, as I was perusing a long
15 and extremely interesting letter of my sister's—which
I had just glanced at in the morning to see that it
contained no very bad news, and kept till now, unable
before to find a quiet moment for reading it,—"Miss
Grey, do put away that dull, stupid letter, and listen to
20 me! I'm sure my talk must be far more amusing than
that."
She seated herself on the low stool at my feet; and
I, suppressing a sigh of vexation, began to fold up the
epistle.
25 "You should tell the good people at home not to
bore you with such long letters," said she; "and, above
all, do bid them write on proper note-paper, and not on
those great vulgar sheets. You should see the charming
little lady-like notes mamma writes to her friends."
30 "The good people at home," replied I, "know very
well that the longer their letters are, the better I like
them. I should be very sorry to receive a charming
little lady-like note from any of them; and I thought
you were too much of a lady yourself, Miss Murray, to
35 talk about the 'vulgarity' of writing on a large sheet of
paper."
"Well, I only said it to tease you. But now I want
to talk about the ball; and to tell you that you positively
must put off your holidays till it is over."
40 "Why so?—I shall not be present at the ball," I
admitted.
"No, but you will see the rooms decked out before
it begins, and hear the music, and, above all, see me in
my splendid new dress. I shall be so charming, you'll

45 be ready to worship me—you really must stay."
"I should like to see you very much; but I shall
have many opportunities of seeing you equally
charming, on the occasion of some of the numberless
balls and parties that are to be, and I cannot disappoint
50 my friends by postponing my return so long."
"Oh, Miss Grey, never mind your friends! Tell
them we won't let you go."
"But, to say the truth, it would be a
disappointment to myself: I long to see them as much
55 as they to see me—perhaps more."
"Well, but it is such a short time."
"Nearly a fortnight by my computation; and,
besides, I cannot bear the thoughts of a Christmas
spent from home: and, moreover, my sister is going to
60 be married," said I.
"Is she—when?"
"Not till next month; but I want to be there to
assist her in making preparations, and to make the best
of her company while we have her."
65 "Why didn't you tell me before?"
"I've only got the news in this letter, which you
stigmatize as dull and stupid, and won't let me read."
"To whom is she to be married?" asked she.
"To Mr. Richardson, the vicar of a neighbouring
70 parish."
"Is he rich?"
"No; only comfortable."
"Is he handsome?"
"No; only decent."
75 "Young?"
"No; only middling."
"Oh, Miss Grey, mercy! what a wretch! What sort
of a house is it?"
"A quiet little vicarage, with an ivy-clad porch, an
80 old-fashioned garden, and—"
"Oh, stop!—you'll make me sick. How can she
bear it?"
"I expect she'll not only be able to bear it, but to
be very happy. You did not ask me if Mr. Richardson
85 were a good, wise, or amiable man; I could have
answered Yes, to all these questions—at least so
my sister thinks, and I hope she will not find herself
mistaken."

*governess: an employed caretaker and educator
of children

CONTINUE

1

The main purpose of the first paragraph is to

A) introduce an event that main characters later discuss.
B) contrast Agnes Grey and Miss Murray's personalities.
C) describe Miss Murray as a snobbish and aloof character.
D) foreshadow an event that occurs later in the passage.

2

It can be inferred from the passage that Agnes' duties in the household most likely include

A) cooking.
B) cleaning.
C) midwifery.
D) companionship.

3

As used in line 11, "wildest" most nearly means

A) immense.
B) excessive.
C) unruly.
D) uncivilized.

4

As used in line 20, "amusing" most nearly means

A) cheerful.
B) humorous.
C) impressive.
D) interesting.

5

In context of the whole passage, Miss Murray's comments in lines 18-21 ("Miss Grey...that.") mainly serve to

A) belittle Agnes by rudely dismissing the things that are important to her.
B) gain Agnes' attention so that Miss Murray can talk about the ball.
C) poke fun at Agnes' family by calling the paper the letter is written on vulgar.
D) prevent Agnes from leaving so early so she can keep Miss Murray company.

6

Which of the following provides the best evidence for the answer to the previous question?

A) Lines 27-29 ("do bid...friends")
B) Lines 37-39 ("Well, I...over")
C) Lines 44-45 ("I shall...stay")
D) Lines 51-52 ("Oh, Miss...go")

7

Which of the following best describes Anges' reaction to Miss Murray's berating remarks concerning Agnes' family?

A) She compliantly agrees with Miss Murray.
B) She reluctantly tolerates them with exasperation.
C) She actively fights back with indignation.
D) She sternly retorts with composed dignity.

8

Which choice provides the best evidence for the answer to the previous question?

A) Lines 22-24 ("She seated...epistle")
B) Lines 33-36 ("I thought...paper")
C) Lines 46-49 ("I should...be")
D) Lines 62-64 ("Not till...her")

CONTINUE

9

The conversation between Miss Murray and Agnes that follows Agnes' announcement of her sister's wedding serves primarily to

A) provide details about Agnes' family and life at home.

B) highlight the differences in Miss Murray's and Agnes' values.

C) reveal the comparably lower social status of Agnes' family.

D) suggest a growing animosity between Miss Murray and Agnes.

10

In lines 71-88 ("Is he...it?"), the author characterizes Miss Murray as

A) apathetic.

B) despicable.

C) selfish.

D) superficial.

CONTINUE

Questions 1-10 are based on the following passage.
Chapter 10.2
Adapted from Sarah Orne Jewett, "A Late Supper." Published in *Old Friends and New* (1907).

Miss Spring had lost part of her already small income, and she did not know what to do. The first loss could be borne; but the second seemed to put the
Line maintenance of her house out of the question, and this
5 was a dreadful thing to think of. She knew no other way of living, beside having her own house and her own fashion of doing things. If it had been possible, she would have liked to take some boarders; but summer boarders had not yet found out Brookton. Mr.
10 Elden, the kind old lawyer who was her chief adviser, had told her to put an advertisement in one of the Boston papers, and she had done so; but it never had been answered, which was not only a disappointment but a mortification as well. . .
15 Miss Spring tapped her thimble still faster on the window-sill, and thought busily. "I'm going to think it out, and settle it this afternoon," said she to herself. "I must settle it somehow, I will not live on here any longer as if I could afford it." There was a niece of hers
20 who lived in Lowell, who was married and not at all strong. . . It had grieved her in her last visit to see the house half cared for, and she remembered the wistful way Mary had said, "How I wish I could have you here all the time, Aunt Catherine!" and at once Aunt
25 Catherine went on to build a little castle in the air, until she had a chilly consciousness that her own house was to be shut up. . .
In a little while she heard the click of the gate-latch; and, with the start and curiosity a village woman
30 instinctively feels at the knowledge of somebody's coming in at the front-door, she hurried to the other front-window to take a look at her visitor through the blinds. It was only a child, and Miss Catherine did not wait for her to rap with the high and heavy knocker,
35 but was standing in the open doorway when the little girl reached the steps.
"Come in, dear!" said Miss Catherine kindly, "did you come of an errand?"
"I wanted to ask you something," said the child,
40 following her into the sitting-room, and taking the chair next the door with a shy smile that had something appealing about it. "I came to ask you if you want a girl this summer."
"Why, no, I never keep help," said Miss Spring.
45 "There is a woman who comes Mondays and

Tuesdays, and other days when I need her. Who is it that wants to come?"
"It's only me," said the child. "I'm small of my age; but I'm past ten, and I can work real smart about
50 house." A great cloud of disappointment came over her face.
"Whose child are you?"
"I'm Katy Dunning, and I live with my aunt down by Sandy-river Bridge. Her girl is big enough to help
55 round now, and she said I must find a place. She would keep me if she could," said the little girl in a grown-up, old-fashioned way; "but times are going to be dreadful hard, they say, and it takes a good deal to keep so many."
60 "What made you come here?" asked Miss Catherine, whose heart went out toward this hard-worked, womanly little thing. It seemed so pitiful that so young a child, who ought to be still at play, should already know about hard times, and have begun to fight
65 the battle of life. A year ago she had thought of taking just such a girl to save steps, and for the sake of having somebody in the house; but it never could be more out of the question than now. "What made you come to me?"
70 "Mr. Rand, at the post-office, told aunt that perhaps you might want me: he couldn't think of anybody else."
She was such a neat-looking, well-mended child, and looked Miss Catherine in the face so honestly! She
75 might cry a little after she was outside the gate, but not now.
"I'm really sorry," said Miss Spring; "but you see, I'm thinking about shutting my house up this summer." She would not allow to herself that it was for any
80 longer. "But you keep up a good heart. I know a good many folks, and perhaps I can hear of a place for you. I suppose you could mind a baby, couldn't you? No: you sit still a minute!" as the child thanked her, and rose to go away; and she went out to her dining-room closet to
85 a deep jar, and took out two of her best pound-cakes, which she made so seldom now, and saved with great care. She put these on a pretty pink-and-white china plate, and filled a mug with milk. "Here," said she, as she came back, "I want you to eat these cakes. You
90 have walked a long ways, and it'll do you good. Sit right up to the table, and I'll spread a newspaper over the cloth."
Katy looked at her with surprise and gratitude. "I'm very much obliged," said she; and her first bite of
95 the cake seemed the most delicious thing she had ever tasted.

CONTINUE

1

Which choice best describes a major theme of the passage?

A) Loss of innocence as a result of malice

B) Solidarity in the face of imminent hardship

C) Fulfillment from assisting those in need

D) Unexpected redemption arising from misfortune

2

The developmental pattern of the passage can best be described as

A) a melancholy account of a traumatic event.

B) a bittersweet reflection on a sudden change.

C) an uplifting narrative of a fortuitous encounter.

D) a heartfelt depiction of an ill-timed request.

3

The main purpose of the first paragraph is to

A) present the sequence of events that led to the financial ruin of Miss Spring.

B) describe Miss Spring's daily life after she experienced a life-changing event.

C) illustrate Miss Spring's desperation after a change in her circumstances.

D) underscore Miss Spring's determination and resourcefulness at solving her crisis.

4

The narrator uses the phrase "chilly consciousness" (line 26) mainly to emphasize Miss Spring's

A) inescapable reality.

B) need for escapism.

C) search for a solution.

D) pragmatic attitude.

5

Which choice provides the best evidence for the conclusion that Miss Spring had become frugal?

A) Lines 7-8 ("If it...boarders")

B) Lines 18-19 ("I must...it")

C) Lines 44-47 ("Why, no...come")

D) Lines 84-87 ("she went...care")

6

The primary impression created by the narrator's description of Katy Dunning over the course of her conversation with Miss Spring is that she is

A) charming.

B) dejected.

C) mischievous.

D) virtuous.

7

According to the passage, the plight of Katy Dunning causes Miss Spring to react in which of the following ways?

A) Miss Spring appears sympathetic but is in fact indifferent about the girl's situation.

B) Miss Spring understands Katy's situation and feels genuine empathy for her.

C) Miss Spring sees an opportunity to further her own needs by assisting Katy.

D) Miss Spring resolves to find a solution that could benefit others in the town.

8

It can be inferred from the passage that Katy Dunning had lost her position at her aunt's house mainly because

A) she was too young to do most of the work required in that position.

B) the seasonal work for which she had been hired came to an end.

C) her cousin had grown sufficiently to take on Katy's responsibilities.

D) she had long been a significant burden on the family.

CONTINUE

9

Which choice provides the best evidence for the answer to the previous question?

A) Lines 49-51 ("I'm small...house")

B) Lines 54-56 ("Her girl...place")

C) Lines 58-60 ("but times...many")

D) Lines 70-73 ("Mr. Rand...else")

10

As used in line 62, "womanly" most nearly means

A) mature.

B) feminine.

C) sophisticated.

D) ladylike.

CONTINUE

Questions 1-10 are based on the following passage.
Chapter 10.3
Adapted from Frank Norris, *McTeague* (1899).

Once every two months Maria Macapa set the entire flat in commotion. She roamed the building from garret to cellar, searching each corner, ferreting
Line through every old box and trunk and barrel, groping
5 about on the top shelves of closets, peering into rag-bags, exasperating the lodgers with her persistence and importunity. She was collecting junks, bits of iron, stone jugs, glass bottles, old sacks, and cast-off garments. It was one of her perquisites. She sold
10 the junk to Zerkow, the rags-bottles-sacks man, who lived in a filthy den in the alley just back of the flat, and who sometimes paid her as much as three cents a pound. The stone jugs, however, were worth a nickel. The money that Zerkow paid her, Maria spent on shirt
15 waists and dotted blue neckties, trying to dress like the girls who tended the soda-water fountain in the candy store on the corner. She was sick with envy of these young women. They were in the world, they were elegant, they were debonair, they had their "young
20 men."
On this occasion she presented herself at the door of Old Grannis's room late in the afternoon. His door stood a little open. That of Miss Baker was ajar a few inches. The two old people were "keeping company"
25 after their fashion.
"Got any junk, Mister Grannis?" inquired Maria, standing in the door, a very dirty, half-filled pillowcase over one arm.
"No, nothing—nothing that I can think of, Maria,"
30 replied Old Grannis, terribly vexed at the interruption, yet not wishing to be unkind. "Nothing I think of. Yet, however—perhaps—if you wish to look." . . .
"Here's this old yellow pitcher," said Maria, coming out of the closet with it in her hand. "The
35 handle's cracked; you don't want it; better give me it."
Old Grannis did want the pitcher; true, he never used it now, but he had kept it a long time, and somehow he held to it as old people hold to trivial, worthless things that they have had for many years.
40 "Oh, that pitcher—well, Maria, I—I don't know. I'm afraid—you see, that pitcher—"
"Ah, go 'long," interrupted Maria Macapa, "what's the good of it?"
"If you insist, Maria, but I would much rather—"
45 he rubbed his chin, perplexed and annoyed, hating to refuse, and wishing that Maria were gone.
"Why, what's the good of it?" persisted Maria. He

could give no sufficient answer. "That's all right," she asserted, carrying the pitcher out.
50 "Ah—Maria—I say, you—you might leave the door—ah, don't quite shut it—it's a bit close in here at times." Maria grinned, and swung the door wide. Old Grannis was horribly embarrassed; positively, Maria was becoming unbearable.
55 "Got any junk?" cried Maria at Miss Baker's door. The little old lady was sitting close to the wall in her rocking-chair; her hands resting idly in her lap.
"Now, Maria," she said plaintively, "you are always after junk; you know I never have anything
60 laying 'round like that."
It was true. The retired dressmaker's tiny room was a marvel of neatness, from the little red table, with its three Gorham spoons laid in exact parallels, to the decorous geraniums and mignonettes growing
65 in the starch box at the window, underneath the fish globe with its one venerable gold fish. That day Miss Baker had been doing a bit of washing; two pocket handkerchiefs, still moist, adhered to the window panes, drying in the sun.
70 "Oh, I guess you got something you don't want," Maria went on, peering into the corners of the room. "Look-a-here what Mister Grannis gi' me," and she held out the yellow pitcher. . .
"Ain't that right, Mister Grannis?" called Maria;
75 "didn't you gi' me this pitcher?" Old Grannis affected not to hear; perspiration stood on his forehead; his timidity overcame him as if he were a ten-year-old schoolboy. He half rose from his chair, his fingers dancing nervously upon his chin.
80 Maria opened Miss Baker's closet unconcernedly. "What's the matter with these old shoes?" she exclaimed, turning about with a pair of half-worn silk gaiters in her hand. They were by no means old enough to throw away, but Miss Baker was almost beside
85 herself. There was no telling what might happen next. Her only thought was to be rid of Maria.
"Yes, yes, anything. You can have them; but go, go. There's nothing else, not a thing."
Maria went out into the hall, leaving Miss Baker's
90 door wide open, as if maliciously. She had left the dirty pillow-case on the floor in the hall, and she stood outside, between the two open doors, stowing away the old pitcher and the half-worn silk shoes. She made remarks at the top of her voice, calling now to Miss
95 Baker, now to Old Grannis. In a way she brought the two old people face to face. Each time they were forced to answer her questions it was as if they were talking directly to each other.
"These here are first-rate shoes, Miss Baker. Look

CONTINUE

100　here, Mister Grannis, get on to the shoes Miss Baker
　　gi' me. You ain't got a pair you don't want, have you?
　　. . ."
　　　　　Nothing could have been more horribly
　　constrained, more awkward. The two old people
105　suffered veritable torture. When Maria had gone, each
　　heaved a sigh of unspeakable relief.

1

Which choice best describes what happens in the passage?

A) Two characters attempt to avoid being approached by
　　another character.

B) Two characters reluctantly acquiesce to another
　　character's demands.

C) Two characters are surprised when met with an
　　unexpected request.

D) Two characters are embarrassed when junk is
　　discovered in their homes.

2

The primary impression of Maria as depicted in the first
paragraph is that she is

A) manic.

B) hardworking.

C) lonely.

D) greedy.

3

The main purpose of the second paragraph is to

A) introduce a situation that will be described for the rest
　　of the passage.

B) characterize Maria as alienated from the other lodgers
　　of the flat.

C) indicate that Maria's appearance at Grannis's room was
　　anticipated.

D) return the narrative to an encounter mentioned earlier in
　　the passage.

4

The passage indicates that Maria relies on which of the
following methods to procure her junk?

A) Clout.

B) Deception.

C) Manipulation.

D) Persistence.

5

Which choice provides the best evidence for the
conclusion that Grannis had an irrational attachment to
his pitcher?

A) Lines 33-35 ("Here's this...it")

B) Lines 37-39 ("he had...years")

C) Lines 40-41 ("Oh, that...pitcher")

D) Lines 47-48 ("Why, what's...answer")

6

In context of the interaction between him and Maria,
Grannis's reaction in lines 75-79 ("He affected...chin")
primarily serves to

A) emphasize the effect Maria has on him.

B) indicate a fact about his childhood.

C) illustrate his impatience with Maria.

D) show the effectiveness of Maria's methods.

7

It can be reasonably inferred that Miss Baker complies
with Maria's request because she

A) feels sympathy for Maria.

B) wants Maria to leave quickly.

C) realizes the validity of Maria's claims.

D) wishes to resume her conversation with Grannis.

CONTINUE

8

According to the passage, one consequence of Maria's encounter with Grannis and Miss Baker is that they

A) become closer with one another.

B) reveal their true selves to each other.

C) become uncomfortable with each other.

D) indirectly communicate with each other.

9

Which choice provides the best evidence for the answer to the previous question?

A) Lines 78-79 ("He half...chin")

B) Lines 93-95 ("She made...Grannis")

C) Lines 95-98 ("In a...other")

D) Lines 103-106 ("Nothing could...relief")

10

As used in line 92, "stowing" most nearly means

A) storing.

B) packing.

C) hiding.

D) carrying.

CONTINUE

Questions 1-10 are based on the following passage.
Chapter 10.4
Adapted from Jack London, "The Unexpected."
Published in 1913 in *Love of Life and Other Stories*.

The effect of civilization is to impose human law upon environment until it becomes machine-like in its regularity. The objectionable is eliminated, the
Line inevitable is foreseen. One is not even made wet by
5 the rain nor cold by the frost; while death, instead of stalking about grewsome and accidental, becomes a prearranged pageant, moving along a well-oiled groove to the family vault, where the hinges are kept from rusting and the dust from the air is swept continually
10 away.

Such was the environment of Edith Whittlesey. Nothing happened. It could scarcely be called a happening, when, at the age of twenty-five, she accompanied her mistress on a bit of travel to the
15 United States. The groove merely changed its direction. It was still the same groove and well oiled. It was a groove that bridged the Atlantic with uneventfulness, so that the ship was not a ship in the midst of the sea, but a capacious, many-corridored
20 hotel that moved swiftly and placidly, crushing the waves into submission with its colossal bulk until the sea was a mill-pond, monotonous with quietude. And at the other side the groove continued on over the land—a well-disposed, respectable groove that
25 supplied hotels at every stopping-place, and hotels on wheels between the stopping-places.

In Chicago, while her mistress saw one side of social life, Edith Whittlesey saw another side; and when she left her lady's service and became Edith
30 Nelson, she betrayed, perhaps faintly, her ability to grapple with the unexpected and to master it. Hans Nelson, immigrant, Swede by birth and carpenter by occupation, had in him that Teutonic unrest that drives the race ever westward on its great adventure. He was
35 a large-muscled, stolid sort of a man, in whom little imagination was coupled with immense initiative, and who possessed, withal, loyalty and affection as sturdy as his own strength.

"When I have worked hard and saved me some
40 money, I will go to Colorado," he had told Edith on the day after their wedding. A year later they were in Colorado, where Hans Nelson saw his first mining and caught the mining-fever himself. His prospecting led him through the Dakotas, Idaho, and eastern Oregon,
45 and on into the mountains of British Columbia. In

camp and on trail, Edith Nelson was always with him, sharing his luck, his hardship, and his toil. The short step of the house-reared woman she exchanged for the long stride of the mountaineer. She learned to look
50 upon danger clear-eyed and with understanding, losing forever that panic fear which is bred of ignorance and which afflicts the city-reared, making them as silly as silly horses, so that they await fate in frozen horror instead of grappling with it, or stampede in blind
55 self-destroying terror which clutters the way with their crushed carcasses.

Edith Nelson met the unexpected at every turn of the trail, and she trained her vision so that she saw in the landscape, not the obvious, but the concealed.
60 She, who had never cooked in her life, learned to make bread without the mediation of hops, yeast, or baking-powder, and to bake bread, top and bottom, in a frying-pan before an open fire. And when the last cup of flour was gone and the last rind of bacon, she
65 was able to rise to the occasion, and of moccasins and the softer-tanned bits of leather in the outfit to make a grub-stake substitute that somehow held a man's soul in his body and enabled him to stagger on. She learned to pack a horse as well as a man,—a task to break the
70 heart and the pride of any city-dweller, and she knew how to throw the hitch best suited for any particular kind of pack. Also, she could build a fire of wet wood in a downpour of rain and not lose her temper. In short, in all its guises she mastered the unexpected. But the
75 Great Unexpected was yet to come into her life and put its test upon her.

The gold-seeking tide was flooding northward into Alaska, and it was inevitable that Hans Nelson and his wife should he caught up by the stream and swept
80 toward the Klondike. The fall of 1897 found them at Dyea, but without the money to carry an outfit across Chilcoot Pass and float it down to Dawson. So Hans Nelson worked at his trade that winter and helped rear the mushroom outfitting-town of Skaguay.
85 He was on the edge of things, and throughout the winter he heard all Alaska calling to him. Latuya Bay called loudest, so that the summer of 1898 found him and his wife threading the mazes of the broken coast-line in seventy-foot Siwash canoes. With them
90 were Indians, also three other men. The Indians landed them and their supplies in a lonely bight of land a hundred miles or so beyond Latuya Bay, and returned to Skaguay; but the three other men remained, for they were members of the organized party. Each had put
95 an equal share of capital into the outfitting, and the profits were to be divided equally. In that Edith Nelson undertook to cook for the outfit, a man's share was to be her portion.

CONTINUE

1

Which choice best describes a major theme of the passage?

A) The consequences of an adventurous life

B) The fulfillment gained from a life of independence

C) The sacrifices made for a significant other

D) The destructive effects of civilization on nature

2

The passage as a whole presents Hans as the type of person who

A) possesses a sense of unwavering determination.

B) relies on instinct without considering consequences.

C) is driven by the opportunity of becoming wealthy.

D) inspires those around him through his hard work.

3

The narrator uses the image of hotels (lines 18-26) most likely to

A) indicate that Edith was able to afford luxurious living quarters.

B) emphasize the uniformity of Edith's life wherever she went.

C) suggest that Edith never settled down in one location for long.

D) underscore Edith's dissatisfaction with her life of monotony.

4

The narrator uses the phrase "her ability to grapple with the unexpected and to master it" (lines 30-31) primarily to

A) hint at a transformation that Edith will eventually undergo.

B) characterize Edith as unique among other city-dwellers.

C) provide context for Edith's remarkable survival skills.

D) indicate a significant shift in Edith's perception of society.

5

Which choice provides the best evidence for the conclusion that Edith undertook the same work as her husband while traveling?

A) Lines 45-47 ("In camp...toil")

B) Lines 68-70 ("She learned...city-dweller")

C) Lines 78-80 ("it was...Klondike")

D) Lines 96-98 ("In that...portion")

6

The narrator states that one unfortunate consequence of city life is that those raised in the city are likely to

A) pursue a path through life that avoids any possible risk.

B) become incapacitated when facing a perilous situation.

C) impose their way of living upon the natural world.

D) be ignorant of the signs that are prevalent in nature.

7

Which choice provides the best evidence for the answer to the previous question?

A) Lines 1-3 ("The effect...regularity")

B) Lines 4-5 ("One is...frost")

C) Lines 53-54 ("they await...it")

D) Lines 57-59 ("Edith Nelson...concealed")

CONTINUE

8

In context of the passage as a whole, the fifth paragraph (lines 57-76) primarily serves to

A) provide context for Edith and Hans's next venture.

B) contrast Edith's former lifestyle to her current one.

C) detail how Edith adapted to life in the wilderness.

D) illustrate the effects of nature on Edith's well-being.

9

As used in line 83, "rear" most nearly means

A) cultivate.

B) support.

C) establish.

D) build.

10

The passage indicates that Hans and Edith were accompanied by "Indians" (line 90) for a portion of their journey because the Indians

A) were experienced gold miners who had joined the expedition as partners.

B) served as guides and provided transportation in an unfamiliar territory.

C) had unique insights about the most promising locations to mine for gold.

D) had a vested interest in the positive outcome of the mining expedition.

CONTINUE

Questions 1-10 are based on the following passage.
Chapter 10.5
The following is an excerpt from *Action Must Be Taken* (2017) by Chris Holliday.

Janet opened the door to Mrs. Maitland's office. "It's time to do it."

The headmistress looked up from reading a
Line letter sent by an angry parent complaining about the
5 school's lack of action over secret transactions going on in the girls' locker room: "Such lack of concern is inacceptable. When something isnt right, action must be taken! and those responsable must be punnished!" Mrs. Maitland resisted the urge to amend the spelling
10 and punctuation and added the letter to the pile of opened correspondence.

"May I do it? I have always wanted to! Oh, please!" Janet was grinning.

Mrs. Maitland laughed. "Why not—if it will
15 lessen your excitement—go ahead." She moved to her desk, switched on the intercom and announced, "Attention all. This is a fire drill. Duty staff and prefects to your posts. Students are reminded to leave all bags behind and move quickly and quietly to the
20 yard outside. Do not run. Walk on the right side of the corridors and stairs."

She switched off the intercom and nodded. Janet grinned again, unlocked the glass box on the wall and pushed the red button. The alarm resonated throughout
25 the building. It was succeeded by the thunderous sound of three hundred children and staff moving from classrooms to the playground. The building trembled.

"Do students ever listen? It sounds like a hundred and one dalmations on the loose!" Mrs. Maitland
30 crossed to the window behind her desk and watched the students quickly assembling in lines outside the building. In the bright sunshine, class teachers were checking off names on their lists. She relaxed a little. "So far, so good. Now, Janet, let's make our sweep of
35 the classrooms."

As the two moved into the empty corridor they heard a door slam. A student burst out from the girls' locker room. She was carrying a stuffed book bag.

Mrs. Maitland's acerbic tone brought the girl to
40 an abrupt halt. "Thank you, Penelope. I will take that. We will discuss this in my office. Go there now. My secretary will escort you: it is so easy to get confused in an emergency."

The fire drill ended successfully. The students,
45 rather exuberant and grateful for the unexpected break, returned to their classrooms. Mrs. Maitland returned

to her office. She placed the book bag on her desk and waited. Soon she heard a knock at the door. Janet ushered in the culprit, then turned to go.
50 "Will you stay, Janet. I should like a witness to be present." Janet nodded and sat by the window through which poured the brilliant afternoon sun. "Penelope, sit down there, please." She indicated the wooden chair before her desk. Penelope shrank into it and intently
55 regarded the carpet. "Look at me, if you please!"

The girl raised her head and stared at the bag on the desk. Beyond it, her inquisitor seemed a dark, intimidating silhouette.

"So, can you explain why you took it upon
60 yourself to deliberately break the rules laid down in the drill? The instructions were clear enough."

Penelope took a deep breath. "It's not my fault. I didn't know it was a drill. I went to the toilet before it came on—you can ask my teacher. I was in the wash
65 room. I never heard what you said. I only heard the alarm going off."

Mrs. Maitland glanced towards Janet who shrugged her shoulders and said, "It's possible. Everything echoes so badly in there."
70 "Perhaps." She turned back to the girl. "Penelope, you are an intelligent girl. Why would you go and find your school bag rather than go straight out to join the others? If the alarm bell had been activated by a real fire, your foolishness could have had very serious
75 consequences. Once it is discovered that something isn't right, then action must be taken immediately."

There was moment of silence. She looked down at the bag, then back at Penelope."Would you like to show me what this bag contains? Just to be sure
80 nothing has come to any harm. You know, a puppy sleeps a lot, but it also needs air, just like you and I do."

Penelope gasped. "Oh, no! Our dog just had three puppies and my dad said we would have to get rid of
85 one of them and this girl in school said she would buy it off me. He was ever so good and quiet and I went and checked on him between lessons. And then the fire alarm went off. I thought it was a real fire and I thought..." She was opening the bag as she spoke. She
90 looked in the bag, then around her. "He is not here!"

"Of course he isn't!" said Mrs. Maitland. "He is playing with the caretaker's son. I may seem like Cruella de Ville but that's as far as it goes. You may collect him after your last class today and take him
95 back home. Your friend, if she still wants the dog, will have to go to your house and take possession of him there. Transactions like these, between students, are not permitted on school property. Is that clear? Penelope

CONTINUE

nodded. "Off you go now, back to class."

100   Mrs. Maitland turned and winked at Janet. "Action taken. I guess."

1

Over the course of the passage, the main focus shifts from a

A) narration of a spontaneous decision to a consequence of that decision.

B) dialogue between two characters to a portrayal of a humorous encounter.

C) description of an unexpected problem to the resolution of that problem.

D) performance of a routine procedure to a depiction of an unusual incident.

2

The main purpose of the second paragraph (lines 3-11) is to

A) hint at an occurrence that is explained later in the passage.

B) characterize Mrs. Maitland as inconsiderate and dismissive.

C) poke fun at a principle that is exemplified later in the passage.

D) highlight the frustration Mrs. Maitland feels towards her duties.

3

As used in line 15, "lessen" most nearly means

A) restrain.

B) control.

C) satiate.

D) calm.

4

It can reasonably be inferred that Mrs. Maitland "nodded" at Janet (line 22) in order to

A) agree with Janet's request to push the button.

B) express her approval at Janet's initiative.

C) instruct Janet to push the button.

D) indicate the seriousness of Janet's task.

5

Mrs. Maitland uses the phrase "a hundred and one dalmatians" (lines 28-29) most likely to show her

A) amusement at the students enjoying the fire drill.

B) exasperation at the students disobeying her directions.

C) annoyance at the students causing chaos in the school.

D) relief at the students having arrived safely outside.

6

According to the passage, Janet's role in Mrs. Maitland's life can best be described as

A) a companion.

B) an apprentice.

C) a teacher.

D) an assistant.

7

The passage indicates that upon being confronted by Mrs. Maitland, Penelope experiences a feeling of

A) nervousness.

B) shame.

C) embarrassment.

D) self-consciousness.

CONTINUE

8

Which choice provides the best evidence for the conclusion that Mrs. Maitland, while lenient, prefers to operate within her rules?

A) Lines 40-43 ("Thank you...emergency")

B) Lines 59-61 ("So, can...enough")

C) Lines 91-93 ("Of course...goes")

D) Lines 95-98 ("Your friend...property")

9

With which of the following statements about Penelope's actions would Mrs. Maitland most likely agree?

A) They were justified because Penelope was unaware that there was a fire drill.

B) They were foolish because Penelope had no reason to retrieve her bag.

C) They were irresponsible because Penelope was putting her safety at risk.

D) They were understandable because Penelope had a dog in her possession.

10

Which choice provides the best evidence for the answer to the previous question?

A) Lines 67-69 ("Mrs. Maitland...there")

B) Lines 70-73 ("She turned...others")

C) Lines 73-75 ("If the...consequences")

D) Lines 78-80 ("Would you...harm")

Answer Key: CHAPTER TEN

Chapter 10.1
1. A
2. D
3. A
4. D
5. B
6. B
7. D
8. B
9. B
10. D

Chapter 10.2
1. B
2. D
3. C
4. A
5. D
6. A
7. B
8. C
9. B
10. A

Chapter 10.3
1. B
2. A
3. A
4. D
5. C
6. A
7. B
8. D
9. C
10. B

Chapter 10.4
1. A
2. A
3. B
4. A
5. A
6. B
7. C
8. C
9. D
10. B

Chapter 10.5
1. D
2. A
3. C
4. C
5. B
6. D
7. A
8. D
9. C
10. C

Answer Explanations

Chapter 10

Chapter 10.1 | *Agnes Grey*

1) CORRECT ANSWER: A
The first paragraph indicates that Miss Murray is going to make her debut at "a magnificent ball" (lines 7-8); much of the discussion that follows concerns either the ball itself or how the marriage in Agnes's family might influence Agnes's attendance at the ball. A is thus the best answer. While the paragraph describes Miss Murray's situation in terms of the ball, it does not in fact explain her personality (a topic only discussed later in the passage, thus eliminating B and C). Moreover, since the ball itself does not occur in the passage, D ("foreshadow") is an inaccurate choice.

2) CORRECT ANSWER: D
In the passage, Agnes listens to Miss Murray's private sentiments regarding both the marriage and the ball; moreover, Miss Murray tells Agnes that Agnes "really must stay" (line 45) for the ball itself. Agnes thus serves as a companion to Miss Murray, so that D is an effective choice. Agnes is not observed cooking (A) or cleaning (B) at any point in the passage, and is not charged with helping to deliver children ("midwifery", C). As a governess, she is most likely required to attend to Miss Murray's education as a primary responsibility.

3) CORRECT ANSWER: A
The word "wildest" refers to Miss Murray's "impatience" (line 11) regarding the ball; she is thus highly or "extremely" impatient for this event, which she eagerly anticipates, to occur. A is the best answer, while B indicates that her impatience is inappropriate, and C and D offer even stronger criticisms. However, the ball is a desired event, so that there is no reason to expect such strong negative tones.

4) CORRECT ANSWER: D
The word "amusing" refers to Miss Murray's "talk" (line 20), which Miss Murray believes must be superior to Agnes's letter in interest and content. D applies an appropriate positive tone for Miss Murray's comparison; A and B both introduce personality traits that are out of scope (since Miss Murray indicates that her "talk" is superior, but does not say HOW exactly). C is a trap answer: Miss Murray's talk is superior to the letter, but it would be wrong to describe either a record of everyday events (the letter) or a young woman's casual discussion as remarkable or "impressive".

5) CORRECT ANSWER: B

In lines 37-39, Miss Murray indicates that she wants to talk about the ball; her earlier comments in lines 18-21 are meant to divert Agnes's attention away from the letter and to the topic of the ball, which is Miss Murray's main preoccupation in the passage. B is thus the best answer; A and C capture the belittling nature of Miss Murray's comments but not the MAIN purpose (calling attention to the ball) as demanded by the question. D is a trap answer: Agnes does not appear to have any interest in leaving Miss Murray. The real objection is that Agnes does not appear to be paying Miss Murray and the ball the desired level of attention.

6) CORRECT ANSWER: B

See above for the explanation of the correct answer. A records Miss Murray's criticism of the correspondence that Agnes has received, and C and D both indicate Miss Murray's desire that Agnes stay for the ball. Make sure not to wrongly take A as evidence for Question 5 C or D (which describes a LATER event) as evidence for Question 5 D.

7) CORRECT ANSWER: D

In lines 33-36, Agnes composedly responds to Miss Murray's comments about the "vulgar sheets" (line 28) that Agnes has received by correcting Miss Murray's manners; Agnes's controlled and somewhat critical tone in these lines is representative of her stern, dignified response to Miss Murray elsewhere in the passage. D is the best answer, while Agnes's willingness to correct Miss Murray can be used to eliminate A and B. C overstates the intensity of Agnes's approach (which relies on controlled correction, not on emotional indignation) and should be eliminated for this reason.

8) CORRECT ANSWER: B

See above for the explanation of the correct answer. A describes some of Agnes's movements (but not her ultimate reaction to Miss Murray's "berating remarks"), and C and D record Agnes's comments once Miss Murray has finished criticizing Agnes's family. Make sure not to mistakenly take A as evidence for Question 7 A or Question 7 B, since Agnes does in fact take a more assertive stance in correcting Miss Murray later on.

9) CORRECT ANSWER: B

While Miss Murray is critical of the fact that Agnes's sister has not married a rich, young, and handsome man, Agnes is more interested in the possibility that her sister's husband will be "good, wise, or amiable" (line 85). The two characters clearly have different criteria or values in regard to marriage; B is an effective answer, while A neglects the important matter of Miss Murray's perspective. Agnes's family may be lower in status, but the conversation mostly indicates a divergence in family VALUES (eliminating C). And while the two women have different opinions, these differences do not lead to strong dislike or "animosity" (eliminating D).

10) CORRECT ANSWER: D

In the relevant line reference, Miss Murray focuses on qualities that are readily apparent (wealth, appearance, and youth) in a prospective husband, as opposed to the moral qualities that Agnes emphasizes. Miss Murray is thus interested in surface-level or "superficial" traits. D is the best answer, while her strong opinions disqualify A ("apathetic" or without emotion). B and C may be tempting, but are much too critical in context (since Agnes does not voice strong antipathy towards Miss Murray, only disagreement with Miss Murray's values) and must be eliminated.

Chapter 10.2 | *A Late Supper*

1) CORRECT ANSWER: B
The passage describes Miss Spring, who faces financial difficulties because she "had lost part of her already small income" (lines 1-2) but offers food and kindness to a young girl who "must find a place" (line 55) and has few real prospects. These two characters thus come together during hard times, so that B is the best answer. A wrongly indicates that the two characters face malice (or purposeful ill will, not bad turns of FORTUNE), while C wrongly indicates that Miss Spring is fulfilled by assisting Katy (rather than that Katy HERSELF is fulfilled when Miss Spring, rather than offering assistance, offers a treat). D overstates the positive tone that arises when Miss Spring comforts Katy, but does not herself feel "redeemed" or delivered from hardship.

2) CORRECT ANSWER: D
The passage centers on Katy's request to be taken into Miss Spring's household (lines 70-72), which Miss Spring, who is going through difficulties of her own, is forced to deny. This information supports D and can be used to eliminate C, since the characters' inability to solve their main problems prevents the passage from being "uplifting". A is problematic because both Katy and Miss Spring are composed and pragmatic (not shocked or "traumatized"), while B wrongly refers to a "sudden change" (when the only major changes, such as Miss Spring's financial worries and Katy's loss of position, have happened in stages rather than occurring suddenly).

3) CORRECT ANSWER: C
The first paragraph explains that Miss Spring "did not know what to do" (line 2) in a time of financial worry; she has tried various options, but none of them have proven viable as ways to improve her position. This information supports C, while the paragraph mainly describes Miss Spring's thoughts AFTER her finances have deteriorated (eliminating A). It would also be wrong to describe this discussion of Miss Spring's remaining, problematic options as an overview of her daily life (since it is limited to her finances, eliminating B) or as a description of determination and resourcefulness (since it mostly delivers objective information about her state of mind, not the narrator's evaluation, eliminating D).

4) CORRECT ANSWER: A
Miss Spring's "chilly consciousness" concerns the fact that "her own house was about to be shut up" (lines 26-27), which she has regarded earlier as a "dreadful" (line 5) option. This sense of a negative and inescapable fact of her life supports A. B wrongly refers to the "castle in the air" (line 25) which CONTRASTS with Miss Spring's "chilly consciousness", while C and D refer to qualities that Miss Spring hopes to summon but not to the NEGATIVE situation that has come to her consciousness.

5) CORRECT ANSWER: D
In lines 84-87, the narrator indicates that Miss Spring "seldom" makes her pound cakes any more and that she saves them up; she conserves the money that was once used to buy ingredients and is unwilling to consume the cakes at will, so that D is the best answer. A and B refer to plans of action that Miss Spring is considering (not to ACTUAL ways in which she has become frugal or saved money), while C simply explains that Miss Spring does not need help around the house.

6) CORRECT ANSWER: A

The narrator initially describes Katy as "shy" (line 41) yet "appealing" (line 42); later, Katy honestly discusses her situation and wins Miss Spring's sympathy. Katy is meant to give a positive and personable or "charming" impression, so that A is the best answer, while B and C introduce faulty negatives. D is a trap answer: Katy may in fact be a morally upright or virtuous person, but her main goal in the passage is to appeal to or "charm" Miss Spring, not to profess a strong system of values or virtues.

7) CORRECT ANSWER: B

After hearing of Katy's need for a household place, Miss Spring tells Katy that she is "really sorry" (line 77) but also offers Katy praise, an offer of assistance, and the treat of a pound cake and milk. This information supports B and can be used to eliminate A, which wrongly indicates that the sympathetic Miss Spring does not care about Katy's plight. C is problematic because Miss Spring REFUSES to assist Katy by bringing the young girl into the household, while D is problematic because Miss Spring only wants to help Katy and herself (not others in the town).

8) CORRECT ANSWER: C

In lines 54-56, Katy explains that she lives with her aunt, and that because her aunt's girl "is big enough to help round now" Katy herself must find a new place to live. The girl has thus taken her position, so that C is the best answer and A (which assumes that the work was inappropriate to Katy's age, NOT the cousin's) uses faulty logic. B is problematic because Katy had grown up in the aunt's house and is only now seeking employment, while D wrongly applies a strong negative tone to Katy (who is no longer needed, but was not clearly a problem or "burden" at any earlier point).

9) CORRECT ANSWER: B

See above for the explanation of the correct answer. A records a testimony about Katy's situation and signals her disappointment (but does NOT indicate why she left the aunt's house), C indicates that bad times may be coming, and indicates that Katy's aunt was told that Miss Spring may need help. Make sure not to wrongly take C as evidence for Question 8 D: the idea of burdens or hard times is a NEW possibility, while Katy was secure in her position around the house until recently.

10) CORRECT ANSWER: A

The word "womanly" refers to Katy, who is "hard-worked" (lines 61-62) and, rather than knowing only childhood recreations, knows about the world of adult difficulties. Katy is thus mature, so that A is the best answer. In context, the narrator is not calling attention to Katy's gender (B, D) or the refinement of her thoughts and accomplishments (C, D); instead, the narrator indicates that Katy's EXPERIENCE of adult struggle and negativity is what makes her "womanly".

Chapter 10.3 | *McTeague*

1) CORRECT ANSWER: B
The passage describes Maria's process of "collecting junks" (line 7), a process that brings her into contact with Old Grannis and Miss Baker, who give Maria various junk items despite their initial reluctance. B is the best answer. A is incorrect because Old Grannis and Miss Baker stay where they are (rather than trying to avoid Maria), while C is incorrect because collecting junk is one of Maria's habits (lines 1-2, indicating that her requests are not surprising). D is a trap answer: Old Grannis and Miss Baker are indeed troubled by Maria's invasive approach, but are not upset about the presence of junk ITSELF.

2) CORRECT ANSWER: A
Maria is described in the first paragraph as setting "the entire flat in commotion" (lines 1-2) and as "ferreting through every old box and trunk and barrel" (lines 3-4); these pieces of evidence and others indicate that she is highly active or "manic". A is the best answer, while B applies the theme of activity to the wrong pursuit (since Maria is active in finding junk, not necessarily at any other employment). C and D both wrongly criticize Maria as selfish or anti-social; in fact, her main flaws are very different, and are linked mostly to her invasive approach and her fixation on trifles (such as the appearance of the other girls).

3) CORRECT ANSWER: A
The second paragraph describes a particular "occasion" (line 21) involving Maria, Old Grannis, and Miss Baker: this scene is considered at length in the remainder of the passage. A is the best answer for this mostly informative and objective paragraph, while B wrongly applies a critical tone to Maria. Keep in mind that the paragraph does not indicate whether or not Old Grannis expected the encounter (eliminating C) and serves mostly to set up the encounter (not to return to an encounter, since Old Grannis and Miss Baker have NOT been mentioned before, eliminating D).

4) CORRECT ANSWER: D
In the passage, Maria points out specific old items and emphatically indicates that she should have them: Old Grannis sums up Maria's approach with the phrase "If you insist" (line 44), indicating that Maria is persistent in obtaining the junk. D is the best answer. A would refer to physical force and B would refer to dishonesty or trickery (both too negative). C is a trap answer: Maria does ask questions, but her desire to for the junk is too blunt and too obvious to make "manipulation" a good description of her approach.

5) CORRECT ANSWER: C
The narrator describes the pitcher as an example of one of the "trivial, worthless things" that old people such as Grannis hold on to with no logical reason. C is the best answer. A indicates that Maria wants the pitcher and that it may be in a state of disrepair (but not that Grannis HIMSELF has no good reason to keep it). B records Grannis's attempt to keep the pitcher (not his motive for keeping it) and D indicates that Grannis cannot justify his attachment to the pitcher. However, on the basis of D alone, he may have reasons OTHER than irrational attachment for his decision; only C truly clarifies his motives.

6) CORRECT ANSWER: A

The narrator has already established that Grannis is unsettled by Maria's persistence; the relevant line reference records the "perspiration" (line 76) and "timidity" (line 77) that result from Maria's comments. A is thus the best answer, while the narrator also compares Grannis to a child (but does not MENTION his childhood, eliminating B). C attributes the wrong negatives to the nervous (not superior or impatient) Grannis, while D misdirects the narrative: Maria's methods ARE effective, but the real topics of the line reference are Grannis and his discomfort, not the methods that unsettle Grannis.

7) CORRECT ANSWER: B

In dealing with Maria's search, Miss Baker's "only thought was to be rid of Maria" (line 86). This information supports B and can be used to eliminate inappropriately positive answers such as A and C. D is a trap answer: Miss Baker does seem positively inclined towards Grannis, but if her "only thought" is getting rid of Maria then she cannot, logically, have any other motive.

8) CORRECT ANSWER: D

In lines 95-98, the narrator explains that Maria intensified the contact between Miss Baker and Old Grannis, making it as though "they were talking directly to each other" when they are in fact answering Maria's questions. D is the best answer, while the same information can be used to eliminate C (which mistakes the old people's discomfort with Maria for discomfort with one another). Keep in mind that the two old people are united primarily by their aversion to Maria, so that A and B (which overstate the closeness and positivity of their relationship) distort the content of the passage.

9) CORRECT ANSWER: C

See above for the explanation of the correct answer. A describes a movement made by Old Grannis, B describes how Maria called out to the two old people, and D indicates that the two old people are relieved by the end of Maria's ordeal. Only D mentions both Old Grannis and Miss Baker, but characterizes them only as temporarily relieved (a theme that does not align with an answer to the previous question).

10) CORRECT ANSWER: B

The word "stowing" refers to what Maria does with the pitcher and old shoes, which she packs in a "dirty pillow-case" (line 91) before she leaves. B is thus the best answer. A refers to a destination where goods are kept for a long time or "stored", C wrongly indicates that the other characters do not know where their junk has gone, and D wrongly indicates that Maria is leaving and carrying the goods. In fact, she remains in the hall and continues to talk.

Chapter 10.4 | *The Unexpected*

1) CORRECT ANSWER: A
The passage as a whole describes the life of Edith Nelson, who joined her husband in the "great adventure" (line 34) of Westward movement and "met the unexpected at every turn" (line 57) of life in the wilderness. This information supports A. B is incorrect because Edith is united with her husband (not "independent"), and C is problematic because Edith does not see her lifestyle as a drawback or sacrifice for her husband's sake (and instead fully accepts her role). D refers to an issue (the destructive effects of civilization) that may be expected in a wilderness narrative, but does not in fact occur in THIS description of how two people adapt to the wilderness (rather than destroying it).

2) CORRECT ANSWER: A
Hans is described as a man of "immense initiative" (line 36); he resolves to go to Colorado and arrives there after a year of hard work. This information indicates that he is determined: choose A and eliminate B (since Hans's sense of initiative is practical in nature and does not lead to any lasting misfortunes). C and D overstate themes from the passage: Hans pursues opportunities (but does not set wealth as a clear goal or prioritize it over adventure) and works with others (but is not seen as an inspiration, since his companions may already be hard workers regardless of Hans's influence).

3) CORRECT ANSWER: B
In explaining Edith's life, the narrator states that Edith has stayed in the "same groove" (line 16) even though she is changing location; she does not always stay in the same hotel, but the "hotels" are a predictable part of her lifestyle. This information supports B, while the fact that Edith travels with her "mistress" or employer can be used to eliminate A. C applies the wrong theme (repetition, NOT instability or restlessness) to the hotels, while D wrongly introduces a strong negative tone into an analytic discussion that is designed simply to explain Edith's lifestyle.

4) CORRECT ANSWER: A
The relevant line reference depicts Edith's marriage as an early manifestation of her "ability" to deal with the unexpected; later, she adapts to a lifestyle of adventure and achieves mastery of unexpected situations (lines 57-59). A captures this sense of an impending transformation, while the people around Edith are not analyzed by the author (aside from her husband, eliminating both B and D). C wrongly raises the topic of survival skills, which does not appear until significantly LATER both in Edith's life and in the passage.

5) CORRECT ANSWER: A
In lines 45-47, the narrator explained that Edith accompanied her husband and shared directly in his "toil" or work. A thus provides effective evidence that the two performed the same work. B indicates that Edith learned to pack a horse (but not that Hans also performed this task), C indicates that the couple traveled together (but not what kind of work Edith performed), and D indicates that Edith served as a cook (a job that is never explicitly given to Hans as well).

6) CORRECT ANSWER: B

In lines 53-54, the narrator explains that, when faced with negative circumstances, city-dwellers "await fate in frozen horror". This evidence supports B and can be used to eliminate A, since city-dwellers DO face negative circumstances but do not know how to react properly. Both C and D wrongly discuss the conflicted relationship between city-dwellers and the world of nature (which is not actually a theme of the passage) and must be eliminated as out of scope.

7) CORRECT ANSWER: C

See above for the explanation of the correct answer. A indicates that the whole of civilization (not city-dwellers specifically) can influence the world of nature, B explains that people find ways to eliminate discomforts related to the natural world, and D describes Edith only (not city-dwellers as a group). Make sure not to take B as evidence for Question 6 D: city-dwellers may understand the signs present in nature, but can still avoid the inconveniences associated with nature itself.

8) CORRECT ANSWER: C

The relevant paragraph indicates that Edith adapted to life in the wilderness "at every turn of the trail" (lines 57-58) and then lists her various skills (cooking, packing a horse, building a fire). These skills show how well she was able to fare in her circumstances, so that C is a highly effective answer. The forthcoming venture is mentioned only after the paragraph concludes (and may take Edith to settings where new skills are required, eliminating A), while Edith's former lifestyle is only mentioned at any length earlier in the passage (eliminating B). D focuses on Edith's "well-being" (her thoughts or attitudes, NOT on the skills that the paragraph primarily explains) and is thus off-topic.

9) CORRECT ANSWER: D

The word "rear" refers to a town that Hans Nelson "worked at his [carpenter] trade" (line 83) to help build up through his contributions. D is the best answer. A and B are appropriately positive but refer to different contexts than the building activity of a carpenter (crops and alliance or goodwill, respectively), while C is tempting but employs faulty logic. Hans is staying in a town, but did not actually create or "establish" the town that he is helping to build.

10) CORRECT ANSWER: B

The narrator explains that the Indians "landed" (line 90) Edith's party in a particular region before returning to the party's starting point, Skaguay. In other words, the Indians help primarily with navigation and transportation before they depart, so that B is the best answer. A, C, and D are illogical because the Indians do NOT have any clear knowledge of gold or definite interest in the ultimate fate of the exhibition, since they depart well before it reaches its conclusion.

Chapter 10.5 | *Action Must Be Taken*

1) CORRECT ANSWER: D
The passage opens with a description of the fire drill, an orderly procedure whose details are well known to Janet, Mrs. Maitland, and the teachers; the narrative then considers Penelope's misadventure with the puppy, a clear departure from routine since Penelope chose to "deliberately break the rules" (line 60). This movement from a routine event to an unusual incident supports D. A wrongly indicates that the fire drill was a "spontaneous" decision (because both Janet and Mrs. Maitland anticipate that it will take place at an appointed time). B focuses entirely on "dialogue" in a manner that neglects the other events that transpire (teachers and students moving) while Janet and Mrs. Maitland speak, while C neglects the fact that the "problem" involving Penelope's puppy is only addressed at length in the SECOND major segment of the passage.

2) CORRECT ANSWER: A
The second paragraph refers to "secret transactions" (line 5) ; it is later revealed that these "Transactions" (line 97) include the exchange of property such as Penelope's puppy. This information supports A. Mrs. Maitland in fact cannot be "inconsiderate" because the person she looks down on in the second paragraph, the sender of the letter, is not present (eliminating B). The poor spelling and punctuation are the only "principles" that are poked fun at (but do not return later, eliminating C), while Mrs. Maitland is at most somewhat mocking towards the parent's writing (NOT frustrated toward her duties overall, eliminating D).

3) CORRECT ANSWER: C
The word "lessen" is used in reference to Janet's "excitement" (line 15) by the laughing and good-natured Mrs. Maitland. She wishes to Janet to enjoy herself, so that C ("satiate" or satisfy) is the best choice. In context, A, B, and D all indicate that Mrs. Maitland wants the excitement removed or hampered in some way (not that she wants Janet to be pleased) and should thus be eliminated.

4) CORRECT ANSWER: C
After Mrs. Maitland "nodded" at Janet, Janet "pushed the red button" (line 24) that set off the fire alarm and thus set the fire drill in motion. C is thus the best answer, while Mrs. Maitland has ALREADY agreed to let Janet initiate the fire drill (lines 14-15, eliminating both A and B). Keep in mind that Mrs. Maitland's demeanor regarding Janet's duty is not overwhelmingly serious (and that she "laughed" at the grinning Janet) and eliminate D as an answer that attributes an inappropriate "serious" tone to the passage.

5) CORRECT ANSWER: B
Mrs. Maitland's reference to "a hundred and one dalmatians" occurs immediately after she asks, "Do those students ever listen?" (line 28); she is tense because the students have disobeyed the instruction not to run and only "relaxed" (line 33) after she sees that the fire drill is proceeding in an orderly manner. B is thus the best answer, while A and D introduce inappropriately positive tones for the line reference. Trap answer C is inappropriate because the students, though noisy, have quickly left the school, rather than staying within the building and creating "chaos".

6) CORRECT ANSWER: D

In the passage, Janet takes over a role that Mrs. Maitland might perform under other circumstances (activating the fire drill) and accompanies Mrs. Maitland on a "sweep of the classrooms" (lines 34-35). She thus assists Mrs. Maitland in performing specific duties, so that D is the best answer. A wrongly indicates a role that is more social than professional, while C wrongly indicates that Janet is Mrs. Maitland's superior (not that she takes directions from Mrs. Maitland). B is a trap answer; while Janet is an apparent subordinate who takes over some of Mrs. Maitland's duties, the narrative never indicates that Janet is training to take over Mrs. Maitland's ENTIRE role in the manner that an apprentice, by definition, would.

7) CORRECT ANSWER: A

The narrator explains that Mrs. Maitland appears to Penelope as "a dark, intimidating silhouette" (lines 57-58) after Penelope has been discovered. Penelope is thus intimidated and made nervous by Mrs. Maitland's presence, so that A is the best answer. B and C are similar answers that do not capture the strength of Penelope's nervous reaction (or the fact that, rather than regretting her action entirely, she tries to justify and explain it to Mrs. Maitland). D wrongly suggests that Penelope is most interested in reflecting on her OWN emotions, not in dealing with the intimidating figure of Mrs. Maitland.

8) CORRECT ANSWER: D

In lines 95-98, Mrs. Maitland allows Penelope to give the dog to her friend but stipulates that the action shall not take place "on school property". This information indicates both that Mrs. Maitland is willing to accept Penelope's course of action and that (as a school authority) she is unwilling to go against set rules. D is thus the best answer. A indicates that Mrs. Maitland is accommodating (but NOT that she is managing Penelope according to any precise rules), B indicates Mrs. Maitland's cognizance of the school rules (but NOT her lenience), and D indicates that Mrs. Maitland has thoughtfully removed the dog (but, again, NOT that there is any rule related to her choice).

9) CORRECT ANSWER: C

In lines 73-75, Mrs. Maitland calls attention to the "serious consequences" that Penelope's actions would have had in the event of a real fire; one consequence was that Penelope, who stayed in the school, could have found herself in danger. C is the best answer, while the same clear criticism of Penelope's actions can be used to eliminate positive or more accommodating answers such as A and D. B is inaccurate because Mrs. Maitland (who knows of the dog's presence) would agree that Penelope had a REASON to protect the animal; she would not, however, agree that Penelope's choice to stay in the building was advisable.

10) CORRECT ANSWER: C

See above for the explanation of the correct answer. A deals primarily with Janet's perspective (not Mrs. Maitland's), B offers praise of Penelope and a question about her motives (not a judgment regarding her actions, as necessitated by the previous question), and D records an inquiry about the contents of the bag (not a statement about Penelope's conduct).

CPSIA information can be obtained
at www.ICGtesting.com
Printed in the USA
LVHW03s0607260718
585011LV00020B/119/P